THIRD EDITION

LITERATURE
FOR
CHILDREN
A Short Introduction

D A V I D   L . R U S S E L L

Ferris State University

 **LONGMAN**

An imprint of Addison Wesley Longman, Inc.

New York • Reading, Massachusetts • Menlo Park, California • Harlow, England
Don Mills, Ontario • Sydney • Mexico City • Madrid • Amsterdam

**Literature for Children: A Short Introduction,
Third Edition**

Copyright © 1997, 1994, 1991 by Longman.
All rights reserved.
No part of this publication may be reproduced,
stored in a retrieval system, or transmitted
in any form or by any means, electronic, mechanical,
photocopying, recording, or otherwise,
without the prior permission of the publisher.

Longman, 10 Bank Street, White Plains, N.Y. 10606

Associated companies:
Longman Group Ltd., London
Longman Cheshire Pty., Melbourne
Longman Paul Pty., Auckland
Copp Clark Longman Ltd., Toronto

Acquisitions editor: Virginia L. Blanford
Associate editor: Arianne J. Weber
Production editor: Linda Moser
Editorial assistant: Michael Lee
Cover design: Robin Hoffmann
Production supervisor: Edith Pullman
Compositor: University Graphics

Library of Congress Cataloging-in-Publication Data

Russell, David L.
      Literature for children / David L. Russell.—3rd ed.
          p.   cm.
      Includes bibliographical references and index.
      ISBN 0-8013-1773-8
      1. Children's literature—History and criticism.   2. Children—
Books and reading.   I. Title.
      PN1009.A1R87   1997
      028.5—dc20   96-14429
                                                         CIP

2 3 4 5 6 7 8 9 10-MA 00999897

CONTENTS

PREFACE TO THE
THIRD EDITION

It is a great privilege to be able to offer a third edition of *Literature for Children*. As with the first two editions, I have aimed this work at college students, many of whom are heading toward careers in education, and many of whom have only a passing knowledge of children's literature. I have found that what these students need most of all is to read, read, and read some more—the classic authors, the contemporary favorites, the lesser-known gems. What they do not need is an exhaustive pedagogical study or endless plot summaries of books they should have read. Consequently, my method has been to require students to read as many of the primary works of literature as is feasible during the academic term and to supplement those readings with this text, which gives them a handle on the study of children's literature in general.

In preparing this edition, I have tried to address the concerns of readers who have used the second edition without infringing on the strengths of that work. Acting on the conviction that the simplest way is often the best, I have returned to the two-part division I used in the first edition: "The Contexts of Children's Literature" and "The Kinds of Children's Literature." This moves the three chapters on cultural diversity, the study of literature, and literature in the classroom from the back to the front of the book, placing all the foundation material together in one section. The second part of the text is then devoted to the various genres of literature. My experience has been that each instructor (including myself) has a preferred method of organization—some like to begin with the chapter on history, others go directly to the chapters on picture books, still others start with the chapters on literary analysis and pedagogy. The chapters are clearly defined and relatively self-contained, and may be used in whatever organizational pattern best suits the instructor's needs and style.

The only other organizational change is in the chapters treating picture books. In an effort to avoid the duplication of content (including bibliographies), I have folded the two chapters on Mother Goose books and Alphabet, Counting, and Concept books into a single chapter entitled "Books for the Very Young." To these I have added material on wordless picture books, toy books, and easy-to-read books. The picture storybooks, those intended for children of about three or four and older, have been placed in the same chapter that deals with illustrators, their styles and techniques. This arrangement seems to provide for a smooth transition from books for infants and toddlers to books for older preschoolers and children in the primary grades. An additional advantage is that storybook texts and pictures can be dealt with in a single manageable chapter. (Some readers of the second edition noted that keeping picture book texts and illustrations in two separate chapters tended to de-emphasize the fact that in the best picture books, the illustrations and the text form an inseparable union.) One final organizational change involves the movement of historical realism into the chapter on contemporary realism. These two types have considerably more in common than do historical realism and biography (which were combined into a single chapter in the second edition), and this new arrangement has proven more economical.

This new organization has permitted me to add a considerable amount of content without vastly increasing the size of the book. Readers will find a more developed chapter on cultural diversity and a fuller discussion of the ways in which picture books function, as well as modest additions to virtually every chapter. The bibliographies have been enlarged with the inclusion of more recent publications, and although space simply will not permit plot or thematic annotations for the children's books, they have so far as possible been categorized according to certain broad types. New to this edition is the classification of most of the books into some general grade classifications: The books of fantasy, realism, and biography, for example, are divided into books for readers in grades two through five and books for readers in grades six and up. These classifications are intended as general guidelines only, for parents and teachers well know how difficult it is to pigeon-hole a child's reading abilities and interests. I have not attempted to recommend age categories for picture books aside from the implied classification in the chapter divisions.

As in the previous editions, the objectives of this revision were to retain the brevity, sharpen the clarity, fill in the gaps, and still have a reasonably priced and attractive book. I trust the readers will find that all of these objectives were achieved in some measure. I would like to reiterate my sentiments from the first two editions that it is my hope that my readers will come away from this work with a keen interest in and healthy respect for children's literature, with an understanding of the complexities of the literature, and an appreciation of the importance of the literature in the lives of young people. Reading is unquestionably the most fundamental of all academic skills, and the love of reading is among the richest gifts we can bestow upon our children. Our justification has been eloquently pronounced by the writer of Ecclesiasticus:

If thou has gathered nothing in thy youth,
how canst thou find anything in thine age?

ACKNOWLEDGMENTS

I would like to thank the following reviewers, whose comments and suggestions enabled me to make this a better book:

Evelyn Butler, San Diego State University

Christine Francis, Central Connecticut State University

Isabel Hasen, Black Hawk College

Mary McNulty, Francis Marion University

Leslie Marlow, Northwestern State University

Carol Nelson, Indiana University

Emilie Warner Paille, Georgia State University

Mary Stanley, Indiana University-Purdue University at Indianapolis

Lorena Stone, Wesley College

Dee Storey, Saginaw Valley State University

Terrell Young, Washington State University

Andrew Kantar, Ferris State University

Part One

THE CONTEXTS OF CHILDREN'S LITERATURE

Chapter 1

THE HISTORY OF CHILDREN'S LITERATURE

"A page of history is worth a volume of logic," wrote the great judge Oliver Wendell Holmes, Jr. History gives us perspective; it helps us to see our role in the great sweep of time. Surveying the landscape of the past may not necessarily provide us with an accurate map for the future, but it will make us more informed and astute observers of the present. Seeing where children's literature has been in the past can help us understand what it is today. Our focus in this chapter will be chiefly on the history of children's literature in the English-speaking world, specifically British and American; however, the roots of this literature are very deep indeed.

THE ANCIENT WORLD

The history of children's literature mirrors the history of childhood. For many thousands of years—from the very beginnings of civilization, as a matter of fact—children were of little interest to society in general. Childhood was viewed as a necessary (sometimes regrettable) stage on the path to adulthood. Consequently, we find little in civilization's first several thousand years on earth that can be labeled "children's literature." In the beginning was the oral tale, which was passed on by word of mouth—a practice reaching beyond antiquity. The earliest cultures were, of course, oral cultures possessing no writing, and children had to be content with listening to the stories their elders told for the entire clan. We may imagine flickering hearth fires, guarding against the chill of night, around which storytellers shared their tales—perhaps to pass the time or to explain some natural phenomenon. Eventually the stories became more elaborate as society grew more complex; in time, fantastic tales of gods and heroes, princes and dragons, foolish peasants and clever animals were being disseminated all over the world.

Naturally, no one thought of these tales as "children's literature," nor were they specifically intended for children, yet today these myths, legends, fables, and epics form the foundation of much that is recognized as literature for children. Children typically appropriated stories from the adult repertoire. Consequently, we hear that the young of classical Greece (around 400 BC) enjoyed the two famous poems attributed to Homer, the *Illiad*—the story of the Trojan War—and the *Odyssey*—the story of the adventures of the Greek hero Odysseus. Whereas the adults might be allured by the passionate love stories and the depth of human emotion in Homer's *Odyssey*, the younger listeners might relish the fanciful monsters and exciting adventures. Today, children still enjoy hearing of the travels of Odysseus, or of the fall of Troy, or of the feats of Hercules or of Jason and the Golden Fleece, or of scores of other magical tales of ancient Greece. Aesop's *Fables*, those familiar animal tales with pointed morals attached, were almost certainly staple reading for young Greek students during this time.

Children of ancient Rome (from about 50 BC to AD 500) read Virgil's *Aeneid*, the story of the legendary progenitor of the Roman race, and Ovid's *Metamorphoses*, poetic versions of the classical myths. Virgil and Ovid drew on the oral tradition, although their works are definitely literary, for the ancient Romans tended to be highly educated. Virgil has not held the same appeal for modern children as Homer has, but it is possible to find modern retellings of the myths in *Metamorphoses*. Their brevity and their imaginative qualities have kept them popular with children for centuries.

THE MIDDLE AGES

By the time of the European Middle Ages (from about AD 500 to 1500), the state of literature for children scarcely changed—except that almost certainly fewer children could read during this period than during the preceding classical ages in Greece and Rome. Education was largely carried on by the Church and almost exclusively for the purpose of spreading Christianity. Childhood itself was not romanticized, and since the average lifespan was scarcely more than 35 years, prolonging childhood into the teenage years as we do today was simply not possible. Most people were wed in their early to middle teens (Shakespeare's Juliet was not yet 13 when she was betrothed). People did not have a great deal of time to spend pursuing the delights of childhood because adulthood beckoned. Childhood was not a great concern of medieval society.

Education was extremely unenlightened and reserved for the privileged classes—hence few people could read. There was also the very practical problem of the scarcity of books. It is difficult for us to imagine an era when every single book had to be laboriously copied by hand, as was the case prior to the introduction of the movable-type printing press. It took up to three years for a single copy of the Bible to be produced. Books were extraordinarily costly in the Middle Ages, and libraries often chained them to the tables. (Forget about checking a book out for the weekend!) The library of the Sorbonne, the principal library of the University of Paris, had an inventory of some 1,700 books in the early fourteenth century—and that must have been one of the finest libraries of the day. Given these circumstances, it is little wonder that the general populace did not bother to learn to read—there would have been very little for them to read anyway.

MEDIEVAL EPICS

It is not surprising that medieval writers were as reluctant as classical writers to devote their talents and energies to writing for children. So medieval children had to be content largely with those adult stories that held some interest for them, as children in ancient times had had to do. Nevertheless, this left much for them to enjoy, for, as with classical literature, medieval literature preserved that capacious quality that made it appealing to a broadly based audience—the same story could be enjoyed by young and old alike. The medieval world produced epics in the vein of the great classical epics of Homer and Virgil, and, like them, they were intended for oral delivery. Surely the Anglo-Saxon epic *Beowulf*, the exciting story of a hero's defeat of a terrible monster, was a favorite among young listeners. Although the poem was originally composed in about the eighth century AD, it can still be read with pleasure today in modern retellings for children, such as Rosemary Sutcliff's *Dragon Slayer*. Medieval children likely knew other epics, such as the French *Song of Roland*, and the Spanish *The Cid*.

MEDIEVAL ROMANCES

The tales of King Arthur and his knights of the Round Table likewise delighted many medieval children. Arthur is a half-legendary, half-historical figure who was made popular during the High Middle Ages (around the twelfth and thirteenth centuries), at least partly to generate patriotic spirit in the English. But the stories of Arthur and his knights were well-known on the Continent as well. These *romances*, as they are called, are stories of high adventure, love, mystery, treachery, and magic. Adults might have been attracted to the love stories (some happy, some tragic) of the knights and the fair damsels; children might have been captivated by the wondrous monsters—ogres and dragons—and the magic spells; and both might have been thrilled by contests and battles. The great reteller of the tales of King Arthur is the fifteenth-century writer Thomas Malory, whose *Morte d'Artur* ("The Death of Arthur") is one of the great pieces of medieval English literature. Four and a half centuries later, Howard Pyle, an American writer, retold some of the tales of Arthur for younger audiences in *The Stories of King Arthur and His Knights* (1903).

Another literary hero of the Middle Ages who has survived into the modern era is Robin Hood. Some believe Robin Hood to have been based upon an historical figure, a twelfth-century outlaw stealing from the rich and giving his booty to the poor. Once again, Howard Pyle wrote one of the most popular adaptations of these tales for children, *The Merry Adventures of Robin Hood* (1883), recounting the stories of this medieval anti-hero and forebear of the gunslingers of the American West.

FABLES AND OTHER TALES

In the late thirteenth century, a collection of tales, including many fables, all with morals prominently attached, appeared in England. This was called the *Gesta Romanorum* ("The Deeds of the Romans"). It proved to be a rich source of plots for many famous writers later on, including the great medieval Italian storyteller Boccaccio and the equally great medieval English writer Geoffrey Chaucer. Children of the Middle Ages must have been very familiar with the tales of the *Gesta Romanorum*.

Animal stories have always been favorites of children, so it is not surprising that the beast epic *Reynard the Fox*, the story of a trickster, was also extremely popular during the Middle Ages and apparently loved by children. Barbara Cooney's *Chanticleer and the Fox* is a twentieth-century picture-book version of this tale, which has remained a favorite since the days of Chaucer.

In addition to these secular entertainments were the biblical stories, the lives of saints (typically embellished and improved), and local legends (celebrating the great deeds of some half-real, half-mythical hero of the neighborhood), all of which sought to improve the moral and spiritual character of the audience. The lively medieval imagination drew no close distinction between fantasy and reality, and medieval storytellers were free to mingle magic, enchantment, and the downright ludicrous alongside the serious. For many medieval people, miracles were as real as taxes. If the children were content to share the literature of their parents, it may be at least partly because that literature was rich with a childlike imagination—full of wonder, mystery, and excitement.

THE EUROPEAN RENAISSANCE

THE PRINTING PRESS

By the mid-fifteenth century, dramatic changes began to take place in Europe. At that time, the movable-type printing press was developed in the West (by Gutenberg and others, building on technology first discovered in China). It became possible to print books in quantity, the time and labor involved were reduced, and books were cheaper and more accessible. It is difficult to exaggerate the impact of this single invention, probably the most important technical innovation since the introduction of the wheel. In a short time, a remarkable revolution took place that resulted in increasing literacy and the rapid dissemination and advancement of knowledge.

SOCIAL CHANGES

At the same time, several other factors were converging that were to change the face of Europe: (1) The Crusades, which had taken place chiefly in the eleventh and twelfth centuries, had opened up trade routes to the East as far as India and helped to bring wealth in the form of trade to Europe; (2) strong central monarchies harnessed warring feudal lords—who had dominated much of the Middle Ages with their petty wars—and encouraged the growth of peaceful commerce and industry;

and (3) the European arrival in the Western Hemisphere (also known rather inaccurately as the "Discovery of the New World") brought untold wealth to some and opportunity to many Europeans (albeit disaster to the native American peoples). The growing wealth during this time saw the rise of a substantial merchant middle class—a class that was almost nonexistent during the Middle Ages, when people were aristocrats, peasants, or clergy. Whereas peasants could not afford to educate their children (and had no reason to anyway), the new middle class valued education. Merchants and traders needed to read and write to keep their accounts.

INSTRUCTIONAL BOOKS

Nevertheless, the children of Renaissance Europe, even though they were more literate than their medieval counterparts, still had to be content largely with reading instructional books or works written primarily for adults. Children continued to enjoy the medieval legends and romances, and some of the classical works. William Caxton's edition of *The Fables of Aesop* (1483) has been called "the first popular illustrated book printed in England" (Wooden 7). It remained popular throughout the Renaissance. Instructional works, such as the books of courtesy, showing children how to behave in society (a sort of Emily Post or Miss Manners for children), sprang up during the fifteenth and sixteenth centuries. Sir Thomas Elyot's *The Boke Named the Governor* (1531) and Roger Ascham's *The Scholemaster* (1570) are the best known. They illustrate society's growing interest in the education of children. John Foxe's *Book of Martyrs* (1563), an anti-Catholic work filled with horrific scenes of violent deaths for the sake of religion, was among the most popular reading material for children. Because of its religious theme, it was considered acceptable reading for children, "pointing little feet down the path of righteousness" (Wooden 8), and was chained to stands in English cathedrals so it would be readily available to adults and children alike. We even hear of children early in the twentieth century still enjoying this work. Two gentler pieces are John Skelton's long poem *Philip Sparrow* (1508), about the assuagement of a little girl's grief over the death of her pet, and Michael Drayton's *Nymphidia* (1627), a fantasy in verse filled with fairy folklore.

Finally it is important to mention John Comenius's *Orbis Sensualium Pictus* (1658), which is generally regarded as the earliest children's picture book (see Figure 1.1). It was, in fact, a Latin vocabulary book—a sort of "Latin through pictures"—that provides us today with an interesting look at seventeenth-century European society. By the end of the seventeenth century, social changes were well under way that would clear the path for a genuine literature for children.

THE PURITANS AND JOHN LOCKE

The seventeenth century saw the rise of at least two specific influences that brought to society a heightened sense of the special needs of the child. First was the rise of Puritanism, an influential branch of Protestantism that placed special emphasis on the individual's need to tend to his or her own salvation. And second was the work of John Locke, the English philosopher.

CXXXVI.

Ludi Pueriles.

Boyes-Sport

Boys used to play either with *Bowling-stones* 1. or throwing a *Bowl*, 2. at *Nine-pins*, 3. or striking a *Ball*, through a *Ring*, 5. with a *Bandy*, 4. or scourging a *Top*, 6. with a *Whip*, 7. or shooting with a *Trunk*, 8. and a *Bow*, 9. or going upon *Stilts*, 10. or tossing and swinging themselves upon a *Merry-totter*, 11.

Pueri solent ludere vel *Globis fictilibus*, 1. vel jactantes *Globum*, 2. ad *Conas*, 3. vel *mittentes* Sphærulam per *Annulum*, 5. *Clava*, 4. versantes *Turbinem*, 6. *Flagello*, 7. vel jaculantes *Sclopo*, 8. & *Arcu*, 9. vel incidentes *Grallis*, 10. vel super *Petaurum*, 11. se agitantes & oscillantes.

FIGURE 1.1 John Comenius's *Orbis Sensualium Pictus* is often considered the first children's picture book. It first appeared in 1658 as a German/Latin textbook and was an immediate success. It revolutionized Latin instruction, a necessity in a society in which Latin was still the language of scholarship. The English/Latin version, from which this illustration is taken, appeared in 1659. Although the woodblock illustrations appear crude, they provide a wealth of information about seventeenth-century European life.

PURITANISM

The Puritans were a very strict religious sect who believed in living simply and work-ing hard. They abhorred fancy church ritual and tended to frown on the pleasures of the flesh. The Puritans suffered persecution in England because they refused to support the established Church of England, and this brought them to North Amer-ica. They believed that one could achieve salvation through individual faith alone and that a thorough knowledge of the Bible was necessary for every human being. Consequently, the ability to read and to understand the Bible was a principal re-quirement for Puritan children. The Puritans were not in America long before they found the need to establish a college, Harvard (1636), as if to emphasize their com-mitment to the primacy of education.

As might be expected, the Bible stories were staple reading for Puritan children, and virtually all the first books for these children were *didactic* books—that is, they were intended to instruct children. Early schoolbooks included the so-called horn books. Commonly found in New England, these consisted of simple wooden slabs, usually with a handle, on which was attached parchment containing rudimentary language lessons (the alphabet, numerals, etc.). The slabs were then covered with transparent horn (from cattle, sheep, goats), which served as a primitive form of lamination, making these books very durable. Battledores, cheap books made of folded cardboard and usually containing educational material, were popularly used into the nineteenth century. Surely the most famous of early schoolbooks was *The New England Primer*, first appearing sometime around 1680 and continuing in print in some form or another until 1886. It was initially a Puritan publication introduc-ing young children to the alphabet through rhymes ("In Adam's fall/We Sinned all" for A) and then to increasingly sophisticated reading material—all with a religious intent (see Figure 1.2). Chapbooks, small and cheaply made books containing fairy tales and other secular works, were also widespread during the period, but the Pu-ritans frowned upon these forerunners of the dime novel.

JOHN LOCKE AND EDUCATIONAL PHILOSOPHY

The second great influence on children's literature during this period was the Eng-lish philosopher John Locke (1632–1704), who, in 1693, wrote a famous essay, "Thoughts Concerning Education." In this work, he formulated his notion that the minds of young children were similar to blank slates (he called them *tabula rasa*) just waiting to be written upon and thus instructed. Locke effectively discounted the influence of heredity by suggesting that every child possessed a similar capacity for learning. Moreover, Locke felt, it was the responsibility of adults to see to the proper education of children. The Puritans were interested in childhood for religious reasons, whereas Locke stressed the importance of childhood for intellectual rea-sons. So it was that the idea of books for children received the considerable support of both religion and philosophy.

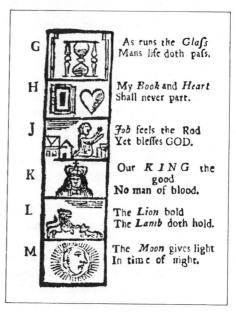

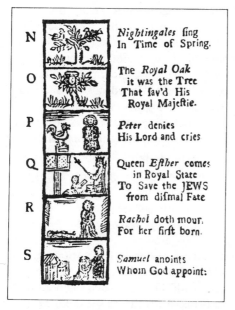

FIGURE 1.2 *The New England Primer* was one of the longest-lived school texts in American history, flourishing from approximately 1680 to 1830. The earliest surviving copy is from 1727, from which these illustrations are taken. Intended to teach the children of the early Puritans how to live a godly life, the book is unabashedly didactic, which is evident even in its rhyming alphabet, recalling a time when church and state were not so completely separate as they are now.

IMAGINATIVE LITERATURE: BUNYAN, DEFOE, AND SWIFT

English children also continued to adopt certain adult works of literature. They were especially drawn to the fanciful allegory of John Bunyan's *A Pilgrim's Progress* (1678), the story of a man's journey to Heaven; children were undoubtedly delighted by the horrific monsters that plagued him on the trip to the religious ecstacy of his safe arrival in Heaven. Bunyan also composed a book of verse, *A Book for Boys and Girls: Country Rhimes for Children* (1686), which proved popular throughout the succeeding century, although in a drastically edited form. Two other works, both originally for adults, were exceedingly popular with children in the early eighteenth century. The first was Daniel Defoe's *Robinson Crusoe* (1719), a shipwreck adventure tale that is the ancestor of numerous survival stories that children relish to this day. The second was Jonathan Swift's *Gulliver's Travels* (1726), a satirical travel fantasy that is still retold from time to time for children and has been the subject of several movies for young people. Young readers' favorite part of Swift's book is Gulliver's visit to Lilliput, a miniature land, and this too has been a recurrent subject of modern children's fantasies. The moral and ethical messages of these works did not concern the youthful readers, who were simply after a good tale.

THE EIGHTEENTH AND EARLY NINETEENTH CENTURIES

JOHN NEWBERY AND CHILDREN'S BOOK PUBLISHING

As a consequence of these influences, the way was paved for the serious publishing of children's books. Although he may not have been the first, John Newbery (1713-1767), an English entrepreneur, was certainly the most successful of the early publishers of books for children. His *Little Pretty Pocket Book* (1744) is now considered a landmark as the first significant publication for children that sought not only their edification but their enjoyment as well. This collection of songs, moral tales, and crude woodblock illustrations marked the successful beginning of a publishing phenomenon that has not yet stopped ballooning.

ROUSSEAU AND THE MORAL TALE

The French philosopher Jean Jacques Rousseau (1712-1778) added yet another point of view to the concept of children's reading. His ideas about education were expressed in a book called *Emile* (1762), where he emphasized the importance of *moral* development. (The Puritans' concern had been *spiritual*; Locke's had been *intellectual*.) For Rousseau, proper moral development could be best accomplished through simplicity of living. (Even 200 years ago people were becoming distressed over the increasing complexity of life.) Rousseau's ideas led to extremely didactic and moralistic books for children, books that supposedly taught them how to be good and proper human beings. (Newbery had, in fact, contributed his fair share of moralistic tales, *Little Goody Two Shoes* being the most famous.) A great many writers, most of them women (men still looked upon writing for children as an inferior occupation), churned out a great number of moralistic tales through the remainder of the eighteenth and well into the nineteenth centuries.

Among the best known of these writers is Maria Edgeworth (1744-1817), whose most famous stories for children are "The Purple Jar" (1796) and her book *Simple Susan*, about a country girl whose goodness helps her to triumph over an ill-intentioned city lawyer. Sarah Trimmer (1741-1810) wrote the *History of the Robins* (1786), an animal story unusual in a time that looked with suspicion on the device of talking animals (the eighteenth-century rationalists thought it was illogical). As one of the first reviewers of children's books, Mrs. Trimmer believed that literature must preach Christian morality above all, and she condemned fairy stories for children because they were sacrilegious and lacked moral purpose. Mrs. Anna Laetitia Barbauld (1743-1825) wrote in a similar vein; her most famous works, *Lessons for Children* (1778) and *Hymns in Prose for Children* (1781), clearly suggest their purpose in their titles. Hannah More (1745-1833) and Mrs. Mary Sherwood (1775-1851) were also part of this moralizing company, and Mrs. Sherwood's *History of the Fairchild Family* (1818) includes frighteningly vivid stories about the souls of impious children moldering in a cold grave or being consigned to the fires of hell. The reputations of most of these women have declined over the years; however, they deserve mention as ardent pioneers in the world of children's literature.

THE RISE OF THE FOLKTALES

The didactic element in children's books remained persistent through the early nineteenth century, and children's books of distinction were exceedingly rare. Concurrent with the heavily moralistic tales, however, was another development that would prove enormously influential. This was the rescue of the old folktales from the quickly fading oral tradition. Actually, folktales had been published in England as early as 1729 when *Tales of Mother Goose*, by the Frenchman Charles Perrault (1628-1703), was first translated and published in English. These stories (originally published in France in the 1690s, apparently for the diversion of the ladies of the Royal Court) were retellings of old folktales, including "Cinderella," "Little Red Riding Hood," and "Sleeping Beauty." Of course, children adored them—as they always have—and throughout the eighteenth century, more and more retellings appeared, despite the admonitions of Mrs. Trimmer.

At the beginning of the nineteenth century, two German brothers, Jacob (1785-1863) and Wilhelm (1786-1859) Grimm, collected a great number of folktales and published them (once again, not expressly for children). In 1846, Hans Christian Andersen's *Fairy Tales* were first published in English and have remained popular ever since. By the end of nineteenth century, the collectors Joseph Jacobs (*English Fairy Tales*) and Andrew Lang (*The Blue Fairy Book, The Red Fairy Book*, etc.) were making available a wealth of folktales from the world over.

THE VICTORIANS: THE GOLDEN AGE

It was during the long reign of Britain's Queen Victoria (1837–1901) that children's literature first blossomed. The Victorians were influenced by the Romantic Movement of the early nineteenth century, a movement that idealized childhood and led to a greater interest in children in general. On both sides of the Atlantic, first-rate authors and illustrators began to turn their talents to children and their books, and the late Victorian period is still referred to as the Golden Age of children's books. (The twentieth century was to see a second golden age and we may still be basking in its glow.)

FANTASIES

In 1865, Lewis Carroll (the pseudonym for Charles Dodgson, a mathematics professor at Oxford University) published *Alice in Wonderland* and thus began a new era in children's literature. *Alice in Wonderland* was the first significant publication for children that abandoned all pretense of instruction and was offered purely for enjoyment. Many consider this to be the book that broke the bonds of didacticism that had so long gripped children's literature and thus opened the gates for a flood of imaginative writing in both England and America. Fantasies in novel form were immensely popular among the Victorians (the British have always had a greater fondness for fantasy than either the continental Europeans or the Americans). Among the great early fantasy writers after Carroll were Charles Kingsley (*The Water Babies*, 1863), George Mac-Donald (*The Princess and the Goblin*, 1872, and *The Princess and the Curdie*, 1877), Rudyard Kipling (*Jungle Books*, 1894–1895), the American L. Frank Baum (*The Wizard of Oz*, 1900), E. Nesbit (*Five Children and It*, 1902), J. M. Barrie (*Peter Pan*, 1904, the name of the play—the book, entitled *Peter and Wendy*, did not appear until 1911), and Kenneth Grahame (*The Wind in the Willows*, 1908).

ADVENTURE STORIES

Also especially popular in the nineteenth century were adventure stories that were written specifically for boys. (The Victorian period drew very clear lines between the sexes.) British children seemed to prefer stories set in faraway and unfamiliar places, and Robert Louis Stevenson's *Treasure Island* (1883), the classic story of pirates and hidden treasure, is one of the hallmarks of this type. The far-flung British Empire may have encouraged this international flavor, and hundreds of (mostly mediocre) adventure stories were published during the period. Captain Marryat, who actually was a seaman, was the first to write historical adventures for children (including *Mr. Midshipman Easy*, 1836, and *Children of the New Forest*, 1847). Other writers of adventure stories include R. M. Ballantyne (*The Coral Island*, 1857, the story of three boys shipwrecked on an island paradise) and G. A. Henty, a war correspondent who traveled widely throughout the British Empire and wrote books such as *With Clive in India* (1884).

American boys were more attracted to adventure stories set in their native land, sometimes in the romantic past of their still young nation. Mark Twain's *The Adventures of Tom Sawyer* (1876) and *The Adventures of Huckleberry Finn* (1884) are among the most enduring of adventure stories, and the latter has been recognized as one of the great American novels. One of the most successful writers of boys' stories was Horatio Alger, Jr., whose immensely popular rags-to-riches stories (*Ragged Dick; or, Street Life in New York*, 1867, and many others) have made his name virtually a household word even today, long after people have ceased to read his books. Alger's heroes were always downtrodden boys who struggled for financial security and respectability, both of which they ultimately gained due to a combination of moral uprightness and hard work. Another favorite was William Taylor Adams, who wrote formula fiction under the pen name of Oliver Optic. His works were only a notch above the so-called dime novels of the day—the forerunners of the modern-day paperbacks. Written by hack writers, dime novels were sensational, lacking in style and depth, cheap, and, therefore, immensely popular.

SCHOOL STORIES

Also primarily for boys was the so-called school story, about the antics of boys at boarding schools. This was largely a British phenomenon, where class-consciousness and the tradition of the public school (which, in England, is actually a private school) remained strong. *Tom Brown's School Days*, 1857, by the British writer Thomas Hughes, is a prototype of this sort of fiction. In 1899, Kipling's school story *Stalky and Co.* appeared, a story remarkable for its lack of sentimentality and its emphasis on harsh realism. The school story was never as popular in America, but it did have its spokespersons. Thomas Bailey Aldrich's *The Story of a Bad Boy* (1870)—who turns out not to be so bad—is among the first American school stories. This was soon followed by Edward Eggleston's *The Hoosier Schoolmaster* (1871), which tells the school story from the teacher's point of view, and eventually *The Hoosier School-Boy* (1883). The school story fairly vanished in the twentieth century, although occasionally vestiges appear in works for older readers, such as John Knowles's *A Separate Peace* (1960) and Robert Cormier's *The Chocolate War* (1974).

DOMESTIC STORIES

Girls of the Victorian period were given the popular domestic stories, tales of home and family life focusing on the activities of a virtuous heroine, usually coming from dire circumstances and achieving good fortune and ultimate happiness in the person of a handsome young man. (If the themes of both the Alger stories and the domestic stories sound vaguely familiar, they should—they are essentially modern versions of the old folktales, in which persons of humble origins rise to wealth, fame, and happiness, primarily because they are moral and upright individuals.) The American Susan Warner, who used the pseudonym Elizabeth Wetherell, wrote one of the earliest Victorian domestic novels, *The Wide, Wide World* (1850), a popular work, both highly sentimental and religious. Charlotte Yonge's *The Daisy Chain* (1856), a British work, is among the best of the early family stories. It is, of course, Louisa May Alcott's *Little Women* (1868) that achieved the greatest fame among the domestic novels, and this story of the four March sisters and "Marmee"—modelled after Alcott's own family—has been accorded the status of a minor classic. Many of the domestic novels sank into maudlin sentimentality. Martha Finlay's *Elsie Dinsmore* (1867) was among the most popular and the most sentimental, with Elsie, a heroine of delicate sensibilities, shedding torrents of tears. Not all domestic novels were so soggy. Margaret Sidney's *The Five Little Peppers and How They Grew* (1880) and Kate Douglas Wiggins's *Rebecca of Sunnybrook Farm* (1903) achieved a measure of restraint. And occasional bright stars appeared, such as L. M. Montgomery's *Anne of Green Gables* (1908) and its sequels.

Some notable early twentieth-century successors to the family story include the works of Laura Ingalls Wilder (*The Little House* series, 1932–1943), Eleanor Estes (*The Moffats*, 1941), and Elizabeth Enright (*The Saturdays*, 1941). And today, such notable writers as Katherine Paterson (*Jacob, Have I Loved*, 1980) and Patricia MacLachlan (*Sarah, Plain and Tall*, 1985) write versions of the domestic story, and the popular problem novels for young teens are also incarnations of this versatile form. These modern stories tend to be much less sentimental, and many deal with the harsher realities of life, but we should see this as evidence of the increasing frankness of children's stories rather than as a commentary on the declining state of the family.

CHILDREN'S BOOK ILLUSTRATION

Victorian children's literature saw extraordinary advances in the field of book illustrations. Children's books of the eighteenth century and earlier either lacked illustrations altogether or contained crude woodblock illustrations, such as those in the *Orbis Sensualium Pictus*. Serious artists could not be enticed to draw for children's books until the end of the nineteenth century, when the growth of children's book publishing and the development of printing technology that allowed for full-color printing attracted many talented artists to the field. The earliest great illustrator of English children's books was George Cruikshank (1792–1878), who in 1823 illustrated the first English translation of Grimms's fairy tales, and he was also the first illustrator for Charles Dickens's works, most notably for *Oliver Twist* (1838). Randolph Caldecott (1846–1886) illustrated William Cowper's *John Gilpin's Ride* (1878) and numerous other poems and nursery rhymes in a stunning series for children (see Figure 1.3). Kate Greenaway (1846–1901) illustrated Browning's *The Pied Piper of Hamelin* (1888) and other works, including some of her own poetry (see Figure 6.5 on page 95). Walter Crane (1845–1915) produced lavish illustrations for many children's books, including *The Baby's Opera* (1877), a collection of nursery rhymes complete with music. Arthur Rackham (1867–1939) was an immensely versatile and highly original artist who contributed works of the finest artistic quality to children's book illustration.

FIGURE 1.3   Randolph Caldecott, the great nineteenth-century English illustrator, was one of the pioneers of children's book illustration. His art is characterized by an economy of line and a playfulness of manner that make his work appealing today, more than a century after his death. The American Library Association annually awards the Caldecott Medal, named in his honor, to what it judges the most distinguished picture book published in the United States. This illustration from *The Frog He Would A-Wooing Go* (1883) depicts Caldecott's lively sense of humor.

THE TWENTIETH CENTURY: WIDENING WORLDS

Children's books of extraordinary quality have continued to appear throughout the twentieth century and have been characterized by even greater diversity in all kinds of children's literature, from picture books to poetry to fantasy to realistic fiction to informational books. A greater appreciation for quality books has surfaced, as evidenced by the numerous book awards now being offered in children's literature, among the earliest being the Newbery Medal, named for John Newbery and honoring the most distinguished American book written for children during a given year, and the Caldecott Medal, named for Randolph Caldecott and honoring the most distinguished American contribution to children's book illustration. The British counterparts of these awards are the Carnegie and Greenaway Medals, respectively, and similar awards can be found in many other countries.

We have come a considerable distance over the past two centuries, from the time when children's literature was relegated to the back room of intellectual life and when children were regarded as embodiments of sin about to happen and therefore in need of constant instruction, admonition, and supervision. We have seen writers and illustrators acquire a greater respect for their child audiences and a deeper awareness of children's needs. Writers are no longer afraid to broach the most serious of subjects with children, from the evils of the Holocaust to the devastations of AIDS. The result has been a body of extremely fine literature, rich in diversity and polished in form.

C. S. Lewis wrote: "When I was ten, I read fairy tales in secret and would have been ashamed if I had been found doing so. Now that I am fifty I read them openly. When I became a man I put away childish things, including the fear of childishness and the desire to be very grownup" (210). He further reminds us that growth or maturation actually consists not of putting away old pleasures, but of adding new ones:

> I now enjoy Tolstoy and Jane Austen and Trollope as well as fairy tales and I call that growth; if I had had to lose the fairy tales in order to acquire the novelists, I would not say that I had grown but only that I had changed. A tree grows because it adds rings; a train doesn't grow by leaving one station behind and puffing on to the next. (211)

One of the purposes of the study of children's literature is to help us recover the old pleasures (or perhaps, in some cases, to introduce them for the first time). It has only been in the later decades of this century that a serious study of children's literature has emerged. It is a far-ranging study—the study of childhood, of human aesthetic development, of human intellectual development, of social development. At its root is the conviction that reading is the great indispensable tool of our culture. Without reading, civilization as we know it would disappear in one generation; the ideas of the past would be lost forever; we would be forced naked into the world. And so, perhaps the greatest end of the study of children's literature is to make readers of our children, to give them the tools they will need to build a better world than their parents have known.

WORKS CITED

Lewis, C. S. "On Three Ways of Writing for Children." In *Only Connect*, 2nd ed., Sheila Egoff. New York: Oxford, 1980. 207–220.

Wooden, Warren W. *Children's Literature of the English Renaissance*. Lexington: University of Kentucky Press, 1986.

RECOMMENDED READINGS

Aries, Philippe. *Centuries of Childhood: A Social History of Family Life*. New York: Knopf, 1962.

Avery, Gillian. *Childhood's Pattern: A Study of the Heroes and Heroines of Children's Fiction, 1770-1950*. London: Hodder and Stoughton, 1975.

Avery, Gillian, and Julia Briggs. *Children and Their Books*. Oxford: Oxford University Press, 1989.

Bator, Robert, comp. *Signposts to Criticism of Children's Literature*. Chicago: American Library Association, 1983.

Butts, Dennis, ed. *Stories and Society: Children's Literature in Its Social Context*. London: Macmillan, 1992.

Carpenter, Humphrey. *Secret Gardens: A Study of the Golden Age of Children's Literature*. Boston: Houghton Mifflin, 1985.

Carpenter, Humphrey, and Mari Prichard. *The Oxford Companion to Children's Literature*. Oxford: Oxford University Press, 1984.

Chevalier, Tracy, ed. *Twentieth-Century Children's Writers*, 3rd ed. Chicago: St. James Press, 1989.

Coody, Betty. *Using Literature with Young Children*, 2nd ed. Dubuque, IA: Wm. C. Brown, 1979.

Cott, Jonathan. *Pipers at the Gates of Dawn: The Wisdom of Children's Literature*. New York: Random House, 1981.

Darton, F. J. Harvey. *Children's Books in England, Five Centuries of Social Life*. Cambridge: Cambridge University Press, 1982.

Demers, Patricia, and Gordon Moyles, eds. *From Instruction to Delight*. Toronto: Oxford University Press, 1982.

Egoff, Sheila A. *Only Connect: Readings on Children's Literature*, 2nd ed. Toronto: Oxford University Press, 1980.

————. *Thursday's Child: Trends and Patterns in Contemporary Children's Literature*. Chicago: American Library Association, 1981.

Fraser, James H., ed. *Society and Children's Literature*. Boston: Godine, 1978.

Harrison, Barbara, and Gregory Maguire, comps. and eds. *Innocence & Experience: Essays & Conversations on Children's Literature*. New York: Lothrop, Lee & Shepard, 1987.

Haviland, Virginia, ed. *Children and Literature: Views and Reviews*. Glenview, IL: Scott, Foresman, 1973.

Hazard, Paul. *Books, Children, and Men*. Boston: The Horn Book, 1983.

Hunt, Peter. *An Introduction to Children's Literature*. Oxford: Oxford University Press, 1994.

Hunter, Mollie. *Talent Is Not Enough*. New York: Harper & Row, 1976.

Inglis, Fred. *The Promise of Happiness: Meaning and Value in Children's Fiction*. Cambridge: Cambridge University Press, 1981.

Jackson, Mary V. *Engines of Instruction, Mischief, and Magic: Children's Literature in England from Its Beginnings to 1839*. Omaha: University of Nebraska, 1990.

MacDonald, Ruth. *Literature for Children in England and America from 1646 to 1774*. Troy: Whitston, 1982.

McLeod, Anne Scott. *A Moral Tale: Children's Fiction and American Culture, 1820-1860*. Hamden: Archon, 1975.

Meek, Margaret, Aidan Warlow, and Griselda Barton. *The Cool Web: The Patterns of Children's Reading*. New York: Atheneum, 1978.

Meigs, Cornelia, Elizabeth Nesbitt, Anne Thaxter Eaton, and Ruth Hill. *A Critical History of Children's Literature: A Survey of Children's Books in English*. New York: Macmillan, 1969.

Nikolajeva, Maria, ed. *Aspects and Issues in the History of Children's Literature*. Contributions to the Study of World Literature, No. 60. Wesport, CT: Greenwood, 1995.

Pickering, Samuel F., Jr. *John Locke and Children's Books in Eighteenth-Century England*. Knoxville: University of Tennessee Press, 1981.

Pollack, Linda. *Forgotten Children: Parent-Child Relations from 1500 to 1900*. Cambridge: Cambridge University Press, 1983.

Sadker, Myra Pollack, and David Miller Sadker. *Now Upon a Time: A Contemporary View of Children's Literature*. New York: Harper & Row, 1977.

Summerfield, Geoffrey. *Fantasy and Reason: Children's Literature in the Eighteenth Century*. Athens: University of Georgia Press, 1983.

Thwaite, Mary F. *From Primer to Pleasure in Reading: An Introduction to the History of Children's Books in England*. Boston: The Horn Book, 1972.

Townsend, John Rowe. *Written for Children: An Outline of English-language Children's Literature*, 3rd rev. ed. New York: Lippincott, 1987.

Tucker, Nicholas. *The Child and the Book: A Psychological and Literary Exploration*. Cambridge: Cambridge University Press, 1981.

Wall, Barbara. *The Narrator's Voice: The Dilemma of Children's Fiction*. London: Macmillan, 1991.

Chapter 2

~

CHILD
DEVELOPMENT AND
LITERATURE

THE IMPACT OF CHILD
DEVELOPMENT ON READING

Children, as we have seen, were once regarded as miniature adults with simple minds and shallow feelings. But today we have taken virtually the opposite view as our understanding of childhood behavior and intellectual development has increased. Modern theories of child development have revealed that children are psychologically complex individuals indeed, possessing a host of special needs on their way to maturity. An awareness of these theories can give us a better understanding of both children and their books—or, more specifically, of their relationships and interactions with books.

MODERN THEORIES
OF CHILD DEVELOPMENT

We will look at three of the more prominent theories of child development, all of which complement each other (see Table 2.1). Jean Piaget was concerned with intellectual or cognitive development, Erik Erikson with social development, and Lawrence Kohlberg with the development of moral judgment. All three see human development as occurring in a series of stages through which most individuals pass on their progress toward maturity.

TABLE 2.1   Comparative chart of developmental stages identified by Piaget, Erikson, and Kohlberg

Piaget	Erikson	Kohlberg
Sensorimotor Period (0–2 years)	Trust vs. Mistrust (0–18 months)	Preconventional Level (0–7 years)
Preoperational Period (2–7 years)	Autonomy vs. Doubt	*Stage 1 Punishment/Obedience*
Preconceptual Stage (2–4 years)	(18 months–3 years)	*Orientation*
Intuitive Stage (4–7 years)	Initiative vs. Guilt (3–7 years)	*Stage 2 Instrumental/Relativist*
		Orientation
Period of Concrete Operations	Industry vs. Inferiority	Conventional Level (7–11 years)
(7–11 years)	(7–11 years)	*Stage 1 Interpersonal Concordance*
		Orientation
		Stage 2 "Law and Order" Orientation
Period of Formal Operations	Identity vs. Role Confusion	Postconventional Level
(11–15 years)	(11–15 years)	(Adolescence/Adulthood)
		Stage 1 Contractual/Legalistic
		Orientation
		Stage 2 Universal/Ethical/Principle
		Orientation

Before these theories are described, a word of caution is in order. Both Piaget and Kohlberg have been criticized for ignoring female development, which, some argue, is not the same as male development. Males generally value competition, self-assertiveness, individual rights, and social rules. Females, on the other hand, value human relationships, responsibilities to others, cooperation, community values, and tolerance for opposing viewpoints. Additionally, some researchers argue, females reach some of these developmental stages more quickly than males. Only lately has a significant amount of work been done in the field of women's psychological development. Also neglected until quite recently was the study of the psychological development of members of minority groups, who often reflect different values from those of the majority group. This is not to say that the work of the three psychologists below is to be invalidated, but that these theories, as all theories, are not infallible. They are offered here as a general guide.

PIAGET'S COGNITIVE THEORY OF DEVELOPMENT

The *Cognitive Theory of Development*, devised by the Swiss psychologist Jean Piaget, is the earliest and perhaps the most famous of the theories. Piaget saw a person's intellectual or mental development as occurring in steps, each building on the previous one. He outlined four major periods of intellectual development, some of which he subdivided into stages. It is important to note that once an individual has moved on to a higher stage some backsliding may occur, some temporary reverting to a previous stage. (It is rather like mountain climbing; if we don't have a sure footing or a firm grasp, we will slip back down the mountain.) Also, the movement between stages is gradual and almost imperceptible, with all individuals developing at different rates. Consequently, the age spans mentioned here can be only approximations and averages.

THE SENSORIMOTOR PERIOD

The first period Piaget identifies is the *Sensorimotor Period*, which he estimates as lasting from birth to about two years of age, during which the child is incapable of establishing *object permanence*—in other words, infants in this period do not realize that objects continue to exist even if they cannot be seen. So far as an infant is concerned, when she can no longer see her mother, her mother simply does not exist; out of sight is out of mind. Consequently, the infant's world is entirely egocentric and the only things that matter to the child are what she sees, feels, hears, tastes, and smells. It is also during this period that the infant is concerned with the development of coordination, figuring out how to use the hands and arms and legs.

What impact does this early period of cognitive development have on reading? It is most important in these early years that we plant the seed of reading, encourage the physical handling of books, and establish habitual story times. The stories themselves are not so important as is a happy experience during the story time. Durable cardboard and cloth books are helpful in providing infants and toddlers with a sense of the book's physical characteristics. Tactile books, such as Dorothy Kunhardt's *Pat the Bunny* in which the young child can touch the cottony fur of the bunny or feel the sandpaper roughness of daddy's facial stubble, can provide considerable entertainment. For the very young, nursery rhymes have appeal with their lilting rhythms and curious sounds (for example, "Higglety, pigglety, my black hen," or "Hickory, dickory dock"). The infant responds to the engaging sounds of the language.

THE PREOPERATIONAL PERIOD

The Preconceptual Stage. Once children have acquired fundamental language skills, they begin to move into the second of Piaget's periods—the *Preoperational Period*—lasting between the ages of two and seven. During the first two or three years of this period, children are in what Piaget termed the *Preconceptual Stage*, characterized by a very subjective logic. This is a time of discovery for children and they still rely heavily on sensory experiences. The concept of classification is beginning to take shape, and children can, at a very young age, grasp certain rudimentary classes, such as colors, shapes, sizes, and so on. Children respond well to concept books that present these ideas. However, children at this stage have a difficult time with abstraction and tend to classify objects according to variable criteria: For instance, they attribute human characteristics to anything that moves (including animals and machines). Consequently, children are fond of books about talking animals and animated machines. Some examples include Hardy Gramatky's

Little Toot, the story of a tugboat, and Virginia Burton's *Mike Mulligan and His Steam Shovel*, the adventures of a steamshovel named Maryanne.

By "preconceptual," Piaget simply refers to the inability to grasp generalizations or abstract concepts. Examples of the kinds of abstractions children do not understand at this stage include the concept of *conservation of quantity* (in Piaget's famous experiment, children believed that a tall thin jar contained more water than a short fat one, even though they observed the same quantity of water being transferred from one to the other). Nor do they comprehend the notion of the *reversibility of operations* (the fact that certain things can be "undone"). The concept of history is difficult for them to grasp because it involves a sort of reversal of time. Additionally, these children have difficulty with adaptation, which includes *assimilation* (using current knowledge to explain or otherwise deal with new information) and *accommodation* (revising current knowledge to respond to new information).

When we consider these characteristics, it is easy to understand how children between the ages of two and four can readily believe in Santa Claus and have no trouble with the fact that they might see a half dozen different Santas in the course of a single shopping trip. Only when they begin to understand such a concept as conservation of quantity do they begin to wonder how Santa can be in so many places at once. Also, it is easy to see why children might have great difficulty with a story containing flashbacks, for that concept requires a grasp of the notion of reversibility. Likewise, we understand why stories with repeated patterns are appealing, or why anthropomorphic tales are popular with these children. Essentially, it has not yet occurred to them to question the logic of such literature.

The Intuitive Stage.   The second stage of this *Preoperational Period* is what Piaget terms the *Intuitive Stage*, which occurs typically between the ages of four and seven. Rather than using formal logic, children at this stage use, for lack of a better term, "intuition" or their feelings to help them make judgments about the world around them. They are developing language skills and they are becoming increasingly aware of their environment and, consequently, they are becoming less egocentric. Now stories about human relationships carry new meaning as do stories that explore inner emotions. Although fantasies remain popular with these children, realism often becomes more meaningful as they grow curious about other people and their own relationships with others. A realistic story such as Robert McCloskey's *One Morning in Maine*, a picture book describing the simple pleasures of family life, will hold appeal for children in this age group. This is an extremely important time for children so far as reading is concerned, since this is a stage of experimentation and it is at this time that children often discover hidden interests. Reading a wide variety of books on many different topics can help them in this discovery process.

THE PERIOD OF CONCRETE OPERATIONS

The third period, the *Period of Concrete Operations*, lasts roughly between the ages of seven and eleven. This is when children begin to use rudimentary logic and problem solving. They begin to understand time and spatial relationships. At this stage, young readers begin to read longer books that are divided into chapters, and they can comfortably pause between chapters and pick up the story at a later time. Time sequencing is no longer a difficult problem, and episodic books (such as Beverly Cleary's *Dear Mr. Henshaw*) and mystery stories (such as Donald Sobol's *Encyclopedia Brown* series) present pleasurable challenges for these readers. Because children at this stage are more aware of people around them and of their own role in society, novels by such writers as Judy Blume (*Blubber* and *Tales of a Fourth Grade Nothing*) and Patricia MacLachlan (*Cassie Binegar* and *Unclaimed Treasures*) are popular. Such books focus on the personal and social problems of this age group and frequently depict the young protagonists in the process of problem solving.

Additionally, historical fiction becomes more meaningful at this period, since the children now have a grasp of the passage of time. Laura Ingalls Wilder's *Little House* series has been a longtime staple for readers in these years, and Patricia MacLachlan's *Sarah, Plain and Tall*, with a similar setting, is a more recent addition to this sort of fiction. Often historical fiction carries social implications, such as the commentary on racial injustice in Mildred Taylor's stories (e.g., *Roll of Thunder, Hear My Cry*, about the South in the 1930s). Stories about other lands, such as Lois Lowry's *Number the Stars*, an exciting story of Denmark during World War II, or the mysterious postwar atmosphere in France described by Steven Schnur in *The Shadow Children*, become appealing as young readers begin to expand their horizons and explore the wider world.

THE PERIOD OF FORMAL OPERATIONS

The final stage is the *Period of Formal Operations*, beginning around the age of eleven and being completed at about fifteen (when full cognitive maturity is established, according to Piaget). During this period, young people become capable of using formal logic, engaging in a true exchange of ideas, comprehending the viewpoints of others, and essentially understanding the world as a social phenomenon requiring human interaction. Most readers at this stage of development have already entered adolescence, or what many prefer to call "young adulthood." Their reading tastes extend beyond the boundaries established for this book, but it is helpful to see where the reading development is headed. Examples of topics found in books for this age group include inner-city gang wars (S. E. Hinton's *The Outsiders*), homosexuality (John Donovan's *I'll Get There. It Better Be Worth the Trip*, Sandra Scoppettone's *Trying Hard to Hear You*, and M. E. Kerr's *Deliver Us from Evie)*, racial prejudice (Mildred Taylor's *Roll of Thunder, Hear My Cry*), premarital sex (Judy Blume's *Then Again, Maybe I Won't*), just to name a few. The controversial works of Robert Cormier (*I Am the Cheese*, *The Bumblebee Flies Anyway*, and others) treat such subjects as social and government corruption and have overall negative tones. They remain popular because they address head-on some of the doubts, fears and anxieties that active young minds naturally experience.

ERIKSON'S PSYCHOSOCIAL DEVELOPMENT THEORY

In addition to developing intellectually, individuals develop in their social interaction. Erik Erikson's Psychosocial Development Theory classifies the maturing process into a series of psychosocial conflicts, each of which must be resolved before one can move on to the next, in much the same way that Piaget sees successive levels in cognitive development. Erikson's theory includes five principal stages of development throughout childhood. As with Piaget's stages, this development can only be approximated and is different for each individual. Also, regression (or backsliding) does occur from time to time.

TRUST VS. MISTRUST

The first stage focuses on the conflict of *Trust versus Mistrust*, from birth to about eighteen months. This is when children have little option but to trust those who are their caregivers, and they must overcome fears of mistrust, such as the fear of abandonment when they are put to sleep in their own bed. Security provided by creature comforts and physical affection is extremely important at this stage when life is so full of new and potentially unsettling experiences. Margaret Wise Brown's classic, *Good Night Moon*, has long been popular as a story for early childhood because it exudes warmth and coziness as we observe a little bunny saying good night to all his favorite possessions in the comfort of his womblike bedroom. Children's preference for hearing familiar books read night after night provides a measure of comfort and security as well.

AUTONOMY VS. DOUBT

Erikson's second stage, *Autonomy versus Doubt*, from eighteen months to about three years, is when children become aware of others around them, especially their caregivers and siblings. As young children become mobile, they begin to exercise their first impulses toward autonomy or independence. But at the same time, they must overcome doubts about whether they can do what they attempt. Consequently, this is a period of exploration, which can be exasperating for parents who have labeled this time "the terrible twos." Beatrix Potter's *The Tale of Peter Rabbit* beautifully illustrates the moral dilemma that faces children at this stage, with the protagonist facing the conflict between acting on his own will and obeying the authority of his mother.

INITIATIVE VS. GUILT

The third stage, *Initiative versus Guilt*, occurs between the ages of three and six, when children begin to realize their own responsibilities and understand the interpersonal conflicts that arise between people. Children want to take the initiative, not only to do things on their own but to decide what to do and when to do it. But they must also struggle with guilt when they make the wrong choices. In Ezra Jack Keats's *Peter's Chair* (1967), Peter exhibits hostility when his parents decide to paint all his baby furniture pink for his new sister. Peter decides to run away but eventually comes to regret his selfish motives in refusing to share his baby things (which he realizes he no longer needs), and he finally offers them to her of his own free will. Peter has arrived at a higher stage of social development than his rabbit counterpart in Beatrix Potter's tale, as he demonstrates by his resolve to alter his behavior.

INDUSTRY VS. INFERIORITY

The fourth stage, *Industry versus Inferiority*, takes place between the ages of seven and eleven and is characterized by a determination to achieve success, often working in concert with others (i.e., engaged in work or industry). At the same time, however, children have a tendency to measure themselves against their peers and find themselves wanting, hence feelings of inferiority may develop. Beverly Cleary's *Ramona* books wonderfully demonstrate these feelings; young readers view Ramona with a sympathetic eye as she strives for acceptance among her peers.

IDENTITY VS. ROLE CONFUSION

The fifth stage, *Identity versus Role Confusion*, is achieved at adolescence. Perhaps the great crisis of adolescence is the discovery of identity (not only personal identity, but cultural and social identity as well). Young adults are anxious to know what their roles in life are to be, what society expects of them, what they expect of themselves. All these are questions of identity. Naturally, because of the wealth of options available to young adults, role confusion is a constant threat. Individuals at this stage often appear to be fickle, and sometimes seem to be in a state of almost constant flux, as they are torn by a reluctance to leave the security of childhood and tempted by the exciting possibilities of adult independence. Add to all this their emerging sexuality, and we can easily understand the turmoil of adolescence. Also at this time, cultural and social differences are first fully realized, and young readers benefit from books that deal honestly and openly with these issues. Although many of the books that address these issues are young adult books and outside the realm of this text, readers in the intermediate grades—approximately fifth through seventh or eighth—can find many good novels that examine these issues. Virginia Hamilton's *M.C. Higgins, the Great*, Katherine Paterson's *The Great Gilly Hopkins*, and the fantasies of Ursula Le Guin's *Earthsea* cycle are all stories of the search for individual identity.

KOHLBERG'S THEORY OF THE DEVELOPMENT OF MORAL JUDGMENT

Lawrence Kohlberg's theories concern the development of moral reasoning and moral judgment—that is, how individuals determine what is right and wrong. He bases his work on that of John Dewey and Jean Piaget, and similarly sees development as occurring in a series of stages through which an individual must pass to reach moral maturity. With particular interest in why moral judgments are made, Kohlberg identifies three different levels of development, each divided into two stages.

THE PRECONVENTIONAL LEVEL

The first level, the *Preconventional Level*, is characterized by children responding in terms of the immediate consequences of an action—to punishment or reward or to the superior strength of another. At this level, children move through two stages. The first, termed the *Punishment/Obedience Orientation*, is when a child judges an action to be good or bad depending upon its physical consequences. What hurts is bad and what gives pleasure is good. (A hot stove is bad; a chocolate chip cookie is good.) The second stage, the *Instrumental/Relativist Orientation*, is when a child judges an action in terms of its ability to satisfy his or her own needs, or perhaps the needs of others, but only when reciprocity is present ("I'll do this for you if you do that for me"). For children to engage in this sort of activity they must have reached Piaget's Preoperational Period and have some facility with language and intuitive logic. Children readily see the actions of Potter's Peter Rabbit as bad because they are likely to cause him harm. His disobedience brings life-threatening consequences and results in loss of property and health.

THE CONVENTIONAL LEVEL

The second level, the *Conventional Level*, corresponding roughly with Piaget's Period of Concrete Opertions (ages seven to eleven), marks the point at which children begin to value the family, group, community, and nation. Conformity and loyalty to societal conventions or norms become important. The first stage in this level is the *Interpersonal Concordance (or "Good Boy/Nice Girl") Orientation*. To be good is to please others and to have the approval of others. "Normal" behavior is frequently the ideal, and what is "normal" is usually a stereotyped image agreed upon by the majority. We can see a relationship between this stage and Erikson's fourth stage, *Industry versus Inferiority*, coming into play here, for this is the time when peer pressure begins to exert itself. Children now want to wear clothes like their friends wear, eat foods like their friends eat, and, perhaps most important, they just want to have friends. What is good for the individual, therefore, is anything that makes him or her look good in the eyes of others. Patricia MacLachlan's *Cassie Binegar* is the story of a girl embarrassed by her unconventional family: "Why can't we be like everyone else?" Cassie laments. Her cry echoes the sentiments of every child going through this stage of life, yearning for acceptance.

The second stage in this level is the *"Law and Order" Orientation*, which occurs when children develop a respect for authority and for abiding by the "rules," and when they realize the necessity for carrying out their part in the social order. Eleanor Estes's classic family story *The Moffats* depicts Janey Moffat, although typically respectful of her elders, one day mimicking the peculiar walk of the superintendent. Then she is convinced that the chief of police is after her for this "crime," and she jumps into a large wooden breadbox at the grocer's to hide from him. It is a comical, but believable, reaction.

THE POSTCONVENTIONAL LEVEL

The final level is the *Postconventional Level*, which occurs when the individual is capable of making rational, independent judgments apart from the authority of the group or society. This is a phenomenon not usually realized until adolescence. The first stage in this level is the *Contractual/Legalistic Orientation* at which individuals define what is right according to broadly based individual standards that a society establishes. The law is no longer blindly accepted, as in the Conventional Level, but instead it is examined and weighed and occasionally found wanting. Books on social problems, such as S. E. Hinton's study of gang violence, *The Outsiders*, and Robert Cormier's unsettling tale of corruption, *The Chocolate War*, address readers at the *Postconventional Level*.

The second stage of the Postconventional Level is the *Universal/Ethical/Principle Orientation*, in which an individual defines what is right by his or her own conscience and what he or she perceives to be logical, consistent, and universal principles of right and wrong. Acting according to the Golden Rule or some other abstract principle is an example of this type of moral reasoning. But it should be pointed out that psychologists disagree as to whether such a stage actually exists—or rather whether human beings are actually capable of attaining this stage (perhaps prophets and saints come close, but few ordinary individuals do).

If we take a simple example (and this does admittedly oversimplify the matter, but it will serve our purposes nevertheless), we can illustrate the various stages of development in this way. When a parent requires a toddler to fasten her seatbelt in the car, the toddler responds because the parent is bigger and stronger and the toddler must do as she is told. This is the first level of moral development, the *Preconventional Level*. A child in early elementary school may fasten her seatbelt because she learns that all her friends fasten theirs, or she may do so because her parents have told her they might get arrested if she is caught out of her seatbelt. She is responding to the pressure of peers or to societal authority and is at the *Conventional Level* of moral development. A teenager fastens her seatbelt not only because she knows it is the law, but because she knows that it is an intelligent law designed to protect her. She is operating at the third level of moral development, the *Postconventional Level*.

THE USES OF DEVELOPMENTAL PSYCHOLOGY

There are probably as many developmental theories as there are developmental psychologists to devise them. Suffice it to say that there is considerable agreement that human beings develop in stages, that these stages can only be roughly approximated in terms of years, that there is much overlapping in these stages, and that there may be occasional regression or a temporary going backwards as children develop. Healthy individuals progress successfully through these stages, generally moving from a period of complete egocentrism to maturity, when the needs and concerns of others begin to play a central role, perhaps even the pivotal role if the development is completely successful. Although they may not always be able to identify developmental stages by name or to recite psychological theory, the best writers are fully cognizant of human behavior. They are keenly aware of the problems, fears, hopes, and dreams of children as they move through childhood.

RECOMMENDED READINGS

Brainerd, Charles J. *Recent Advances in Cognitive Developmental Research*. New York: Springer-Verlag, 1983.

Brief, Jean-Claude. *Beyond Piaget: A Philosophical Psychology*. New York: Teachers College Press, 1983.

Cullinan, Bernice. *Literature and the Child*, 2nd ed. San Diego, CA: Harcourt, 1989.

Donelson, Kenneth L., and Alleen Pace Nilsen. *Literature for Today's Young Adults*, 2nd ed. Glenview, IL: Scott, Foresman, 1985.

Erikson, Erik. *Childhood and Society*. New York: Norton, 1950.

Fields, M. V., K. Spangler, and D. M. Lee. *Let's Begin Reading Right*, 2nd ed. Columbus, OH: Merrill, 1991.

Gilligan, Carol. *In a Different Voice: Psychological Theory and Women's Development*. Cambridge, MA: Harvard University Press, 1982.

Huck, Charlotte S., Susan Hepler, and Janet Hickman. *Children's Literature in the Elementary School*, 4th ed. New York: Holt, Rinehart & Winston, 1987.

Hyde, Janet Shibley. *Half the Human Experience: The Psychology of Women*. Lexington, MA: D. C. Heath, 1985.

Kohlberg, Lawrence. *The Philosophy of Moral Development*. San Francisco: Harper & Row, 1981.

———. *Essays on Moral Development. Vol. II: The Psychology of Moral Development, the Nature and Validity of Moral Stages*. San Francisco: Harper & Row, 1985.

Lindfors, J. W. *Children's Language and Learning*, 2nd ed. Englewood Cliffs, NJ: Prentice-Hall, 1987.

Piaget, Jean. *The Language and Thought of the Child*. New York: Harcourt, Brace, 1926.

———. "Piaget's Theory." In *Handbook of Child Psychology*, 4th ed., P. H. Mussen, Ed. New York: John Wiley & Sons, 1983.

Sugarman, Susan. *Piaget's Construction of the Child's Reality*. Cambridge: Cambridge University Press, 1987.

Walsh, Mary Roth, ed. *The Psychology of Women: Ongoing Debates*. New Haven, CT: Yale University Press, 1987.

Chapter 3

CULTURAL AND SOCIAL DIVERSITY

This chapter will address two somewhat different avenues of human diversity. *Cultural diversity* (also termed *multiculturalism*) deals with people of different ethnic, cultural, and religious groups. *Social diversity*, an admittedly ambiguous term, is meant to deal with any persons, regardless of cultural background, who have traditionally been left out of the mainstream or disenfranchised by those in power. Under the heading of social diversity, we will briefly examine the issues of gender, alternative lifestyles, and individuals with special needs—physical, emotional, or intellectual.

Let's note before we go further into this discussion that whenever we consider the social implications of literature we make it a political issue. When literature becomes political, it risks falling into didacticism and polemicism. Two schools of thought exist: (1) those who believe that literature is purely aesthetic and should be judged only on its artistic merit; and (2) those who believe that literature is necessarily a social document and should also be judged on the strength and integrity of its message. This is a longstanding debate—going back to ancient Greece. Is literature purely a creation of beauty, or does it have a social and moral obligation as well? Dangers lurk in the extremes of both views. On the one hand, literature may become effete and obscure; on the other, it may devolve into mere propaganda. We should keep these cautions in mind as we consider the issues in this chapter. The best literature provides a balance between the form and the content—giving us both pleasure and wisdom.

CULTURAL DIVERSITY

Cultural diversity in literature is exhibited in works about people of color (in the United States, these include African Americans, Asian Americans, Hispanic Americans, and Native Americans), people of foreign cultures (regardless of their color), and people of cultural or religious groups outside the mainstream (such as the Amish). The appearance of heroes from minority cultural groups has been a belated one in children's literature—as indeed it has been in most literature. The social reality in the United States, as demographers have shown us, is that we are moving from a culture dominated by European Americans to one of greater ethnic diversity, and our literature should reflect this dramatic shift. Rather than reinforcing outmoded values, literature can provide us with the intellectual apparatus to effect greater tolerance and understanding. The critic Northrop Frye once wrote:

> So you may ask, what is the use of studying the world of imagination where anything is possible and anything be assumed, where there are no rights or wrongs and all arguments are equally good? One of the most obvious ones, I think, is its encouragement of tolerance. In the imagination our own beliefs are also only possibilities, but we can see the possibilities in the beliefs of others. Bigots and fanatics seldom have any use for the arts, because they're so preoccupied with their beliefs and actions that they can't see them as also possibilities. (77–78)

In the best literature, we are exposed to the world of possibilities, removed from our own narrow confines, and challenged to spread our wings. In short, literature can prepare us for the multicultural society in which we all live.

One of the significant controversies surrounding culturally diverse literature is whether or not an author outside a specific cultural social group can write authentically about that group. One African-American playwright, August Wilson, says that "Someone who does not share the specifics of a culture remains outside, no matter how astute a student or well-meaning the intentions" (Harris 42). In other words, those who believe as Wilson does insist that only African Americans can write credibly and sensitively about African Americans, only Native Americans can write about Native Americans, and so on. However, another African American, the critic Henry Louis Gates, Jr., disagrees: "No human culture is so inaccessible to someone who makes the effort to understand, to learn, to inhabit another world" (Gates 30). Those who believe as Gates does feel that true empathy is possible between individuals from different cultures, that cultural differences can be bridged, that human beings have the capacity to embrace other traditions and other peoples. Perhaps it should be our hope that Gates is correct, for therein lies the promise of a better world in the future.

Rudine Sims Bishop has very clearly identified the necessity for culturally diverse literature, as well as the dangers for not having it:

> If literature is a mirror that reflects human life, then all children who read or are read to need to see themselves reflected as part of humanity. If they

are not, or if their reflections are distorted and ridiculous, there is the danger that they will absorb negative messages about themselves and people like them. Those who see only themselves or who are exposed to errors and misrepresentations are miseducated into a false sense of superiority, and the harm is doubly done. (quoted in Harris 43)

So, culturally diverse literature enriches everyone. It provides the majority culture with exposure to the various minority cultures and thus helps to break down old prejudices and dispel misunderstandings. Not least, it provides the minority cultures with positive role models and bolsters cultural pride and individual dignity. All these considerations must be weighed against the drawbacks of using literature for political and social ends. Obviously, when we focus on the multicultural aspect of literature, we are concerning ourselves with the message first and foremost, and the aesthetic value second. Many critics—going back as far as Plato—believe that literature cannot help being political and that good literature does indeed carry important moral and social implications. But that does not mean that a revealing novel about contemporary Native American society cannot also be a work of the highest literary achievement, such as we find, for example, in N. Scott Momaday's books for adult readers. It is this balance between the art and the message that we should be seeking in cross-cultural literature for children.

There are several important features to be considered about culturally diverse literature, regardless of its subject matter. Following are some guidelines we may use in evaluating a literary work for its attention to cultural consciousness:

1. The characters are portrayed as individuals, with genuine feelings, thoughts, and beliefs, and not as types representing a specific cultural group.
2. There is no cultural stereotyping suggesting that all members of a specific cultural group share the same socioeconomic status, similar occupations, and so on.
3. The culture is accurately portrayed, neither exaggerated nor romanticized.
4. The problems facing the group are dealt with seriously, faithfully, and honestly, not oversimplified.
5. All factual details are accurate, and there are no omissions or distortions that may cast an unfair light on the picture.
6. The author demonstrates a sincere understanding of and respect for the cultural group being portrayed.

Next we will consider the literature about the four principal non-European cultural groups in the United States, with a word on cultures worldwide.

AFRICAN AMERICANS

Fortunately, in recent years there has been an increase in African-American literature for children, which begins to offset the decades of sore neglect. Earlier literature tended to focus on young, white, middle-class Americans of Christian backgrounds. In 1945, Jesse Jackson (not the minister/politician/activist) wrote what was considered a groundbreaking book, *Call Me Charley*. It is the story of a young African-American boy attempting to assimilate into the white middle-class neighborhood where his parents have moved. The conflict in the book is racial, and the author's intent is made clear from the very beginning, when Charley responds to a boy who refers to him as "Sambo": "My name is Charles. . . . Sometimes I'm called Charley. Nobody calls me Sambo and gets away with it" (8). The story seems dated now, with its emphasis on the essentially white middle-class values shared by Charley and his family, which we take to be the principal reason he is finally accepted as an equal in the white community. Later African Americans would decry the necessity for Charley to abandon his identity and his cultural roots in order to gain entry into the white world. But Charley was only operating in accordance with the widely accepted practices of the day, when everyone believed the ideal society to be that of the melting pot in which all distinguishing cultural features were abandoned in favor of those of the dominant white culture.

It is virtually impossible to find a picture book about an African-American child published prior to the 1960s. All of the widely used elementary basal school readers of the first half of the twentieth century depicted European-American families, and reading them we would never guess that the society included any people of color. Ezra Jack Keats's *The Snowy Day* and its sequels are among the first to use an African American as a protagonist. Keats's critics point out that his books lack "cultural specificity"—i.e., nothing except Peter's skin color identifies him as an African American, but they remain important groundbreakers. Lucille Clifton's moving picture books about Everett Anderson trace the joys and heartaches of a young African-American boy who experiences the separation of his parents, the remarriage of his mother, the birth a new half-sister, and the death of his father. Such books recognize current social realities, which make them particularly appealing.

Culturally conscious African-American literature avoids stereotypes (such as implying that all African Americans are musically inclined or talented in sports or fond of specific foods). African-American traditions are included as matters of course. These books will mention such rituals as "church attendance, Sunday suppers, beautification rituals, double dutch jump rope rhymes," and other features characteristic of the African-American cultural experience (Harris 71). Modern writers (e.g., Eloise Greenfield, Rosa Guy, Virginia Hamilton, Sharon Bell Mathis, Walter Dean Myers, and Mildred Taylor) aim at capturing what is unique about the African-American culture. A wide variety of literature about African Americans is available, ranging from contemporary novels to historical novels to biographies to retellings of African and African-American folktales. All help to remind us of the pervasive and important influence of African-American culture on American life.

Rosa Guy, a distinguished writer of books for young adults (*The Friends, Ruby*, and others) and a native of the former British colony of Trinidad, has issued this call to arms for all cultural groups:

> I reject the young of each succeeding generation who dare to say: "I don't understand *you* people. . ." "I can't stand *those people*. . ." or, "Do you see the way *they* act . . .?" They are us! Created by us for a society which suits our ignorance.

I insist that Everychild understand this. I insist that Everychild go out into the world with this knowledge: there are no good guys. There are no bad guys. We are all good guys. We are all bad guys. And we are all responsible for each other. (34)

NATIVE AMERICANS

Perhaps more than any other cultural minority in the United States, Native Americans have been the subject of a mythology that continues to cloud the general public's perception. Too many children today tend to lump together all Native Americans (some Native Americans prefer the term *American Indian* and still others prefer *Amerind*) into one vision of a beaded, feathered, and moccasined warrior. Formerly, children's picture books either ignored the Native American altogether or fell back on the stereotypes. Native Americans argue that even the modern picture books rely on the old images and fail to portray the modern American Indian realistically. Indeed, by and large, picture books on Native Americans still tend to focus on the traditional images—feathered headresses, teepees, tomahawks, and papooses—and ignore the fact that about two million Native Americans live in America today without these trappings.

One of the difficulties in finding culturally sensitive Native American literature lies in the fact that Native American writers are relatively few, and much of the literature to which children are directed has been written by European Americans. A need exists for more Native American spokespersons, a need that is happily being filled with the appearance of such writers as Craig Kee Strete (*Big Thunder Magic*, 1990), Rosebud Yellow Robe (*Tonweya and the Eagles and Other Lakota Tales*, 1979), Joseph Bruchac (*Iroquois Stories: Heroes and Heroines, Monsters and Magic*, 1985), and Virginia Driving Hawk Sneve (*Dancing Teepees: Poems of American Indian Youth*, 1989).

Several types of literature by and about Native Americans exists. Most very young children are exposed first to the Native American folktales. Some of these have resulted in handsomely illustrated books. (Those by Paul Goble, such as *Iktomi and the Berries*, 1989, have been among the most admired for their faithfulness to the oral character of the tales and his sensitive use of form and color to capture the spirit of the works.) Because many Native American tales are still essentially within the oral tradition and remain a significant aspect of the culture, it is important that the sources of these tales be respected. More and more children's versions of these folktales are identifying not only the specific Native American society where the tales originated (e.g., Iroquois, Sioux, Ojibway, etc.), but the Native tellers themselves. (Richard Erdoes's *The Sound of Flutes and Other Indians Legends*, 1976, specifically names the storytellers, for example.) Joseph Bruchac and Rosebud Yellow Robe are both Native American collectors and retellers whose work has acquired respect.

A second type of Native American literature is that dealing with the history of Native Americans. It is in this category that we have historically seen the most damage done to the image of the Native American. Consequently, we find ourselves looking for modern books that counter the deplorable stereotypes of the past. Books such as Ignatia Broker's *Night Flying Woman: An Ojibway Narrative* (1983), which describes the life of the author's great-great-grandmother and the uprooting of her people by nineteenth-century white men, provide extraordinary testaments about the plight of the Ojibway nation and the indomitable spirit that enabled the people's survival. Russell Freedman's *Indian Chiefs* (1987) is a much-praised historical study that sets out to correct myths and misconceptions. Freedman refuses to sugarcoat his material and is assiduous about relying on primary sources, using photographs from the period, and quoting people who lived at the time. Still, too many histories and biographies fall back on a subtle racism, implying that the white way of life is superior to the Native American. Such books display a white bias, portray Native Americans as objects rather than as individuals, and imply a smug superiority of European culture over all others.

Perhaps the rarest type of Native American book is the contemporary novel— a story of Native Americans in modern society. We can have no truly adequate understanding of modern Native American culture if we do not see Native Americans as citizens of late twentieth-century America, wearing modern dress, using modern appliances, entering professions just like everyone else. At the same time, just as with African-American literature, we should expect the important cultural issues facing Native Americans, such as poverty, prejudice, and rapidly vanishing cultural traditions and identity, to be addressed faithfully. Hal Borland's *When the Legends Die* (1963), for older readers, is a ground-breaking work on contemporary life. More recent are such works as A. E. Cannon's *The Shadow Brothers* (1990), Barbara Girion's *Indian Summer* (1990), and Craig Kee Strete's *When Grandfather Journeys into Winter* (1979).

Culturally conscious books eliminate demeaning vocabulary and artificial dialogue, cruel and insensitive Indian stereotypes, and the depiction of white authority figures who solve all the problems. These books include portraits of Native Americans as individuals, sensitive descriptions of Native American cultural traditions, and an awareness that each Native American society is a distinct cultural entity—that there are Ojibway, Iroquois, Sioux, and so on. Finally, when considering books about Native Americans we will do well to keep in mind these questions posed by Donnarae MacCann: "Is there anything in the book that would make a Native American child feel embarrassed or hurt to be what he or she is? Can the child look at the book and recognize and feel good about what he or she sees?" (quoted in Harris 161).

HISPANIC AMERICANS

Among the largest commonly recognized minority groups in the United States are the Hispanic Americans. Particularly in the southwestern states, the Hispanic American is on the way to becoming the dominant cultural group. Literature has not yet reflected that influence, however. Until very recently, very few good books on Hispanic Americans have been available. Many of the books in existence present an inaccurate picture of the culture and perpetuate stereotypes. For example, despite the fact that most Hispanic Americans live in cities, books have more typically depicted rural people, often migrant workers, usually living in poverty (see Wagoner). The earliest works depicting Hispanic Americans were pieces of historical fiction or pieces that focused exclusively on the Hispanic American culture in isolation. Joseph Krumgold's . . . *and now Miguel* (1953), a Newbery award winner from the early 1950s, is the story of the coming of age of an Hispanic American boy from a family of shepherds in northern New Mexico. Although a sensitive and well-told narrative, the book unfortunately contributes to the stereotype of the rural and poor Hispanic, uneducated and out of the mainstream. In picture books, circumstances were little different. The writer and illustrator Leo Politi was among the first to use Hispanic Americans in picture books. His works include at least two award winners, *Pedro, the Angel of Olvera Street* (Caldecott Honor Book in 1947) and *Song of the Swallows* (Caldecott Medalist in 1950), both set in California. Marie Hall Ets's *Nine Days to Christmas*, winner of the 1960 Caldecott Medal, is another that has remained popular. Because they focused on earlier time periods and relied on stereotypical rural settings, these books contribute little to our understanding of the modern Hispanic American culture.

In the 1970s, we finally saw books to counter the stereotypes promulgated in the 1940s—the stereotype of the Hispanic migrant worker in need of saving by a benevolent representative of the white community. Today we can find works that depict the urbanized Hispanic American facing the modern world. Hila Colman's *The Girl from Puerto Rico* (1961) and Frank Bonham's *Viva Chicano* (1970) are pioneering examples. Theodore Taylor's *The Maldonado Miracle* (1986) has been praised as a work by an "outsider" that captures the spirit of the Mexican-American experience, a rare accomplishment.

By the 1990s, a growing number of Hispanic American writers began to appear on the scene. Among the most celebrated are Gary Soto, who writes both prose (*Baseball in April* and *The Cat's Meow)* and poetry (*A Fire in My Hands*); Pat Mora, who also writes both prose (*Communion*) and poetry (*Borders* and *Chants*); and Carmen Lomas Garza, whose *Family Picture/Cuadros de Familia* is an example of the dual-language book in English and Spanish. Hispanic American writers draw frequently on the rich oral traditions of their cultures, and many are poets. In literature about Hispanic Americans, the Spanish language is a key element. Hispanic Americans in large numbers speak Spanish, many as their first language, and writers from outside the culture attempting to portray the Hispanic Americans must have a secure knowledge of not only the culture, but the language.

Perhaps one of the most important aspects of Hispanic culture that children must realize is that it is not a unified experience. Very much like the Native American cultures, the Hispanic cultures are diverse and continually changing. Hispanic American cultures include, among others, Mexican-Americans, Puerto Ricans, and immigrants from Central and South America, all of whom have distinctive backgrounds. The largest group is the Mexican-American, concentrated in, but not confined to, the Southwest and California. Hispanic Americans will unquestionably become a powerful force in the American socioeconomic-political arena by the turn of the century. It is time that this presence was noted in children's literature, and that we all become more sensitive to the diversity and richness of this culture.

ASIAN AMERICANS

As with the other cultural groups we have examined, we must realize that Asian Americans are a diverse group (in fact, we should more accurately refer to this group as Asian Pacific Americans, since we generally refer to those whose ancestry derives from Asian countries bordering on the Pacific Ocean). Naturally, Japanese differ from Chinese who differ from Vietnamese and so on. To lump all these cultures together as if they were a single national/ethnic group is not only inaccurate, it is insensitive. Ideally, the literature should reflect these differences and celebrate these distinctions.

With that said, Asian Americans are becoming a prominent part of the American culture, and they too, like almost every minority in this nation's history, have suffered indignities at the hands of the dominant European culture. In the middle of the nineteenth century, large numbers of Chinese workers were brought to the American West where they provided cheap labor for the railroads. For the Chinese, as for the European immigrants, America promised to be a land of opportunity, but those promises did not always come to fruition. J. S. Wong's *Fifth Chinese Daughter* (1950) is among the earliest books to portray Chinese Americans with realism; it is the story of a girl growing up in San Francisco and her desire to become an artist. Laurence Yep's *Dragonwings* (1975) provides us with a view of San Francisco's Chinatown in the early 1900s through the eyes of a young Chinese immigrant, giving us valuable insight into the difficulties of assimilating two very different cultures. The same author's *The Child of the Owl* (1977) provides a modern setting with a similar theme—the clash of two cultures, out of which the protagonist learns the value of her Chinese heritage.

The Japanese are even less often found in children's books, which is surprising given the economic influence of Japan in recent years. It is interesting to note that virtually no books exist on the difficulty of Japanese characters in adapting to life in America, but there are significant books on the difficulty of the Americans adapting to Japanese living in America, more specifically, the cultural conflict that erupted during World War II. The autobiographical *Farewell to Manzanar* (1973) by Jeanne Wakatsuki Houston and James D. Houston is the harrowing story of the internment of Japanese-American families during the war, a tale little-known among Americans until recent years. Yoshiko Uchida's *Journey to Topaz* (1971) is a book on the same theme, also drawn from personal experience.

Today we find a growing selection of literature about Asian Americans. This literature exists in several forms. Historical fiction frequently focuses on the trials of immigrants in a new land, such as Laurence Yep's *Dragon's Gate* (1993), which deals with the building of the transcontinental railroad by Chinese immigrants. Contemporary fiction depicts the personal conflicts that arise from the mingling of two cultures, such as is described in Betty Bao Lord's *The Year of the Boar and Jackie Robinson* (1984). And we have seen an increasing number of traditional Asian folktales retold in beautiful picture books—particularly Ed Young's award-winning *Lon Po Po: A Red-Riding Hood Story from China* (1990). Such works as these can help all young readers to combat the old prejudices and the unfair stereotyping of Asian Americans and Asian cultures.

WORLDWIDE CULTURES

In addition to these four, the United States can boast myriad cultural groups that contribute to our rich diversity. The nature of the modern world demands that we all become more aware of and sensitive to the diverse cultures found not only in our own nation, but in the world at large. Books can be found on a wide variety of cultures from around the globe, from the Cholistan Desert tribes of Pakistan in Suzanne Fisher Staples's *Shabanu: Daughter of the Wind* to the Australian outback in Mavis Thorpe Clark's *The Min-Min* to the Welsh coal-mining district in Richard Llewellyn's *How Green Was My Valley* to modern-day Africa in Bess Clayton's *Story for a Black Night.*

Some of the most eye-opening books are those based on historical events. The moving *Anne Frank: The Diary of a Young Girl*, which recounts the horrors of Nazi occupation in The Netherlands, is among the most famous of these. Aranka Siegal's *Upon the Head of the Goat: A Childhood in Hungary, 1939–1944*, describes the Nazi attrocities against the Jews from the perspective of yet another nation. The terror of the Holocaust a half-century ago was the grim culmination of centuries of persecution for the Jewish people. But anti-Semitism still thrives—most obviously, but not only, in the Middle East. Chaim Potok's *My Name Is Asher Lev*, Yuri Suhl's *The Merrymaker*, and the wonderful works of Isaac Bashevis Singer, including the autobiographical stories of *In My Father's Court*, his popular *Yentl, the Yeshiva Boy*, and *The Death of Methuselah*, are lovely expressions of the Jewish culture that can bring readers to a more sympathetic understanding. But persecution knows no cultural bounds, as demonstrated in David Kherdian's *The Road from Home: The Story of an Armenian Girlhood*. This is a biographical account of the author's mother's experiences during the period of the massacre of Armenian Christians in Turkey just after World War I and brings to light one of the lesser-known, but no less horrifying, crimes against humanity. This cataloguing sounds like a grim list indeed, but keeping before us these deplorable chapters in the world's history may serve in some small way to prevent future atrocities.

SOCIAL DIVERSITY

GENDER AWARENESS

For thousands of years, most of human society has been patriarchal, dominated by the male. Our patriarchal culture has effectively relegated woman's position to one of subservience and has caused us to see feminine traits as inferior to masculine traits. Society has come to value physical strength, assertiveness, independence, power, aggressiveness, ambition—all of which we tend to see as masculine features. Conversely, we denigrate passivity, docility, emotionalism, physical weakness, dependence, resignation—all of which we tend to see as feminine features. These values have been so ingrained in our culture that we generally accept them unquestioningly. For a woman to be taken seriously, she must perform as a man, and such behavior is just as likely to win her ridicule from both sexes. It has only been in the last half of the twentieth century that significant measures have been taken to counter this male bias in Western culture.

In literature, as we might expect, the bias is reflected in several ways, most notably in the prevalence of male protagonists over female, the celebration of the typically male traits of physical strength and aggression, and the perpetuation of the image of the female as weak and ineffectual. Children's books have not escaped such stereotyping, and they reflect in their own way society's subtle anti-feminine bias. There are three principal ways literature conveys this negative message.

Gender-Biased Language.   Language can perpetuate cultural bias, and English is particularly notable for this transgression. The use of the masculine pronoun "he" to refer to everyone, for example, effectively eliminates over half of the human race. Compound words such as "chairman," "mailman," "policeman," and "businessman" indicate the historical dominance of the male. We use "sissy" as a disparaging term, but it's seen as good for someone to stand up and take it like a "man."

Gender Roles.   Society has traditionally assigned certain roles to men—generally roles of leadership and authority—and certain roles to women—generally roles of caregivers and assistants. In the past, children's books have portrayed doctors, airline pilots, school principals, and corporate executives as male, whereas nurses, stewardesses, teachers, and secretaries have been depicted as female. This is the result of centuries of patriarchal domination, which has cast men in positions of power and kept women at the lower rungs of the social ladder. Additionally, the tasks performed by women have been typically undervalued—ask those in the nursing profession or in secretarial positions, for example. These two areas are still dominated by underpaid women.

Gender Behavior.   In addition to casting men and women in predetermined roles, society has traditionally differentiated between what it perceives to be male and female behavior or standards of conduct. Women have been cast as the fairer and weaker sex—weaker physically, emotionally and intellectually. The male child is expected to be physically active, even mischievous. The female child who shows such traits may be labeled a "tomboy," another disparaging term. Tears are expected of a female and condemned in a male. Males are expected to be clever and inventive, but similar traits in females are often acknowledged with surprise. Studies of gender behavior in children's books point out how often girls are depicted as passive observers, whereas the boys are actively engaged. (A boy climbs a tree, but a girl observes from the safety of the ground, for example. On the other hand, who is the wiser?)

It is important that children read books that give them positive images of women and that avoid ignorant stereotyping of roles and behavior. These might include such books as Louise Fitzhugh's *Harriet the Spy*, about a clever young girl who decides she wants to be a spy, or Jean Craighead George's *Julie of the Wolves*, about a courageous Eskimo girl with painful decisions to face, or Mildred Taylor's *Roll of Thun-*

der, *Hear My Cry*, about a young African-American girl facing prejudice during the Great Depression. Books that provide positive adult role models are equally important, such as Peggy Mann's *Amelia Earhart, First Lady of Flight*, one of the many biographies of this pioneer pilot, or Patricia MacLachlan's *Cassie Binegar*, with its portrait of a remarkable grandmother.

Not to be neglected are books that depict males in other than stereotypical roles. John Steptoe's *My Daddy Is a Monster . . . Sometimes* depicts a nurturing father as seen through the eyes of children. And Mark Wandro and Joanie Blank's *My Daddy Is a Nurse* describes ten fathers in professions traditionally associated with women. Books in which males are depicted as sensitive, artistic, or anything other than macho sports fanatics are also helpful. Patricia MacLachlan's *Arthur, for the Very First Time* and Katherine Paterson's *Bridge to Terabithia* are two notable examples.

Two principles must be stressed here. The first is that gender bias in children's books does not create the problem, but it may reinforce it. When obvious gender bias is found in a book, we as adults should be ready to point it out to young readers and to discuss it. Gender bias is frequently found in many of the classics that predate this era of consciousness raising. But rather than eliminate these books altogether and deprive children of some great stories, we can use the books to advantage and show children how times have changed. One of the purposes of literature, in addition to entertainment, is to give us food for thought.

The second principle is that eliminating gender bias from our society does not help females alone. Males are just as much victims of social bondage, weighted down with great expectations and permitted no acceptable emotional outlet except, perhaps, for aggressive behavior on the playing fields. The liberation of women must necessarily mean the liberation of men as well, leaving all people free to choose their places in society unshackled by ignorance and bias.

Following are some guidelines to use when evaluating a literary work for gender awareness. Literature that shows a positive gender awareness will have these characteristics:

1. The author uses inclusive language, avoiding the generic "he" and gender-specific words, such as "mailman" and "chairman." (Of course, we may not fault earlier writers for not observing this practice, for only since the 1980s has inclusive language become the norm.)
2. The author avoids blanket casting of males and females into stereotyped roles—especially roles that cast females as subservient to males, such as males as breadwinners, females as housewives; males as doctors, females as nurses; and so on. (This is not to suggest that all roles be reversed out of a sense of fairness, but only that we should not expect all nurses to be females, all mayors to be males, and so on.)
3. The author avoids stereotyping certain behaviors and personality traits as "feminine"—especially those suggesting weakness, docility, and passivity.
4. The author avoids stereotyping certain behaviors and personality traits as "masculine"—especially those suggesting toughness, insensitivity, and aggressiveness.

ALTERNATIVE FAMILIES AND LIFESTYLES

A third issue recognizes the fact that no longer do most children grow up in homes in the suburbs with two parents, a sibling, and a dog. No longer do most mothers don their aprons in the morning and spend their days cleaning and cooking for their families. Divorce is as common as marriage; and women virtually outnumber men in the work force. Modern children's books are now coming to reflect this reality. The traumas of dealing with divorce are related in Beverly Cleary's *Dear Mr. Henshaw*. Children who have stepparents, stepsiblings and half-siblings may find comfort in books depicting other families like theirs. Of course, many popular folktales have some very unflattering portraits of stepmothers. Rather than deprive children of the enchantment of "Cinderella," we might balance it with a book about a positive experience with stepmothers, such as Patricia MacLachlan's *Sarah, Plain and Tall*. There are also those more unconventional families, such as that depicted in Norma Klein's *Mom, the Wolfman, and Me*, which focuses on an unmarried mother and her daughter who must make adjustments to her mother's new boyfriend. Katherine Paterson's *The Great Gilly Hopkins* deals with the issues of foster care. And Cynthia Voigt's *Homecoming* and *Dicey's Song* tell the story of four children, abandoned by their mother, who seek to make a home with their formidable grandmother. Arnold Adoff's *Black Is Brown Is Tan*, a picture book for the very young, is one that deals with interracial marriages. Adoff celebrates the joy of diversity in the relationship. In the future, we should expect more books for children on this subject.

For children approaching the middle school years—sixth, seventh, and eighth grades—even more delicate lifestyle issues are broached in their reading. Perhaps none is so delicate as homosexuality. Virtually ignored—even taboo—in children's literature until the 1980s, sexual preference is now being recognized by many writers as an important social issue about which children need sensitive education. Pioneering works in this field include John Donovan's *I'll Get There. It Better Be Worth the Trip* and Isabelle Holland's *The Man Without a Face* (the recent movie eliminated the homosexual references, which, in fact, played a key role in the book). More recently, works by well-established writers have focused attention on homosexuality, such as Marion Dane Bauer's *Am I Blue?: Coming Out from the Silence* (a selection of short stories by various writers), M. E. Kerr's *Deliver Us from Evie* (about a teenage lesbian), and Paula Fox's *The Eagle Kite*. Michael Willhoite's *Daddy's Roommate* is a picture book describing the weekends a young boy spends with his father and his father's live-in boyfriend. The ultimate theme of all these works is that of understanding and acceptance of an individual's sexual orientation. This is just one more hurdle of bigotry and prejudice that we must help our children overcome. Following are some guidelines to use in evaluating books about alternative families and lifestyles:

1. The author treats the subject with sensitivity.
2. Any suggestion that the alternative family life is somehow less desirable than the so-called traditional family is avoided.

3. The author treats the subject with honesty and frankness. (There is no pretense that children in these circumstances will not face problems, doubts, fears—in other words, they are treated just like all other children.)

THE PHYSICALLY, EMOTIONALLY, AND INTELLECTUALLY CHALLENGED

Another change taking place in our society is a more receptive attitude developed toward individuals with special needs. These individuals were once virtually ignored in children's books, undoubtedly a holdover from the time when people with physical, emotional, or intellectual differences were largely hidden away from society— either institutionalized or kept secluded at home. Thankfully society has become more sensitive to the needs of this group. Our laws now recognize the existence of physically challenged individuals, and our schools are now far more accommodating to the intellectually challenged. Gradually, children's books are addressing the interests of these people. We can now find books dealing with emotional needs, such as Taro Yashima's picture book, *Crow Boy*, about an inordinately shy boy, or Betsy Byars's *The Summer of the Swans*, about a boy with a mental disability and his relationship with other family members, or Virginia Hamilton's *Sweet Whispers, Brother Rush*, about a family coping with an inherited mental disorder. Physical disabilities are featured in such books as Elizabeth Fanshawe's *Rachel* and Joan Fassler's *Howie Helps Himself*, both stories about younger children in wheelchairs.

It is important that people face their fears and ignorance regarding others with special needs, and reading books is one way of ovecoming prejudices and combatting stereotypes. Of course, it is important that the books we read deal fairly with disabilities and special needs. Following are some guidelines to use in evaluating literary works focusing on characters with special needs:

1. The characters with special needs are portrayed in a positive light without sentimentality or romanticism.
2. The characters are treated realistically and not as superhuman or as helpless children.
3. The characters are integrated naturally into the story and not depicted as anomalies or pecularities in society or as comic sidekicks.
4. The author avoids using language or terminology that stereotypes, such as "handicap," "retarded," and other words that may be construed as offensive.
5. The author portrays people with special needs as capable of ordinary human feelings—love, anger, joy, hate.
6. The author avoids paralleling physical or mental disabilities with personality traits—spinal deformities as a sign of wickedness, for example.

OTHER ISSUES

Other issues to look for in children's books include old age, death and dying, war, and sexuality. The best books deal honestly with these subjects. In recent years, we have seen more books appear that portray old age in a positive light, books that present images of old people as distinct individuals rather than cruelly stereotyped cranks, for example. Many books depict positive relationships between young people and the elderly, such as Miska Miles's *Annie and the Old One*, Tomie de Paola's *Nana Upstairs, Nana Downstairs*, and Barbara Cooney's *Miss Rumphius*—all delightful picture books. Cynthia Voigt's *Dicey's Song*, Patricia MacLachlan's *Cassie Binegar*, and Laurence Yep's *Child of the Owl* are all excellent books that help to break down traditional stereotypes of old age.

The portrayal of death in children's literature is really nothing new. In the eighteenth century, children read books with vivid descriptions of death and dying, but usually death was viewed as punishment for wickedness or godlessness or, conversely, as the gateway to the heavenly reward for a pious life. In the twentieth century, however, as life spans have been lengthened and child mortality has declined, death has become far less visible—both in our lives and our literature. Earlier in this century, death was considered an unsuitable topic for children; it was simply too morbid, people seemed to feel. But we are now coming to realize what our ancestors well knew, that death is a natural part of life and our children should not be sheltered from it. A young child's first experience with death is often with the death of an animal. Margaret Wise Brown's *The Dead Bird* is the simple story of children finding a dead bird, giving it a proper funeral, and then going about their play; death is seen as a natural part of things, requiring both observance and acceptance. Doris Buchanan Smith's *A Taste of Blackberries* is about how a boy copes with the tragic death of his best friend. It is a story both sad and beautiful.

Following are some general guidelines to use in evaluating books on any contemporary issue, death, old age, sexuality, and so on:

1. The author avoids stereotyping any situation, but instead treats it as an individual experience having a specific effect on the characters involved.
2. The author avoids prejudgment, but instead allows the reader to examine the details and arrive at a conclusion.
3. The author treats the situation with sensitivity and openness, helping the reader to understand the varied emotions as they are revealed in the characters.
4. The author treats the situation with honesty and frankness, without sentimentality, exaggeration, or romanticism.

With these and other issues that are now being confronted in books for children our primary concern is that the subject matter is treated intelligently, sensitively, and honestly. Perhaps the most important message of this entire chapter is that children's literature can provide a positive influence on young people's lives by unveiling for them the rich variety of human life.

WORKS CITED

Frye, Northrop. *The Educated Imagination.* Bloomington, IN: Indiana University Press, 1969.
Guy, Rosa. "Innocence, Betrayal, and History." *School Library Journal* November 1985: 33–34.

Harris, Violet, ed. *Teaching Multicultural Literature in Grades K–8*. Norwood, MA: Christopher-Gordon, 1993.

Jackson, Jesse. *Call Me Charley*. New York: Dell, 1945.

RECOMMENDED READINGS

Broderick, Dorothy M. *Image of the Black in Children's Fiction*. New York: Bowker, 1973.

Carlson, Ruth Kearney. *Emerging Humanity: Multi-Ethnic Literature for Children and Adolescents*. Dubuque, IA: Wm. C. Brown, 1972.

Gates, Henry Louis, Jr. " 'Authenticity,' or The Lesson of Little Tree." *New York Times* 24 November 1991: 1, 26–30.

Gilliland, Hap. *Indian Children's Books*. Billings, MT: Montana Council for Indian Education, 1980.

John, L., and S. Smith. *Dealing with Diversity Through Multicultural Fictions: Library-classroom Partnerships*. Chicago: American Library Association, 1993.

LeBeau, Patrick R. *The Codical Warrior: The Codification of American Indian Warrior Experience in American Culture*. Unpublished dissertation, University of Michigan, 1993.

Lo, Suzanne, and Ginny Lee. "Asian Images in Children's Books: What Stories Do We Tell Our Children?" *Emergency Librarian* 20.5 (May–June 1993): 14–18.

Luecke, Fritz J., comp. *Children's Books: Views and Values*. Middletown, CT: Xerox Education Publications, 1973.

Manna, Anthony L., and Carolyn S. Brodie, eds. *Many Faces, Many Voices: Multicultural Literary Experiences for Youth*. Fort Atkinson, WI: Highsmith, 1992.

McCann, Donnarae, and Gloria Woodard. *The Black American in Books for Children: Readings in Racism*. Metuchen, NJ: Scarecrow, 1985.

———. *Cultural Conformity in Books for Children*. Metuchen, NJ: Scarecrow, 1977.

McIntosh, Peggy. "White Privilege: Unpacking the Invisible Knapsack." *Peace and Freedom* July/August 1989: 10–12.

Miller-Lachman, L., ed. *Our Family, Our Friends, Our World: An Annotated Guide to Significant Multicultural Books for Children and Teenagers*. New Providence, NJ: R. R. Bowker, 1992.

Rudman, Masha K. *Children's Literature: An Issues Approach*, 3rd ed. New York: Longman, 1995.

Sims, Rudine. *Shadow & Substance: Afro-American Experience in Contemporary Children's Fiction*. Urbana, IL: National Council of Teachers of English, 1982.

———. "Walk Tall in the World: African-American for Today's Children." *Journal of Negro Education* 58 (1990): 556–565.

Wagoner, Shirley A. "Mexican-Americans in Children's Literature Since 1970." *The Reading Teacher* December 1982: 274–279.

CULTURAL DIVERSITY IN CHILDREN'S LITERATURE: A SELECTED BIBLIOGRAPHY

The following list contains books about diverse cultural groups. Books on social issues have been excluded since many of those are included in the bibliographies following Chapters 6, 12, 13, and 14, and to list them here would be redundant.

In those bibliographies, you will find books addressing gender awareness, alternative families and lifestyles, and the phsysically, emotionally, and intellectually challenged. The suggested reading levels are only approximations.

AFRICAN-AMERICAN BOOKS FOR YOUNGER READERS (GRADES 2–5)

Bryan, Ashley. *All Night, All Day: A Child's First Books of African-American Spirituals*. New York: Atheneum, 1991.

———. *Beat the Story Drum, Pum-pum*. New York: Atheneum, 1980.

———. *The Dancing Granny*. New York: Atheneum, 1977.

Caines, Jeanette. *Abby*. New York: Harper, 1973.

———. *Daddy*. New York: Harper, 1977.

———. *I Need a Lunchbox*. New York: Harper, 1988.

———. *Just Us Women*. New York: Harper, 1982.

Clifton, Lucille. *All Us Come Cross the Water*. New York: Holt, 1973.

———. *My Friend Jacob*. New York: Dutton, 1980.

———. *Some of the Days of Everett Anderson*. New York: Holt, 1970.

———. *Sonora Beautiful*. New York: Dutton, 1981.

Dunbar, Paul. *Little Brown Baby* (1895). New York: Dodd, Mead & Co., 1968.

Greenfield, Eloise. *Big Friend, Little Friend*. New York: Black Butterfly Children's Books, 1991.

———. *Grandpa's Face*. New York: Philomel, 1988.

———. *Honey, I Love*. New York: Harper, 1973.

———. *Night on Neighborhood Street*. New York: Black Butterfly Children's Books, 1991.

———. *Under the Sunday Tree*. New York: Harper, 1988.

Howard, Elizabeth. *Aunt Flossie's Hats*. New York: Clarion, 1991.

———. *Chita's Christmas Tree*. New York: Bradbury, 1989.

———. *The Train to Lulu's*. New York: Bradbury, 1988.

Johnson, Angela. *Do Like Kyla*. New York: Orchard, 1990.

———. *One of Three*. New York: Orchard, 1991.

———. *Tell Me a Story, Mama*. New York: Orchard, 1989.

———. *When I Am Old with You*. New York: Orchard, 1990.

Jordan, June. *His Own Where*. New York: Crowell, 1971.

Lowry, Lois. *Anastasia's Chosen Career*. Boston: Houghton Mifflin, 1987.

Mathis, Sharon Bell. *Listen for the Fig Tree*. New York: Viking, 1974.

———. *Teacup Full of Roses*. New York: Viking, 1972.

Steptoe, John. *Baby Says*. New York: Harper, 1988.

———. *Daddy Is a Monster . . . Sometimes*. New York: Viking, 1980.

———. *Mufaros' Beautiful Daughters*. New York: Lothrop, 1947.

———. *Stevie*. New York: Harper, 1969.

———. *Uptown*. New York: Harper, 1970.

AFRICAN-AMERICAN BOOKS FOR OLDER READERS (GRADES 6 AND UP)

Bonham, Frank. *Durango Street*. New York: Dutton, 1965.

———. *The Nitty Gritty*. New York: Dutton, 1968.

Brooks, Bruce. *Everywhere*. New York: Harper, 1990.

Burch, Robert. *Queenie Peavy*. New York: Viking, 1966.

Cameron, Eleanor. *To the Green Mountains*. New York: Dutton, 1975.

Childress, Alice. *A Hero Ain't Nothin's But a Sandwich*. New York: Coward, 1973.

Colman, Hila. *Classmates by Request*. New York: Morrow, 1964.

Fair, R. L. *Cornbread, Earl, and Me*. New York: Bantam, 1975.

Fox, Paula. *The Slave Dancer*. New York: Bradbury, 1973.

Giovanni, Nikki. *Spin a Soft, Black Song*. New York: Farrar, Straus & Giroux, 1987.

Graham, Lorenz. *North Town*. New York: Thomas Crowell, 1965.

———. *South Town*. New York: Thomas Crowell, 1958.

Greene, Bette. *Get on Out of Here, Philip Hall*. New York: Dial, 1981.

———. *Philip Hall Likes Me, I Reckon Maybe*. New York: Dial, 1974.

Guy, Rosa. *The Disappearance*. New York: Delacorte, 1979.

———. *The Friends*. New York: Holt, 1973.

———. *Ruby*. New York: Viking 1976.

———. *The Ups and Downs of Carl Davis*. New York: Delacorte, 1989.

Hamilton, Virginia. *Anthony Burns*. New York: Knopf, 1988.

———. *The House of Dies Drear*. New York: Macmillan, 1968.

———. *The Magical Adventures of Pretty Pearl*. New York: Harper, 1983.

———. *M. C. Higgins, the Great*. New York: Macmillan, 1974.

———. *The People Could Fly*. New York: Knopf, 1985.

———. *The Planet of Junior Brown*. New York: Macmillan, 1971.

———. *Zeely*. New York: Macmillan, 1967.

Hentoff, Nat. *Jazz Country*. New York: Harper, 1965.

Hunter, Kristin. *Guests in the Promised Land*. New York: Scribner's, 1973.

———. *The Soul Brothers and Sister Lou*. New York: Scribner's, 1968.

Langstaff, J. *What a Morning! The Christmas Story in Black Spirituals*. New York: Margaret K. McElderry, 1987.

Lester, Julius. *To Be a Slave*. New York: Dial, 1966.

McKissack, Patricia. *Mirandy and Brother Wind*. New York: Knopf, 1988.

———. *Nettie Jo's Friends*. New York: Knopf, 1989.

McKissack, Patricia, and Frederick McKissack. *The Long Hard Journey*. New York: Knopf, 1989.

Myers, Walter Dean. *Fallen Angels*. New York: Scholastic, 1988.

———. *Me, Mop, and the Moondance Kid*. New York: Dell, 1988.

———. *The Mouse Rap*. New York: Harper, 1990.

———. *Now Is Your Time!* New York: HarperCollins, 1991.

———. *Scorpions*. New York: Harper, 1988.

Neufeld, John. *Edgar Allan*. Chatham, NY: Phillips, 1968.

Ringgold, Faith. *Tar Beach*. New York: Crown, 1991.

Sebastian, Ouida. *Words by Heart*. Boston: Little, 1979.

Taylor, Mildred. *Let the Circle Be Unbroken*. New York: Dial, 1981.

———. *Mississippi Bridge*. New York: Dial, 1990.

———. *The Road to Memphis*. New York: Dial, 1990.

———. *Roll of Thunder, Hear My Cry*. New York: Dial, 1976.

Yates, Elizabeth. *Amos Fortune, Free Man*. New York: Dutton, 1967.

Wilkinson, Brenda. *Ludell*. New York: Harper, 1975.

———. *Ludell and Willie*. New York: Harper, 1977.

NATIVE AMERICAN BOOKS FOR YOUNGER READERS (GRADES 2–5)

Bruchac, Joseph. *Iroquois Stories: Heroes and Heroines, Monsters and Magic.* Freedom, CA: The Crossing Press, 1985.

Dorris, Michael. *Guests.* New York: Hyperion/Disney, 1994.

———. *Morning Girl.* New York: Hyperion/Disney, 1992.

Manitonquat (Medicine Story), reteller. *The Children of the Morning Light: Wampanoag Tales.* New York: Macmillan, 1994.

Sneve, Virginia Driving Hawk. *Dancing Teepees: Poems of American Indian Youth.* Illus. Stephen Gammell. New York: Holiday House, 1989.

———. *High Elk's Treasure.* New York: Holiday, 1972.

Strete, Craig Kee. *Big Thunder Magic.* Illus. Craig Brown. New York: Greenwillow, 1990.

———. *The Bleeding Man and Other Science Fiction Stories.* New York: Greenwillow, 1977.

———. *When Grandfather Journeys Into Winter.* Illus. Hall Frenck. New York: Greenwillow, 1979.

Yellow Robe, Rosebud. *Tonweya and the Eagles and Other Lakota Stories.* Illus. Jerry Pinkney. New York: Dial, 1979.

NATIVE AMERICAN BOOKS FOR OLDER READERS (GRADES 6 AND UP)

Armer, Laura Adams. *Waterless Mountain.* New York: McKay, 1931.

Borland, Hal. *When the Legends Die.* Philadelphia: Lippincott, 1963.

Brown, D. *Creek Mary's Blood.* New York: Franklin Library, 1980.

Cannon, A. E. *The Shadow Brothers.* New York: Delacorte, 1990.

Clark, Ann Nolan. *Medicine Man's Daughter.* New York: Farrar, 1963.

Craven, Margaret. *I Heard the Owl Call My Name.* New York: Bantam, 1973.

Embry, Margaret. *Shadi.* New York: Holiday, 1971.

Fuller, Iola. *The Loon Feather.* New York: Harcourt, 1940.

George, Jean Craighead. *Julie of the Wolves.* New York: Harper, 1972.

———. *The Talking Earth.* New York: Harper, 1983.

———. *Water Sky.* New York: Harper, 1987.

Highwater, Jamake. *Anpao: An American Indian Odyssey.* New York: Harper, 1977.

Houston, John. *Ghost Fox.* New York: Harcourt, 1977.

Hudson, Jan. *Sweetgrass.* New York: Philomel, 1989; Tree Frog, 1984.

LaFarge, Oliver. *Laughing Boy.* Boston: Houghton Mifflin, 1929.

Lauritzen, Jonreed. *The Ordeal of the Young Hunter.* Boston: Little, Brown, 1954.

Lampman, Evelyn Sibley. *The Potlatch Family.* New York: Crowell, 1953.

Means, Florence Crannell. *Our Cup Is Broken.* Boston: Houghton Mifflin, 1969.

O'Dell, Scott. *Black Star, Bright Dawn.* Boston: Houghton Mifflin, 1988.

———. *Island of the Blue Dolphins.* Boston: Houghton Mifflin, 1960.

———. *Sing Down the Moon.* Boston: Houghton Mifflin, 1970.

Richter, Conrad. *Light in the Forest.* New York: Knopf, 1953.

Speare, Elizabeth George. *The Sign of the Beaver.* Boston: Houghton Mifflin, 1983.

HISPANIC-AMERICAN BOOKS FOR YOUNGER READERS (GRADES 2–5)

Brown, Tricia. *Hello, Amigos!* New York: Holt, 1986.

Garcia, Maria. *The Adventures of Connie and Diego / Las adventuras de Connie y Diego.* San Francisco: Children's Book Press, 1978.

Garza, Carmen Lomas. *Family Picture / Cuadros de Familia.* San Francisco: Children's Book Press, 1990.

Griego, M. C. et al. *Tortillitas para Mama and Other Nursery Rhymes, Spanish and English.* New York: Holt, n.d.

Hewett, Joan. *Hector Lives in the United States Now: The Story of a Mexican-American Child.* New York: Lippincott, 1990.

Krumgold, Joseph. *. . . and now Miguel.* New York: Crowell, 1953.

Mora, Pat. *Borders.* Houston, TX: Arte Público Press, 1985.

———. *Chants.* Houston, TX: Arte Público Press, 1984.

———. *Communion.* Arte Público Press, 1991.

———. *Pablo's Tree.* New York: Macmillan, 1993.

———. *Tomás and the Library Lady.* New York: Knopf, 1993.

Soto, Gary. *The Cat's Meow.* San Francisco: Strawberry Hill, 1987.

Tafolla, Carmen. *Patchwork Colcha: A Children's Collection.* Flagstaff, AZ: Creative Educational Enterprises, 1987.

Torres, Leyla. *Subway Sparrow / Gorrión del Metro.* New York: Farrar, Straus & Giroux, 1993.

Ulibarrí, Sabine. *Pupurupú: Cuentos de Ninos / Children's Stories.* Mexico: Sainz Luiselli Editores, 1987.

Viramontes, Helena Maria. *The Moths and Other Stories.* Houston, TX: Arte Público Press, 1985.

HISPANIC-AMERICAN BOOKS FOR OLDER READERS (GRADES 6 AND UP)

Anaya, Rodolfo. *Bless Me, Ultima.* Berkeley, CA: Tonatiuh International, 1972.

———. *The Farolitos of Christmas: A New Mexico Christmas Story.* Santa Fe: New Mexico Magazine, 1987.

Bonham, Frank. *Viva Chicano.* New York: Dutton, 1970.

Buss, Fran Leeper, and Daisy Cubias. *Journey of the Sparrows.* New York: Lodestar, 1991.

Chavez, Denise. *The Last of the Menu Girls.* Houston, TX: Arte Público Press, 1988.

Colman, Hila. *The Girl from Puerto Rico.* New York: Morrow, 1961.

Foresman, Bettie. *From Lupita's Hill.* New York: Atheneum, 1973.

Galarza, Ernesto. *Barrio Boy.* Notre Dame, IN: University of Notre Dame Press, 1971.

Means, Florence Crannell. *Us Malthbys.* Boston: Houghton Mifflin, 1966.

Meltzer, Milton. *The Hispanic Americans.* New York: Crowell, 1982.

Mohr, Nicholasa. *El Bronx Remembered: A Novella and Stories.* New York: Harper, 1975.

———. *Nilda.* New York: Harper, 1973.

Pinchot, Jane. *The Mexicans in America.* Minneapolis, MN: Lerner, 1989.

O'Dell, Scott. *The Black Pearl.* Boston: Houghton Mifflin, 1967.

Soto, Gary. *Baseball in April.* San Diego: Harcourt, 1990.

———. *A Fire in My Hands: A Book of Poems*. New York: Scholastic, 1990.

Taylor, Theodore. *The Maldonado Miracle*. New York: Avon, 1986.

ASIAN-AMERICAN BOOKS FOR YOUNGER READERS (GRADES 2–5)

Bang, Molly. *The Paper Crane*. New York: Greenwillow, 1985.

Coutant, Helen, and Vo-Dinh Coutant. *First Snow*. New York: Knopf, 1974.

Lord, Bette Bao. *In the Year of the Boar and Jackie Robinson*. New York: Harper, 1984.

Say, Allen. *El Chino*. Boston: Houghton Mifflin, 1990.

———. *Grandfather's Journey*. Boston: Houghton Mifflin, 1994.

———. *The Lost Lake*. Boston: Houghton Mifflin, 1989.

Surat, Michele Maria. *Angel Child, Dragon Child*. Illustrated by Vo-Dinh Mai. Milwaukee: Carnival/Raintree, 1983.

Uchida, Yoshiko. *The Rooster Who Understood Japanese*. New York: Scribner's, 1976.

Yashima, Taro, and Mitsu Yashima. *Umbrella*. New York: Viking, 1958.

Young, Ed. *Lon Po Po: A Red-Riding Hood Story from China*. New York: Philomel, 1990.

ASIAN-AMERICAN BOOKS FOR OLDER READERS (GRADES 6 AND UP)

Houston, Jeanne Wakatsuki, and James D. Houston. *Farewell to Manzanar*. New York: Bantam, 1973.

Ignacio, Melissa M. *The Philippines: Roots of My Heritage*. Filipino Development Associates, 1977.

Lewis, Elizabeth Foreman. *Young Fu of the Upper Yangtze*. New York: Holt, 1932.

Takashima, Shizue. *A Child in Prison Camp*. New York: Morrow, 1971.

Uchida, Yoshiko. *The Best Bad Thing*. New York: Atheneum, 1983.

———. *The Happiest Ending*. New York: Atheneum, 1985.

———. *A Jar of Dreams*. New York: Atheneum, 1991.

———. *Journey Home*. New York: Atheneum, 1978.

———. *Journey to Topaz*. New York: Scribner's, 1971.

———. *The Promised Year*. New York: Harcourt, 1959.

Wong, J. S. *Fifth Chinese Daughter*. New York: Harper, 1950.

Yagawa, Sumiko. *The Crane Wife*. Illustrated by Suekichi Akabas. New York: Morrow, 1981.

Yee, Paul. *Tales from Gold Mountain: Stories of the Chinese in the New World*. New York: Macmillan, 1990.

Yep, Laurence. *Child of the Owl*. New York: Harper, 1977.

———. *Dragon's Gate*. New York: Harper, 1993.

———. *Dragonwings*. New York: Harper, 1975.

———. *The Rainbow People*. New York: Harper, 1989.

———. *The Star People*. New York: Harper, 1991.

BOOKS ABOUT OTHER CULTURES PRIMARILY FOR OLDER READERS (GRADES 6 AND UP)

Achebe, Chinua. *Things Fall Apart*. Greenwich, CT: Fawcett, 1969. (First published in 1958.) (Nigerian)

Beskow, Elsa. *Pelle's New Suit*. New York: Harper, 1929. (Swedish)

Boissard, J. A. *A Matter of Feeling*. Boston: Little, Brown, 1981. (French)

Case, Dianne. *Love, David*. New York: Dutton, 1991. (South African)

Clark, Ann Nolan. *Secret of the Andes*. New York: Viking, 1952. (Peruvian Indian)

Clark, M. T. *The Min-Min*. New York: Macmillan, 1978. (Australian)

Cunningham, Julia. *The Silent Voice*. New York: Dutton, 1981. (French)

Degens, T. *On the Third Ward*. New York: Harper, 1990. (Chinese)

DeJong, Meindert. *The House of Sixty Fathers*. New York: Harper, 1956. (Chinese)

————. *Journey from Peppermint Street*. New York: Harper, 1968. (Dutch)

Fritz, Jean. *Homesick: My Own Story*. New York: Putnam, 1982. (Chinese)

Hall, Lynn. *Danza!* New York: Scribner's, 1981. (Puerto Rican)

Ho, Minfong. *Rice without Rain*. New York: Lothrop, 1990. (Thai)

————. *The Clay Marble*. New York: Farrar, 1991. (Cambodian)

Kherdian, David. *The Road from Home: The Story of an Armenian Girlhood*. New York: Greenwillow, 1979. (Armenian)

Lingard, Joan. *Tug of War*. New York: Lodestar, 1990. (Latvian)

Naidoo, Beverley. *Chain of Fire*. New York: Lippincott, 1990. (South African)

Moeri, Louise. *The Forty-third War*. Boston: Houghton Mifflin, 1989. (Central American)

Newth, Mette. *The Abduction*. New York: Farrar, Straus & Giroux, 1989. (Norwegian)

O'Dell, Scott. *My Name Is Not Angelica*. Boston: Houghton Mifflin, 1989. (African, Caribbean Islanders)

Orlev, Uri. *The Man from the Other Side*. Boston: Houghton Mifflin, 1991. (Jewish, Eastern European)

Potok, Chaim. *My Name Is Asher Lev*. New York: Knopf, 1972. (Jewish)

Rubinstein, Gillian. *Beyond the Labyrinth*. New York: Watts, 1990. (Australian)

Siegal, Aranka. *Upon the Head of the Goat: A Childhood in Hungary, 1939-1944*. New York: Farrar, Straus & Giroux, 1981. (Hungarian)

Singer, Isaac Bashevis. *The Death of Methuselah and Other Stories*. New York: Farrar, Straus & Giroux, 1971. (Jewish)

Sperry, Armstrong. *Call It Courage*. New York: Macmillan, 1940. (Pacific Islands)

Staples, Suzanne Fisher. *Shabanu: Daughter of the Wind*. New York: Knopf, 1989. (Pakistani)

Suhl, Yuri. *The Merrymaker*. New York: Four Winds, 1975. (Jewish)

Wojciechowska, Maia. *Shadow of a Bull*. New York: Atheneum, 1964. (Spanish)

Chapter 4

UNDERSTANDING LITERATURE

APPROACHES TO LITERARY CRITICISM

An entire field of literary study wrestles with the problem of how we are to interpret literature, how we derive meaning from a collection of words on a page. Each generation seems compelled to devise its own theory, and we should not view this as confusion but as evidence that a literary text is rich and enjoys a many-faceted life. Our understanding of the various ways a piece of literature can be read and interpreted will help to make us more perceptive readers, better judges, and wiser purveyors of literature for our children. The critic Peter Hunt writes: "Literary criticism may seem arcane to many, but it does provide ways of talking about texts, and without some vocabulary, there is considerable danger that those who want to talk about children's books will not understand each other—or not seem worthy of anyone else's attention" (19). With that in mind, we will look briefly at "ways of talking about texts," and we will acquaint ourselves with some "vocabulary" to make our talking comprehensible to others.

It was once popular to discuss the merits of a literary work in terms of how well it fit into an accepted standard—consequently, new works were compared to the "classics" (also called the *canon*) to see how they measured up. In recent times, the idea of the canon has been brought to task—Who decides what the classics are? What criteria are being used? What biases have crept into these criteria? The definition of literature has been challenged—Are some works "literature" and others not? Whose definition is it? But more important, the whole notion of how a reader approaches a piece of writing ("literature" or otherwise) has been reexamined. Whereas once literary works were regarded "primarily as reflecting the world . . . as isolated specimens to be examined" (Purves et al. 43), today it is more common to see literary texts as part of a complex structure of interrelated experiences, with the meaning varying from individual to individual and from time to time. Or, as it has been summed up: "Texts are written by authors, deal with something called 'the world,' and are read by readers" (Purves et al. 43). Until we take all these factors into account, we have not fully understood the literary experience for ourselves. Of course, this theory suggests that it is not always (and perhaps never is) possible to understand the literary experiences of others. The following discussion will review four of the more common approaches to studying literature and will provide just a sampling of the many ways a book or poem can be read and understood.

THE READER-RESPONSE APPROACH

Although reader-response criticism can be traced as far back as the 1920s, it is the work of Louise Rosenblatt in the 1930s (and culminating with her 1978 work, *The Reader, the Text, the Poem*) that has most clearly defined this approach to literature. For years, students had been taught that a literary text held a specific meaning and that the study of literature involved the discovery of that meaning. Students often believed they were expected to discover the "correct" interpretations of poems, stories, and novels with the assistance of their teachers who were somehow privy to the answers. In other words, the text was assumed to hold all the meaning, and the reader was a passive participant whose role was to soak up the meaning. However, we now acknowledge that readers hold widely different interpretations of the same literary work and that the reading process is a highly complex one.

Reader-response criticism attempts to account for these differences in interpretation by seeing the reader and the text as equal partners in the interpretative process. The text is no longer an object whose meaning we are supposed to unlock. Rather, the text is a stimulus that elicits responses from us based on our past experiences, our previous reading, our thoughts, and our feelings. Furthermore, if we read the same text a second or third time, it is newly created for us, since the circumstances surrounding the reading are different each time. Consequently, according to reader-response criticism, it is not possible to scientifically analyze (or dissect, as many students prefer to think of it) a text for meaning, since meaning is constantly evolving and emerges ultimately from the interaction of a reader and the text. (Some call this *transaction*, hence this method is often referred to as transactional analysis.)

If we take the familiar folktale "Rumpelstiltzkin" and look at it from a reader-response or transactional approach, several options are open to us. "Rumpelstiltskin," you will remember, is the story of a miller who lied to the king about his daughter's ability to spin straw into gold. The greedy king promised to take her as his wife if she would spin a roomful of straw into gold each night for a year. The daughter is then aided by a mysterious dwarfish stranger—Rumpelstiltzkin—who demands her first-born child in return for his help. The girl promises, but when the time comes to surrender her child she begs another chance and Rumpelstiltzkin agrees to let her off the hook if she can guess his name, which she ultimately does with the unwitting assistance of a messenger who had learned the name by chance.

It is possible for readers to examine their own ethical attitudes by rank-ordering the characters—Rumpelstiltzkin, the miller, the daughter, the king—according to their ethical behavior. A comparison of student responses to this exercise reveals a wide range of attitudes, and there is almost never absolute agreement on any character; indeed, virtually every time, each of the characters will be ranked first by some of the respondents and each of the characters will be ranked last by some. What is the reason for this discrepancy? Why do readers or listeners not agree on which character is the hero or which the villain? The answer is to be found in the varying attitudes and value systems the readers bring to the text—attitudes and value systems formulated over a lifetime of experiences, readings, thoughts, and feelings. Some readers, very sensitive to the issue of child abuse, are likely to be horrified at the thought of the daughter bargaining with the life of her own child (and these readers likewise find some sympathy for Rumpelstiltzkin whom they believe to be genuinely lonely and in need of human companionship). Others react very negatively toward the miller for his basic dishonesty and the careless way in which he puts his daughter's life in jeopardy, whereas others say he was simply trying to give his daughter a break in life by arranging for her marriage to the king. Many people regard the king as merely greedy, but some see him as a victim, deceived by the miller and his daughter, and the only character who remains true to his bargain. The ranking causes the readers to evaluate their own ethical beliefs, to prioritize their own values. And as readers share their ideas, they soon discover how difficult it is to establish absolutes—and reader-response critical theory teaches us that there are no absolutes. Such an exercise points out the complexity of human behavior and motivation, the difficulty in ascertaining right and wrong, and the interdependencies involved in any social construct.

THE HISTORICAL APPROACH

The historical approach to reading literature asks such questions as these:

1. Who is the author and what is his or her object in writing the work?
2. How did the political events of the time influence what the writer wrote?
3. How did the predominant social customs of the time influence the writer's outlook?
4. What is the predominant philosophy that influenced the work?
5. Were there any special circumstances under which the work was written?

In general, the historical approach looks at how the period in which a work was written has influenced the work itself. The historical approach examines the external political, social, and intellectual influences on literature. Although a grasp of this historical context is not always necessary for our enjoyment of a particular work of literature, it does give us a better understanding as to why the author wrote what he or she did. Knowing the historical context can answer some perplexing questions about a literary work.

Let's take, for example, the popular folktale of "Hansel and Gretel." How can the parents be so callous as to abandon their children? What is the significance of the gingerbread house? Why does the witch die in the oven? Because this tale in its present form is of Western European origin, some of these questions can be answered by examining the historical context out of which the tale grew.

In medieval Europe, where the story undoubtedly originated, numerous factors contributed to widespread famine, and peasants lived on the verge of starvation. The historian Barbara Tuchman writes that during the fourteenth century "reports spread of people eating their own children, of the poor in Poland feeding on hanged bodies taken down from the gibbet" (24). In light of this ghastly information, the tale of "Hansel and Gretel" seems tame indeed. The abandonment of children might not have been so unusual a thing in a society that still did not necessarily condemn infanticide (particularly if the infant was a female). The overwhelming emphasis on food—the children drop breadcrumbs; they are enticed by a gingerbread house from which they eat delicious candies; the witch is killed in her own oven where she had planned to bake Hansel—can be viewed as the product of an age when providing food indeed occupied much of the average person's daily activities.

Another example of the way society influences literature can be seen in Daniel Defoe's *Robinson Crusoe*, first published in 1719. In that story, the hero is cast upon the proverbial desert isle, and, through industry and ingenuity, he tames the wilderness, creates a comfortable life, and even makes a personal servant out of the native, Friday. Modern readers are likely to frown upon Crusoe's transforming the environment to suit him, not to mention the enslavement of Friday. But Defoe is a product of his time when society believed its mission was to tame the wilderness and convert the "heathen." In Scott O'Dell's *Island of the Blue Dolphins*, published in 1960, the heroine, Karana, stranded on a desert island, does not conquer nature, but learns to respect it and live in harmony with it. This message is more in tune with modern ideas about the ecology.

Reading a book with the historical perspective in mind can help us to understand (and sometimes appreciate) the literary accomplishment.

THE PSYCHOANALYTICAL APPROACH

Whereas a historical reading of a work of literature examines it from the point of view of the social climate of the time in which it was written, a psychoanalytical reading examines a work in relation to its author. The most common psychoanalytical approach is the Freudian approach, based on the work of Sigmund Freud (1856–1939), regarded as the father of modern psychoanalysis, who believed that the motivations for much of our behavior (such as our fear of heights, our compulsion to be neat, our love of a certain color) lay hidden in our unconscious minds. Freud also believed that in our dreams and our art (including literature, music, the graphic and plastic arts) these unconscious motivators appeared.

To examine a work psychoanalytically is to probe the unconscious of the characters, to determine what their actions really reveal about them. The most famous modern example in children's literature of psychoanalytical reading is Bruno Bettelheim's study of folktales, *The Uses of Enchantment* (1976). Here is a brief summary of Bettelheim's psychoanalytical interpretation of "Hansel and Gretel." He interprets the story as a symbolic representation of the child emerging from the developmental stage of oral fixation, and he points to the importance of food in the tale for his support—the children must be abandoned because of lack of food; the children find a gingerbread house that they begin to eat; the house is inhabited by a cannibal witch. Bettelheim sees in Hansel's initial efforts to find his way back home "the debilitating consequences of trying to deal with life's problems by means of regression and denial, which reduce one's ability to solve problems" (160). The return home is seen as denial and regression—Hansel's denying that the parents do not want him and his desire to return to the tenuous security of home and Hansel's own resistance to move beyond the oral stage. The gingerbread house, Bettelheim contends, "stands for oral greediness and how attractive it is to give in to it" (161). He goes yet a step further in suggesting that the house is also a symbol of the body, "usually the mother's," and that the children's devouring of the house symbolically represents their nursing. The witch personifies "the destructive aspects of orality," and she also represents the threatening mother. On the other hand, the witch has jewels that the children inherit, but only when they have reached a higher stage of development, represented by the clever way they deceive the witch (by substituting the bone for the finger and tricking her into the oven). Bettelheim concludes:

> This suggests that as the children transcend their oral anxiety, and free themselves of relying on oral satisfaction for security, they can also free themselves of the image of the threatening mother—the witch—and rediscover the good parents, whose greater wisdom—the shared jewels—then benefit all. (162)

Bettelheim's analysis is a great deal more complex than this, but such a summary does reveal some of the basic tenets of psychoanalytical criticism.

Freud's student, the psychologist and physician Carl Gustav Jung (1875-1961), further developed his mentor's ideas in analytical psychology. The result was yet another literary approach, which we refer to as archetypal criticism. Jung believed in a collective unconscious that lay deep within all of us and where are housed the "cumulative knowledge, experiences, and images of the entire human race" (Bressler 92). This explains, Jung argued, why people the world over respond to the same myths and stories (why we find, for example, the Cinderella story everywhere from Vietnam to Egypt to northern Europe). Jung identified certain archetypes, which are simply repeated patterns and images of human experience—the changing seasons; the cycle of birth, death, rebirth; the heroic quest; the beautiful temptress, and so on. Archetypal criticism therefore depends heavily on symbols and patterns operating on a universal scale.

Some readers, for example, have seen in Cinderella a sort of Christ figure—her virtues are goodness and humility, and she must be accepted in her servant's rags and not in royal raiments, just as Christ appeared to his followers in the guise of a carpenter's son. Another example would be that interpretation of "Little Red Riding Hood" that sees the girl in her red cloak as symbolic of the sun and the wolf who devours her as the night. The tale then becomes an archetypal narrative of the sun's daily progress across the sky to its final envelopment in the bowels of night. Jungians would argue that these interpretations are valid since these images are part of our collective unconscious; the stories' creators themselves would not have been fully aware of the symbolic implications of their tales. The most evident danger in all psycholoanalytical criticism—whether Freudian or Jungian—is in overreading, in seeing a symbol in every object, in seeing unconscious desires and fears lurking in every utterance.

THE FEMINIST APPROACH

Feminist criticism actually combines other critical methods while placing its focus on the questions of how gender affects a literary work, writer, or reader. The feminist approach might ask such questions as these:

1. How are women portrayed in the work? As stereotypes? As individuals?
2. How is the woman's point of view considered?
3. Is male superiority implied in the text?
4. In what way is the work affected because it was written by a woman? or a man?

A major concern of feminist criticism is the masculine bias in literature. Historically, most works (including those written by women) have been written from a masculine point of view and for male audiences. Literature has traditionally celebrated the masculine traits and cast aspersion on the feminine. Among the first works to come under attack were the folktales with their stereotypically beautiful, helpless princesses who needed only a good man to set their lives aright and enable them to live happily ever after. The feminist critic looks for the presence of female stereotypes—for example, the woman as the dark-haired, sensuous, submissive femme fatale, or as the fair-haired, virginal, plaster saint. If we look again at "Hansel and Gretel," we can see that the feminist critic might object to the portrayal of the woman as either selfish wife or cannibalistic witch. The mother/wife is, on the other hand, simply taking a desperate situation in hand, assuming authority where her ineffectual husband will not. Hansel, the boy, proves equally ineffectual, marking the path with breadcrumbs that are quickly eaten by the birds, and then finding himself imprisoned by the witch. It is Gretel who must take the decisive action and rescue them by cleverly deceiving the witch and then killing her. Gretel is, of course, an exception to the rule and refuses to fit into the traditional feminine mold. But the feminist critic looks for societal misconceptions that treat the masculine viewpoint as the norm and the feminine viewpoint as a deviation.

Our point here is to emphasize the need to challenge the way we have traditionally read literature—and that is from the point of view of a male-dominated society. The feminist critic believes that, in the words of Simone de Beauvoir, "One is not born, but rather becomes, a woman." Or, to put it another way, one critic says, "Feminists do not deny that women exhibit group characteristics. However, they do not accept the thesis that similarities in female behavior are biologically determined" (Register 13). Looking at a literary text from a feminist point of view can enrich a reading, making us aware of the complexity of human interaction. To read a text as a woman would, according to some theorists, is to read it with "the skeptical purity of an outcast from culture" (Auerbach 156). To read a text as a woman "means questioning its underlying assumptions about differences between men and women that usually posit women as inferior" (Waxman 150). Feminist criticism therefore ultimately becomes cultural criticism.

THE FORMALIST APPROACH

The formalist approach is also called *New Criticism*, although it was "new" over half a century ago and was popular from the 1930s to the 1960s. This was once the standard way of examining a literary text. According to this approach, a literary text should be regarded as an object to be analyzed for meaning apart from the values or beliefs of the author or reader—quite the opposite from the transactional approach. There was once a time when formalist critics believed that we should disregard everything except the literary elements of a work. Few critics or readers go that far today, but formalism, with its emphasis on the architecture of a poem or story or novel, is still a useful approach in helping us to understand and appreciate a literary work.

A formalist approach to "Hansel and Gretel" would examine the tale from a structural perspective, illustrating the essential unity of the text. The focus would be on the rising and falling dramatic action and on the building of suspense as the children overhear their parents plotting. The formalist critic looks for the chief tension—the conflict—in a text as the source of its unity, and in "Hansel and Gretel" it is the tension between the children and the stepmother/witch, who, if they are not the same person, represent the same perverted values and must be defeated in order to resolve the tension. Of particular importance would be the foreshadowing of the witch in the person of the children's mother and the parallels (and differences) found between the woodcutter's house and the witch's gingerbread cottage. The formalist would also examine the language, paying special attention to its figurative meaning (in one version of the tale, Gretel says, upon seeing the witch's gingerbread cottage, "It looks good enough to eat," an ironical statement when we consider the witch's intentions). Formalist criticism demands the close reading of a text, which, the formalist maintains, will reveal the text's deeper meaning.

THE PURPOSE OF CRITICISM

Literary criticism is an old preoccupation, going back as far as Aristotle in the fourth century BC. And ever since Aristotle, it has been the critic's task to study the art of literature, to explore the ways that poems, plays, stories, and novels affect us emotionally, intellectually, and aesthetically. So long as there are thinking people to read, there will be fresh and inventive ways of looking at literature. And we all become critics when we react to what we read. When we begin to think about the reasons for our responses, when we try to discover why we feel the way we do, when we search for relationships between the works we read, when we draw connections between our reading and our life experiences, then we are responding like informed critics. The results will be reading experiences that bring us both deeper understanding and greater pleasure.

THE ELEMENTS OF LITERATURE

The study of literature seemed at one time to be largely the study of terminology. We should recognize that classifications and terminology play only a supporting role in the study of literature and are decidedly not the end of criticism. However, if we are to have meaningful discussions of literary texts, we must have some vocabulary by which we may express our ideas, feelings, and beliefs. That is the purpose of the following. The terms described here can be used for fiction, drama, and poetry (although poetry also has its own specialized vocabulary).

POINT OF VIEW

Every story is told from someone's point of view, and we should not assume that the narrator, or storyteller, is the author. It is important for us as readers to be aware of who is telling the story and how that narrator affects the story itself. There are essentially three distinctive points of view.

First-Person Point of View.   If the narrator refers to him- or herself as "I" in the story, the story has a *first-person point of view.* The first-person narrator is usually a character in the story and may or may not be the protagonist. The first-person narrator is readily identified, usually in the very first paragraph, such as in this first sentence of Irene Hunt's Newbery Award–winning novel, *Up a Road Slowly:* "Three children stood outside our gate in the bright October sunlight, silent and still as figurines in a gift shop window, watching each step I took as I came slowly down the flagstone walk across the lawn" (1).

Omniscient Point of View.   An *omniscient point of view* is one in which the author exercises unlimited powers of knowing the thoughts and actions of anyone in the story at any time and any place. The word *omniscient* means literally "all-knowing." The omniscient narrator is not a character in the story but an outside commentator, able to delve into the hearts and minds of the characters. In E. B. White's fantasy, *Charlotte's Web,* the omniscient narrator can show us the thoughts and actions of Wilbur the pig in one scene, of Fern Arable and her family in another, of Mrs. Arable's conversation with the family physician in still another scene. The omniscient narrator provides a great deal of flexibility for the writer, allowing the writer, for instance, to comment on the action and explain the thematic intentions. The danger, however, is that the omniscient point of view, if not skillfully handled, may devolve into moral didacticism or polemical writing.

Limited Point of View.   A *limited point of view* (also called the *subjective consciousness*) is used when the story is told from the viewpoint of a single character in the story—but not told *by* that character. The limited narrator takes on features of both the first-person narrator and the omniscient narrator. Like the omniscient narrator, the limited narrator is not a character in the story but a storyteller outside the events. Also like the omniscient narrator, the limited narrator can tell us the innermost thoughts and actions of the character. But unlike the omniscient narrator, the limited narrator comments only on a single character's observations, describing only what that character sees, knows, and feels. Laura Ingalls Wilder's popular *Little House in the Big Woods* and its sequels are told from a limited narrator's point of view. The narrator allows us to see only those things that Laura experiences, but the writer is not confined to the vocabulary of a six-year-old narrator.

It is important that we realize who is telling the story and why. As was mentioned above, we should never confuse the narrator with the author, for many authors of fiction assume a *persona* (which means "mask") when they write; that is, they pretend to be someone else. Readers expect the point of view to be logical and consistent—for example, a narrator should not reveal material he or she could not have known at the time. And, of course, we must not forget that the narrator may not always be trustworthy.

SETTING

The setting refers to the time, the geographical place, the general environment and circumstances that prevail in a narrative. Every story must happen in some time and in some place. The setting helps to establish the mood of a work of fiction. In Laura Ingalls Wilder's *Little House on the Prairie*, the setting is on the Great Plains in the latter half of the nineteenth century. But the setting goes beyond simply establishing the time and place. It includes descriptions of the daily occupations of the Ingalls family—poor settlers eeking out a living in a fairly inhospitable environment, where wells have to be dug by hand, the nearest neighbor is miles away, and a family must huddle in a log cabin behind a blanket for a door while wolves lurk perilously close outside.

In some books the setting is more crucial than in others. For example, works of fantasy or historical fiction rely quite heavily on the setting to help establish the feeling or milieu of places unfamiliar to the readers. C. S. Lewis's *Chronicles of Narnia* (including *The Lion, the Witch, and the Wardrobe* and others), describing events happening chiefly in the mythical land of Narnia, requires fairly detailed descriptions of the land, the inhabitants, and their customs. And Wilder's *Little House* books include thorough explanations of the details of pioneer life. On the other hand, when a story is set in a familiar place—such as a modern city as we find in many of Judy

Blume's novels (e.g., *Are You There, God? It's Me, Margaret*)—a writer can eliminate much of the emphasis on the setting. However, the setting is almost always a significant factor in defining character and establishing the predominate mood in any story.

CHARACTERS

Regardless of the type of fiction, readers demand believable and memorable characters. The principal characters include the *protagonist*, the hero or heroine, the main character with whom we sympathize. And there is the *antagonist*, the villain, or the character who works against the protagonist. Usually several supporting characters are included as well. We generally want the characters to be properly *motivated*, that is, there should be believable reasons for their doing what they do. The characters behave as they do because of the circumstances into which they have been placed and because they are the kind of people they are. We usually expect the story's action to develop out of the character and not the other way around.

Flat and Round Characters.   All characters may be identified as either flat or round. A *flat character* is one who exhibits only one side of his or her personality. Usually these characters are functionaries, needed to advance the plot, such as servants, police, store clerks, and so on—they might be parents (such as Fern's in *Charlotte's Web*) or siblings (such as Peter Rabbit's sisters) or teachers, gardeners, and so on. Many times a flat character will also be a *stereotype* or a *stock character*, possessing the traits considered to be typical of a group (such as disagreeable mothers-in-law; haughty English butlers; giddy schoolgirls; impish schoolboys, and so on). In any case, we expect the stereotype to be used with discretion. Whether it be ignorance or insensitivity, nothing should excuse offensive stereotypes in modern literature.

Our chief focus, however, is usually on the *round* characters, those who are fully developed personalities—the Wilburs and Charlottes, the Huck Finns, and even the Long John Silvers (we're not only interested in the good guys). The round characters experience a range of emotions—joy, sorrow, worry, confidence, dejection, elation. They are the characters we get to know best, and because of their complexity, we seldom find more than a handful in any story—sometimes we find only one or two.

Static and Dynamic Characters.   All characters may also be identified as either static or dynamic, and most fiction will include both types. A *static character*—who may also be either a flat or a round character—remains essentially the same thoughout the story and has no noticeable development. Static characters may be flat, such as Mrs. Rabbit or Mr. McGregor in Potter's *The Tale of Peter Rabbit*, characters about whom we learn very little, or round, such as Charlotte the spider in *Charlotte's Web*, about whom we learn a great deal. But in each case, the character does not change significantly. In contrast, a *dynamic character*—who must always be a round character—undergoes some important character transformation during the course of the story. In *Charlotte's Web*, Wilbur the pig grows from an immature, self-centered, and insecure character into a mature, caring, and confident creature.

Foil Characters.   A *foil character* is one who possesses personality traits opposite to those of another character, often the main character. *Foil* is a jeweler's term for a gem setting, and just as the proper setting can make a diamond appear larger and more brilliant, so can certain character traits be emphasized when compared to the opposite traits in others. To use *Charlotte's Web* again, Templeton serves as a foil to Charlotte—his selfishness makes her own ultimate sacrifice that much more impressive.

Character Development and Consistency.   *Character development* is simply the means the author uses to tell us about a character. We learn about characters in a variety of ways.

1. The narrator may tell us about the characters, although this is usually the least memorable way (this is like getting our information about someone from a lecture).
2. We may hear about them through what other characters say of them, although we must be wary of possible hidden motives or prejudices and realize that what others say may not necessarily be true (this is like getting our information about someone from what their friends—and enemies—say about them).
3. We may learn about characters through what they say themselves, although we must remember that people do not always mean what they say.
4. We may learn about characters through observing their actions. Actions, we all know, speak louder than words, and it is through actions that the most convincing evidence about character is revealed.

Character consistency means that we expect fictional characters to behave in ways consistent with their nature as presented in the story. Huckleberry Finn may be a troublesome child, but he is also generous and good-hearted. It would have been inconsistent with his character if Mark Twain had caused Huck to turn into a drug dealer or racketeer.

PLOT AND CONFLICT

The novelist E. M. Forster provides us with this definition of a plot:

> "The king died and then the queen died" is a story. "The king died, and then the queen died of grief" is a plot (86).

The point is that a plot is more than a simple sequence of events, it is a sequence of interrelated events linked by causality. (The king's death *caused* the queen's death.) But most of us would still feel that this plot wants for something. It lacks conflict; in the most gripping plots, something must be at stake; some difficulty must be overcome; some goal must be achieved. It is to see the resolution of the conflict (which, of course, is the outcome of the plot) that most readers continue to read until the end of the story.

Types of Conflict.   As the most important single feature of the plot, the conflict commonly takes one of five directions.

1. *The Individual against Another* occurs when two persons are struggling for the same goal, or perhaps one person is determined to prevent another from achieving a goal. Folktales, such as "Little Red Riding Hood," pointedly demonstrate this type of conflict, as do *The Tale of Peter Rabbit, The Wizard of Oz,* and *Treasure Island*.

2. *The Individual against Society* shows the protagonist (and sometimes the protagonist's family or close associates) pitted against the values and mores of mainstream society. This struggle is most evident in some of the stories of racial prejudice, such as Mildred Taylor's *Roll of Thunder, Hear My Cry* or Ouida Sebestyen's *Words by Heart*; or in stories dealing with such social problems as alienation, as in S. E. Hinton's story of inner-city gangs, *The Outsiders*; or in stories dealing with individual differences, such as Taro Yashima's picture book *The Crow Boy*.

3. *The Individual against Nature* is a popular conflict with older children who enjoy reading about protagonists striving to survive in the wilderness as in Elizabeth George Speare's *The Sign of the Beaver*, or perhaps in the Arctic wasteland as in Jean Craighead George's *Julie of the Wolves*, or on a deserted tropical island as in Theodore Taylor's *The Cay* or Scott O'Dell's *Island of the Blue Dolphins*.

4. *The Individual against Self* occurs when the conflict is an emotional or intellectual struggle within the protagonist him- or herself. Maurice Sendak's *Where the Wild Things Are* is an interesting example of a picture-book rendition of this sort of conflict, where Max is torn by the conflicting desires to do exactly as he pleases or to obey his mother. In Beverly Cleary's *Dear Mr. Henshaw*, Leigh Botts attempts to blame others for his problems, for his feelings of inadequacy, and for his loneliness, but he realizes eventually that these are his own problems, and ones that only he can work out.

5. *The Individual against God* occurs in stories of individuals wrestling with religious beliefs, a conflict seldom found in literature for the very young. We do find it in books for older children, and Judy Blume's *Are You There, God? It's Me, Margaret* is a popular example.

Plot Credibility.   Plots do not have to be realistic, but most readers insist that they be credible or believable according to the standards constructed by the author. (Naturally, for a comic work or a fantasy, those standards are different from those for a serious piece of realism.) We ask questions such as does this action make sense in the story? Have we been sufficiently prepared for the turn of events (through fore-shadowing or the dropping of hints, for example)? Is the plot unnecessarily con-trived or too full of coincidences? One of the principal differences between art and life is that life is random, whereas art is often quite meticulously planned. In real life, we may receive a telephone call during dinner or late at night that turns out to be a wrong number, and that event may have no significance whatever on the fu-ture course of events. However, in a novel or a play, should the telephone ring dur-ing a dinner scene, we expect it to be important. In literature, whenever a charac-ter enters a room or whenever a change in the weather is noted or whenever a cup of coffee is spilled, that event will likely have some meaning, whether it be to es-tablish the atmosphere or to advance the plot or to help us evaluate a character or a situation or to reinforce the theme.

Dramatic Plot Structure.   Plot structure may follow one of two general pat-terns. A *dramatic plot structure* first establishes the setting and conflict, then fol-lows the action through to a *climax* (the peak of the action and turning), and con-cludes with a *denouement* (a wrapping up of loose ends). This structure is probably the most familiar; it is the structure of most folktales, and it is used by most televi-sion dramas. It is also the plot structure of such familiar works as *The Tale of Peter Rabbit* and *Charlotte's Web*. A dramatic plot structure is typically arranged chrono-logically—that is, events are described from first to last, beginning to end.

Sometimes, two dramatic plots are interwoven into a single book, creating a parallel plot structure. Often one of the plots is decidedly secondary to the main plot. The Finnish writer Tove Jansson has created a marvelous parallel plot in her fantasy *Moominsummer Madness*, in which several characters are inadvertently sep-arated during a flood and encounter a variety of experiences before finally being re-united at the conclusion. Likewise, Robert Lawson uses a parallel plot structure in his comic biography of Benjamin Franklin, *Ben and Me*, told from the point of view of Amos, a mouse (who takes most of the credit for Franklin's achievements—a good example of an unreliable first-person narrator). In *Ben and Me*, paralleling the Rev-olutionary War activities of the humans is a similar struggle taking place among the mouse population.

Episodic Plot Structure.   An *episodic plot structure* consists of a series of loosely related incidents tied together by a common theme and/or characters. Wilder's *Little House* books are organized episodically. Each chapter is capable of standing on its own much like a short story, but taken together the episodes give us a complex picture of the family relationships and other issues important to the story. Unity is provided by the predominant theme of love and family togetherness overcoming hardship. Episodic plots work best when the writer wishes to explore the personalities of the characters, the nature of their existence, and the flavor of an era. Episodic plots may be arranged chronologically—or they may be arranged using flashbacks, a technique that takes us back and forth between two or more time periods. Older readers (upper elementary school and beyond) are quite capable of handling such shifts as those found in Robert Cormier's complex *I Am the Cheese*, which freely moves back and forth in both time and place.

THEME

If the plot tells us what happens in a story, the theme tells us why it happens and what it means. The theme is the main, underlying idea. In the most enduring works of literature, the theme is substantial, not trivial—although this does not imply that the work must be serious. Sometimes even nonsense literature contains its own logic and expresses a serious theme. If readers often prefer the significant and thoughtful theme over the silly and vacuous, they do *not* like to be browbeaten. Most find it much preferable to have the themes woven subtly into the fabric of the story or the poem. Literature for young readers offers many important themes (and a single book often includes several minor themes in addition to the major one). The problems of growing up and maturing are probably the themes most frequently found in children's literature. These include the individual's adjustment to society, the importance of love and friendship, the acceptance of a stepparent, achieving one's identity, and finding one's place in the world.

STYLE

Style refers to the use of language, the choice of words, the way sentences are constructed, the use of imagery, and so on. It is not enough that a writer has a good story to tell. The story must be told well.

Exposition.   Exposition refers to the information provided by the narrator—usually this is descriptive and gives us background information necessary for us to understand the events. Exposition may be used to introduce a character: "Dorothy lived in the midst of the great Kansas prairies, with Uncle Henry, who was a farmer, and Aunt Em, who was the farmer's wife" (Baum 7). Sometimes exposition is used to move the action along:

> When Laura and Mary had said their prayers and were tucked snugly under the trundle bed's covers, Pa was sitting in the firelight with the fiddle. Ma had blown out the lamp because she did not need its light. On the other side of the hearth she was swaying gently in her rocking chair and her knitting needles flashed in and out above the sock she was knitting.
>
> (Wilder 236)

Other times, exposition is used to summarize and focus ideas presented in a scene, and to suggest future directions:

> Wilbur was merely suffering the doubts and fears that often go with finding a new friend. In good time he was to discover that he was mistaken about Charlotte. Underneath her rather bold and cruel exterior, she had a kind heart, and she was to prove loyal and true to the very end.
>
> (White 41)

Dialogue.   *Dialogue* refers to the words spoken by the characters to each other, as opposed to exposition, which consists of the words of the narrator to the reader. Most works of fiction rely on both dialogue and exposition. Young readers, especially, enjoy dialogue as a realistic and convincing way of defining character. Dialogue allows the author to convey individual peculiarities, such as the goose's quirky speech in *Charlotte's Web* when she replies to Wibur's inquiry about the time: "Probably-obably-obably about half-past eleven . . . Why aren't you asleep, Wilbur?" (33). Charlotte's intellectual superiority over the other barnyard animals is clearly demonstrated by her greeting to Wilbur: "'Salutations!' said [Charlotte]. Wilbur jumped to his feet. 'Salu-*what?*' he cried" (35). Dialogue makes the most sense when it is suited to the character who speaks it; otherwise it appears stilted and unnatural.

Vocabulary.   For children, word choice is particularly important because of the child's naturally limited vocabulary. Consequently, we would not expect to find sophisticated, multisyllabic, and bombastic orations in a work intended for preschoolers. On the other hand, if the vocabulary is too simple, the reader is never given a chance to grow and may ultimately become bored with reading. Beatrix Potter does not hesitate to use such words as "exert," "fortnight," and "camomile tea." She had faith that young children would either pick up the meanings from the context or, if it were very important, they would ask somebody. Of course, some abstract terms— "vicarious" or "altruistic," for example—are beyond the grasp of younger children, but concrete terms are usually easily explained and we should not complain if a work requires a child to learn new words.

Imagery.   *Imagery* is the use of words to create sensory impressions, and an *image* conveys sights, sounds, textures, smells, and tastes. Imagery refers to a collection of images, the effect of which is intended to create emotional responses in the reader. Notice how L. Frank Baum uses a collection of bleak images to portray the drabness of Kansas in *The Wizard of Oz:*

> Not a tree nor a house broke the broad sweep of flat country that reached the edge of the sky in all directions. The sun had baked the plowed land into a gray mass, with little cracks running through it. Even the grass was not green, for the sun had burned the tops of the long blades until they were the same gray color to be seen everywhere. Once the house had been painted, but the sun blistered the paint and the rains washed it away, and now the house was as dull and gray as everything else. (8)

The desolation is heightened by the use of the verbs describing the sun's effects: baked, burned, blistered. Not even the sun can give joy to this scene.

Sentences.   Sentences, both by their length and their construction, can contribute to or inhibit our enjoyment of a work. Short sentences best convey suspense, tension, and swift action. Longer sentences work best when explanations and descriptions are needed. A well-written long sentence can be just as easy to understand as a short sentence. Notice how E. B. White, in the following paragraph from *Charlotte's Web*, effectively combines short and long sentences as he moves from describing action to thought and back to action:

> Wilbur looked everywhere. He searched his pen thoroughly. He examined the window ledge, stared up at the ceiling. But he saw nothing new. Finally he decided he would have to speak up. He hated to break the lovely stillness of dawn by using his voice, but he couldn't think of any other way to locate the mysterious new friend who was nowhere to be seen. So Wilbur cleared his throat. (34)

Prose has rhythm as well as poetry. The best writers can make a prose paragraph read as beautifully as a well-crafted poem. The right juxtaposition of sounds, the right measure of repetition, the right variety of patterns, the right choice of images, and the author produces a lyrical passage such as this final paragraph from Patricia MacLachlan's *Sarah, Plain and Tall:*

> Autumn will come, then winter, cold with a wind that blows like a wind off the sea in Maine. There will be nests of curls to look for, and dried flowers all winter long. When there are storms, Papa will stretch a rope from the door to the barn so we will not be lost when we feed the sheep and the cows and Jack and Old Bess. And Sarah's chickens, if they aren't living in the house. There will be Sarah's sea, blue and gray and green, hanging on the wall. And songs, old ones and new. And Seal with yellow eyes. And there will be Sarah, plain and tall. (58)

TONE

By the effective use of language and literary elements, an author may convey a specific attitude toward the subject; this attitude is called the *tone*. In children's literature, a wide variety of tones can be found, including humor in its numerous forms (such as the nonsense of Dr. Seuss or the comical, realistic escapades of Harriet in Fitzhugh's *Harriet the Spy*), tenderness (as in Margaret Wise Brown's popular bedtime story, *Good Night Moon*), didacticism (that is, instructional reading or reading with moral messages, such as Aesop's fables), and, for older readers, satire (as in Lawson's spoof, *Ben and Me*), or even cynicism (as in the novels of Robert Cormier, such as *I Am the Cheese* or *The Chocolate War*). In some books the tone may even vary from chapter to chapter, as in Alice Childress's *A Hero Ain't Nothin' but a Sandwich*.

Critics generally frown upon some literary tones as inappropriate to children's literature (or to serious adult literature, for that matter)—didacticism, sentimentalism, sensationalism, and condescension.

Didacticism simply means that a work is intended for instructional purposes.

Didacticism is not necessarily a weakness—textbooks are didactic, for example, and that's the way they're supposed to be. But if a novel or a story tries too hard to teach a lesson, readers often react against it. And too often, when an author has a particular lesson in mind, some of the other literary features suffer, such as plot credibility or character development.

Sentimentalism is unrestrained or overindulgent emotionalism. It occurs whenever readers are asked to respond with more emotion than the situation calls for. Sentimentalism often arises from a writer's exaggerated sense of the goodness of human nature, resulting in an overly sweetened view of the world and the people in it. Its opposite is cynicism, a view of the world as worse than it probably is. In children's books, sentimentalism can be seen in the "cuteness" with which some authors and illustrators imbue their characters, or in the creation of characters who are just too good to be true. We should note that some critics believe the derision of sentimentalism is, in part at least, a masculine point of view that has traditionally pervaded literary criticism.

Sensationalism is akin to thrill-seeking. We call books sensational when they emphasize grisly horror or steamy passion. Little true sensationalism is found in young children's books, but in books for teenagers it has become commonplace and very popular. For some, it is an essential ingredient for a good story; for many others it is meaningless exploitation.

Condescension is something that is found in books for the very young and it refers to the author's talking down to the reader and treating the reader as an inferior human being. Condescension is similar to sentimentalism. (Once again, the penchant toward "cuteness" in children's picture books seems to assume that young children can only handle subjects when they are sweetened and softened.) Anyone who has shared some of the franker folktale versions with young children (such as Margot Zemach's *Three Little Pigs* in which the wolf devours the first two and then is himself eaten by the third) knows that children themselves love a good no-nonsense story, devoid of its sugarcoating, just as well as the rest of us.

LITERATURE AS ART

The philosopher Alfred North Whitehead wrote that "Art is the imposing of a pattern on experience, and our aesthetic enjoyment in recognition of the pattern." As the painter takes lines, colors, and shapes, and imposes some order on them to create a painting, as the composer takes sounds and gives them form to create a piece of music, so the writer takes words and crafts them into a work of literature. Just as we must respond to a painting or a musical composition with both our intellect and our emotions, so we must respond to a poem, a story, or a novel with our minds and our hearts. So far as we know, human beings alone among all of creation are able to create and enjoy art. This is a love we should cherish in ourselves and nurture in our children. It is good to keep in mind President John Kennedy's admonition: "When power corrupts, poetry cleanses, for art establishes the basic human truths which must serve as the touchstone of our judgment."

WORKS CITED

Baum, L. Frank. *The Wizard of Oz*. 1900. Ed. Michael Patrick Hearn. Illus. W. W. Denslow. New York: Schocken, 1983.

Childress, Alice. *A Hero Ain't Nothin' but a Sandwich*. New York: Coward, 1973.

Forster, E. M. *Aspects of the Novel*. New York: Harcourt, Brace, 1954.

Hunt, Irene. *Up a Road Slowly*. New York: Follett, 1966.

Hunt, Peter. *An Introduction to Children's Literature*. Oxford: Oxford University Press, 1994.

MacLachlan, Patricia. *Sarah, Plain and Tall*. New York: Harper and Row, 1985.

Purves, Alan, et al. *How Porcupines Make Love: Teaching a Response-Centered Literature Curriculum*. White Plains, NY: Longman, 1990.

Tuchman, Barbara. *A Distant Mirror: The Calamitous 14th Century*. New York: Knopf, 1978.

White, E. B. *Charlotte's Web*. New York: Harper, 1952.

Wilder, Laura Ingalls. *Little House in the Big Woods*. Illus. Garth Williams. New York: Harper and Row, 1953.

RECOMMENDED READINGS

Auerbach, Nina. "Engorging the Patriarchy." In *Feminist Issues in Literary Scholarship*, ed. Shari Benstock. Bloomington: Indiana University Press, 1987: 150–160.

Bettelheim, Bruno. *The Uses of Enchantment: The Meaning and Importance of Fairy Tales*. New York: Knopf, 1976.

Bressler, Charles E. *Literary Criticism: An Introduction to Theory and Practice*. Englewood Cliffs, NJ: Prentice-Hall, 1994.

Cameron, Eleanor. *The Seed and the Vision: On the Writing and Appreciaton of Children's Books*. New York: Dutton, 1993.

Carlson, Ruth Kearney. *Emerging Humanity: Multi-Ethnic Literature for Children and Adolescents*. Dubuque, IA: Wm. C. Brown, 1972.

Cullinan, Bernice, and Carolyn Carmichael, eds. *Literature and Young Children*. Urbana, IL: National Council of Teachers of English, 1977.

Hearne, Betsy, and Roger Sutton, eds. *Evaluating Children's Books: A Critical Look*. Urbana: University of Illinois Press, 1993.

Hilkick, Wallace. *Children and Fiction*. Cleveland: World, 1971.

Lukens, Rebecca J. *A Critical Handbook of Children's Literature*, 5th ed. Glenview, IL: Scott, Foresman, 1995.

Nodelman, Perry. *The Pleasures of Children's Literature*, 2nd ed. New York: Longman, 1995.

Otten, Charlotte F., and Gary D. Schmidt, eds. *The Voice of the Narrator in Children's Literature: Insights from Writers and Critics*. New York: Greenwood, 1989.

Purves, Alan C., and Dianne L. Monson. *Experiencing Children's Literature*. Glenview, IL: Scott, Foresman, 1984.

Register, Cheri. "American Feminist Literary Criticism: A Bibliographic Introduction." In *Feminist Literary Criticism: Explorations in Theory*, ed. Josephine Donovan. Lexington: University Press of Kentucky, 1975: 1–28.

Rosenblatt, Louise. *The Reader, the Text, the Poem*. Carbondale, IL: Southern Illinois Press, 1978.

Shapiro, Jon, ed. *Using Literature & Poetry Affectively*. Chicago: International Reading Association, 1979.

Smith, James Steel. *A Critical Approach to Children's Literature*. New York: McGraw-Hill, 1967.

Smith, Lillian. *The Unreluctant Years*. Chicago: American Library Association, 1953 (report Viking, 1967).

Stewig, John Warren, and Sam L. Sebesta, eds. *Using Literature in the Elementary Classroom*. Urbana, IL: National Council of Teachers of English, 1978.

Waxman, Barbara Frey. "Feminist Theory, Literary Canons, and the Construction of Textual Meanings." In *Practicing Theory in Introductory College Literature Courses*, eds. James M. Cahalan and David B. Downing. Urbana, IL: National Council of Teachers of English, 1991: 149–160.

Chapter 5

RESPONDING TO LITERATURE

LANGUAGE ACQUISITION

Language acquisition is how children learn to speak and understand language in the first place. Because we are so accustomed to using language daily, we can easily forget what a miracle human speech is. It is actually a very abstract concept employing a complex set of symbols and rules that enable us to communicate virtually any human thought to another. Modern researchers believe that language is acquired through a combination of heredity (the inborn human potential for speech) and environment (the imitation of others and the reinforcement of habits).

As adults dealing with children, we can benefit from understanding the importance of our role in language acquisition. Most authorities agree that as early as three years of age, children have developed a significant proficiency in language—even to the point of comprehending grammatical structure. This means that we cannot wait until kindergarten to begin stressing language skills. Even infancy is not too early to expose a child to a variety of language experiences, from talking to the child to reading the child stories and poems. We can be assured that even very young children absorb both vocabulary and linguistic patterns that will eventually result in the power of communication. In language acquisition, as in so many other areas of life, we will do well not to underestimate our children.

SHARING LITERATURE
WITH CHILDREN

Perhaps the principal responsibility of adults when it comes to children and books is simply to make sure that children and books come together often, and to see that, when they do, the experience is happy and stimulating. So it is crucial that we do everything we can to make our children readers, lovers of books, and seekers of knowledge.

Happily, the trend in most schools today is away from using textbooks to teach reading and toward using much of the fine literature—fiction, poetry, and nonfiction—that is currently available for young people. Books are an integral part of every good preschool and elementary school classroom. Our goal should be that every classroom have plenty of books on hand; that ample time for sharing books, reading aloud, and silent reading is scheduled; that children look forward to the time when they can read. Simply put, books should be seen as an inseparable part of education, an invaluable part of life.

Books present a multitude of opportunities for classroom discussions and activities. What follows are suggestions that encourage thoughtful responses and student interaction. A teacher is limited only by his or her imagination.

THE READER-CENTERED
APPROACH TO LITERATURE

A reader-centered approach to talking and writing about literature emphasizes the individual as a reader-responder. Because of its reader-friendly attitude, this approach is ideal for use in the elementary classroom (and it is enormously successful with older readers as well). In *How Porcupines Make Love: Teaching a Response-Centered Literature Curriculum*, Purves, Rogers, and Soter identified four "Objectives" of the reader-centered approach, which are helpful to keep in mind as we prepare to share books with young readers (47).

Objectives of the Reader-Centered Approach
1. To encourage individual readers to feel comfortable with their own responses to a literary work,
2. To encourage the readers to seek out the reasons for their responses and thereby come to understand themselves better,
3. To encourage the readers to recognize, in the responses of others, the differences among people and to respect those differences, and
4. To encourage readers to recognize, in the responses of others, the similarities among people.

Such an approach does not attempt to "teach" literature; rather its primary goal is to bring children and literature together.

In a response-centered approach, we, as adults interested in the interaction of children with books, do a variety of things. Again, Purves, Rogers, and Soter (56) have suggested specific actions that define the role of adults in effecting a successful reading experience in young people:

The Role of Adults

1. We bring children and books together;
2. We give them as many different types of literature as possible;
3. We encourage honest and open responses;
4. We challenge children to explore those responses and learn something about themselves;
5. We provide them with the critical language that they might clearly express their responses;
6. We encourage tolerance;
7. We encourage mutual understanding.

The following are activities for bringing about a connection between children and the books they read. This is in no way an exhaustive list, but rather a suggestive one.

READING ALOUD

From the parent's gentle singing of a lullaby while rocking an infant to sleep to the reading of such childhood classics as *Alice in Wonderland* or *Pinocchio*, sharing literature orally with children can be one of the most fulfilling of human experiences. The relaxing moments of story time with two-, three-, and four-year-old children are among the most cherished memories of parenthood. But the times are equally magical when young children want to read the stories to us. Jim Trelease's *Read-Aloud Handbook* is an excellent resource for adults who wish to cultivate the skill of effective reading aloud.

If the book is a picture book, then we have to take care that the illustrations can be easily seen by everyone in the audience. This is easy enough with one or two children, but somewhat more difficult when sharing a picture storybook with a classroom of 30. Of course, an alternative is to break larger classes into small groups for story sharing.

Selecting books to read aloud to children in the upper elementary grades requires just as much care. The story ought to be one that the reader enjoys as well as the listener. It pays to select the book thoughtfully, considering the emotional level of the children, their primary social and psychological concerns—even the time of year may have an impact on the selection. This is also a great opportunity to introduce subjects and themes that children may not ordinarily seek but would find rewarding.

Reading aloud entails something more than simply pronouncing the words on the page. Careful enunciation, the proper inflections, the correct tone, thoughtful pacing—all these help to make the experience more rewarding for reader and listener alike. Reading aloud is not, however, acting, and exaggerated threatrics may actually detract from the story itself and defeat the entire purpose. Generally, the best reading is slow and deliberate—listening audiences miss a great deal of what is said to them anyway, and reading too rapidly only increases the chances of their becoming lost or confused. And finally, nothing beats rehearsing the story ahead of time, practicing the pronunciation and making certain there are no words to stumble over. The reward—a grateful and delighted audience—is well worth the effort.

STORYTELLING

Storytelling, the art of narrating a tale from memory rather than reading it, is one of the oldest of all art forms—undoubtedly reaching back to prehistoric times. Through storytellers, virtually all the traditional folktales were preserved for centuries, most having been committed to paper only in the past two or three centuries. Storytelling involves two elements—selection and delivery. A successful storyteller chooses good stories, and most storytellers prepare a repertoire of stories, often specializing in certain types of stories—tall tales, tales of a specific culture or region, and so on. An effective storyteller is also a performer, for the delivery is crucial and requires considerable preparation and rehearsal.

An important part of the success of any storytelling lies in the choice of an effective story, one that builds up to a climax and then ends quickly while the audience's interest is still at a peak. Folktales are natural sources for storytellers. They include easily memorized patterns, with ample dialogue to enliven the story, and they are brief enough to be relayed in a single sitting. Also, they lend themselves well to adaptation so the storyteller can adjust the tale to the audience.

Of course, a rich, mellifluous voice is an asset to any would-be storyteller, but few of us are so blessed. However, this means only that we need to develop some other assets—effective body movement, eye contact, clear enunciation, meaningful inflection, and appropriate pauses. And, with practice, it is possible to develop a greater vocal range and a voice that will project. The best storytellers know how to pace the telling, when to slow down, when to pause, when to speed up, when to talk in near whispers, when to shout, and so on. Movement on a staging area can be significant. Natural body gestures (and at times even exaggerated ones, depending on the nature of the story) and direct eye contact help to totally engage the audience.

BOOK DISCUSSIONS

One of the most common classroom approaches to literature is the book discussion, which, if successful, will go beyond a simple series of questions from the teacher and the expected "correct" answers from the students. A good book discussion evolves and metamorphoses as it proceeds. It should be stimulating and provocative, and to ensure that it is, the leader of the discussion needs to be prepared. Asking the right questions is the key to a provocative discussion, and at least four different levels of questions can be identified.

At the first level, *memory or factual questions* ask the audience to recall facts from the story or poem: plot incidents, character identifications, details of the setting, and so on. It is good to begin a discussion with memory questions for they can help determine if the readers understand the basic elements of the work.

An example of a good memory question might be, "In Beatrix Potter's *The Tale of Peter Rabbit*, what happened to Peter's father?" The answer to this question has a direct bearing on the theme of the story, since it shows that Peter was aware of the dangers of entering Mr. McGregor's garden. In a discussion of E. B. White's classic book *Charlotte's Web*, for example, we may begin with memory questions such as these: "Why was Wilbur's life in danger?" "How did Fern save Wilbur?" "How did Charlotte save Wilbur?" or "How did Wilbur repay Charlotte?" All these questions can be answered from a reading of the book, and all have some thematic significance. It would be unproductive to ask such questions as "What color was Wilbur?" or "What was Charlotte's oldest child's name?" These details have little bearing on the story, and there is no reason to expect a reader to recall every bit of minutiae. There is no virtue in memory questions that seem designed to trick even the most careful reader; if we can think of no good reason for asking a question, it probably should not be asked.

The second level of questioning consists of *interpretation questions*, questions requiring the readers to make inferences and draw conclusions from the facts of the story or poem. These questions may require *analysis* (lifting individual facts from the story and examining them carefully) or *synthesis* (putting together disparate facts in a new way). "Why does Peter's mother not punish him for his disobedience?" might be a good interpretation question, for it will lead into a discussion of one of the major ideas of the story. For *Charlotte's Web*, we might ask such questions as these: "How does the relationship between Fern and Wilbur change over the course of the book?" or "How does Wilbur's character change from the beginning to the end of the book?" In any case, it is important that readers understand that any conclusions they draw be based soundly on the evidence found in the work itself. Personal opinions should be supported by specific details from the text.

The third level of questioning is that of *application*. These questions ask the readers to consider the work in a larger context, and they tend to focus on further extensions of the theme as well as on matters of style, imagery, symbolism, and so on. Application refers to the transfer of information acquired from the literary work to another experience (one's own life, for example, or another literary work). Children might be asked, "Compare *The Tale of Peter Rabbit* with Potter's *Tale of Benjamin Bunny*" or "Discuss a time when you were in a situation similar to Peter's." While discussing *Charlotte's Web*, students might be asked, "In what ways do Templeton, Charlotte, and Wilbur remind you of people you know?" Application questions should ultimately help us to see the relationships between literature and life, and should, when possible, ask us to draw on our own experiences. Here are where the personal responses to literature come into play. These questions can result in some of the more meaningful and exciting discussions.

Ultimately, we may bring young readers to the fourth level of questioning, which involves *critical evaluation*. As children read more and more, and become sophisticated in their literary knowledge, we can ask them to make critical judgments about the works they read. It is not realistic to expect the very young to read on this level, but with older children we might ask, "Compare *Charlotte's Web* with Kenneth Grahame's *Wind in the Willows* or with Robert Lawson's *Rabbit Hill*." "How are they alike?" "How are they different?" "Which is most believable and why?" "Compare *Charlotte's Web* with another of E. B. White's fantasies—*Stuart Little* or *Trumpet of the Swan*." "What similarities do you see?" "What differences?" "If you prefer one over another, why?" Asking young readers which of two books they prefer is only useful if we can get them to articulate their reasons and thereby help them to understand their own tastes a little better. This is also the beginning of the acquisition of critical taste and judgment. It is good to remember that with most interpretation and evaluation questions, there are no clear wrong or right answers, only answers that are more convincingly supported than others.

WRITING EXPERIENCES

As early as second grade, most children are capable of responding to literature through writing, and certainly by the time they reach the middle elementary grades, children should be writing as a regular part of their total curriculum. Several possibilities are available at all grade levels.

Webbing.   Webbing, also known as mapping, is a visual means of demonstrating relationships between story elements or concepts. A web consists of a figure (the simplest resembles a spider's web, which is where the term comes from) on which labels are placed by which we can see the connections between aspects of a piece of literature. For example, the web in Figure 5.1 illustrates the ways in which the principal characters in the folktale *Cinderella* are opposites. Countless variations on webs are possible. Any visual representation is a potential tool for webbing or map-

FIGURE 5.1   Web for *Cinderella*.

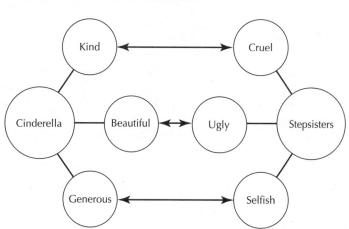

ping a story. The petals of a flower, the steps of a stairway, the points of a star can all be transformed into images that demonstrate connections in a work of literature. And if the web or map is truly successful, the image itself makes a statement. For example, we might label the petals of a flower with a character's personality traits to show how the individual grows (or "blossoms") throughout the course of a story. Since many people are visual learners, that is, they grasp ideas more quickly if they can see them illustrated, webbing is an effective tool for examining relationships in a poem, story, or play. Virtually any aspect of literature can be applied to a web or map—character development, plot, symbols or imagery, themes. A good webbing or mapping exercise can not only help readers better understand a literary work, it can also provide a great deal of fun during the preparation.

Journals. Keeping journals in which they are free to record their feelings without fear of a recriminating grade can be a very effective way for children to become more thoughtful readers. When we have to commit our ideas to writing we are compelled to think them through more thoroughly. Thus, writing helps us to analyze and evaluate our thoughts.

Journal sharing can be a rewarding variation on this exercise. Students can share journal entries with others, who can respond with their own feelings. One way to do this is to draw a line down the middle of the page, with the original writer using the left-hand side and the respondent using the right-hand side. It can also be done by using facing pages in a spiral-ring notebook. Teachers can also be respondents. It is important that children fully understand the nature of the journal assignment before they write—an entry in a private journal would be much different from an entry intended for another reader. Journal writing is most effective when it is habitual and when the entries are long enough to explore ideas and feelings.

Reader-Response Essays. Other writing exercises might include reader-response essays, in which young readers are asked to record various responses to their reading. These responses may be emotional, responding to particular characters or situations, especially as they relate to their own lives and experiences. They may be interpretative, as when a reader makes an inference about what he or she reads, or draws some conclusion based on the evidence in a story. Responses may be critical or evaluative, as when a reader makes some judgment about the literary quality of a written work.

Another interesting writing experiment is to have young readers write a preliminary essay in preparation for a reading assignment. For example, prior to reading Natalie Babbitt's *Tuck Everlasting*, students might be asked to write on the following topic: "If you discovered the fountain of immortality, would you drink from it? Why or why not?" Then, once the students have read the book, in which such a question is actually posed to the protagonist, they might be asked to write a follow-up essay reconsidering the same issue in the new light shed by the novel. A comparison of the two responses—before and after—can be quite interesting.

Book Reports: Variations on an Old Theme. There are countless imaginative exercises available to replace the old "book report." Children may enjoy making up their own endings to stories, for example, or writing new episodes with their favorite characters: Peggy Parrish's *Amelia Bedelia* series or Beverly Cleary's *Ramona* books provide wonderful starting points for younger readers. Newspaper stories based on events in books can also be fun to write: Roald Dahl's *James and the Giant Peach* or *Charlie and the Chocolate Factory* offer some delightful opportunities here. Some children may enjoy reading and writing about the life of a favorite author. Students might write open letters to authors—living or dead—in which the students discuss their own attitudes and opinions toward a book. They do not need to be mailed. Read Beverly Cleary's *Dear Mr. Henshaw* for an example of the value of letter writing, even if those letters are not mailed. Writing the imaginary diary of a fictional character can help children understand the concept of point of view. Having children create a story from their own life experiences can help them gain firsthand knowledge of plot. Script-writing, in which children must devise dialogue for characters, can enrich their understanding of language differences, characterization, and setting.

Creating Books.   A particularly enjoyable activity for children of all ages is that of making their own books. Very young children can create alphabet, counting, or concept books, or do takeoffs on favorite nursery rhymes or poems. Older children may want to experiment with ghost stories, adventure stories, family stories, or poetry. Of course, much of the fun lies in illustrating the books, and a variety of media can be used—crayon, watercolor, collage, montage, pencil, and so on. Individuals can write their own books, or, if the budget permits, an anthology of stories, poems, or illustrations created by the members of the class can be assembled and duplicated for everyone.

Binding the books can be as simple as fastening them in a loose-leaf folder or as elaborate as sewing the leaves and making cloth-covered cardboard covers. Not only does this project give children firsthand experiences in designing books and laying out pages, it can also result in an attractive finished product that is fit for a gift or a keepsake. Such a project can bring a writing exercise to a satisfying climax, and the children can see themselves as young authors.

DRAMATIC RESPONSES TO LITERATURE

Dramatic responses to literature include a wide range of activities, from oral interpretation (a one-person performance of a piece of literature) to creative dramatics and role playing (impromptu inventions of the actors). We will briefly consider a few of these approaches.

Oral Interpretation.   Oral interpretation typically involves a one-person performance of a poem or brief prose passage, usually, but not necessarily, memorized (that is, it may be read). The effectiveness of oral interpretation lies in the performer's vocal talents and meaningful gestures. It is very much like storytelling, except that oral interpretation does not allow for variation in the original material. In other words, the speaker is expected to recite the piece exactly as it was written. Oral interpretation works best with children in the middle and upper elementary grades and older.

Many wonderful, humorous poems are available that might make this experience a pleasurable one for both performer and audience. (In fact, if it is not pleasurable, it should be discontinued at once.) Whenever possible, children should be allowed to select their own material for oral interpretation. Memorization becomes rather pointless when the children do not like or understand what it is they are supposed to memorize—then the purposes of enjoyment and sharpening mental skills are both defeated. In oral interpretation an important emphasis is on the careful pronunciation and enunciation of the words, projection, and, to the extent possible, in conveying the appropriate feeling behind the language. Shyness is inevitable with many students, but it can only be overcome with continued practice and experience.

Story Theater.   Story theater is a pantomime accompanied by a narrator who reads or tells the story while others act out the plot. Since even inanimate objects (such as a tree) might be portrayed by an actor, story theater allows for a very flexible number of performers (some children may enjoy the idea of portraying objects like the moon, for example). The performance can be as simple or elaborate as the means dictate. Pantomime does not require line memorizing, making it one of the least threatening dramatic forms for children. It does require one good reader, however, and some uninhibited actors. Since the youngest children tend to be the least inhibited, story theater is a good exercise to begin in the early elementary years. The best tales for a story theater presentation are those with plenty of action; otherwise the pantomimes would be little more than furniture. Many folktales provide wonderful opportunities for story theater, particularly the farcical tales, such as "Clever Gretel," where action rather than dialogue dominates. Story theater can be enhanced by costumes, scenery, and props, and can be a great way to introduce play production.

Reader's Theater.   Reader's theater, as the name implies, involves the reading of a script as opposed to acting it out. The participants assume various speaking roles in a story—usually one reader for each speaking character and one narrator to read the exposition. True reader's theater is traditionally performed without any action whatever, with the readers sitting on chairs and using only their voices to convey meaning. The old-time radio dramas were, in essence, reader's theater, and that is very much the effect that good reader's theater has. All the audience's attention is directed to the language, so the readers must be expressive and must read with clarity and precision.

To avoid distraction from the reading, performers in reader's theater often wear simple, uniform clothing—usually in black, or black and white. Since no memorization, physical movement, scenery, or properties are involved, reader's theater provides a convenient and affordable outlet for self-expression. Without the advantage of action—as with story theater—greater responsibility is placed on the readers to work with the voice of their respective characters. For this reason, considerable practice in oral interpretation is essential for successful reader's theater.

Although reader's theater is designed for the reading of plays, many stories can be adapted to reader's theater, including (once again) many folktales. It is important that each reader have a substantial part—and there is no reason a single person cannot read more than one part. But stories with few speaking parts may leave most of the reading for the narrator, with little for the other readers to do. "The Three Bears" is an example of a story that is primarily narration; there is really very little for the characters to say. The best reader's theater stories are those with several speaking parts, ample dialogue, a fairly easy vocabulary, distinctive and identifiable characters, and, finally, good conflict, such as "Hansel and Gretel." It is always possible to edit the tales as well, abbreviating the narration or even replacing narration with dialogue.

Creative Dramatics.   Creative dramatics is the dramatization of a story with improvised dialogue. This allows children to perform their own versions of stories without strict adherence to script—although in creative dramatics, the actors are expected to remain faithful to the storyline. This activity requires considerable preparation and may be as elaborate in setting, properties, and theatrical accouterments as the director desires. Creative dramatics can be less threatening than a more traditional play, since there is no need for memorization. It also allows for more individual expression than either story theater or reader's theater, providing children with the opportunity to update old stories and give them their own peculiar twists. At the same time, this exercise can result in a more meaningful consideration of character, plot, and theme. One of the great advantages to creative dramatics is that many folktales and other short stories or even chapters from favorite books (e.g., *Winnie-the-Pooh* or *The Wind in the Willows*) can be readily adapted to the form.

Role Playing.   Role playing is similar to creative dramatics, but it removes us one step further from the literary source. The actors assume specific character roles and are expected to invent not only the dialogue but the action as they proceed. Typically, a problem is posed and through the role-playing exercise, the children arrive at a solution, which allows them to examine the issues from different points of view. Role playing is only marginally connected with literature, but it is a widely used and effective method of exploring personal and social values. Children, for example, could be assigned the roles of various characters (such as those from Cleary's *Ramona* books), and they could then be presented with a dilemma to solve. The important element in a successful role-playing exercise is to be sure that each assigned role is a distinct personality type who will respond appropriately as the personality suggests. This exercise, as with many of the dramatic responses, works best with children in the middle or upper elementary grades, since younger children have not yet grasped the fundamental concepts of drama.

Puppet Theater.   Puppet theater is a favorite medium of children, and combines both dramatic and artistic responses to literature. An elaborate and time-honored art form, puppetry can be very simple (puppets made from a sock or decorated paper bag stuck on a hand) or very complex (string-operated marionettes with movable hands, feet, eyes, and mouth). Puppet-making is an art in itself, and one in which children can readily participate. In addition to socks and paper bags, puppets can be made from construction paper and sticks, vegetables (they make wonderful puppets, but don't wait too long to do the show), cardboard boxes, rubber balls and cloth, cardboard cylinders (such as paper towel tubes), and shadow puppets (created by using overhead projectors, with great possibilities available through the use of colored acetate sheets for background).

Once the puppet is made, the dramatic part of the experience begins. Stories with ample dialogue and action work best. And, since lines need not be memorized and since the puppeteers are hidden from the audience's view, puppet theater can be an ideal form for beginning thespians. It is also perfect for shy children, for behind the mask of the puppet, many have found an exhilarating outlet for their deepest feelings.

ARTISTIC RESPONSES TO LITERATURE

Another popular means of extending literature is through art. As soon as they can handle a crayon or pencil, even the youngest children can be asked to draw pictures in response to a story. The means by which art can enrich the literary experience are many. Following are a few of the more widely used methods.

The Graphic Arts.   Children love working with paints, watercolors, crayons, and pencil. These are usually the simplest art projects, requiring rather basic tools and minimal instruction to get started. And they allow for a great deal of originality. Even having young children draw pictures suggested by picture storybooks can be a means of getting them to explore different artistic styles as they try to copy Maurice Sendak's impressionistic style in Charlotte Zolotow's *Mr. Rabbit and the Lovely Present*, or Beatrix Potter's delicate representational style in *The Tale of Peter Rabbit*, or Ludwig Bemelmans's expressionistic style in *Madeline*. Allowing children to draw pictures after hearing stories read to them can result in some of the most highly individualistic creation, for they do not have another artist's work to imitate.

Collage, not technically a "graphic" method except that it can make use of pens, pencils, and other drawing instruments, is a picture created from nonpainterly materials (cloth, wood, cotton, leaves, rocks, and so on). These materials are typically fixed to a posterboard to make a unified work. This was the favorite method of Ezra Jack Keats (*The Snowy Day*, *Peter's Chair*, and many other fine picture books) and Leo Lionni (*Frederick* and *Inch by Inch*, among others). Creating a collage about a favorite story is especially appealing for young children since it does not require highly developed drawing skills. The materials used and their arrangment may be suggested by the story itself.

Similar to the collage is the *montage*, which is a collection of pictures arranged into a single composite. Both the collage and the montage can be used as responses to literature if children are asked to create, for example, a poster that reflects their feelings about a particular work. Doing this, young readers are being asked to focus on a specific aspect of the literature—usually either character or theme. This is the great advantage of incorporating artwork into the literature program, for the readers can be encouraged to distill all their thoughts on a story into a single visual image. As a result, they may better understand the work's plot or theme or characterization.

The Plastic Arts.   The plastic arts include the three-dimensional, nonpainterly works, such as sculpture. The *diorama* is a three-dimensional scene easily created from a shoebox or other carton (an unused fish aquarium, with its glass sides, provides some interesting opportunities as well) and decorated with cardboard cutouts, plastic figures, or any other suitable objects. Like the montage and collage, the diorama focuses on a single thematic idea. By a further extension of the diorama, children can create miniature stages and puppet figures with which to reenact a story, thus combining an artistic and a dramatic response to literature. A natural development of the miniature stage is for the children to create stories of their own to dramatize. The diorama requires attention to detail, which is why this form is used so frequently for social studies projects—such as dioramas of the ice age or of Colonial America and so on.

Mobiles are free forms, usually cut from paper or cardboard, interconnected and suspended by string or wire so that when hung they turn freely in the breeze. These are popular with children from infancy, and many babies enjoy some form of mobile hung over their cribs. *Stabiles* are similar to mobiles in that they are abstract sculptural forms, but, unlike the mobile, they remain stationary. Modeling with clay or working with other craft materials, such as the proverbial popsicle sticks, can provide further imaginative outlets as responses to stories or poems. Such projects can help children see relationships in a story, and they can cause them to consider such things as character, plot, and theme more seriously. Children could create a mobile or stabile representing the theme of a story or the nature of a character, for example. As with any art project associated with literature, such projects are extensions of the literary study, not just meaningless time-fillers.

Cooking.   A recently popularized extension to literature is cooking, which can be considered an art form in itself, one in which the artistic creation is eaten. Some children's books even include recipes suitable for children, and there are, in fact, some very fine cookbooks written for children—for example, Virginia Ellison's *Pooh's Cookbook* is for the very young. Jean Fritz's *George Washington's Breakfast* readily lends itself to a cooking experience as a capstone to the reading.

Regardless of the art project, it is important to remember that if the art is seen as a true extension of the literature it should not be regarded as the end itself. In other words, we are not reading *Pinocchio* for the purpose of making our own puppet when we are finished. And, if the art is to be a true extension of the literature, it should not be simply gratuitous—"Now that we have read *Pinocchio*, let's all draw a picture of his nose." If the art project cannot become a meaningful part of the study of the literature, helping children to better focus on the ideas and the structure of the work itself, it is perhaps best not to fabricate a relationship between the art and the literature. Both, after all, are valuable in their own right.

CHILDREN'S BOOKS AND THE CENSOR

A regrettable fact that many educators ultimately have to face is the self-proclaimed censor wielding a swift and wrathful sword against the supposedly dangerous ideas presented in books. Literature, as we have noted, is not for the bigot, for literature encourages tolerance as it presents us with endless possibilities. The bigot and the despot both fear literature because it helps to keep people's minds open and receptive to new ideas, so it should be of no surprise to us that the bigots and despots are also the bookburners and censors.

For centuries, censorship has been pervasive in children's literature—it derives from the natural inclination to protect childhood innocence. Unfortunately, not everyone agrees on what is suitable for children and, to complicate matters further, banning a book usually backfires and makes the book even more popular. We have seen the folktales tidied up and rid of much of their gore, and that may be to accommodate delicate modern tastes (usually of adults). But we have also seen the banning of such books as E. B. White's *Charlotte's Web* (some find the whole concept of talking animals unnatural and disturbing), William Steig's *Sylvester and the Magic Pebble* (the author portrays the police as pigs in this animal fantasy), Robert Cormier's *I Am the Cheese* (too negative a view of society), J. D. Salinger's *The Catcher in the Rye* (all those four-letter words)—the list is legion. Censorship is alive and well in the United States. We should view this with alarm, for it threatens our intellectual freedom, our personal freedom, and it undermines one of the most fundamental tenets of our Constitution. It can, at its worst, threaten democracy.

Our problem as purveyors of children's literature is to be prepared to defend our choices if parents or the community objects to any literature we might wish to use. It is wise for teachers to have a written justification prepared for each book in the curriculum. In this way, we can try to anticipate objections and be ready to address them if it becomes necessary.

Books have little power to turn good children into bad or bad children into good. No reliable evidence exists that a child was ever ruined by a book. At most, a book can probably only reinforce attitudes already held by the reader. The seventeenth-century English thinker Sir Francis Bacon wrote, "Some books are to be tasted, other to be swallowed, and some few to be chewed and digested." We have suggested ways in which we can help children taste, swallow, and—in some cases—chew and digest the books they read. If we have done our jobs well, the young people in our care will look forward to a feast of rich and pleasurable reading, lasting throughout their entire lives.

WORK CITED

Purves, Alan, et al. *How Porcupines Make Love: Teaching a Response-Centered Literature Curriculum*. White Plains, NY: Longman, 1990.

RECOMMENDED READINGS

Aquino, John. *Fantasy in Literature*. Washington, DC: National Education Association, 1977.

Bauer, Caroline Feller. *This Way to Books*. Bronx, NY: Wilson, 1982.

Barton, Bob, and David Booth. *Stories in the Classroom*. Portsmouth, NH: Heinemann, 1990.

Blatt, Gloria T., ed. *Once Upon a Folktale: Capturing the Folklore Process with Children*. New York: Teachers College Press, 1993.

Bosma, Betty. *Fairy Tales, Fables, Legends, and Myths: Using Folk Literature in Your Classroom*, 2nd ed. New York: Teachers College Press, 1992.

Bromley, Karen D'Angelo. *Webbing with Literature: Creating Story Maps with Children's Books*. Boston: Allyn and Bacon, 1991.

Bruno, Janet, and Peggy Dakan. *Cooking in the Classroom*. Belmont, CA: Fearon Pitman, 1974.

Chambers, Aidan. *Introducing Books to Children*, 2nd ed. Boston: The Horn Book, 1983.

———. *The Reluctant Reader*. Elmsford, NY: Pergamon, 1969.

Cioni, Alfred J., ed. *Motivating Reluctant Readers*. Newark, DE: International Reading Association, 1981.

Coody, Betty. *Using Literature with Young Children*, 4th ed. Dubuque, IA: Wm. C. Brown, 1992.

Currell, David. *The Complete Book of Puppetry*. Boston: Plays, 1975.

Gillies, Emily. *Creative Dramatics for All Children*. Wheaton, MD: Association for Childhood Education International, 1973.

Hanford, Robert Ten Eyck. *Puppets and Puppeteering*. New York: Sterling, 1981.

Leonard, Charlotte. *Tied Together: Topics and Thoughts for Introducing Children's Books*. Metuchen, NJ: Scarecrow, 1980.

MacDonald, M. R. *The Storyteller's Sourcebook: A Subject, Title and Motif Index to Folklore Collections for Children*. Detroit, MI: Heal-Schuman, 1982.

Pellowski, Ann. *World of Storytelling*. Ann Arbor, MI: R. R. Bowker, 1977.

Raines, Shirley, and Rebecca Isbell. *Stories: Children's Literature in Early Education*. Albany, NY: Delmar, 1994.

Rothlein, Liz, and Anita Meyer Meinbach. *Legacies: Using Children's Literature in the Classroom*. New York: HarperCollins, 1996.

Routman, Regie. *Transitions: From Literature to Literacy*. Portsmouth, NH: Heinemann, 1988.

Rudman, Masha, ed. *Children's Literature: Resource for the Classroom*. Norwood, MA: Christopher-Gordon, 1989.

Sawyer, Ruth. *The Way of the Storyteller*. New York: Penguin, 1942.

Schickedanz, J. A. *More Than the ABCs: The Early Stages of Reading and Writing*. Washington, DC: National Association for the Education of Young Children, 1986.

Shapiro, Jon E., ed. *Using Literature & Poetry Affectively*. Newark, DE: International Reading Association, 1971.

Shedlock, Marie. *The Art of the Storyteller* (1915). New York: Dover, 1951.

Sloan, Glenna Davis. *The Child as Critic: Teaching Literature in Elementary and Middle*

Schools, 3rd ed. New York: Teachers College Press, 1991.

Strickland, D. S., and L. M. Morrow, eds. *Emerging Literacy: Young Children Learn to Read and Write*. Newark, DE: International Reading Association, 1989.

Trelease, Jim. *The Read-Aloud Handbook*, rev. ed. New York: Penguin, 1985.

Troeger, Virginia Bergen. "Student Storytelling." *Teaching K-8* March 1990: 41–43.

Watson, Dorothy J., ed. *Ideas and Insights: Language Arts in the Elementary School*. Urbana, IL: National Council of Teachers of English, 1987.

Yopp, Ruth Helen, and Hallie Kay Yopp. *Literature-Based Reading Activities*. Boston: Allyn and Bacon, 1992.

Part Two

THE KINDS OF CHILDREN'S LITERATURE

Chapter 6

~

BOOKS FOR THE
VERY YOUNG

Few things in life are more rewarding than sharing a good picture book with an eager young child. The picture book—a collaboration of the talents of the writer and the artist—has the power to shape a child's lifelong tastes and attitudes toward reading. This and the next chapter will examine the wide assortment of picture books and their accompanying art that are available for children. The focus of this chapter will be those books of early childhood—Mother Goose books, wordless books, toy books, and alphabet, counting, concept, and easy-to-read books. In Chapter 7 we will consider the picture storybook and the art of picture-book illustration.

MOTHER GOOSE BOOKS

Mother Goose rhymes share the characteristics of two types of literature. First they are folk literature—songs that were passed down by word of mouth long before they were written down. Second, they are a form of poetry, with rhyme and rhythm being a large part of their charm. Mother Goose rhymes (in England they are called "nursery rhymes") are typically a child's first introduction to literature, beginning with the parents' singing of lullabies, such as "Rock-a-bye, Baby," or counting out tiny toes with "This little pig went to market."

A great deal of time has been devoted to speculations on the origin of the term *Mother Goose*. We know that the seventeenth-century French reteller of folktales, Charles Perrault, named his book *Tales from Mother Goose*, and that by the end of the eighteenth century "Mother Goose" was clearly associated with a mythical teller of nursery rhymes for young children—at least in the United States. No one is really sure where Perrault found the name. It may have been the appellation given to the woman who, in earlier times, kept the village geese and who was the traditional community storyteller.

Whereas some nursery rhymes are exceedingly old (the counting-out rhyme "Eena, meena, mona, my" and its variations seem to harken back to the sounds of ancient names for the numbers), most date from the sixteenth, seventeenth, and eighteenth centuries. "The Three Blind Mice" was set to music as early as 1609; "Jack Sprat" may have ridiculed a certain Archdeacon Spratt in the mid-seventeenth century, and some identify "Jack Horner" with Thomas Horner of Mells whose "plum" was valuable land he acquired through Henry VIII's dissolution of the monasteries in 1536. Nursery rhymes are derived from a number of sources: war songs, romantic lyrics, proverbs, riddles, political jingles and lampoons, and street cries (the early counterparts of today's television commercials). But one thing can be said for certain: Few of these rhymes were initially intended forchildren.

The heroes of nursery rhymes typically come from the lower walks of life: Simple Simon, Tom the Piper's Son, Mother Hubbard, the Old Woman in the Shoe, and so on. Those that do include kings and queens ("Sing a Song of Six Pence" or "Old King Cole," for example) are typically comical and irreverent. Scarcely hidden beneath the surface of these rhymes and jingles are the jibe and the barb.

It has often been pointed out that the nursery rhymes contain their share of violence. Some of this realism could be shocking if we take it literally: babes dropping from treetops, cradle and all; a farmer's wife cutting off the tails (some say "heads") of three blind mice; a beleaguered old woman giving her children broth without bread and soundly whipping them; a man imprisoning his troublesome wife in a pumpkin shell; and so on. One assiduous critic, Geoffrey Handley-Taylor, noted that in a single collection of 200 familiar nursery rhymes, he discovered clearly 100 rhymes with "unsavoury elements," including eight allusions to murder, two cases of choking to death, one case of decapitation, seven cases of severing of limbs, one case of body snatching, four cases of breaking of limbs, and the list goes on (Baring-Gould 20). The important thing to realize is that this "violence" is not sensationalized, that any grisly element is eliminated, and the context of the violence is not only fictional but absurd. (Who puts wives in pumpkin shells? Who really lives in a shoe?) It can also be argued that this verbal expression of aggressive behavior may help children to vent those natural hostilities and pent-up anxieties. Further, there is not a single recorded instance of a child being transformed into a vicious human being from the influence of nursery rhymes. We may suspect, in fact, that exposure to such literature has a cathartic effect on children, relieving them of the need to engage in any physical violence.

Perhaps the only defense that Mother Goose rhymes need is that they are purely fun; their delightful nonsense and wonderful characters remain with us long beyond childhood. We should never underestimate the value of the sheer pleasure that literature can offer, but these rhymes, in fact, provide much more than an enjoyable pastime. Mother Goose rhymes may actually contribute significantly to a child's development in a surprising variety of ways.

COGNITIVE DEVELOPMENT

With such rhymes as "One, two, buckle your shoe/Three, four, shut the door," and "One, two, three, four, five/Once I caught a fish alive," young children are encouraged to learn numbers and counting. The letters of the alphabet are subjects of such rhymes as "A—apple pie." Nursery rhymes—perhaps because many of them were originally intended for adults—often include challenging words. "Mary, Mary, quite *contrary*," "Jack be *nimble*" and "Peter Piper picked a *peck of pickled peppers*" all provide opportunities for young children to expand their vocabularies painlessly. There is never any need to shy away from big words in children's books so long as they are words that can be easily explained and do not involve abstract thinking beyond the children's capacity. And it is also good to remember that because the nursery rhymes are easily memorized, young children frequently are able to "pretend" to read them, and soon, almost without realizing it, they actually begin to recognize the words. In this way, Mother Goose rhymes can be a tremendous stimulant to reading.

Finally, the appreciation of nonsense, such as that in most nursery rhymes, requires a firm grasp of reality. Nonsense is only amusing if we see its absurdity and incongruity when we place it next to what we know to be real. Therefore, it might be argued that Mother Goose rhymes help children in developing a sense of humor and that the rhymes force intellectual comparisons between fantasy and reality.

AESTHETIC DEVELOPMENT

Aesthetic development is the forming of an appreciation for beautiful things; in the case of literature, we are referring specifically to an appreciation of the beauty of language. Mother Goose rhymes with their lively meter appeal to a child's natural sense of rhythm—perhaps learned in the womb from the steady rhythm of the mother's heartbeat. The repeated refrains also provide children with the pleasures of anticipating something familiar. The playful sounds, including those wonderful nonsense words ("Hickory, dickory dock," "Diddle, diddle dumpling, my son John," "Higgledy, piggledy, my black hen"), appeal to the natural delight most children find in language. The rhymes encourage the very young children to experiment in creating sounds—a necessary developmental process toward learning to speak.

In addition to providing children with an introduction to linguistic sounds, the nature of rhyming, and the joy of rhythm, nursery rhymes also develop a child's sensitivity to pattern. The idea of pattern forms the basis of much art, for pattern imposes form, order, and logic on life. "A little girl was sitting on the ground eating and was scared away by a spider" describes an event in life. But notice how much more memorable the scene is when we impose a pattern on it:

Little Miss Muffet sat on a tuffet
Eating her curds and whey;
   Along came a spider
   And sat down beside her
And frightened Miss Muffet away.

Naturally, we hope that, with maturity, readers come to appreciate more sophisticated poetry than this, but without this foundation—verse forms and the repetition of sound that we call *rhyme*—a deeper appreciation is not very likely to develop.

SOCIAL AND PHYSICAL DEVELOPMENT

Many nursery rhymes are based on cooperative play—"Pat-a-cake, pat-a-cake" requires physical coordination and interpersonal contact, for example. Other rhymes, such as "Ring-a-ring o' roses" or "London Bridge Is Falling Down," call for the interaction of several children and thus encourage games and social interaction. Jump-rope rhymes are simply nursery rhymes gone to the playground, and they appear to be an almost worldwide childhood pastime (see Francelia Butler, *Skipping Around the World*). They also exhibit a considerable amount of aggression and even hostility. Take this popular jump-rope jingle, for instance:

> Fudge, fudge, tell the judge
> Mother has a newborn baby;
> It isn't a girl and it isn't a boy;
> It's just a fair young lady.
> Wrap it up in tissue paper
> And send it up the elevator:
> First floor, miss;
> Second floor, miss;
> Third floor, miss;
> Fourth floor,
> Kick it out the elevator door.

In one playful action, the skipping children are developing large motor coordination skills, engaging in a cooperative social activity, and rather harmlessly verbalizing some of the hostility that is an inevitable part of every sibling relationship. It is more socially acceptable than punching out one's kid brother—and almost as efficacious.

CHOOSING MOTHER GOOSE BOOKS

Scores of Mother Goose books are on the market, and they are of varying quality. Here are some points to consider when selecting a good volume:

1. Is there a balance between the familiar rhymes and those that are less-often anthologized?
2. Are rhymes from other cultures included—African, Asian, Native American, for example? (Mother Goose may be American, but cultures the world over have their equivalent of the child's folk rhyme.)
3. Are the illustrations examples of good illustrative art, both imaginative and well executed?
4. Are the pages uncluttered in appearance and are the rhymes juxtaposed with the proper pictures?
5. Are there enough rhymes to justify the cost of the book?

6. Is there an index so specific rhymes can be easily located?

7. Does the book present an overall attractive appearance?

Every household should possess at least one good collection of Mother Goose rhymes, and it is almost guaranteed that it will be well worn and that the investment will be returned manifold.

ILLUSTRATORS OF MOTHER GOOSE

Mother Goose rhymes are widely illustrated and have attracted some of the best children's artists. On the following pages are comparative examples of illustrations of two favorite rhymes—"Jack Sprat" and "Little Miss Muffet" —which will demonstrate the interpretative possibilities that these songs hold for the imaginative artist.

Jack Sprat.   *"Jack Sprat" has been especially popular among illustrators of Mother Goose rhymes and has inspired a wide variety of individual interpretations. The appeal of this nursery rhyme for illustrators has undoubtedly been the opportunity afforded by its two distinctive characters—each with a clearly defined character trait.*

FIGURE 6.1   Raymond Briggs's little drawing is quite different from the ones that follow in that it captures the Sprats in their most bizarre behavior—that of licking the platter clean. Appropriate to the subject, Briggs's style is cartoon, which heightens the effect of the absurd.

SOURCE: Illustration by Raymond Briggs. Reprinted by permission of Coward, McCann & Geoghegan from *The Mother Goose Treasury* by Raymond Briggs, © 1966 by Raymond Briggs.

JACK SPRAT could eat no fat,
His wife could eat no lean:

And so, betwixt them both, you see,
They lick'd the platter clean.

FIGURE 6.2 L. Leslie Brooke depicts a decidedly older couple and from an earlier time—the costumes are Renaissance. As always with Brooke, a close examination of his illustration reveals his wry humor: notice the bovine fattened for market prominently displayed on the Sprats's coat-of-arms. Like many Victorian children's artists, Brooke imbued his representational drawings with rich, subtle details.

SOURCE: From *The Nursery Rhyme Book* by Andrew Lang. Illustrated by L. Leslie Brooke. Copyright 1972 by Dover Publications, Inc. Reprinted by permission.

FIGURE 6.3 Blanche Fisher Wright depicts an eighteenth-century husband and his solicitous mate. Typical of her illustrations for the popular collection, *The Real Mother Goose*, the lines are clean and sharp and her characters well-defined.

SOURCE: From *The Real Mother Goose*. Illustrated by Blanche Fisher Wright. Copyright 1916, 1944 Checkerboard Press, a division of Macmillan, Inc. All rights reserved. Used by permission.

FIGURE 6.4 Marguerite de Angeli's lush painting of the Sprats, from her *Book of Nursery and Mother Goose Rhymes,* is a feast for the eye. Her illustration contrasts interestingly with Wright's, for although both artists have chosen virtually the same pose (even to the dog before the table), de Angeli's use of line makes her vision much more animated. De Angeli's style comes closer to expressionism, although she is still seeking that pictorial quality of representational art.

SOURCE: Excerpt(s) from *Book of Nursery and Mother Goose Rhymes* by Marguerite de Angeli, copyright © 1954 by Marguerite de Angeli. Used by permission of Doubleday, a division of Bantam, Doubleday, Dell Publishing Group, Inc.

Little Miss Muffet. *"Little Miss Muffet" is a wonderfully constructed tale, complete with setting, characters, conflict, climax, and resolution. With its clearly defined beginning, middle, and end, and its distinct characterization, this rhyme has been among the most popular of all Mother Goose verses. Most illustrators understandably choose to depict the moment just prior to the verse's climax: it provides the most drama and the greatest possibilities for interpretation.*

Little Miss Muffet,
Sat on a tuffet,
Eating some curds and whey ;
There came a great spider,
And sat down beside her,
And frightened Miss Muffet away.

FIGURE 6.5 Kate Greenaway could not bring herself to include unsavory elements in her illustrations; consequently she detracts from the drama by focusing all attention on the prim and proper Miss Muffet. The spider is barely noticeable off to the left. The colors are subdued and contribute to the air of quietness belying the circumstances.

SOURCE: Kate Greenaway, *Mother Goose Nursery Rhymes.* London: Frederick Warne & Co., Ltd.

FIGURE 6.6 Arthur Rackham, on the other hand, portrays a truly monstrous-looking, but not ungentlemanly, spider. The spider's appearance completely overwhelms the picture, and there is a wonderful contrast between the sedate Miss Muffet (somewhat more mature than Greenaway's), her lip daintily pursed, and the grotesque creature about to interrupt her. Rackham's surrealistic, frequently nightmarish quality is tempered here by a bit of wry humor as the spider gallantly doffs his hat.

SOURCE: Arthur Rackham, *Mother Goose Nursery Rhymes*. London: Chancellor Press.

LITTLE MISS MUFFET

Little Miss Muffet
Sat on a tuffet,
Eating her curds and whey;
There came a big spider,
Who sat down beside her
And frightened Miss Muffet away.

FIGURE 6.7 Raymond Briggs portrays a looming creature, but his Miss Muffet looks more like a nineteenth-century school marm. The fact that Briggs's spider does not have the anatomically correct number of legs need not bother us, since the illustration is in a cartoon style, and exaggerations and distortions are to be expected.

SOURCE: Illustration by Raymond Briggs. Reprinted by permission of Coward, McCann & Geoghegan from *The Mother Goose Treasury* by Raymond Briggs, © 1966 by Raymond Briggs.

FIGURE 6.8 Alice and Martin Provensen depict the real moment of drama in the rhyme—Miss Muffet actually encountering the spider and her spilling of the curds and whey. The old-fashioned flavor of the illustration, reminiscent of eighteenth-century New England folk art, helps to distance the viewer from the action, so Miss Muffet's horror is not necessarily shared by the audience.

SOURCE: From *The Mother Goose Book* by Alice and Martin Provensen. Copyright © 1976 by Alice and Martin Provensen. Reprinted by permission of Random House, Inc.

WORDLESS PICTURE BOOKS

A *wordless picture book* contains only pictures and no text—and there is much controversy over whether these works actually constitute "literature." They surely cannot be evaluated according to the same criteria as a book with a written text. On the other hand, many wordless picture books (Mitsumasa Anno's *Anno's Journey*, Lynd Ward's *The Silver Pony*, and Raymond Briggs's *The Snowman*, for example) do tell stories and include points of view, themes, character studies, settings, tones—all literary elements we recognize in written texts. Also, wordless picture books, because they seem to demand an oral response from the "reader," can help to develop linguistic and storytelling skills, and can play an important role in the development of positive reading habits and attitudes among children. (See Cianciolo 1984 and Groff 1984 for two different viewpoints on the value of wordless picture books.)

TOY BOOKS

The so-called toy books—cardboard books, cloth books, pop-up books—are those that include some gimmick in addition to (or in place of) a story. Toy books have to be judged differently from the typical picture storybooks (in a toy book, for example, we might be concerned with the very practical question of how well the pop-up mechanism operates). Usually these books are intended for the very youngest children, even babes in arms. Cardboard and cloth books are durable, can be easily washed, and will withstand rough treatment. They are excellent books with which to instruct children on the proper handling of books. And even the very young children can be taught respect for books. Pop-up books provide great fun, and they can be extraordinarily intricate. The Victorians developed the pop-up book and other books with movable parts (such as wheels, sliding panels, and so on) into an intricate art form. In this century, Mitsumasa Anno has produced *Anno's Sundial*, recalling the nineteenth-century sophistication in this medium.

ALPHABET BOOKS

Alphabet books are designed to teach children the letters and sounds of the alphabet. They are therefore didactic books (in the good sense of the word). Alphabet books are generally organized around one of three general patterns:

1. A *theme book* is one that provides a thematic or topical focus for the objects depicted, an animal alphabet book or an animal counting book, for example. Jan Garten's *The Alphabet Tale*, using wild animals to represent the letters of the alphabet, or Ezra Jack Keats's *Over in the Meadow*, us-

ing various animals in a meadow as the countable objects, are examples of theme books, as is Margaret Musgrove's *Ashanti to Zulu: African Traditions* (Figure 6.9), illustrated by Leo and Diane Dillon, and using words from African culture to represent the letters of the alphabet.

2. A *potpourri book* disregards uniformity in subject matter—virtually anything goes—but the book is usually given some sense of unity through the style of its illustrations or its overall tone. *Anno's Alphabet* by Mitsumasa Anno uses sophisticated *trompe l'oeil* artwork, in which each picture plays tricks with us. *Dr. Seuss's ABC,* on the other hand, uses decidedly unsophisticated but thoroughly enjoyable cartoons. The potpourri book allows the artist the greatest freedom—but that, at the same time, is its limitation if an artist is a bit short of imagination. (Consequently we end up with a multitude of "A is for Apple" books.)

3. The rarest is the *sequential-story book*, which illustrates the alphabet or numbers through a continuous storyline. Wanda Gág's *ABC Bunny* or Miska Miles' *Apricot ABC* are examples, and they are also books that demonstrate the difficulties of teaching the alphabet through well-plotted stories. Usually, the challenge of learning to recognize letters and their sounds is difficult enough for small children, without further complicating matters for them by incorporating a plot line to follow as well.

CONTENT OF ALPHABET BOOKS

Perhaps the most fundamental feature of the content of an alphabet book is clarity, or the purpose of teaching children the sounds of letters is defeated. *Dr. Seuss's ABC* comically reinforces the phonetic associations with such rollicking lines as "Big A, little a, what begins with A? Aunt Annie's Alligator—A—A—A" or "Y—A yawning, yellow yak and young Yolanda Yorgenson is yelling on his back." Three- or four-year-olds may not initially know what an alligator or a yak is, but the illustrations will quickly teach them. After all, how are they to learn new concepts and facts if their reading never introduces them? However, Jane Walsh Anglund's *A Is for Always* uses such concepts as "C [for] Courteous"; "D [for] Determined"; "E [for] Exuberant"—abstract words that will have little meaning for the preschoolers for whom the book is presumably written.

Additionally, we are usually dealing with phonetic sounds when teaching the alphabet. In other words, the purpose of the alphabet is to help the child associate the shape of a letter with the sound it customarily makes. This is not as simple as it sounds. Vowels, for instance, make several sounds, from long to short to everything in between. So the letter "A" can be accurately represented by an "apple" or by an "ape" or by an "auto." Some alphabet books (such as Gyo Fujikawa's *A to Z Picture Book*) take care of this problem by offering several objects on the same page to represent the letter. *Dr. Seuss's ABC* demonstrates the various sounds in the text: "Oscar's only ostrich oiled an orange owl today."

I The Ikoma (ik·oh'·muh) gather honey to eat and sell. There is a tiny bird in their land which loves honey but cannot get into the beehives. When this bird sees a person, it becomes excited and flies to him. Fluttering and chattering, it leads the way through the bush to a hive. The Ikoma always reward the bird with a gift of honeycomb—otherwise, they say, it may never help them find honey again.

FIGURE 6.9 This illustration by Leo and Diane Dillon is taken from Margaret Musgrove's *Ashanti to Zulu: African Traditions*, a sophisticated alphabet book for older readers that associates the letters of the English alphabet with various African cultural traditions. This is an example of an alphabet book that is not really intended to teach the alphabet, but its exquisite artwork and informative text hold appeal to a wide range of readers.

SOURCE: From *Ashanti to Zulu: African Traditions* by Margaret Musgrove, illustrated by Leo and Diane Dillon. Copyright © 1976 by Penguin Books, Inc. Reprinted by permission of Penguin USA, Inc.

Consonants can also present problems. Two consonants—"C" and "G"—can be hard or soft. So "G" may be represented by a giraffe or a gorilla, for example. And then there is the troublesome "X." Most books rely on "Xylophone" for "X"—but the phonetic sound is closer to "Z." Dr. Seuss perhaps has a sensible compromise, by using such words as "Ax" and "Extra Fox." Occasionally in alphabet books for the very young, we find a letter such as "K" with a word such as "Knife" or "G" with "Gnat." A difference exists between phonics—the sounds of letters—and spelling. We should be careful not to create unnecessary and frustrating confusion for beginners.

It is unlikely that a single alphabet book will accommodate all the quirks of the English language. On the bright side, this simply gives us an excuse to read several different alphabet books to our children, so their language experiences will become richer and more varied and they will begin to understand the extraordinary flexibility of English.

DESIGN OF ALPHABET BOOKS

The design and the illustrations of a good alphabet book are appropriate for the intended age level. This means that the visual representation of the letter is understandable to the young reader. If the letters are drawn too fancifully ($\mathcal{A}$, $\mathcal{B}$, $\mathcal{C}$, for example), children may have a difficult time recognizing them in other contexts. It is helpful if both upper and lower case letters are illustrated because children need to understand that letters appear in different forms. And there are, of course, distinctions between the way some letters are printed in texts and the way we normally write them in handwriting ("*a*" and "a" or "*g*" and "g", for instance). Eventually children will have to learn all forms of the letter, and no single picture book can be expected to provide all this information.

Most alphabet books juxtapose the letters and the pictures that represent them—that is they are on the same page or facing pages, which, of course, makes the most sense. Chris Van Allsburg departs from this tradition in *Z Was Zapped*—a book depicting all manner of violence befalling the letters of the alphabet. Many alphabet books, including Van Allsburg's, demonstrate picture-book art at its most creative. The works of Anno, Bert Kitchen, John Burningham, Helen Oxenbury, and Alice and Martin Provensen (Figure 6.10 on p. 102), to name only a few, clearly indicate that alphabet books have achieved a very high status among illustrators.

COUNTING BOOKS

Like alphabet books, counting books have an educational purpose, and that purpose is best served when the book effectively combines design and content. Counting books are intended to present the concept of numbers and to help children with number recognition. Many of the statements we have made about alphabet books apply equally to counting books.

ERIWINKLE,

Ermine,   Katydid,   Hawk,

FIGURE 6.10   The spirit of the simple, industrious way of the Shakers, an early American religious sect, is depicted in this illustration by Alice and Martin Provensen for *A Peaceable Kingdom: The Shaker Abecedarius*. The lack of depth and the disproportionate scale (notice the woman's tiny feet and hands and the overly large katydid) are all characteristic of the folk art of rural New England, where many Shakers lived.

SOURCE: From *A Peaceable Kingdom: The Shaker Abecedarius* illustrated by Alice and Martin Provensen, afterword by Richard Meran Barsam. Ilustrations copyright © 1978 by Alice and Martin Provensen. Reprinted by permission of the publisher, Viking Penguin, a division of Penguin Books USA Inc.

CONTENT OF COUNTING BOOKS

Sometimes, as with simple alphabet books, counting books contain virtually no text, just the numbers and the objects to be counted. Although as adults we take counting for granted, we must remember that it is an extremely abstract concept. We assign both names (*one, two, three*) and symbols (1, 2, 3 or I, II, III, and so on) to numbers, and these numbers in turn identify quantities—so we are dealing with more than one level of abstraction. Because of this complexity, perhaps the most important aspect of the content of a counting book is that the objects to be counted are clearly identifiable. It usually makes the most sense to count similar objects—how many cows? how many apples?

On the other hand, counting books need not be totally simplistic. Only a writer's or illustrator's imagination need restrict the possibilities. Molly Bang's award-winning *Ten, Nine, Eight* is an example of an effective counting book that counts backwards. Children can benefit from this kind of number play once they have mastered the fundamental elements of enumeration. Pat Hutchins's *The Doorbell Rang* includes the concepts of division and addition. Tom and Muriel Feelings's very beautiful counting book, *Moja Means One: A Swahili Counting Book*, introduces cultural information along with counting concepts. Such books go far beyond teaching numbers and letters, and suggest that we do not necessarily outgrow alphabet and counting books. For the somewhat more sophisticated reader is Russell Hoban's *Ten What? A Mystery Counting Book*. In the same vein is Arthur Geisert's *Pigs from 1 to 10*, which requires the reader to find the hidden numerals along with ten little pigs on the full-page spreads that are replete with inventive detail. Also, there are the familiar counting rhymes, such as "Over in the Meadow," which has inspired counting books by such noted illustrators as Feodor Rojankovsky and Ezra Jack Keats. The beautiful counting rhyme by S. T. Garne, *One White Sail*, takes the reader to the magic of the Caribbean with such evocative lines as "Five blue doors / in the baking hot sun / Six wooden windows / let the cool wind run."

DESIGN OF COUNTING BOOKS

As with alphabet books, the simplest design in a counting book is best for beginners. In counting books, of course, we expect to see the arabic numerals depicted (1, 2, 3), but even some very simple counting books include the spelling of the number words (*one, two, three*). As in alphabet books, juxtaposition is an important feature in the design of counting books. Since most counting books go only up to ten, they are often shorter than other books and make use of full-page spreads. Or, they may depict the number on one page with the illustrations on the facing page. Ample white space can be a sign of a successful counting book, for it is important that the young child be able to point to the appropriate objects as they are being counted. When a large number of items appear on a single page, the artist can avoid a jumbled appearance by clustering the objects into groups.

CONCEPT BOOKS

A great many picture books are designed to teach very young children *cognitive concepts* beyond letters and numbers, including scientific and social ideas. Concept books can be found dealing with almost any subject, such as opposites (Bernice Kohn's *How High Is Up?*), colors (E. L. Konigsburg's *Samuel Todd's Book of Great Colors*), spatial relationships (Shirley Hughes's *All Shapes and Sizes* or Tana Hoban's *Is It Larger, Is It Smaller?*) or sounds (Margaret Wise Brown's *The Indoor Noisy Book*, *The Outdoor Noisy Book*, *The Country Noisy Book*, and others).

Another type of concept book that is becoming increasingly popular is that dealing not with factual material, but with the formation of attitudes and coping with emotions; these books deal with the child's *psychosocial development*. Catherine and Laurence Anholt's *All about You* is an example of a type of book becoming increasingly popular, encouraging children to examine their world, ask questions, and think about their lives. Norma Simon's *All Kinds of Families* was an early concept book that sought to break down narrow stereotypes. Linda Walvoord Girard's *Jeremy's First Haircut* is a book that attempts to put into focus potentially traumatic experiences for young children. Books can also be found on visits to the dentist, the first day of school, and other "firsts" in life. Also by Girard, *Alex, the Kid with AIDS* demonstrates the degree of openness that both writers and publishers have adopted in recent years. Many storybooks, which will be discussed in the next chapter, deal with similar thematic concerns, although they incorporate the message into the fabric of a fictional story.

Sometimes a concept book will consist of a narrative or story; sometimes it will consist simply of a series of vignettes or individual pictures illustrating a concept. Whatever the book's purpose and design, we should look for imaginative illustration, clearly defined concepts, and an attractive and generally uncluttered layout.

EASY-TO-READ BOOKS

By the time most children reach kindergarten (and often before), they are eager to begin reading on their own. As has been suggested, Mother Goose books provide good opportunities for young readers, but a great many storybooks are designed with controlled vocabularies so the very young can practice their reading. Among the earliest and most famous easy-to-read books are those of Dr. Seuss—*The Cat in the Hat, Fox in Sox*, and others. Some easy-to-read books have achieved status as childhood classics—Arnold Lobel's *Frog and Toad Are Friends* and Elsie Minarek's *Little Bear* and their sequels are examples of delightful stories, beautifully written with memorable characters. Animal stories are favorites among easy-to-read stories, and occasionally folktales are rewritten with controlled vocabularies. These books serve as bridges between picture books and more sophisticated novels.

This chapter has provided only the briefest survey of the multitude of specialized books for the very young. No one is too young for a book, and it is never too early to begin nurturing a love of literature.

WORK CITED

Baring-Gould, William S., and Ceil Baring-Gould, eds. *The Annotated Mother Goose*. New York: Potter, 1962.

RECOMMENDED READINGS

RESOURCES FOR BOOKS FOR THE VERY YOUNG

Bodger, Joan. "Mother Goose: Is the Old Girl Relevant?" *Wilson Library Bulletin* December 1969: 402–408.

Bodmer, George R. "The Post-Modern Alphabet: Extending the Limits of the Contemporary Alphabet Book, from Seuss to Gorey." *Children's Literature Association Quarterly* Fall 1989: 115–117.

Bremmer, Moyra. "The World According to Mother Goose." *Parents Magazine* December 1983: 61–67.

Butler, Francelia. "Skip-Rope Rhymes as a Reflection of American Culture." *Sharing Literature with Children*, ed. Francelia Butler. New York: Longman, 1977.

——. *Skipping Around the World: The Ritual Nature of Folk Rhymes*. New York: Ballantine, 1989.

Chaney, Jeanne H. "Alphabet Books: Resources for Learning." *The Reading Teacher* 47.2 (October 1993): 96–104.

Chisolm, Margaret. "Mother Goose—Elucidated." *Elementary School English* December 1972: 1141–1144.

Cianciolo, Patricia. "Use Wordless Picture Books to Teach Reading, Visual Literacy and to Study Literature." *Jump Over the Moon*, eds. Pamela Petrick Barron and Jennifer Q. Burley. New York: Holt, 1984.

Debes, John L., and Clarence M. Williams. "The Power of Visuals." *Instructor* December 1974: 32–39.

Eckenstein, Lina. *Comparative Studies in Nursery Rhymes* (1906). Detroit: Singing Tree, 1968.

Freeman, Evelyn B., and Diane Goetz Person, eds. *Using Nonfiction Trade Books in the Elementary Classrooms: From Ants to Zeppelins*. Urbana, IL: National Council of Teachers of English, 1992.

Green, Percy B. *A History of Nursery Rhymes*. Detroit: Singing Tree, 1968.

Groff, Patrick. "Children's Literature Versus Wordless Books?" *Jump Over the Moon*, eds. Pamela Petrick Barron and Jennifer Q. Burley. New York: Holt, 1984.

Hall, Mary Anne, and Jane Mantango. "Children's Literature: A Source for Concept Enrichment." *Elementary English* April 1975: 487–494.

Hopkins, Lee Bennett. "Pop Go the Books." *CLA Bulletin* 16 (Fall 1990): 10–12.

Kiefer, Barbara. "Critically Speaking: Literature for Children." *The Reading Teacher* January 1985: 458–463.

Lindauer, Shelley L. Knudson. "Wordless Books: An Approach to Visual Literacy." *Children's Literature in Education* 19.3: 136–142.

MacCann, Donnarae, and Olga Richard. *The Child's First Books*. New York: Wilson, 1973.

Nadasan, Ardell. "Mother Goose Sexist?" *Elementary School English* March 1974: 375–378.

Opie, Iona, and Peter Opie. *The Oxford Dictionary of Nursery Rhymes*. Oxford: Oxford University Press (Clarendon Press), 1951.

Pritchard, David. " 'Daddy, Talk!' Thoughts on Reading Early Picture Books." *The Lion and the Unicorn* 7/8 (1983/84): 64–69.

Rollins, Lucy. *Cradle and All: A Cultural and Psychological Study of Nursery Rhymes*. Jackson: University Press of Mississippi, 1992.

Schoenfield, Madalynne. "Alphabet and Counting Books." *Day Care and Early Education* 10 (Winter 1982): 44.

Stewig, John Warren. "Alphabet Books: A Neglected Genre." *Jump Over the Moon*, eds. Pamela Petrick Barron and Jennifer Q. Burley. New York: Holt, 1984.

Thomas, Della. "Count Down on the 1-2-3's." *School Library Journal* 15 March 1971: 95–102.

Thomas, Katherine Lewis. *The Real Personages of Mother Goose*. New York: Lothrop, 1930.

SELECTED BIBLIOGRAPHY OF BOOKS FOR THE VERY YOUNG

The following books are organized according to types described in this chapter. This is only a representative selection of the many wonderful picture books available to young readers and an effort has been made to balance the enduring classics with the brightest newcomers. Unless otherwise indicated, the author is also the illustrator.

MOTHER GOOSE BOOKS

Alderson, Brian, comp. *The Helen Oxenbury Nursery Rhyme Book*. Illus. Helen Oxenbury. New York: Morrow, 1986.

Briggs, Raymond, illus. *The Mother Goose Treasury*. New York: Coward, McCann & Geoghegan, 1966.

de Angeli, Marguerite, illus. *Book of Nursery and Mother Goose Rhymes*. Garden City: NY: Doubleday, 1953.

Glazer, Tom. *The Mother Goose Songbook*. Illus. David McPhail. New York: Doubleday, 1990.

Hader, Berta, and Elmer Hader. *Picture Book of Mother Goose*. 1930. New York: Crown, 1987.

Lang, Andrew, ed. *The Nursery Rhyme Book*. Illus. L. Leslie Brooke. New York, 1972.

Lines, Kathleen, ed. *Lavender's Blue*. Illus. Harold Jones. New York: Watts, 1973.

Lobel, Arnold, illus. *The Random House Book of Mother Goose*. New York: Random House, 1986.

Marcus, Leonard S., and Amy Schwartz, selectors. *Mother Goose's Little Misfortunes*. Illus. Amy Schwartz. New York: Bradbury, 1990.

Opie, Iona. *Tail Feathers from Mother Goose: The Opie Rhyme Book*. Boston: Little, Brown, 1988.

Opie, Iona, and Peter Opie, eds. *I Saw Esau*. Illus. Maurice Sendak. New York: Candlewick, 1992.

———. *The Oxford Nursery Rhyme Book*. New York: Oxford University Press, 1955.

Petersham, Maud, and Miska Petersham, illus. *The Rooster Crows: A Book of American Rhymes and Jingles*. New York: Macmillan, 1945.

Provensen, Alice, and Martin Provensen, illus. *The Mother Goose Book*. New York: Random House, 1976.

Rackham, Arthur, illus. *Mother Goose* (1913). New York: Marathon, 1978.

Reed, Philip, illus. *Mother Goose and Nursery Rhymes*. New York: Atheneum, 1963.

Scarry, Richard, illus. *Richard Scarry's Mother Goose*. New York: Western, 1983.

Smith, Jessie Willcox, illus. *The Jessie Willcox Smith Mother Goose*. New York: Derrydale, 1986.

Sutherland, Zena, comp. *The Orchard Book of Nursery Rhymes*. Illus. Faith Jaques. New York: Orchard, 1990.

Tripp, Wallace, illus. *Granfa' Grig Had a Pig and Other Rhymes Without Reason from Mother Goose*. Boston: Little, Brown, 1976.

Tudor, Tasha, illus. *Mother Goose: Seventy-Seven Verses with Picture by Tasha Tudor*. New York: Oxford University Press, 1944.

Watson, Wendy. *Wendy Watson's Mother Goose*, ed. Dorothy Briley. New York: Lothrop, 1989.

Wildsmith, Brian, illus. *Brian Wildsmith's Mother Goose*. New York: Watts, 1965.

Withers, Carl, collector. *A Rocket in My Pocket: The Rhymes and Chants of Young America*. Illus. Susane Suba. New York: Holt, 1946.

Wright, Blanche Fisher, illus. *The Real Mother Goose*. New York: Rand McNally, 1916.

WORDLESS PICTURE BOOKS

Alexander, Martha. *Bobo's Dream*. New York: Dial, 1970.

Aliki. *Tabby*. New York: HarperCollins, 1995.

Anno, Mitsumasa. *Anno's Britain*. New York: Philomel, 1982.

———. *Anno's Journey*. New York: Philomel, 1978.

———. *Anno's U.S.A.* New York: Philomel, 1983.

Banyai, Istvan. *Zoom*. New York: Viking, 1995.

Briggs, Raymond. *Father Christmas*. New York: Puffin, 1973.

———. *The Snowman*. New York: Random House, 1978.

Carle, Eric. *Do You Want to Be My Friend?* New York: Crowell, 1971.

de Paola, Tomie. *The Hunter and the Animals: A Wordless Picture Book*. New York: Holiday House, 1981.

Geisert, Arthur. *Oink*. Boston: Houghton Mifflin, 1991.

Goodall, John S. *The Adventures of Paddy Pork*. New York: Harcourt, 1968.

———. *An Edwardian Summer*. New York: Atheneum, 1976.

———. *The Story of an English Village*. New York: Atheneum, 1979.

———. *The Story of Main Street*. New York: Macmillan, 1987.

Hutchins, Pat. *Changes, Changes*. New York: Macmillan, 1971.

Mayer, Mercer. *Oops!* New York: Dial, 1977.

McCully, Emily Arnold. *New Baby*. New York: Harper, 1988.

———. *School*. New York: Harper, 1987.

Spier, Peter. *Noah's Ark*. New York: Doubleday, 1977.

———. *Peter Spier's Rain*. New York: Doubleday, 1982.

Tafuri, Nancy. *Have You Seen My Duckling?* New York: Greenwillow, 1984.

———. *Junglewalk*. New York: Greenwillow, 1988.

Vincent, Gabrielle. *Ernest and Celestine's Patchwork Quilt*. New York: Greenwillow, 1985.

Ward, Lynn. *The Silver Pony*. Boston: Houghton Mifflin, 1973.

Weisner, David. *Free Fall*. New York: Lothrop, 1988.

———. *Tuesday*. New York: Clarion, 1991.

Winter, Paula. *Sir Andrew*. New York: Crown, 1980.

Young, Ed. *The Other Bone*. New York: Harper, 1984.

TOY BOOKS

Anno, Mitsumasa. *Anno's Faces*. New York: Philomel, 1989.

Brown, Margaret Wise. *The Goodnight Moon Room: A Pop-Up Book*. Illus. Clement Hurd (a variation on the 1947 classic). New York: Harper & Row, 1984.

Carle, Eric. *The Very Hungry Caterpillar*. Cleveland: World, 1968.

————. *The Very Quiet Cricket*. New York: Putnam, 1990.

Hoban, Tana. *Look! Look! Look!* New York: Greenwillow, 1988.

Kundhardt, Dorothy. *Pat the Bunny*. Racine, WI: Golden, 1962.

Pienkowski, Jan. *Haunted House*. New York: Dutton, 1979.

ALPHABET BOOKS

Anno, Mitsumasa. *Anno's Alphabet*. New York: Harper, 1975.

Bourke, Linda. *Eye Spy: A Mysterious Alphabet*. New York: Chronicle, 1991.

Brown, Marcia. *Peter Piper's Alphabet*. New York: Scribner's, 1959.

Burningham, John. *John Burningham's ABC's*. New York: Crown, 1985.

Duvoisin, Roger. *A for the Ark*. New York: Lee & Shepard, 1952.

Feelings, Muriel. *Jambo Means Hello: A Swahili Alphabet Book*. Illus. Tom Feelings. New York: Dial, 1974.

Fujikawa, Gyo. *A to Z Picture Book*. New York: Grosset & Dunlap, 1974.

Gág, Wanda. *The ABC Bunny*. New York: Coward-McCann, 1933.

Garten, Jan. *The Alphabet Tale*. New York: Random House, 1964.

Grover, Max. *The Accidental Zucchini: An Unexpected Alphabet*. New York: Harcourt, 1993.

Hoban, Tana. *A, B, See*. New York: Greenwillow, 1982.

Isadora, Rachel. *City Seen from A to Z*. New York: Greenwillow, 1983.

Kitamura, Satoshi. *From Acorn to Zoo: And Everything in Between in Alphabetical Order*. New York: Farrar, 1992.

Kitchen, Bert. *Animal Alphabet*. New York: Dial, 1984.

Lionni, Leo. *The Alphabet Tree*. New York: Pantheon, 1968.

MacDonald, Suse. *Alphabatics*. New York: Bradbury, 1986.

Martin, Bill, Jr., and John Archambault. *Chicka Chicka Boom Boom*. Illus. Lois Ehlert. New York: Simon & Schuster, 1989.

Merriam, Eve. *Where Is Everybody? An Animal Alphabet*. New York: Simon & Schuster, 1989.

Miles, Miska. *Apricot ABC*. Illus. Peter Parnall. Boston: Little, Brown, 1969.

Mullins, Patricia. *V for Vanishing: An Alphabet of Endangered Animals*. New York: HarperCollins, 1994.

Munari, Bruno. *Bruno Munari's ABC*. New York: Philomel, 1960.

Musgrove, Margaret. *Ashanti to Zulu: African Traditions*. Illus. Leo and Diane Dillon. New York: Dial, 1976.

Oxenbury, Helen. *Helen Oxenbury's ABC*. New York: Delacorte, 1983.

Poulin, Stephane. *Ah! Belle Cité!/A Beautiful City ABC*. Montreal: Tundra, 1985.

Rankin, Laura. *The Handmade Alphabet*. New York: Dial, 1991.

Seuss, Dr. (pseud. of Theodore Geisel). *Dr. Seuss' ABC*. New York: Random House, 1988.

Tudor, Tasha. *A Is for Annabelle*. New York: Walck, 1954.

Van Allsburg, Chris. *Z Was Zapped*. Boston: Houghton Mifflin, 1987.

Viorst, Judith. *The Alphabet from Z to A (With Much Confusion on the Way)*. New York: Atheneum, 1994.

Wildsmith, Brian. *Brian Wildsmith's ABC*. New York: Watts, 1962.

COUNTING BOOKS

Anno, Mitsumasa. *Anno's Counting Book*. New York: Crowell, 1977.

————. *Anno's Magic Seeds*. New York: Philomel, 1995.

Bang, Molly. *Ten, Nine, Eight*. New York: Greenwillow, 1983.

Burningham, John. *John Burningham's 1,2,3's*. New York: Crown, 1985.

Carle, Eric. *1, 2, 3 to the Zoo*. Cleveland: World, 1968.

————. *The Very Hungry Caterpillar*. Cleveland: World, 1970.

Feelings, Muriel. *Moja Means One: A Swahili Counting Book*. Illus. Tom Feelings. New York: Dutton, 1971.

Garne, S. T. *One White Sail*. San Marcos, CA: Green Tiger, 1992.

Geisert, Arthur. *Pigs from 1 to 10*. Boston: Houghton Mifflin, 1992.

Hoban, Russell. *Ten What? A Mystery Counting Book*. New York: Scribner's, 1974.

Hoban, Tana. *Count and See*. New York: Macmillan, 1972.

————. *26 Letters and 99 Cents*. New York: Greenwillow, 1987.

Hutchins, Pat. *The Doorbell Rang*. New York: Greenwillow, 1986.

Keats, Ezra Jack. *Over in the Meadow*. New York: Scholastic, 1971.

Kitchen, Bert. *Animal Numbers*. New York: Dial, 1987.

Langstaff, John. *Over in the Meadow*. Illus. Feodor Rojankovsky. New York: Harbrace, 1973.

McMillan, Bruce. *Eating Fractions*. New York: Scholastic, 1991.

————. *Here a Chick, There a Chick*. New York: Lothrop, 1983.

Merriam, Eve. *Twelve Ways to Get to Eleven*. Illus. Bernie Karlin. New York: Simon & Schuster, 1993.

O'Keefe, Susan Heyboer. *One Hungry Monster: A Counting Book in Rhyme*. Boston: Little, Brown, 1989.

Oxenbury, Helen. *Numbers of Things*. New York: Watts, 1968.

Reiss, John. *Numbers*. New York: Bradbury, 1971.

Scott, Ann Herbert. *One Good Horse: A Cowpuncher's Counting Book*. Illus. Lynn Sweat. New York: Greenwillow, 1990.

Sis, Peter. *Waving*. New York: Greenwillow, 1989.

Wildsmith, Brian. *Brian Wildsmith's 1,2,3's*. New York: Watts, 1965.

CONCEPT BOOKS—COGNITIVE DEVELOPMENT

Anno, Mitsumasa. *Anno's Sundial*. New York: Philomel, 1987.

Brown, Marcia. *Listen to a Shape*. New York: Watts, 1979.

Charles, N. N. *What Am I? Looking Through Shapes at Apples and Grapes*. New York: Scholastic, 1994.

Clouse, Nancy L. *Puzzle Maps U.S.A.* New York: Holt, 1990.

Cole, Joanna. *Evolution*. New York: Crowell, 1987.

Brown, Margaret Wise. *The Indoor Noisy Book*. Illus. Leonard Weisgard. New York: Harper, 1942.

Burningham, John. *John Burningham's Opposites*. New York: Crown, 1986.

Crews, Donald. *Freight Train*. New York: Greenwillow, 1978.

————. *Truck*. New York: Greenwillow, 1980.

Ehlert, Lois. *Color Farm*. New York: Lippincott, 1990.

————. *Color Zoo*. New York: Lippincott, 1989.

Emberley, Rebecca. *City Sounds*. Boston: Little, Brown, 1989.

————. *Jungle Sounds*. Boston: Little, Brown, 1989.

Fisher, Leonard Everett. *Look Around! A Book about Shapes*. New York: Viking, 1987.

Gillham, Bill, and Susan Hulme. *Let's Look for Opposites*. Photographs by Jan Siegieda. New York: Coward, 1984.

Grifalconi, Ann. *The Village of Round and Square Houses*. Boston: Little, Brown, 1986.

Hoban, Tana. *Circles, Triangles and Squares*. New York: Macmillan, 1974.

————. *Is It Larger, Is It Smaller?* New York: Greenwillow, 1985.

————. *Push-Pull, Empty-Full*. New York: Macmillan, 1972.

————. *Shapes and Things*. New York: Macmillan, 1970.

Hughes, Shirley. *All Shapes and Sizes*. New York: Lothrop, 1986.

Kohn, Bernice. *How High Is Up?* Illus. Jan Pyk. New York: Putnam, 1971.

Konigsburg, E. L. *Samuel Todd's Book of Great Colors*. New York: Atheneum, 1990.

————. *Samuel Todd's Book of Great Inventions*. New York: Atheneum, 1991.

MacKinnon. *What Shape?* New York: Dial, 1992.

Macmillan, Bruce. *Dry or Wet?* New York: Lothrop, 1988.

————. *Super Super Superwords*. New York: Lothrop, 1989.

McNaughton, Colin. *Autumn*. New York: Dial, 1983.

McPhail, David. *Farm Boy's Year*. New York: Atheneum, 1992.

Maestro, Betsy, and Guilio Maestro. *Traffic: A Book of Opposites*. New York: Crown, 1981.

Oakes, Bill, and Suse MacDonald. *Puzzlers*. New York: Dial, 1989.

Pienkowski, Jan. *Shapes*. New York: Simon & Schuster, 1981.

Reiss, John. *Colors*. New York: Macmillan, 1987.

————. *Shapes*. New York: Macmillan, 1987.

Robbins, Ken. *Tools*. New York: Macmillan, 1983.

Rockwell, Anne, and Harlow Rockwell. *Machines*. New York: Macmillan, 1972.

————. *The Supermarket* . New York: Macmillan, 1979.

Ruben, Patricia. *True or False?* New York: Harper, 1978.

Schwartz, David M. *If You Made a Million*. Illus. Steven Kellogg. Photographs by George Ancona. New York: Lothrop, 1989.

Spier, Peter. *Fast-Slow, High-Low: A Book of Opposites*. New York: Doubleday, 1972.

Tafuri, Nancy. *All Year Long*. New York: Penguin, 1984.

Testa, Fulvia. *If You Look Around You*. New York: Dial, 1983.

Walsh, Ellen Stoll. *Mouse Paint*. New York: Harcourt, 1989.

CONCEPT BOOKS—PSYCHOSOCIAL DEVELOPMENT

Aliki. *Feelings*. New York: Greenwillow, 1984.

————. *We Are Best Friends*. New York: Greenwillow, 1982.

Anno, Mitsumasa. *The King's Flower*. Cleveland: World, 1979.

Anholt, Catherine, and Laurence Anholt. *All about You*. New York: Viking, 1992.

Aruego, José, and Ariane Dewey. *We Hide, You Seek*. New York: Greenwillow, 1979.

Brenner, Barbara. *Faces*. Photographs by George Ancona. New York: Dutton, 1970.

Corey, Dorothy. *Tomorrow You Can*. Illus. Lois Axeman. Morton Grove, IL: Whitman, 1977.

Fujikawa, Gyo. *Let's Play!* New York: Grosset, 1975.

Girard, Linda Walvoord. *Alex, the Kid with AIDS*. Morton Grove, IL: A. Whitman,1990.

————. *The Growing Story*. Illus. Phyllis Rowand. New York: Harper, 1947.

————. *Jeremy's First Haircut*. Morton Grove, IL: A. Whitman, 1986.

————. *We Adopted You, Benjamin Koo*. Morton Grove, IL: A. Whitman, 1989.

Maestro, Betsy, and Giulio Maestro. *Where Is My Friend?* New York: Crown, 1976.

Myers, Walter. *Where Does the Day Go?* Illus. Leo Carty. New York: Parents' Magazine, 1969.

Oxenbury, Helen. *Dressing*. New York: Simon & Schuster, 1981.

————. *Shopping Trip*. New York: Dial, 1982.

Rockwell, Harlow. *My Dentist*. New York: Greenwillow, 1975.

————. *My Doctor*. New York: Harper, 1985.

Rogers, Fred. *Moving*. Photographs by Jim Judkis. New York: Putnam, 1987.

Rosen, Michael J. *Home: A Collaboration of Thirty Distinguished Authors and Illustrators of Children's Books to Aid the Homeless*. New York: Harper, 1992.

Simon, Norma. *All Kinds of Families*. Illus. by Joe Lasker. Morton Grove, IL: Whitman, 1976.

EASY-TO-READ BOOKS

Many of the books in the storybook bibliography at the end of Chapter 7 can serve as easy-to-read books as well.

Cole, Joanna, and Stephanie Calmenson, compilers. *Ready . . . Set . . . Read!: The Beginning Reader's Treasury*. Illus. Anne Burgess and Chris Demarest. New York: Doubleday, 1990.

Leeuwen, Jean Van. *Tales of Oliver Pig*. New York: Dial, 1981.

Lobel, Arnold. *Frog and Toad Are Friends*. New York: Harper, 1970.

————. *Frog and Toad Together*. New York: Harper, 1972.

————. *Mouse Soup*. New York: Harper, 1977.

Minarek, Elsie Holmes. *Little Bear*. Illus. Maurice Sendak. New York: Harper, 1957.

————. *Little Bear's Friend*. Illus. Maurice Sendak. New York: Harper, 1960.

Rylant, Cynthia. *Henry and Mudge*. Illus. Sucie Stevenson. New York: Bradbury, 1987.

Seuss, Dr. *The Cat in the Hat*. New York: Random House, 1957.

————. *Fox in Sox*. New York: Random House, 1965.

Chapter 7

~

PICTURE
STORYBOOKS

In this chapter we will consider the picture storybook, which combines the art of storytelling with that of illustration. We have reserved until this chapter a fuller discussion of artistic styles and techniques, although much of what we say of picture-book art applies to the picture books for the very young explored in Chapter 6. We will begin with an overview of types of storybook narratives and then proceed to picture-book illustrations.

STORYTELLING ELEMENTS

Picture-book stories consist of the same narrative elements of storytelling as described in Chapter 4—that is, point of view, character, plot and conflict, theme, style, and tone. Plots tend to be simple and fast-paced—a picture book's brevity will not permit convoluted plot-lines, nor would they be appreciated by the typical picture-book reader. Often picture-book plots rely on repetitive patterns that are particularly suited to the rhythmic nature of the picture-book design. Characterization is likewise simple, and characters tend to be identified by clearly outlined traits—Peter Rabbit is daring and curious with a propensity toward impish rebellion. However, we learn very little about his likes and dislikes, or how he gets along with his sisters or what his ambitions in life are.

Picture-book themes are naturally addressed to younger readers, but that does not mean they must be condescending or sugarcoated. Today few themes are taboo even in picture books; we can find provocative picture books on the Holocaust (Roberto Innocenti and Christophe Gallaz's *Rose Blanche*) and the Hiroshima atomic bomb (Toshi Maruki's *Hiroshima No Pika*) and social violence (Louise Fitzhugh and Sandra Scoppettone's *Bang, Bang, You're Dead*) and homosexuality (Michael Willhoite's *Daddy's Roommate*). If told from the child's point of view, these stories can sensitively raise important issues in an arena where meaningful discussion can take place—the family home. A good picture-book style is typified by carefully chosen words (picture books average only about 2,000 words, so they should be carefully chosen indeed) and they rely on sharp images to help carry their meaning. Many picture books rely heavily on dialogue, which can be great fun to read aloud—an important consideration since most picture books are read aloud or are intended to be. In tone, we most often find humor in picture books—sometimes rollicking slapstick as in Dr. Seuss's work; sometimes the subtler, quieter humor, as in the work of Margaret Wise Brown, Robert McCloskey, or Patricia MacLachlan. Excitement, even suspense, as in *The Tale of Peter Rabbit* or in Maurice Sendak's *Where the Wild Things Are*, is another staple of the picture book. And there are books of a more serious, reflective nature, such as Lucille Clifton's series of books about an inner-city African-American boy, Everett Anderson, who experiences the divorce of his parents, the remarriage of his mother, the birth of a new sibling, and, finally, the death of his father.

Certainly we should have the same high literary standards for picture books as we expect from books for older readers. However, at the same time, we must realize that picture books are only "literature" in part—we cannot consider them without understanding how the pictures and the text complement each other to produce the whole.

TYPES OF PICTURE STORYBOOKS

FOLKTALES, LEGENDS, AND MYTHS

These remain age-old favorites and include the familiar stories that have been passed down, at least in the beginning, by word of mouth. They adhere to the traditional storytelling patterns (often opening with "Once upon a time" and ending with the hero or heroine living "happily ever after"); and they typically take place in some never-never land where magic is commonplace. Innumerable versions of "Cinderella," "Little Red Riding Hood," and "The Three Little Pigs" are available (and they make for interesting comparisons). The oral folktales are also the basis for many *literary folktales*, which are original stories meant to imitate the style of the traditional folktale (James Thurber's *Many Moons* comes to mind). Although some people believe that folktales should not be illustrated because the illustrations deprive children of their own imaginative flights, others point out that a good illustrated folktale can introduce children to things they might not have imagined themselves. Recently we have seen the appearance of lovely books of folktales from many distant cultures, such as Ed Young's Caldecott Award–winning *Lon Po Po: A Red-Riding Hood Story from China*.

MODERN FANTASY STORIES

These include those tales, usually with modern settings, that employ magic as a principal feature. Unlike folktales, modern fantasies can be ascribed to specific authors and therefore do not appear in multiple versions. Maurice Sendak's classic, *Where the Wild Things Are*, fits into this category, as do Chris Van Allsburg's Christmas enchantment, *The Polar Express*, and Crockett Johnson's imaginative tale, *Harold and the Purple Crayon*. As with folktales, modern fantasies build on the child's delight in make-believe worlds, but whereas folktales generally distance the magic through time and place, many modern fantasies bring the magic into contemporary life. In this way, they appeal to the same drive that causes a child to want to believe in Santa Claus or the Tooth Fairy. (And, by the same token, most modern fantasies omit the potentially threatening forces of evil that characterize the folktales—wicked witches and big bad wolves.) Inanimate objects are the protagonists in many modern fantasies; for example, we can find boats (Hardie Gramatky's *Little Toot*), houses (Virginia Burton's *The Little House*), and machines (Virginia Burton's *Mike Mulligan and His Steam Shovel*).

TALKING ANIMAL STORIES

Talking animals are popular with children and can be found in folktales (for example, "The Musicians of Bremen," in several picture-book editions), modern fantasy (William Steig's *Sylvester and the Magic Pebble*), and in a class of books that are essentially realistic in nature—except for the anthropomorphism. Beatrix Potter's *The Tale of Peter Rabbit* and *Benjamin Bunny* or Russell Hoban's many tales about Frances the Badger are examples of this last type. Many talking animal stories avoid magic (outside of the fact that the animal characters can talk and think as humans do) and attempt to focus on everyday issues in realistic contemporary settings. In Arnold Lobel's *Frog and Toad Are Friends*, we witness the pleasant antics of the frog and toad, who wear clothes, go on outings together, and generally do everything that humans do and in the same manner. These stories are realistic in that they eschew any type of fantasy element and deal entirely with human nature—human dilemmas, human emotions and responses, human hopes and dreams (Hunt 169–170). Children have little trouble imagining animals with human traits (in fact, they may have difficulty imagining animals without human traits), and, given the fascination most children have with animals, these stories are great favorites. Nor should we worry that talking animal stories might unduly confuse children. Quite early in life, children learn to distinguish fact from fiction, and the metaphorical use of animals in human roles seems to be an effective tool for conveying life concepts to children. Besides, who would wish to deprive a young reader of the joys and wisdom of an animal story such as Jean de Brunhoff's *The Story of Babar, The Little Elephant* or Bernard Waber's *Lyle, Lyle, Crocodile?*

REALISTIC STORIES

Realistic stories depict reality as we understand it. They may be historical, such as Brinton Turkle's warm tale of colonial New England, *Thy Friend, Obadiah*, or Donald Hall and Barbara Cooney's *The Ox-Cart Man*, set in New Hampshire in the early 1800s. Or they may take on a modern setting, as does Lucille Clifton's *Some of the Days of Everett Anderson*, about a contemporary African-American boy growing up in a big city. Realistic stories can introduce children to other cultures, such as the traditional Chinese in Thomas Handforth's *Mei Lei*. Many contemporary realistic stories deal with social and psychological issues (including death, divorce, and sibling rivalry) and suggest the faith that many writers place in the abilities of young children to face the complexities of the modern world. A pleasant addition has been the bilingual picture book, such as Sandra Cisneros's *Hairs/Pelitos*, illustrated by Terry Ybánez, a warm family portrait told in English and Spanish. The appeal of realistic stories is often in their ability to depict sympathetic characters with whom young readers can identify or emphathize. In other words, children like to read stories about other children very much like themselves.

THE CONVENTIONS
OF PICTURE-BOOK ART

A good picturebook must have not only an engaging story, but appealing art as well. Picture-book art is more sophisticated than many people think. And children are often more discerning critics than adults. It will therefore be helpful if we consider illustration in some detail.

Above all, picture-book art is narrative art; that is, it tells a story. (Even art in alphabet and counting books can be said to be narrative in that it depicts the meaning expressed by the limited text—so on a page illustrating the letter *A* we may see the picture of an apple or, as in *Dr. Seuss's ABC*, of Aunt Annie riding on the alligator, although a true story seldom develops.) As narrative art, picture-book art is, then, a representation of reality as the artist sees it—but this can take in many artistic styles from purely photographic realism to abstractionism. But as with all art, our understanding depends on our familiarity with the conventions of the art—art is, of course, not reality (remember that the word "artificial" is etymologically related to "art"). A *convention* is simply a mutually agreed-upon rule or method of understanding. Graphic art is two-dimensional, but through the artist's use of certain conventions we are able to visualize the third dimension—depth. For instance, making an object smaller and placing it toward the top of the picture can make it seem farther away and thus add depth to an illustration. So when we look at Ludwig Bemelmans's illustration (Figure 7.1) of the twelve little girls leaving for their walk with Miss Clavel, we understand that they are going away from us and not climbing upwards. We have accepted the illusion that objects toward the top of the picture are

FIGURE 7.1 Ludwig Bemelmans's popular picture storybook *Madeline* is a delightful comedy about a spunky little girl in a Parisian convent school. The illustrations are interesting examples of expressionistic art. Notice the angularity of the figures and the exaggerated height of the nun, Miss Clavel, accompanying the twelve little girls who walk, as we are told, in "two straight lines" (surely a commentary on convent school discipline). The trees are more like ideas of trees; there is no attempt at realistic depiction. There is a carefree jocularity in these pictures that aptly characterizes the mood of the story.

SOURCE: From *Madeline* by Ludwig Bemelmans. Copyright © 1939 by Ludwig Bemelmans, renewed © 1966 by Madeline Bemelmans and Barbara Bemelmans Marciano. Reprinted by permission of the publisher, Viking Penguin, a division of Penguin Books USA Inc.

farther away than those at the bottom. In this same illustration, we also accept the conventions Bemelmans uses to depict grass and trees. They do not really look that way, but in the context of this picture we have no trouble identifying them—and, in fact, if they were drawn more realistically they would seem out of place given the cartoonish nature of the human figures. To understand the artist's use of convention better, we will look briefly at the various artistic elements that comprise an illustration, including line, space, shape, color, texture, composition, and perspective.

LINE

Lines are used both to define objects and to suggest emotional responses. We all realize that lines outline figures and therefore give them definition or shape, but lines can also suggest movement, distance, and even feeling. Curves and circles suggest warmth, coziness, and security (perhaps recalling the safety of the womb and its circular shape). Sharp and zigzagging lines suggest excitement and rapid movement. Horizontal lines suggest calm and stability (recalling firm, solid ground), whereas vertical lines suggest height and distance. Margot Zemach's lines in *Duffy and the Devil* (Figure 7.2) are deliberately angled and crooked, capturing the rollicking spirit of the folktale. Bemelmans's very straight lines in the illustration from *Madeline* (Figure 7.1) may have been intended as a commentary on the rigid conduct expected at the convent school.

SPACE

We often do not think of space—literally the empty parts of the page—as an artistic element, but it is, in fact, very powerful. There is an old story about a Japanese artist who, when asked what was the most important part of a painting, replied, "The part that is left out." The use of space is actually what draws our attention to specific forms depicted on the page. If a page contains very little empty space but is instead crowded with images, our attention is divided among the many objects depicted. Also, the lack of open space on a page may contribute to a claustrophobic feeling (see *Jumanji*, Figure 7.3) or confusion or even chaos. However, if a page contains a great deal of space surrounding a single object, that object acquires great importance. Generous use of space in a picture can suggest emptiness, loneliness, isolaton. Space may also create the illusion of distance.

SHAPE

The predominant shapes in an illustration help to elicit emotional reactions. Grouped massive shapes may suggest stability, enclosure or confinement, or perhaps awkwardness (*Jumanji*, Figure 7.3). On the other hand, lighter, delicate shapes may suggest movement, grace, and freedom (*One Morning in Maine*, Figure 7.4). Sometimes illustrations consist chiefly of shapes to the exclusion of lines, as in collage. Rounded shapes may suggest emotional reactions similar to those of the curved and circular lines (*The Tale of Peter Rabbit*, Figure 7.5, and *Millions of Cats*, Figure 7.6),

FIGURE 7.2 Margot Zemach's illustrations for *Duffy and the Devil* (retold by Harve Zemach) capture the lively, comical nature of this Cornish Rumpelstiltskin tale. Notice how movement and chaos are suggested by the ragged lines moving in every direction.

SOURCE: Illustration from *Duffy and the Devil* by Harve and Margot Zemach. Copyright © 1973 by Farrar, Straus and Giroux, Inc. Reprinted by permission of Farrar, Straus and Giroux, Inc.

and squarish, angular shapes may elicit more excitable responses (*Duffy and the Devil*, Figure 7.2).

COLOR

Color is one of the most emotionally evocative artistic elements, although in picture books color is chiefly used in a conventional fashion—skies are blue, grass is green, and so on. But color presents far more possibilities than this, and children themselves often prove to be particularly responsive to the subtleties of color. Donnarae MacCann and Olga Richard tell us of a seven-year-old who used 32 shades of blue in a painting and asked for the names of each separate color.

Colors have the ability to evoke emotional responses. Psychologists tell us that reds and yellows are warm or hot colors and suggest excitement, whereas blues and greens are cool or cold colors and suggest calm or quiet. These reactions may be imbedded in our responses to the natural world—red and yellow suggest warmth and happiness, and they are also the colors of sunlight and fire; blue we find to be soothing and melancholy perhaps because we associate it with calm waters or the broad expanse of the sky. There are also certain conventional responses to color—purple signifying royalty, green envy or illness, blue depression, yellow cowardice, and so on. (These conventions are cultural phenomena: In imperial China, the color yellow was reserved for the emperor, white is a traditional color of mourning in the Orient, and brides often wear red.)

Additionally, colors are used to convey cultural distinctions. When illustrating a Navajo Indian story, *Arrow to the Sun*, Gerald McDermott used the colors of the Southwest—golds, yellows, desert browns, and oranges. In *Anansi the Spider* (Figure 7.7), a traditional folktale of Africa, McDermott turns to the bold, bright reds, greens, and sharply contrasting black reminiscent of the colorful regalia often associated with the folk culture of western Africa.

We should not think that children require brightly colored pictures (just as we should probably not think that brightly colored pictures might unduly excite young children). Some of the most enduringly popular picture books are illustrated in black and white or monochrome (with pictures done in a single hue, such as blue or sepia). Wanda Gág's *Millions of Cats* (Figure 7.6), Munro Leaf and Robert Lawson's *The Story of Ferdinand* (Figure 7.8), Robert McCloskey's *One Morning in Maine* (Figure 7.4) and, more recently, Chris Van Allsburg's *Jumanji* (Figure 7.3) are only a few of these classics. And most of these books would be far less effective if they were done in full color. Artists who choose to illustrate in black and white or monochrome usually compensate for the absence of color by the effective use of line, space, and shape. Color, in fact, can often detract from a text, particularly if the color is garish, overpowering, or inappropriate.

TEXTURE

One of the illusions the artist creates is to give a flat surface (the paper) the characteristics of a three-dimensional surface—the suggestion of fur, wood grain, smooth silk, and so on. We refer to this quality of art as *texture*. An artist who wants to em-

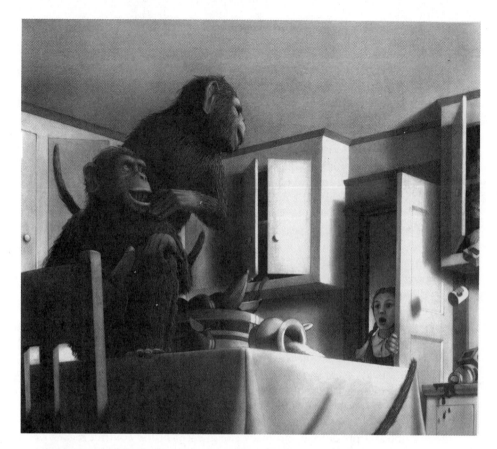

FIGURE 7.3 We, the viewers, are at a child's eye level looking over the table and up at the menacing monkeys (made even more disturbing from this point of view) in this surrealistic pencil drawing from Chris Van Allsburg's *Jumanji*. The figures seem to crowd us, adding an almost claustrophobic feeling, and the whole scene appears to be a moment uncomfortably frozen in time—an appropriate mood for this story of a mysterious board game come to life.

SOURCE: Illustration from *Jumanji* by Chris Van Allsburg. Copyright © 1981 by Chris Van Allsburg. Reprinted by permission of Houghton Mifflin Company.

phasize the realistic quality of a picture may pay great attention to texture (*Jumanji*, Figure 7.3, and *One Morning in Maine*, Figure 7.4). However, less realistic styles may make use of texture to enrich the visual experience and to stimulate the viewer's imagination (*Daddy Is a Monster . . . Sometimes*, Figure 7.9).

COMPOSITION AND PERSPECTIVE

The *composition* of an illustration refers to the arrangement of the details in the picture. Composition is important to the narrative quality of the picture as well as to its emotional impact. The artist must consider where best to place the focal point, from what angle the picture is to be viewed, and what mood is to be conveyed. One

FIGURE 7.4 The stone lithography of Robert McCloskey's illustrations for *One Morning in Maine* helps to provide the textured appearance—the fine grain we see in the pictures is actually created by the stone surface on which the drawing was made. McCloskey's style is a fine example of representational art; he has, in fact, used himself and his daughters as models in this true-to-life tale.

SOURCE: From *One Morning in Maine* by Robert McCloskey. Copyright © 1952, renewed © 1980 by Robert McCloskey. Reprinted by permission of the publisher. Viking Penguin, a division of Penguin Books USA Inc.

important aspect of composition is the point of view or perspective—that is, from what vantage point are we, the viewers, looking at the objects or events depicted? The closer we appear to be to the action, the more engaged we are likely to be (*Jumanji*, Figure 7.3). The farther away we seem to be, the more detached we are (*A Peaceable Kingdom*, Figure 6.10). We may view events from a worm's-eye view or

FIGURE 7.5 This watercolor from Beatrix Potter's *The Tale of Peter Rabbit* exudes warmth and security, appropriate after Peter's harrowing experience in Mr. McGregor's garden. The soft, warm yellows and earthy browns are complemented by gently curved lines and rounded shapes, from the oval mass of Mrs. Rabbit bent before the embracing hearth to the little round tails of each of Peter's sisters. Peter himself, having caught cold from his mischief, is distanced to the right, but nonetheless secure under the rounded folds of his bed blankets.

SOURCE: Beatrix Potter, *The Tale of Peter Rabbit*. London: Warne, 1901.

a small child's perspective or a bird's-eye view, for example. The artist may wish to change points of view from illustration to illustration—perhaps to avoid monotony, but more likely to make us see and think about things in special ways. In fact, Perry Nodelman points out that most picture books give us the "middle shot." We see few closeups and few panoramic views. This is probably because each picture book has only a limited number of "shots"—the typical picture book has approximately 32 pages, and the artist must compromise on the variety of perspectives. Nodelman observes that "picture books are more like the theater in their storytelling conventions than they are like films . . . we are always at the same distance and angle from the action" (231).

DESIGN AND MEANING

Closely related to the composition of the individual illustration is the design of the entire book and how that design contributes to the meaning of both the text and pictures, for it is here that the picture book is truly a unique art form. Among the features important to the design and meaning of picture books are rhythm and movement, tension, and page layout.

RHYTHM AND MOVEMENT

John Warren Stewig defines rhythm as "controlled repetition in art" (76). Good picture-book design creates a sense of rhythm as we move from page to page—a rhythm that is suited to the nature of the narrative. Among the conventions of picture-book design is the simple fact that we read our books, and therefore our pictures, from

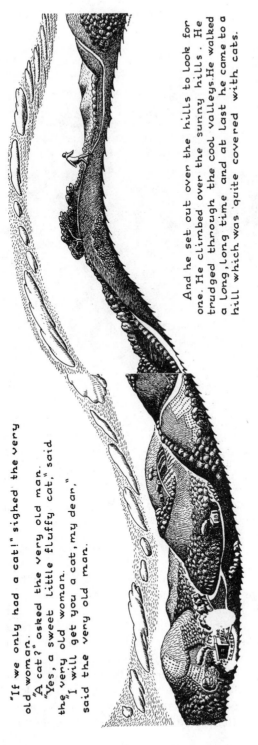

"If we only had a cat!" sighed the very old woman.

"A cat?" asked the very old man.

"Yes, a sweet little fluffy cat," said the very old woman.

"I will get you a cat, my dear," said the very old man.

And he set out over the hills to look for one. He climbed over the sunny hills. He trudged through the cool valleys. He walked a long, long time and at last he came to a hill which was quite covered with cats.

FIGURE 7.6 Wanda Gág's *Millions of Cats* is considered a classic example of the union of picture and text. In this two-page spread, the artist captures the lilting rhythm of the words through an almost rhythmic use of shape and flowing design. The layout also emphasizes the concept of the journey on which the old man has embarked to find a cat. The incorporation of various textures adds both depth and interest to the simple and direct illustrations.

SOURCE: Millions of Cats. Wanda Gág. New York: Coward, McCann, 1928. Renewed © 1956 Robert Janssen.

FIGURE 7.7   Gerald McDermott's illustrations for the African folktale *Anansi the Spider* were inspired by African folk art. The stylized figures are decorated with geometric shapes and colored boldly in primary colors. Despite the abstract quality of the pictures, children have no difficulty in identifying the scene as that of a fish swallowing a spider.

SOURCE: From *Anansi the Spider* by Gerald McDermott. Copyright © 1972 by Gerald McDermott. Reprinted by permission of Henry Holt and Company, Inc.

left to right. Consequently, it is argued that we tend to identify most closely with objects on the left—protagonists typically appear on the left and antagonists on the right. For example, in Figure 7.7, the spider Anansi, the hero, is on the left. But notice that in Figure 7.3, the presumed protagonist, the girl in the doorway, is on the right with the unsettling figures of the monkeys on the left. This reversal of the normal order of things may contribute to the eerie, almost jarring, feeling that this illustration evokes—quite suited to the surrealistic story of an innocent game board mysteriously coming to life. (It is interesting to note that the left-to-right orientation is purely conventional. Israeli picture books, for example, are designed to be read from right to left, since Hebrew texts are written in exactly the reverse of Western texts—right to left, back to front—and, as a result, the movement in the pictures is also from right to left.)

This movement also suggests another anomaly in the picture book—the interrupted rhythm that occurs when we read it. The movement is not continually forward; rather we look at the pictures, then we read, then we look at the pictures again. The pictures create a starting and stopping pattern for which the text must accommodate. This is why many picture-book texts make little sense when read without the pictures. (Of course, we should hasten to point out that typically the pictures often make little sense without the information provided by the text, a problem that the successful wordless picture book must overcome.) Picture books are usually designed so that a natural pause occurs between the turning of pages, or so that some tension is set up that invites us to turn the page (either to be surprised or to have our expectations confirmed).

FIGURE 7.8   This illustration by Robert Lawson for *The Story of Ferdinand* by Munro Leaf is a good example of the correlation of picture and text (without the text we might not understand what is about to happen to the unwary bee). Notice also how the various textures are depicted—the bull's hair, the bee's body, the clover. We should not overlook the comically expressive eye of the bee as it realizes it is about to be sat upon.

SOURCE: From *The Story of Ferdinand.* Munro Leaf. Illustrated by Robert Lawson. New York: Viking, 1936. Renewed © 1964 by Munro Leaf and John W. Boyd.

He didn't look where he was sitting and instead of sitting on the nice cool grass in the shade he sat on a bumble bee.

FIGURE 7.9   A child of expressionism, Les Fauves art includes distinctive strong, black lines separating parts of the picture—much like the lines made by the lead framing in stained-glass windows. Also characteristic of this artistic style is a certain vibrance of line that suggests motion—and emotion—as in this illustration from John Steptoe's *Daddy Is a Monster . . . Sometimes,* a story of parent/child relationships.

SOURCE: Father/Daughter illustration, p. 13, from *Daddy Is a Monster . . . Sometimes* by John Steptoe. (J.B. Lippincott). Copyright © 1980 by John Steptoe. Reprinted by permission of HarperCollins Publishers, with the approval of the estate of John Steptoe.

TENSION

Good picture books also create what Nodelman refers to as "directed tension"—a tension between what the words say and what the illustrations depict, resulting in our heightened interest and excitement. A book without such tension—where, for example, the pictures do no more than mimic the words, or vice versa—soon loses our interest. (For good examples of the tension an artist can create see figures 7.2,

7.3 and 7.7; notice how each picture invites speculation, urges us on to see what will happen next.)

Words in picture books accomplish three things: (1) They explain the "emotional or narrative significance of visible gestures"; (2) They explain the relationship (cause-and-effect or otherwise) of the various parts of a single picture within a series of pictures; and (3) They explain what is important and what is not (Nodelman 215). Take, for example, the two-page spread from Leaf and Lawson's famous picture book, *The Story of Ferdinand* (Figure 7.8). Without the text, the picture would be perplexing. The words explain the bee's wary expression (it is about to be sat upon), what the looming figure at the top of the page is, and, by not mentioning them, the words suggest that the building in the background and the clover in the foreground are relatively unimportant. Without the words, as a matter of fact, we might suppose that the bee is the main character who demands our sympathy, when, in reality, the protagonist is Ferdinand, the gentle bull. Finally, the words and pictures together set up a dramatic tension that makes us want to turn the page to see what happens next.

This illustration is also a good example of how the narrative nature of the picture book often prevents the individual pictures from functioning as artistically complete units in themselves. That is, the picture in Figure 7.8 is only complete when we see it in sequence with the rest of the illustrations in the book, not unlike a cartoon strip, with which picture books have a great deal in common.

PAGE LAYOUT

Another key element of book design is the arrangement of the pictures and the text on the page: Are all the pictures on the same side of the page? Are they all the same size? Do the placement and size vary from page to page? Is there a good reason for the placement and size; that is, do they reinforce some aspect of the whole story? What size and shape are the pages? For example, most picture books are wider than they are high and this makes them especially suited to narrative illustration. The characters (whether human or animal) tend to be taller than they are wide and this gives the artist ample space to depict the setting around the characters, expanding the narrative quality of the pictures (Nodelman 46). Books that are narrower than they are wide typically focus on character at the expense of setting. The size of a book also affects us. We tend to associate very small books and very large books with the youngest readers—small books are easy for little hands to handle and large books are eye-catching. Medium-sized books, on the other hand, tend to be more complex. The point is that these issues must be considered by the writer, artist, and editor before a book is produced; and how these issues are handled will affect our response to a book.

Maurice Sendak's *Where the Wild Things Are* provides a good example of the way in which the layout of pictures and text can enrich each other. As the story opens, Max, a rather naughty boy, is causing all manner of havoc about his house. (It is significant that we do not actually see Max being destructive, for that might cause us to have less empathy for him—he is, instead, depicted just *about* to pound a nail into the wall or just *about* to pounce on the dog.) The initial pictures are small with large white borders around them. Max is then sent to his room for his misbehavior (and significantly, we do not see his mother, for the focus is entirely on Max). Soon the room is transformed into a forest and an ocean tumbles by. Each picture takes up more space on the page than the preceding one, and the border recedes in size until it disappears altogether. Eventually the pictures overlap onto the facing page and finally become full-page spreads. The text, in the meantime, is describing an apparently extraordinary event. Max steps into his private boat and sails to the land where the Wild Things are to become their king and preside over a "wild rumpus" where they all do whatever they like (the dream of Everychild?). During the wild rumpus the pictures completely overtake the page, and both text and borders vanish. In other words, when Max is at his most animal-like, the limits of reality (represented by the picture border) and human speech disappear entirely. Finally, Max longs to be "where someone loved him best of all," and he sails back to the comfort of his bedroom where he finds his supper waiting for him, and, we are told, "it was still hot."

The pictures depicting his return gradually recede in size and the border is restored at the same time that order is restored to Max (or his psyche). At the end of the story, we see Max obviously awakening from a dream and looking very much like a little boy, no longer the wild thing who terrorized the household at the story's beginning. The final words—"and it was still hot"—appear on a page with no illustration whatever, causing us to focus entirely on their meaning without pictorial assistance. We are left to ponder the statement, which signifies unconditional parental love and seems to contradict earlier statements in the book about the passage of time (we are told, for instance, that Max's boat trip took "almost over a year"). The illustrations are far richer than this brief analysis can reveal, but this should suggest the possibilities that exist in the collaboration of words and pictures.

Of course, we do not always find such powerful symbolism in a book's layout. But the best books demonstrate that the size and placement of illustrations is not (or should not be) a random process, but rather a carefully conceived plan that carries out the overall intent of the book. The point is that words and pictures are not separate from each other, and when they work together as they do in a good picture book, the resulting sum is something far greater and more rewarding than the individual parts. Our awareness of some of the intricacies of the workings of the picture book can help us make children better respondents to their reading. Meaningful experiences with picture books contribute significantly to a child's emotional and intellectual development. By learning how the words can enrich the pictures, and how the pictures, in turn, can enrich the words, young readers grow in human awareness, understanding, and sensitivity.

ARTISTIC STYLES

Modern picture-book illustrations come in a rich variety of artistic styles—from photographic realism to impressionism to folk art—and exhibit every imaginable graphic technique—from woodblock prints to oils to collage. Many artists working in children's books today are consummate professionals who have brought a standard of quality to picture-book art unmatched at any time before.

Children are very eclectic in their tastes; that is, they enjoy a wide variety of artistic styles and often seem to enjoy new and unusual techniques. Children have not yet learned artistic prejudice or narrow-mindedness, and are not nearly so set in their ways as are adults. We will do well to remember this and allow children the broadest possible experience with picture-book art. We should also remember that children are often more perceptive about art than adults—children are often more sensitive to color, more astute at picking out minor details, and more responsive to new and unusual artistic styles. Our task as purveyors of art and literature is simply to share with them a generous sampling of all that the world of picture books has to offer. Next we will briefly consider some of the principal artistic styles found in children's picture books.

CARTOON

Cartoon art is one of the most widely used styles in picture-book illustration, probably because it is perfectly suited to the narrative mode. In its simplification of figures and in reducing a drawing to its essentials, cartoon art can show us both emotion and movement. Exaggerated caricatures (as in political cartoons) dwell on these two features. Because of their broad and easily grasped humor, cartoons are particularly appealing to young children. Cartoon art avoids any subtlety; instead it relies on solid lines and absence of shading for its distinctive style. If color is used, it is almost always bold and never exhibits any subtlety of hue. Despite its simplicity, cartoon art can reveal an artist's individual style. Wanda Gág's illustrations for *Millions of Cats* (Figure 7.6) are examples of black and white cartoon art and are characterized by rounded figures and flowing lines. Dr. Seuss's beloved books display his own special brand of cartoon art—and the cartoon style is particularly suited to his rollicking, comical tales. Whereas the animated Walt Disney cartoons can hardly be surpassed, the Disney-inspired books are often disappointing because the cartoon illustrations lack originality—all the characters in all the books resemble each other. (Disney books are largely the products of committees of artists, and consequently any individuality is discouraged.)

REPRESENTATIONALISM

Representational art seeks to present objects realistically, although not necessarily photographically. Nor does representational art necessarily depict realistic subjects. For example, Beatrix Potter (*The Tale of Peter Rabbit*, Figure 7.5) was almost fanatical in her desire to realistically depict the little animal characters in her books; nevertheless she felt compelled to clothe them in human clothes. We still regard her art as representational art, and we see her goal as wishing us to believe that her characters are real. On the other hand, Robert McCloskey's *One Morning in Maine* (Figure 7.4) faithfully depicts an extremely realistic tale—the adventures of an average family on a typical day at their summer vacation home. McCloskey used his own family for his models, and his attention to detail heightens the sense of immediacy and realism. Representational art deals with recognizable shapes, realistic color (if color is used), and proper perspectives and proportions. Representational art allows us to enter into the experience and readily become a part of it, but at the same time, if the artist is good, we are shown a fresh way of looking at the world. Robert Lawson's drawings for *The Story of Ferdinand* (Figure 7.8) illustrate a deft blending of cartoon (note the bee's expression) and representational art—because of their delightful individualism, many artists stubbornly resist being neatly categorized into styles.

EXPRESSIONISM

Expressionism as a school of painting was quite specific and flourished toward the end of the nineteenth century. It was a reaction to the photographic realism of earlier styles (styles made somewhat obsolete by the invention of photography). Since it was no longer necessary to portray objects or people with exacting accuracy, artists sought new ways to express themselves. Painters such as Vincent van Gogh found a new freedom in expressionism, for it allowed them to use color, line, space, and other elements, in a highly individualistic and subjective manner—they could paint what they *felt* rather than simply what they *saw*.

Expressionistic art includes deliberate distortion and exaggeration, accompanying wide-ranging experiments with line, space, color, shape, texture, and composition. Expressionism represents an emotional response to objects and is therefore highly subjective. Notice in Ludwig Bemelmans's *Madeline* (Figure 7.1) how the artist has distorted shapes, included exaggerated lines, and drawn everything with a childlike simplicity. This is the artist's *idea* of a convent of girls going on a walk with their teacher; the illustration is not a faithfully detailed rendering of the event.

IMPRESSIONISM

Impressionism derives from the late nineteenth-century French art movement of the same name, a movement characterized by experimentation with ways of looking at objects. Monet and Cezanne were among the most famous impressionists, but many modern artists have experimented with the style. Impressionistic art uses an interplay of color and light—usually created with splashes, speckles, or dots of paint as opposed to longer brush strokes—to create a dreamlike effect. Many of Maurice Sendak's illustrations for Charlotte Zolotow's *Mr. Rabbit and the Lovely Present* capture this dreamlike quality of impressionism. John Burningham's illustrations for his *Mr. Gumpy's Outing*, Donald Carrick's delicate watercolors for Carol Carrick's *In the Moonlight, Waiting*, and John Schoenherr's Caldecott Medal–winning illustrations for Jane Yolen's *Owl Moon* all evoke the magical, almost dreamlike quality that is characteristic of impressionistic art. Through impressionistic art, we, the audience, are distanced from the action and rarely allowed to fully participate in it. Instead we view it from afar with detachment—and often with wonder. Impressionism evokes a quiet, pensive mood. It is the one artistic style that seems to demand color.

SURREALISM

Surrealism, an artistic style explored most fully by the painter Salvador Dali, represents the artist's *intellectual* response to a subject (as opposed to the *emotional* response of expressionism). In surrealistic art, objects may be depicted quite realistically, but they are subjected to unnatural juxtapositions and bizarre incongruities. Chris Van Allsburg's *Jumanji* (Figure 7.3.) is a prime example of surrealistic art in a picture book. Van Allsburg's illustrations display the disturbing qualities of surrealistic art—almost nightmarish at times—which may make it more appropriate for older readers.

FOLK ART

One of the most commonly used styles of picture-book art is folk art. Folk art is also the most widely varied of art forms and sometimes the most difficult to pinpoint. Folk art is based upon the designs and images peculiar to a specific culture (Native American, Eastern European, Middle Eastern, African, Japanese, and so on). Folk art is derived from an earlier, simpler time and a predominantly agrarian society, which makes the style particularly suited to the illustration of folktales derived from such cultures. There are as many different folk styles as there are folk cultures. Alice and Martin Provensen's *A Peaceable Kingdom: The Shaker Abecedarius* (Figure 6.10) and Margot Zemach's lively depiction of the Cornish folktale *Duffy and the Devil* (Figure 7.2) demonstrate two widely varied versions of folk art. Leo and Diane Dillon's illustrations for Margaret Musgrove's *Ashanti to Zulu: African Traditions* (Figure 6.9) are exquisite art works capturing the flavor of native African culture. Gerald McDermott's illustrations for the West African folktale *Anansi the Spider* carry suggestions of African folk art in their use of color and geometric shapes (Figure 7.7). In spite of the great differences in these illustrations, all attempt to recreate the atmosphere or the pervasive mood of a specific culture.

OTHER ARTISTIC STYLES

Many other styles of art can be found in children's picture books. Some of these are variations of expressionism. In *Brian Wildsmith's 1,2,3*, the artist uses *cubism*, an early offshoot of expressionistic art that relies principally on the juxtaposition of various geometric shapes. Another distinctive style is found in the bold, black lines, richly contrasting colors, and almost shimmering effect of John Steptoes's *Daddy Is a Monster . . . Sometimes* (Figure 7.9). These are all characteristic of another derivative of expressionism termed *Les Fauves* (the "wild beasts" in French). The influence of the Art Deco movement of the 1930s can be seen in some of the illustrations in Rachel Isadora's *Ben's Trumpet*, with their bold, sleek designs and sharp contrast. *Pointillism* sprang from the impressionist movement and is distinguished by pictures composed of carefully positioned colored dots of equal size. Miroslav Sasek's *This Is New York* demonstrates a variation of this style.

Of course, all talented artists create their own highly individualized styles, drawing their inspiration from many varied schools and sources, often, as pointed out above, combining features of more than one style or school to achieve their ends. Some artists, such as Chris Van Allsburg, prefer to specialize in a distinctive style that becomes their signature; whereas others, Marcia Brown, for instance, experiment with a great variety of styles and techniques, adapting each to the specific story being illustrated.

ARTISTIC MEDIA

An artist, in addition to deciding the style of an illustration, must also decide upon the method of producing that illustration: Shall it be drawn with pencil or ink? Shall it be painted in oils or watercolors or tempera? Shall it be cut out on a block of wood or linoleum? Each illustration may represent an artistic style, but the illustration must be accomplished through a specific medium. By *medium* we mean essentially the tools and materials the artist chooses to work with. We can group media generally into the following four broad categories.

PAINTERLY TECHNIQUES

Painterly techniques are those using paint as the primary medium. Paint itself consists of pigment (usually powdered) mixed with some liquid or paste to make it spreadable. Many variations are possible depending upon the medium used to mix with the pigment.

> *Watercolors*, as their name implies, use water as the medium, resulting in transparent, typically soft, delicate pictures, as in Beatrix Potter's *The Tale of Peter Rabbit* (Figure 7.5).
>
> *Tempera* is made by mixing pigments with egg yolk—or some other albuminous substance. Tempera is not so transparent as watercolor and can produce some brilliant hues. It was used by Maurice Sendak in his classic *Where the Wild Things Are*.
>
> *Gouache* is a powdered paint similar to tempera, but mixed with a white base, resulting in a delicate hue. Gouache was the favorite medium of Margot Zemach (*Duffy and the Devil*, Figure 7.2).
>
> *Poster color* is a coarser version of gouache and can be found in Jacob Lawrence's *Harriet and the Promised Land*. The colors tend to be bolder than in gouache.
>
> *Oil paint* typically uses linseed oil as a base and is among the most opaque of media. One of the best examples is found in Paul O. Zelinsky's version of *Rumpelstiltskin*.
>
> *Acrylics* use a plastic base, a product of twentieth-century technology, and they produce very brilliant colors; Barbara Cooney's illustrations for *The Ox-Cart Man* by Donald Hall are an excellent example.
>
> *Pastels* differ from the rest in that they are typically applied in powdered form (often with the fingers). Chris Van Allsburg used pastels in his *The Wreck of the Zephyr*.

Chalk, pencil, and ink drawings, while technically not painting, follow the same general principles as painterly techniques. Chris Van Allsburg used pencil for *Jumanji* (Figure 7.3).

Crayons were used by John Burningham in his fanciful story *Come Away from the Water, Shirley*.

Each of these media produces differing effects, and two or more may be used in combination as well. See Figure 6.9, Leo and Diane Dillon's illustration for *From Ashanti to Zulu*, for an example of art combining watercolors, pastels, and acrylics.

GRAPHIC TECHNIQUES

Graphic techniques refer to those techniques in which the artist prepares blocks or plates that are then inked and imprinted upon paper. As with painterly techniques, there are several varieties.

Woodblocks are the oldest form of reproduceable art. The very first printed book illustrations—dating from the late Middle Ages—were made from blocks of wood on which the artist carved away all the areas that were not to be printed. Today, woodblock illustrations can still be found is such books as Ed Emberley's *Drummer Hoff* (retold by Barbara Emberley), in which stylized woodblock illustrations give an old-fashioned flavor to a folk rhyme.

Linocuts are similar to woodblocks in principle, but the artist uses blocks of linoleum rather than wood. Barbara Cooney's *Dick Whittington and His Cat* is an example.

Scratchboard illustration is a technique in which the artist first paints a deep, black ink over a smooth board (called, appropriately, a "scratchboard") and then, when the ink dries, scratches the design onto the surface with a sharp instrument. Leonard Everett Fisher is a master of this technique, using it in many of his informational books for children (*The Doctors, The Schoolmasters*, and many others).

Stone lithography is a complex process involving the drawing of a design with a grease mixture onto a flat stone, treating the stone with chemicals and oils so that the ungreased areas repel water. Then water and ink are successively applied, the greased areas absorb the ink but repel the water, and when paper is pressed onto the stone, an impression is made from the greased, inked areas. Robert McCloskey's *One Morning in Maine*, Figure 7.4, is an example of stone lithography; if we look closely at the illustration we can detect the grainy surface of the stone imprinted on the paper.

PHOTOGRAPHY

Photography may be considered an artistic style as much as a technique, but it is, nevertheless, an art. And the art of photography is the art of composition—of arranging objects within a frame so that the result is intellectually stimulating. In picture storybooks, we normally expect something more creative than Polaroid snaps.

Photographs are used principally for realistic stories, and they can also be especially effective in informational or concept books. Imaginatively used in black and white or in color, photography can be dramatic, beautiful, and highly expressive. Tana Hoban's *Count and See* and *Look Again* demonstrate the uses of photography in concept books for very young children.

MONTAGE, COLLAGE, AND MORE

Montage (the collection and assembling of a variety of different pictures or designs to create a single picture) and *collage* (similar to montage, but employing materials in addition to pictures—string, cotton, weeds, anything that will work—to create a single picture) have been styles effectively used by Ezra Jack Keats in *The Snowy Day* and its sequels and by Leo Lionni in such works as *Frederick* and *Fish Is Fish*.

There are no limits to an artist's ingenuity, and today's book illustrators are using techniques and media in new and varied ways, many of which were unavailable to their predecessors. Fabric art, such as batik, is becoming popular, such that used by Patricia MacCarthy in Margaret Mahy's *The Horrendous Hullabaloo*. And even computer-generated graphics (in which lies the danger of eliminating the artist's individual touch) have appeared in picture books—J. Otto Seibold's *Mr. Lunch Takes a Plane Ride*, for example.

STYLE AND TECHNIQUE AND THE APPRECIATION OF THE PICTURE BOOK

It is often not easy to discover what medium an artist has used in a picture book, and sometimes the only certain way for us to know is for the publisher to supply that information in the book. And few do so. Surely it may matter little to the child's initial enjoyment of a book whether an artist has used watercolors or pastels or has created impressionistic or East Asian folk illustrations. But the greater the child's knowledge of the way a picture works—even of the way it was made—the deeper the child's perception will be and the richer her understanding of both the picture and the text surrounding it. And, as an additional boon, what a wonderful opportunity picture books provide us for introducing artistic principles, techniques, and styles to young children. What a marvelously painless way to nuture in young readers an acuity of vision that they may develop a sensitivity to the beauty that is possible in the world. And, if we are truly successful, they may grow up with a desire to preserve and add to that beauty.

RECOMMENDED READINGS

Alderson, Brian. *Looking at Picture Books 1973.* New York: Children's Book Council, 1974.
Bader, Barbara. *American Picturebooks from Noah's Ark to the Beast Within.* New York: Macmillan, 1976.

Barrett, Terry, and Kenneth Marantz. "Photographs as Illustrations." *The New Advocate* 17 (Fall 1989): 103–153.

Benedict, Susan, and Leonore Carlisle, eds. *Beyond Words: Picture Books for Older Readers and Writers*. Portsmouth, NH: Heinemann, 1992.

Cianciolo, Patricia. *Picture Books for Children*, 3rd ed. Chicago: American Library Association, 1990.

Cummins, Julie, ed. *Children's Book Illustration and Design*. Glen Cove, NY: PBC International, 1992.

Dooley, Patricia. "The Window in the Book: Conventions in the Illustrations of Children's Books." *Wilson Library Bulletin* October 1980: 108–112.

Freeman, La Verne, and Ruth Sunderlin Freeman. *The Child and His Picture Book*. New York: Century House, 1967.

Gainer, Ruth Straus. "Beyond Illustration: Information about Art in Children's Picture Books." *Art Education* March 1982: 16–19.

Gombrich, E. H. *The Image and the Eye: Further Studies in the Psychology of Pictorial Representation*. Ithaca, NY: Cornell University Press, 1982.

Gottlieb, Gerald. *Early Children's Books and Their Illustrations*. Boston: Godine, 1975.

Hubbard, R. *Authors of Pictures, Draughtsmen of Words*. Portsmouth, NH: Heinemann, 1989.

Hunt, Peter. *An Introduction to Children's Literature*. Oxford: Oxford University Press, 1994.

Hurlimann, Bettina. *Picture-Book World*. Cleveland: World, 1969.

Kiefer, Barbara Z. *The Potential of Picturebooks: From Visual Literacy to Aesthetic Understanding*. Columbus, OH: Merrill; Englewood Cliffs, NJ: Prentice-Hall, 1995.

Kingman, Lee, ed. *The Illustrator's Notebook*. Boston: Horn Book, 1978.

Kingman, Lee, Joanna Foster, and Ruth Giles Lontoft, comps. *Illustrators of Children's Books, 1957–1966*. Boston: Horn Book, 1968. (Also, *Illustrators of Children's Books, 1744–1945* and *Illustrators of Children's Books, 1946–1956*.)

Kingman, Lee, Grace Hogarth, and Harriet Quimby. *Illustrators of Children's Books, 1967–1976*. Boston: Horn Book, 1978.

Lacy, L. E. *Art and Design in Children's Books: An Analysis of Caldecott Award Winning Illustrations*. Chicago: American Library Association, 1986.

Lanier, V. *The Visual Arts and the Elementary Child*. New York: Teachers College Press, 1985.

MacCann, Donnarae, and Olga Richard. *The Child's First Books: A Critical Study of Pictures and Texts*. New York: H. W. Wilson, 1973.

Matthias, Margaret, and Graciela Italiano. "Louder Than a Thousand Words." In *Signposts of Criticism of Children's Literature*, comp. Robert Bator, Chicago: American Library Association, 1983.

Nodelman, Perry. *Words About Pictures: The Narrative Art of Children's Picture Books*. Athens, GA: University of Georgia Press, 1988.

Pitz, Henry C. *Illustrating Children's Books: History, Technique, Production*. New York: Watson-Guptill, 1963.

Roxburgh, Stephen. "A Picture Equals How Many Words? Narrative Theory and Picture Books for Children." The Lion and the Unicorn 7/8 (1983/84): 20–33.

Schwarcz, Joseph H. *Ways of the Illustrator: Visual Communication in Children's Literature*. Chicago: American Library Association, 1982.

Shulevitz, Uri. *Writing with Pictures: How to Write and Illustrate Children's Books*. New York: Watson-Guptill, 1985.

Stewig, John Warren. *Looking at Picture Books*. Fort Atkinson, WI: Highsmith Press, 1995.

SELECTED BIBLIOGRAPHY
OF PICTURE STORYBOOKS

FOLKTALES

Aardema, Verna. *Bringing the Rain to Kapiti Plain*. Illus. Beatriz Vidal. New York: Dial, 1981.

———. *Subgugugu, the Glutton: A Bantu Tale from Rwanda*. Illus. Nancy Clouse. Grand Rapids, MI: William B. Eerdmans, 1993.

———. *Why Mosquitoes Buzz in People's Ears*. Illus. Leo and Diane Dillon. New York: Dial, 1975.

Andersen, Hans Christian. *The Nightingale*. Tr. Eva LeGallienne. Illus. Nancy Ekholm Burkert. New York: Harper, 1965.

Bishop, Claire Huchet. *The Five Chinese Brothers*. Illus. Kurt Wiese. New York: Coward, 1938.

Brown, Marcia. *Cinderella*. New York: Scribner's, 1954.

———. *Dick Whittington and His Cat*. New York: Scribner's, 1950.

———. *Once a Mouse*. New York: Scribner's, 1961.

Cendrars, Blaise. *Shadows*. Illus. Marcia Brown. New York: Scribner's 1982.

Climo, Shirley. *The Egyptian Cinderella*. Illus. Ruth Heller. New York: Crowell, 1989.

Cooney, Barbara. *Chanticleer and the Fox*. New York: Crowell, 1958.

De Paola, Tomi. *Strega Nona*. New York: Prentice-Hall, 1975.

Domanska, Janina. *Little Red Hen*. New York: Macmillan, 1973.

Ehlert, Lois. *Mole's Hill: A Woodland Tale*. New York: Harcourt, 1994.

Emberley, Barbara. *Drummer Hoff*. Illus. Ed Emberley. New York: Prentice-Hall, 1967.

Geisert, Arthur. *After the Flood*. Boston: Houghton Mifflin, 1994.

Hodges, Margaret. *Saint George and the Dragon*. Illus. Trina Schart Hyman. Boston: Little, Brown, 1984.

———. *The Wave*. Illus. Blair Lent. Boston: Houghton Mifflin, 1964.

Hogrogian, Nonny. *One Fine Day*. New York: Macmillan, 1971.

Jarrell, Randall, reteller. *Snow White and the Seven Dwarfs*. Illus. Nancy Ekholm Burkert. New York: Farrar, Straus & Giroux, 1972.

Johnston, Tony. *The Cowboy and the Black-eyed Pea*. Illus. Warren Ludwig. New York: Putnam, 1992.

Lester, Julius. *John Henry*. Illus. Jerry Pinkney. New York: Dial, 1994.

Louie, Ai-Ling. *Yeh-Shen: A Cinderella Story from China*. Illus. Ed Young. New York: Philomel, 1982.

McDermott, Gerald. *Anansi the Spider*. New York: Holt, 1972.

———. *Arrow to the Sun*. New York: Viking, 1974.

———. *Zomo the Rabbit*. New York, Harcourt, 1992.

Mosel, Arlene. *The Funny Little Woman*. Illus. Blair Lent. New York: Dutton, 1972.

———. *Tikki Tikki Tembo*. Illus. Blair Lent. New York: Holt, 1968.

Ness, Evaline. *Tom Tit Tot*. New York: Scribner's, 1965.

Nic Leodhas, Sorche (pseud. of LeClaire G. Alger). *Always Room for One More*. Illus. Nonny Hogrogian. New York: Holt, 1965.

Ransome, Arthur. *The Fool of the World and the Flying Ship*. Illus. Uri Shulevitz. New York: Farrar, Straus & Giroux, 1968.

Robbins, Ruth. *Baboushka and the Three Kings*. Illus. Nicolas Sidjakov. Boston: Houghton Mifflin, 1960.

Sawyer, Ruth. *Journey Cake, Ho!* Illus. Robert McCloskey. New York: Viking, 1953.

Scieszka, John. *The Stinky Cheese Man and Other Fairly Stupid Tales*. Illus. Lane Smith. New York: Viking, 1992.

———. *The True Story of the Three Little Pigs*. Illus. Lane Smith. New York: Viking, 1989.

Singer, Isaac Bashevis. *The Fearsome Inn*. Illus. Nonny Hogrogian. New York: Macmillan, 1984.

Slobodkina, Esphyr. *Caps for Sale*. Reading, MA: Addison-Wesley, 1940.

Steptoe, John. *Mufaro's Beautiful Daughters: An African Tale*. New York: Lothrop, 1987.

Young, Ed. *Lon Po Po: A Red Riding Hood Story from China*. New York: Philomel, 1989.

Zemach, Harve, reteller. *Duffy and the Devil*. Illus. Margot Zemach. New York: Farrar, Straus & Giroux, 1973.

Zemach, Margot, reteller. *The Little Red Hen*. New York: Farrar, Straus & Giroux, 1983.

———. *The Three Little Pigs*. New York: Farrar, Straux & Giroux, 1988.

MODERN FANTASY STORIES

Aiken, Joan. *The Moon's Revenge*. Illus. Alan Lee. New York: Knopf, 1987.

Babbitt, Natalie. *Bub: Or The Very Best Thing*. New York: HarperCollins, 1994.

Birney, Betty G. *Tyrannosaurus Rex*, illus. John O' Brien. Boston: Houghton Mifflin, 1994.

Blos, Joan. *Lottie's Circus*, illus. Irene Trivas. New York: Morrow, 1989.

Brown, Margaret Wise. *The Little Island*, illus. Leonard Weisgard. New York: Doubleday, 1946.

———. *The Steamroller*, illus. Evaline Ness. New York: Walker, 1974.

Burton, Virginia L. *The Little House*. Boston: Houghton Mifflin, 1942.

———. *Mike Mulligan and His Steam Shovel*. Boston: Houghton Mifflin, 1939.

Burningham, John. *Come Away from the Water, Shirley*. New York: Harper, 1977.

———. *Mr. Gumpy's Motorcar*. New York: Crowell, 1976.

———. *Mr. Gumpy's Outing*. New York: Holt, 1971.

Conrad, Pam. *Call Me Ahnighito*. New York: HarperCollins, 1995.

———. *The Tub People*, illus. Richard Egielski. New York: Harper, 1989.

Daugherty, James. *Andy and the Lion*. New York: Viking, 1938.

De Regniers, Beatrice Schenk. *May I Bring a Friend?*, illus. Beni Montressor. New York: Atheneum, 1964.

Ehrlich, Amy. *Parents in the Pigpen, Pigs in the Tub*, illus. Steven Kellogg. New York: Dial, 1993.

Freeman, Don. *Corduroy*. New York: Viking, 1968.

———. *Will's Quill*. New York: Penguin, 1977.

Gág, Wanda. *Millions of Cats*. New York: Coward, McCann, 1928.

Gramatky, Hardie. *Hercules*. New York: Putnam, 1960.

———. *Little Toot*. New York: Putnam, 1978.

Hale, Lucretia. *The Lady Who Put Salt in Her Coffee*, illus. and adapted by Amy Schwartz. New York: Harcourt, 1989.

Johnson, Crockett. *Harold and the Purple Crayon*. New York: Harper, 1981.

———. *Harold's Circus*. New York: Scholastic, 1959.

Leaf, Munro. *The Story of Ferdinand*. Illus. Robert Lawson. New York: Viking, 1936.

Mahy, Margaret. *The Horrendous Hullabaloo*. Illus. Patricia MacCarthy. New York: Viking, 1992.

Rey, A. H. *Curious George*. Boston: Houghton Mifflin, 1973.

Sendak, Maurice. *In the Night Kitchen*. New York: Harper, 1970.

———. *Outside Over There*. New York: Harper, 1981.

———. *Where the Wild Things Are*. New York: Harper, 1963.

Seuss, Dr. (pseud. of Theodore Geisel). *And to Think That I Saw It on Mulberry Street*. New York: Vanguard, 1973.

Sis, Peter. *A Small Tall Tale from the Far Far North*. New York: Knopf, 1993.

Swift, Hildegarde. *The Little Red Lighthouse and the Great Gray Bridge*. Illus. Lynd Ward. New York: Harcourt, 1974.

Thomassie, Tynia. *Feliciana Feydra LeRoux: A Cajun Tall Tale*. Illus. Cat Bowman Smith. Boston: Little, Brown, 1995.

Thurber, James. *Many Moons*. Illus. Marc Simont. New York: Harcourt, 1990.

Titus, Eve. *Anatole in Italy*. Illus. Paul Galdone. New York: McGraw-Hill, 1973.

Ungerer, Tonie. *The Beast of Monsieur Racine*. New York: Farrar, Straus & Giroux, 1971.

Van Allsburg, Chris. *The Garden of Abdul Gasazi*. Boston: Houghton Mifflin, 1979.

——. *Jumanji*. Boston: Houghton Mifflin, 1981.

——. *The Wreck of the Zephyr*. Boston: Houghton Mifflin, 1983.

Willard, Nancy. *The Nightgown of the Sullen Moon*. Illus. David McPhail. New York: Harcourt, 1983.

——. *The Sorcerer's Apprentice*. Illus. Leo and Diane Dillon. New York: Scholastic, 1993.

——. *A Visit to William Blake's Inn*. Illus. Alice and Martin Provensen. New York: Harcourt, 1981.

Willis, Val. *The Secret in the Matchbox*. Illus. John Shelley. New York: Farrar, Straus & Giroux, 1988.

Wood, Audrey. *King Bidgood's in the Bathtub*. Illus. Don Wood. New York: Harcourt, 1985.

Zemach, Margot. *Jake and Honeybunch Go to Heaven*. New York: Farrar, Straus & Giroux, 1982.

Zolotow, Charlotte. *Mr. Rabbit and the Lovely Present*. Illus. Maurice Sendak. New York: Harper, 1962.

TALKING ANIMAL STORIES

Akass, Susan. *Number Nine Duckling*. Illus. Alex Ayliffe. Honesdale, PA: Boyds Mills, 1993.

Allen, Jeffrey. *Mary Alice, Operator Number 9*. Illus. James Marshall. Boston: Little, Brown, 1975.

Brooke, L. Leslie. *Johnny Crow's Garden* (1903). London: Warne, 1978.

——. *Johnny Crow's Party* (1907). London: Warne, 1966.

Brown, Margaret Wise. *Goodnight Moon*. Illus. Clement Hurd. New York: Harper, 1947.

——. *The Runaway Bunny*. Illus. Clement Hurd. New York: Harper, 1962.

Dana, Doris. *The Elephant and His Secret*. Illus. Antonio Frasconi. New York: Knopf, 1989.

de Brunhoff, Jean. *The Story of Babar, the Little Elephant* (1933). New York: Knopf, 1989. (This was the first of a series.)

Duvoisin, Roger. *Petunia*. New York: Knopf, 1950.

Fatio, Louise. *The Happy Lion*. Illus. Roger Duvoisin (1954). New York: Scholastic, 1986.

Ford, Miela. *Little Elephant*. Illus. Tana Hoban. New York: Greenwillow, 1994.

Gerstein, Mordicai. *Arnold of the Ducks*. New York: Harper, 1983.

Henkes, Kevin. *Chrysanthemum*. New York: Greenwillow, 1991.

——. *Owen*. New York: Greenwillow, 1993.

Hutchins Pat. *Good-Night Owl*. New York: Macmillan, 1972.

Kellogg, Steven. *The Island of the Skog*. New York: Dial, 1973.

Kraus, Robert. *Leo the Late Bloomer*. Illus. Jose and Ariane Aruego. New York: Simon & Schuster, 1987.

Kuskin, Karla. *The Bear Who Saw the Spring*. New York: Harper, 1961.

Langstaff, John M. *A Frog Went A-Courtin'*. Illus. Feodor Rojankovsky. New York: Scholastic, 1985.

Lionni, Leo. *Alexander and the Wind-Up Mouse*. New York: Pantheon, 1969.

———. *Frederick*. New York: Pantheon, 1967.

———. *Fish Is Fish*. New York: Knopf, 1987.

Meddaugh, Susan. *Martha Speaks*. Boston: Houghton Mifflin, 1992.

Pearce, Philippa. *Emily's Own Elephant*. Illus. John Lawrence. New York: Greenwillow, 1988.

Peet, Bill. *Encore for Eleanor*. Boston: Houghton Mifflin, 1985.

Piatti, Celestino. *The Happy Owls*. New York: Atheneum, 1964.

Potter, Beatrix. *The Tale of Peter Rabbit*. London: Warne, 1901.

Rayner, Mary. *Garth Pig Steals the Show*. New York: Dutton, 1993.

Shannon, Margaret. *Elvira*. Boston: Houghton Mifflin, 1993.

Soto, Gary. *Chato's Kitchen*. Illus. Susan Guevara. New York: Putnam, 1995.

Steig, William. *Sylvester and the Magic Pebble*. New York: Windmill, 1969.

Waber, Bernard. *The House on East 88th Street*. Boston: Houghton Mifflin, 1975.

———. *Lyle, Lyle, Crocodile*. Boston: Houghton Mifflin, 1987.

Walsh, Vivian. *Mr. Lunch Takes a Plane Ride*. Illus. J. Otto Seibold. New York: Viking, 1993.

Wells, Rosemary. *Morris's Disappearing Bag*. New York: Dial, 1978.

———. *Noisy Nora*. New York: Dial, 1980.

REALISTIC STORIES

Ackerman, Karen. *Song and Dance Man*. New York: Knopf, 1988.

Adoff, Arnold. *Black Is Brown Is Tan*. Illus. Emily McCully. New York: Harper, 1973.

Alexander, Lloyd. *The Fortune-Tellers*. Illus. Trina Schart Hyman. New York: Dutton, 1992.

Alexander, Martha. *Nobody Asked Me If I Wanted a Baby Sister*. New York: Dial,1971.

Allard, Harry, and James Marshall. *Miss Nelson Is Missing*. Illus. James Marshall. Boston: Houghton Mifflin, 1977.

Ardizzone, Edward. *Little Tim and the Brave Sea Captain* (1936). New York: Penguin, 1983.

Asch, Frank. *Sand Cake*. New York: Crown, 1987.

Bang, Molly. *The Grey Lady and the Strawberry Snatcher*. New York: Four Winds, 1980.

———. *The Paper Crane*. New York: Greenwillow, 1985.

Bates, Artie Ann. *Ragsale*. Boston: Houghton Mifflin, 1995.

Bedard, Michael. *Emily*. Illus. Barbara Cooney. New York: Doubleday, 1992.

Bemelmans, Ludwig. *Madeline*. New York: Viking, 1937.

———. *Madeline's Rescue*. New York: Penguin, 1953.

Beskow, Elsa. *Pelle's New Suit*. New York: Harper, 1929.

Brown, Margaret Wise. *The Dead Bird*. Reading, MA: Addison-Wesley, 1958.

Bunting, Eve. *Fly Away Home*. Illus. Ronald Himler. New York: Clarion, 1991.

———. *Smoky Night*. Illus. David Diaz. New York: Harcourt, 1994.

Carrick, Carol. *In the Moonlight, Waiting*. Illus. Donald Carrick. New York: Clarion, 1990.

Cisneros, Sandra. *Hairs/Pelitos*. Illus. Terry Ybánez. New York: Knopf, 1994.

Clifton, Lucille. *Some of the Days of Everett Anderson*. Illus. Evaline Ness. New York: Holt, 1970.

Cooney, Barbara. *Island Boy*. New York: Viking, 1988.

———. *Miss Rumphius*. New York: Viking, 1982.

Crews, Donald. *Sail Away*. New York: Greenwillow, 1995.

de Angeli, Marguerite. *Thee Hannah!* New York: Doubleday, 1940.

de Paola, Tomie. *Nana Upstairs, Nana Downstairs*. New York: Penguin, 1978.

Dorros, Arthur. *Abuela*. New York: Dutton, 1991.

Dunrea, Olivier. *The Painter Who Loved Chickens*. New York: Farrar, Straus & Giroux, 1995.

Ets, Marie Hall. *Play with Me*. New York: Penguin, 1955.

Fitzhugh, Louise, and Sandra Scoppettone. *Bang, Bang, You're Dead*. New York: Harper, 1969.

Flack, Marjorie. *The Story about Ping*. Illus. Kurt Weise. New York: Penguin, 1933.

Fleischman, Sid. *The Scarebird*. Illus. Peter Sis. New York: Greenwillow, 1988.

Fox, Mem. *Night Noises*. Illus. Terry Denton. New York: Harcourt, 1989.

Goble, Paul. *The Girl Who Loved Wild Horses*. New York: Bradbury, 1978.

Greenfield, Eloise. *She Come Bringing Me That Little Baby Girl*. Illus. John Steptoe. Philadelphia: Lippincott, 1974.

Hader, Berta, and Elmer Hader. *The Big Snow*. New York: Macmillan, 1948.

Hall, Donald. *The Farm Summer 1942*. Illus. Barry Moser. New York: Dial, 1994.

———. *The Ox-Cart Man*, illus. Barbara Cooney. New York: Penguin, 1983.

Handforth, Thomas. *Mei Lei*. New York: Doubleday, 1938.

Hawkins, Colin. *Take Away Monsters*. New York: Putnam, 1984.

Hellen, Nancy. *The Bus Stop*. New York: Watts, 1988.

Hoban, Julia. *Amy Loves the Rain*. Illus. by Lillian Hoban. New York: Harper, 1989.

Hoestlandt, Jo. *Star of Fear, Star of Hope*. Illus. Johanna Kang. New York: Walker, 1995.

Hoffman, Mary. *Amazing Grace*. Illus. Caroline Binch. New York: Dial, 1991.

Hol, Colby. *A Visit to the Farm*. New York: North-South, 1989.

Innocenti, Roberto, and Christophe Gallaz. *Rose Blanche*. New York: Creative Education, 1985.

Keats, Ezra Jack. *Peter's Chair*. New York: Harper, 1967.

———. *The Snowy Day*. New York: Viking, 1962.

Keeping, Charles. *Joseph's Yard*. New York: Watts, 1969.

Kraus, Ruth. *The Backward Day*. Illus. Marc Simont. New York: Harper, 1950.

Locker, Thomas. *Where the River Begins*. New York: Dial, 1984.

MacLachlan, Patricia. *All the Place to Love*. Illus. Mike Wimmer. New York: HarperCollins, 1994.

———. *What You Know First*. Illus. Barry Moser. New York: HarperCollins, 1995.

Mahy, Margaret. *The Rattlebang Picnic*. New York: Dial, 1994.

Martin, Jacqueline Briggs. *Washing the Willow Tree Loon*. Illus. Nancy Carpenter. New York: Simon, 1995.

Maruki, Toshi. *Hiroshima No Pika*. Boston: Lothrop, Lee, and Shepard, 1982.

McCloskey, Robert. *Blueberries for Sal*. New York: Viking, 1948.

———. *Make Way for Ducklings*. New York: Viking, 1941.

———. *Time of Wonder*. New York: Viking, 1957.

McCully, Emily Arnold. *Mirette on the High Wire*. New York: Putnam, 1992.

MacDonald, Golden (pseud. of Margaret Wise Brown). *The Little Island*. Illus. Leonard Wiesgard. New York: Doubleday, 1946.

Milhous, Katherine. *The Egg Tree*. New York: Macmillan, 1971.

Mitchell, Margaree King. *Uncle Jed's Barbershop*. Illus. James Ransom. New York: Simon & Schuster, 1993.

Ness, Evaline. *Sam, Bangs & Moonshine*. New York: Holt, 1966.

Patron, Susan. *Dark Cloud Strong Breeze*. Illus. Peter Catalanotto. New York: Watts, 1994.

Pinkney, Brian. *JoJo's Flying Side Kick*. New York: Simon, 1995.

Pinkney, Gloria Jean. *The Sunday Outing*. Illus. Jerry Pinkney. New York: Dial, 1994.

Politi, Leo. *Song of the Swallows*. New York: Macmillan, 1986.

Provensen, Alice, and Martin Provensen. *The Glorious Flight: Across the Channel with Louis Bleriot*. New York: Viking, 1983.

Raskin, Ellen. *Nothing Ever Happens on My Block*. New York: Macmillan, 1966.

Rylant, Cynthia. *The Relatives Came*. Illus. Stephen Gammell. New York: Bradbury, 1985.

———. *When I Was Young in the Mountains*. Illus. Diane Goode. New York: Dutton, 1982.

Say, Allen. *Grandfather's Journey*. Boston: Houghton Mifflin, 1993.

Sheppard, Jeff. *Splash, Splash*. New York: Macmillan, 1994.

Shulevitz, Uri. *Rain, Rain, Rivers*. New York: Farrar, Straus & Giroux, 1969.

Simon, Norma. *The Saddest Time*. Illus. Jacqueline Rogers. Morton Grove, IL: A. Whitman, 1989.

Sis, Peter. *Komodo!* New York: Greenwillow, 1993.

Smith, Janice Lee. *The Baby Blues*. Illus. Dick Gackenbach. New York: HarperCollins, 1994.

Steptoe, John. *My Daddy Is a Monster . . . Sometimes*. New York: Viking, 1980.

Stewart, Sarah. *The Library*. Illus. David Small. New York: Farrar, Straus & Giroux, 1995.

Stoeke, Janet Morgan. *A Hat for Minerva Louise*. New York: Dutton, 1994.

Tejima, Keizaburo. *Fox's Dream*. New York: Philomel, 1987.

———. *Owl Lake*. New York: Philomel, 1987.

Tresselt, Alvin. *Hide and Seek Fog*. Illus. Roger Duvoisin. New York: Lothrop, 1965.

———. *White Snow, Bright Snow*. Illus. Roger Duvoisin. New York: Lothrop, 1947.

Turkle, Brinton. *Thy Friend, Obadiah*. New York: Viking, 1967.

Udry, Janice M. *The Moon Jumpers*. Illus. Maurice Sendak. New York: Harper, 1959.

———. *A Tree Is Nice*. Illus. Marc Simont. New York: Harper, 1956.

Viorst, Judith. *Alexander and the Terrible, Horrible, No Good, Very Bad Day*. Illus. by Ray Cruz. New York: Atheneum, 1972.

———. *The Tenth Good Thing About Barney*. Illus by Erik Blegvad. New York: Atheneum, 1971.

Waber, Bernard. *Do You See a Mouse?* Boston: Houghton Mifflin, 1995.

———. *Ira Sleeps Over*. Boston: Houghton Mifflin, 1972.

Wandro, Mark, and Joanie Blank. *My Daddy Is a Nurse*. Reading, MA: Addison-Wesley, 1981.

Ward, Lynd K. *The Biggest Bear*. Boston: Houghton Mifflin, 1952.

Watanabe, Shigeo. *It's My Birthday!* Illus. Yasuo Ohtomo. New York: Philomel, 1988.

Wells, Rosemary. *Waiting for the Evening Star*. New York: Dial, 1993.

Wild, Margaret. *The Queen's Holiday*. New York: Watts, 1992.

Willhoite, Michael. *Daddy's Roommate*. Boston: Alyson, 1990.

Williams, Vera B. *A Chair for My Mother*. New York: Greenwillow, 1982.

———. *"More More More," Said the Baby: Three Love Stories*. New York: Greenwillow, 1990.

Winthrop, Elizabeth. *That's Mine!* Illus. Emily McCully. New York: Holiday, 1977.

Yashima, Taro (pseud. of Jun Iwamatsu). *The Crow Boy*. New York: Viking, 1955.

———. *Umbrella*. New York: Viking, 1958.

Yolen, Jane. *Owl Moon*, illus. John Schoenherr. New York: Philomel, 1987.

Yorinks, Arthur. *Hey Al*. Illus. Richard Egielski. New York: Farrar, Straus & Giroux, 1988.

Zion, Gene. *Harry, the Dirty Dog*. Illus. Margaret Bloy Graham. New York: Harper, 1956.

———. *Harry and the Lady Next Door*. Illus. Margaret Bloy Graham. New York: Harper, 1960.

Zolotow, Charlotte. *The Moon Was the Best*. Illus. Tana Hoban. New York: Greenwillow, 1993.

———. *William's Doll*. Illustrated by William Pene DuBois. New York: Harper, 1972.

Chapter 8

~

FOLK LITERATURE

Folk literature (also referred to as *traditional literature*) consists of all those stories handed down from generation to generation, from old to young, by word of mouth. By definition, folk literature is not written down (at least not at its inception). The body of folk literature includes not only what we somewhat inaccurately refer to as "fairy tales," but also the myths, legends, fables, tall tales, and other inventions associated with preliterate societies. Although now most of these stories have been committed to paper, for centuries they survived only in the oral tradition of the people. Consequently, folktales were apt to change with each successive telling (much as complicated phrases get altered as they pass from person to person in that childhood game of "Telephone"). We may find hundreds of variations for a single tale, each variation containing elements peculiar to the society and time that produced it. These tales form the roots of all literature, and their story lines are the foundations for virtually every book we read. They speak to our most basic human emotions, to our deepest hopes and fears, and it is little wonder that even the youngest children feel a great affinity with these stories that have been with us for as long as civilization.

Folk literature (and, we may therefore suppose, all literature) arose initially from a variety of human needs, including:

1. the need to explain the mysteries of the natural world in the absence of scientific information;
2. the need to articulate our fears and dreams, thus making them accessible and manageable;

3. the need to impose some order on the apparent random, even chaotic, nature of life, thus helping us to understand our place in the universe; and

4. the need to entertain ourselves and each other.

Even today we see the vestiges of traditional literature in the ghost stories told around campfires, in the double dutch jump-rope rhymes chanted on the playground and in city streets, in the family stories exchanged at holidays and reunions.

We cannot overemphasize the importance of cultural tradition in folk literature. The folk literature of each specific culture has its own traditions and the tellers of the tales usually assume that their audience has a knowledge of these traditions. Western European folktales do not need to explain magical objects, enchanted castles, the power of witches, or the transformation of princes into frogs because these features are all parts of the tradition of the folktale. They are embedded in the culture, and European (and American) audiences are familiar with them. Conversely, it is often difficult for audiences to identify with or immediately understand the meaning and purpose of another culture's folk literature without some background (so it helps to know that Native Americans, for instance, regard the number four to be sacred or that many Japanese folktales are imbued with a combination of Buddhist philosophy and ancestral and nature worship). The folktale's reliance on tradition is a significant difference between a folktale and a fantasy.

THE ORIGIN AND PURPOSES OF FOLK LITERATURE

When the study of folk literature began in earnest in the nineteenth century, scholars were surprised to learn how remarkably similar were the tales in societies as widely separated as those of ancient China, South America, Africa, and Europe. Cultural distinctions existed, of course, but the basic themes, even plots, were found to be very much alike. Cinderella stories, for examples, have been discovered the world over. Since that discovery, two principal theories have arisen in an attempt to explain how folktales originated.

Monogenesis—meaning literally "one beginning"—is the theory that all tales were ultimately derived from a single source (such as a Mesopotamian culture) and were disseminated throughout the world gradually. *Polygenesis*—meaning "many beginnings"—is the theory that tales emerged independently of each other in many different places throughout the world. Polygenesis attributes these marked similarities in form and content to the fundamental similarities in the human psyche—people around the world having similar human hopes, fears, dreams, and psychological needs. Neither theory has yet been absolutely substantiated, and the truth may lie somewhere in between—some tales emerging independently and others having been adopted from neighboring cultures.

Folk literature, as was pointed out above, originally served a multitude of purposes, and so it should not be surprising that this literature appears in a wide variety of types. Folktales and fables, myths, legends, and epics are among the most common. Some stories served as educational tools for preliterate societies, passing on knowledge essential for survival. Others helped to reinforce cultural practices and social mores—the importance of certain virtues, the significance of marriage or of the established social or political order, the superiority of one's clan or tribe over its neighbors, and so on. Vital to nearly all peoples were creation myths—how the world, *their* world, came to be. And we should not forget what must have been one of the driving forces behind the telling of these tales—entertainment. These tales served primitive societies in place of books, plays, movies, and television, and as such they embodied the popular attitudes, beliefs, and values of the culture. They retain their meaning for us because we still share a great deal more with our ancestors than we at first imagine.

TYPES OF FOLK LITERATURE

Folk literature comes in a variety of forms, some of it in secular tales, some in instructional stories, some in religious narratives. Folk literature may be serious or comical. Some of the predominant forms popular among children follow.

ANIMAL TALES

Animal tales are perhaps the oldest of all tales. Early people had a strong affinity with animals. Not only did animals pose the greatest threats for them, but they also provided them with food, clothing, companionship, and even served as guides and protectors, so it is not surprising that animals would play significant roles in early stories and legends. In most animal tales, the animals act as human types, and in no way do they behave as real-life animals would behave. These tales tend to be very popular with young children who are fascinated by animals of all kinds. Nor is it a difficult leap for a young child to believe that an animal can speak and feel just as humans do.

Animals that talk appear in a great number of folktales—remember the magic fish in "The Fisherman and His Wife" or the wolf in "Little Red Riding Hood." But a true animal tale (also called a *talking beast tale*) is one in which the principal characters are anthropomorphized animals, that is, animals that talk and act like humans. Animals in these tales may, and often do, interact with humans, although the human roles are negligible and usually not depicted in the best light. In "The Bremen-Town Musicians," we may recall that the humans are the heartless farmers, who are ready to dispose of the aging animals, and the thieves whom the animals cleverly rout from their hideout.

FABLES

Fables are a form of animal tale in which animals portray human virtues and vices for the purpose of conveying a moral message. Most fables conclude with a blatantly stated moral ("And the moral of the story is . . .") directed toward human behavior and are therefore openly didactic. Aesop, a popular teacher of ancient Greece, is credited with the most famous fables, and it is usually assumed that he used them in his teaching. Ironically, even though their form would suggest a strong appeal among young children, most fables demand abstract thinking and their points are often lost on children. Nevertheless, adults continue to provide children with fables, occasionally with lavish illustrations—but we must suspect that, for the most part, the adults are the ones who chiefly appreciate them.

MÄRCHEN OR WONDER TALES

The best-known of the traditional folktales are the *märchen* or *wonder tales*. Focusing on magical wonders long ago in faraway lands, these tales typically depict the conflict between good and evil, usually enacted by characters of royal birth. They typically conclude with the triumph of virtue and a happy marriage. "Cinderella," "Snow White and the Seven Dwarfs," and "Sleeping Beauty" are the classic examples. It is largely from these stories that the term "fairy tale" emerged, although most do not actually contain fairies. In *märchen*, the supernatural is a dominant element, whether it be a magical person (a fairy godmother, a wicked witch) or a magical object (a wondrous beanstalk and a goose that lays golden eggs) or an enchantment (a miraculous sleep that lasts until love's first kiss). Sometimes these stories are narratives of the hero's or heroine's life from childhood through the accomplishment of some great deed, which more often than not concludes with a marriage. Because of the ages of the protagonists (usually they are in late adolescence) and the fact that matrimony is the end of many of these tales, we may wonder what appeal they have for preschoolers. Their popularity undoubtedly springs from their imaginative characters, their supernatural elements, their focus on action, their simple sense of justice, and their happy endings.

POURQUOI TALES

A *pourquoi tale* (the name derives from the French word for "why") seeks to explain natural phenomena—why the beaver has a flat tail, why the mulberry is red, and so on. Many familiar Native American folktales fall into this category. One particularly moving tale is that explaining the creation of the Sleeping Bear Dunes on the northwest coast of Michigan's lower peninsula. The massive dunes, according to the tale, cover the body of a mother bear mourning the loss of her two cubs who drowned in Lake Michigan, and North and South Manitou islands, just off the coast, represent the two cubs themselves. Many pourquoi tales assume religious significance—such as creation tales—and are more properly considered myths, discussed subsequently.

NOODLEHEAD TALES

Noodlehead tales (also termed *merry*, *droll*, or *simpleton tales*) include as their principal characters fools, albeit lovable fools. "Hans in Luck," in which the title character successively trades one possession for another of lesser value until he is left with nothing (except happiness), is an excellent example of such a tale. "The Three Wishes" is the story of a poor couple who are granted three wishes by a grateful magical creature whom they helped out of a jam. The foolish couple proceed to waste all three wishes, however, and end up no better off than they were at the beginning—although they are usually depicted as contented anyway. Noodlehead tales typically focus on a single episode in the hero's life. The appeal of these tales is usually found in their pure nonsense and jocularity, and sometimes we enjoy the triumph of the good-hearted simpleton over the craftier evil characters of the story. Occasionally, the simpleton proves in the end to be far wiser than anyone else, suggesting that it is the world at large that is foolish and unable to recognize true wisdom. The noodlehead tale is fundamentally that of the underdog, always a popular character.

CUMULATIVE TALES

Most folktales include repetitious patterns—three wishes to be made, three deeds to be accomplished, and four trials to endure, and so on. But certain tales rely on repetition for their total effect. As each new detail is added, the entire list is repeated in order, so that the accumulation becomes a kind of chorus—and a challenge to the memory of the audience. *Cumulative tales* are generally brief, else they become tiresome, but their appeal lies in their musical quality and, often, in their flippant humor. That old rhyme, "This Is the House that Jack Built," is an example of repeated language patterns, and those familiar tales, "The Gingerbread Boy" and "The Turnip," wherein additional characters are summoned to help accomplish some feat, are examples of the accumulation of repetitive action. Young children especially love the repeated patterns, which test their memories and allow them to join in the telling.

TALL TALES

The numerous tales about Paul Bunyan's extraordinary exploits are examples of the American *tall tale*. Tall tales are comic stories of preposterous exaggeration. Early examples may be the stories of Jack the Giant Killer in England, although in the United States these tales assumed some of the quality of the local legend, focusing on local heroes (sometimes real persons, such as Davy Crockett). These stories illustrate the American preference for broad humor and overstatement. Tall tales defy logic and are usually without moral lessons. Their delight is in their absurdity and in the wildly imaginative yarns, each succeeding one seeming to outdo the other.

GHOST STORIES

Most young people enjoy, under the right circumstances, being frightened. The immense popularity of horror movies among teenagers and Halloween celebrations among younger children attest to the appeal of spinetinglers. Telling *ghost stories* around a campfire or beneath the blankets at a pajama party has long been a staple of childhood entertainment. Most cultures have their own versions of chilling tales, ghosts and evil spirits walking the night, or tales that Richard Chase calls "jump tales," because the teller jumps out toward the listeners at the climax to surprise them. Since most children prefer to hear these stories in groups where there is safety in their numbers, and since many of these stories are more effective when delivered orally, ghost stories are perfect examples of the living folktale, told *by* the folk *to* the folk with each tale adapted to the occasion.

MYTHS

Myths are the stories of gods, goddesses, and heroes of a given culture, and these stories serve a variety of purposes, combining science, religion, and even sociology and psychology. Myths may explain the ultimate origin of the world and of human beings—virtually every culture from the most primitive to the most advanced has some creation myth. Myths also help explain the origins of customs and societal beliefs—ancient Greeks and Romans placed coins in the mouths of their dead that they might have the fare for Charon who would ferry them over the River Styx to the Underworld. Myths also provide explanations for natural phenomena. Early peoples devised myths to explain the rising and setting of the sun, the phases of the moon, the change of seasons, the occurrence of thunderstorms, and so on.

Myths also help to define human relationships with the god (or gods and goddesses). Myths may reinforce cultural values, drawing attention to what the culture sees as primary good and evil. Not least, myths help to resolve humanity's fear of the unknown—whether it be fear of thunder and lightning (explained as activities of the gods) or fear of death (typically explained as a passage from one world into another).

Classical Greek and Roman Myths.   To people of Western cultures, the most familiar mythology outside the Judaeo-Christian tradition for Western culture is that of ancient Greece and Rome. Our daily lives are imbued with references to the extensive pantheon and the notable heroes of that civilization—note the names of the planets, stars and galaxies, and, on a more mundane level, months of the year, body parts (Achilles tendon), cleaning agents (Ajax), synthetic fibers (Herculon), automobiles (Mercury and Saturn), tires and mapbooks (Atlas), athletic games (Olympics), and so on. A knowledge of these myths is important if only to make us aware of our cultural debts. But, in addition to recognizing the multitude of references to Greek and Roman mythology in the modern world, our interest in these tales might be both entertaining and spiritually edifying, in that these exciting stories also tell us—as do the folktales—a great deal about human nature. In classical Greece, the gods and goddesses were powerful figures who often struggled against one another for human favor and typically were pragmatic in their dealings with humans ("I'll do that for you if you do this for me"). The questions of humanity's obedience to a higher power, the relationships of men and women to one another, the power of love, and the strength of parental devotion are all addressed in this body of mythology.

Norse Myths.   Second only to Greek and Roman mythology in its influence on the Western tradition, Norse mythology reflects the harsh way of life engendered by the severe, yet dramatically beautiful, Scandinavian lands. In Norse mythology, the gods and goddesses were defenders of humanity against the mighty forces of evil. Like the Greek and Roman gods and goddesses, the Norse deities were anthropomorphic—that is, the gods and goddesses had human forms (a practice not all that common, when we consider the many monsters, demons, multi-armed deities, feathered serpents, and animal forms worshipped throughout the world). But compared to the Greek deities, the Norse gods and goddesses tend to be a much more serious lot, engaged in a perpetual struggle with the forces of evil, a struggle that they were destined eventually to lose. Individual codes of honor were highly esteemed in this war-conscious society. Among the most familiar images from Norse mythology is the god of thunder, Thor, who is remembered weekly in our own culture, for Thursday was named for him. Tuesday, Wednesday, and Friday were named for other Norse deities: Tiw (the god of war), Woden (father of the gods), and Fria (goddess of fruits).

Native American Myths.   The cultures of Native America (including North, Central, and South America) lived—and those surviving still do—in close harmony with the rhythms of the natural world. Indeed, the modern Native American "still lives connected to the nurturing womb of mythology. Mysterious, but real power dwells in nature—in mountains, rivers, rocks, even pebbles" (Erodes and Ortiz xi). The belief that spirits inhabit natural objects is referred to as animism and it is quite common throughout the world. The stories Native Americans tell are, not surprisingly, stories of nature and the associations of nature and human beings. In the Native American storytelling tradition, stories are frequently presented in chains of episodes—sometimes incomplete—each building on the last. Disorganized by the standards of European folktales, the Native American tales are more spontaneous—largely because they are still relatively close to their oral beginnings.

Types of stories found in Native American myths and legends include creation stories, describing the foundation of the world; pourquoi tales, describing the origins of other natural phenomena; and trickster tales, which often resemble the heroic legend—the hero being a wily character outwitting his compatriots. Unlike many of the world's mythical stories, the Native American tales are still part of a living tradition.

African Myths.   Like Native American mythology, African mythology is widely diverse, with each civilization or society having developed its own set of beliefs. Also like Native American mythology, most African mythology prominently features the natural world with spirits inhabiting virtually everything. Magic and ancestor worship also form important parts of African religious practice. Most of the tales that have been retold for children include creation stories and stories of animal heroes—including the trickster. (The trickster is a familiar character in folk literature, usually a clever animal, often whimsical and devilish. The trickster delights in bringing havoc to the world, and is an ambivalent character—often an anti-hero and troublemaker who makes life interesting and keeps the rest of the us on our toes.) Many of the African myths and legends were carried to America in the seventeenth and eighteenth centuries by Africans who had been sold into slavery. The stories of Anansi the spider are trickster tales originating in Africa, later popular in the West Indies and now widely disseminated throughout the English-speaking world.

Oriental Myths.   India and the Far East developed highly complex and sophisticated mythologies. Unlike Greek, Roman, and Norse mythologies with their anthropomorphic deities, the deities of these cultures are frequently polymorphic, combining the forms of animals and/or humans. In some oriental religions, as in that of Hindu India, the gods and goddesses take extraordinary forms—humans having many arms, heads, eyes, and so on, or being part human, part animal. The early religions of China and Japan were animistic, much like the Native American and African religions, but these were supplanted by Buddhism, Confucianism, Shintoism, and Taoism—often in the Orient two or more religions are observed simultaneously (in part because they tend to be more ethical than eschatological). Each religion has its stories—the beautiful humanistic tales of the compassionate Buddha or the adventures of the Hindu gods, for example. The mythology of the Orient is not particularly well known in the English-speaking world, although in recent years more myths and legends from this region have been published. What all these disparate mythologies have in common is a need to explain our relationship to the wondrous and mysterious forces that drive the universe, and to give some validity to our existence. These are needs that we have neither outgrown nor entirely satisfied.

EPICS AND HEROIC LEGENDS

Epics and heroic legends initially grew out of mythology, but instead of focusing on gods and goddesses, these stories had human beings as their heroes. Among the most popular of the Greek and Roman heroes are Achilles, Odysseus, Hector, Jason, and Perseus. They were indeed the first superheroes, the prototypes of Superman, Batman, and Wonder Woman. Although Homer's *Iliad* and *Odyssey* were obviously aimed at an adult audience, there is much in them to attract young readers, for they are adventure-filled and wrought with unworldly wonders. Padraic Colum also wrote fine versions for children (*The Children's Homer* and *The Golden Fleece*).

Medieval Europe saw the rise of epic tales deriving from Christian sources—King Arthur and the Knights of the Round Table, the Quest for the Holy Grail, and the Life of Charlemagne provided sources for the most popular tales. These epics and legends are often more secular than religious, Malory's *The Death of Arthur* and the French epic *The Song of Roland* being among the most famous, and some of these tales have been successfully retold for young readers—for example, Rosemary Sutcliff's story of the Quest for the Holy Grail, *The Light Beyond the Forest*.

SAINTS' LIVES AND LOCAL LEGENDS

Also popular in the Middle Ages were the *saints' legends*, recounting often apocryphal tales of the lives and miracles of saints. These enjoy little modern popularity, but as late as the early part of the twentieth century, John Foxe's *Book of Martyrs*, a sixteenth-century work about the deaths of persecuted Christians, was still read by children. In a similar fashion, *local legends* emerged, focusing on local secular (as opposed to religious) heroes and usually departing rather dramatically from reality. The typical local legend grows up around real people, although the facts are soon lost—George Washington's chopping down the cherry tree, Davy Crocket's frontier exploits, Johnny Appleseed's horticultural contributions.

THE LITERARY FAIRY TALE

The traditional folktales have inspired modern counterparts—original tales by modern writers that have all the flavor of an old tale. These tales fall somewhere between traditional literature and fantasy. Sometimes, unless we know the origin, it is difficult to distinguish the difference between the *literary fairy tale* (the product of a specific author) and the oral folktale—and perhaps the writers of the literary fairy tales would take that as a sign of their success. Hans Christian Andersen was one of the earliest creators of the literary fairy tale, and he has proved one of the most enduring. His popularity inspired others, and by the last half of the nineteenth century many writers were experimenting with this form. George Macdonald's *The Light Princess* and *The Princess and the Curdie* and *The Princess and the Goblin* are all book-length works that we can label literary fairy tales. The literary fairy tale exhibits many of the same features as its oral counterparts: conventional settings in a distant "generic" kingdom, predominately flat and stereotyped characters, an accepted magical element, and, of course, an inevitable happy ending. A modern variation of the literary fairy tale is a spoof or satire on the form, such as James Thurber's delightful *Many Moons*, which takes a comic twist, and Sid Fleischman's Newbery-Award winning novel, *The Whipping Boy*. Satire results when writers feel a literary form has been exhausted and that it offers no other serious possibilities; consequently they begin to poke fun at it, and, in doing so, they give the form new life.

FOLKTALE CONVENTIONS

Folktales can be recognized by certain conventions, accepted components common to virtually all tales. The most familiar include setting, character, plot, theme and conflict, and style.

SETTING

"Once upon a time in a kingdom far, far away" typically defines the time and place in a folktale. The purpose of most folktale settings would seem to be to remove the tale from the real world, taking the events to a world where magic can easily occur. Only occasionally do we find actual place names in tales, and even then we find little that is geographically specific.

CHARACTER

The characters in folk literature are usually flat, simple, and direct. In the folktale, everything is externalized; consequently characters do not internalize their feelings and they are seldom plagued by mental torment. Stereotypical characters—powerful, wicked stepmothers and weak-willed, ineffectual fathers, jealous siblings—populate most tales. A character is typically either all good or all evil, and it is usually not difficult for the audience to separate the good from the bad. Physical appearance often readily defines a character—wicked witches are ugly, good princesses are beautiful, noble princes are fair, but disguises are common. The beast in "Beauty and the Beast" has been transformed from his handsome self into a monstrosity by a jealous witch. And in another popular tale, a witch transforms a handsome prince into a frog. When the spell is broken, the prince is restored to his handsome self. Only rarely do we find a truly beautiful character to be wicked—Snow White's stepmother is an example, but even her beauty is outshone by that of her virtuous stepdaughter, and she performs her most powerful magic when she assumes the disguise of an ugly hag. Truth cannot long remain hidden.

PLOT

The plots, or the sequence of events, are among the most identifiable features of folk literature. Suspense and action are far more important to these tales than character development. Conflicts are quickly established and events move swiftly to their conclusion; although there may be subsidiary plots or the events may at times seem to get sidetracked, the action never slows down.

The hero or heroine is often isolated and is usually cast out into the open world or is apparently without any human friends. The evil, on the other hand, seems overwhelming. Consequently, to offset the apparent imbalance, the hero/heroine must be aided by supernatural forces (such as a magical object or an enchanted creature). In short, the folktale heroes/heroines are very much like young children picture themselves—the helpless victims of evil forces (sometimes appearing in the form of their parents!). And the evil characters symbolize human fears and frustrations. The folktales are also wish-fulfilling, with the good triumphing over the evil.

THEME AND CONFLICT

Themes in most folk literature are usually quite simple, but they are always serious and powerful. Among the commonly found themes in folktales are:

1. the struggle to achieve autonomy or to break away from parents ("Beauty and the Beast");
2. the undertaking of a rite of passage—sometimes to sexual maturity ("Rapunzel");
3. the discovery that eventually we are all alone on our journey to maturity ("Hansel and Gretel");
4. coping with the failure to meet the parent's expectations ("Jack and the Beanstalk");
5. coping with one's displacement in the family by another—the "new arrival" ("Cinderella").

These are not the only themes we find in folk literature, but we can easily see why children might be drawn to tales that emphasize these issues, for they are at the very heart of growing up.

If we had to make a general statement about themes in folktales, we might well turn to themes of Greek tragedy: *Wisdom comes through suffering*. The message is loud and clear that for every benefit there is a condition, that nothing in life comes without strings attached, responsibilities to be met, and bargains to be kept. And folktale themes—especially in the Western tradition—espouse the virtues of *compassion, generosity*, and *humility* over the vices of *greed, selfishness*, and *excessive* or *overweening pride*.

STYLE

Formula and Repetition. The style in folktales is largely regulated by the oral nature of their origins. The language is typically economical, with a minimal amount of description and a heavy reliance on formulaic patterns—conventional openings and closings, for instance ("Once upon a time in a kingdom far, far away" and "They lived happily ever after"). Repetitious phrases are common; they supply a rhythmical quality desirable in oral tales and undoubtedly once served as mnemonic devices to make the tales easy to memorize. Folktales also use a technique known as *stylized intensification*, which occurs when, with each repetition, an element is further exaggerated—with each Billy Goat Gruff we get a larger billy goat, for example, or with each visit Rumpelstiltskin's price for spinning straw into gold increases, and so on. Dialogue is frequently used, and in the best-told tales the dialogue captures the nature of the character speaking—hence, a lowly peasant will speak in a folksy manner whereas the speech of a king or princess will be more refined. (The English retellings of Joseph Jacobs wonderfully capture these differences in speech patterns.)

Imagery and Motifs. Most folktales include examples of simple, but concrete and very powerful, images that leave us with indelible mental pictures. Many tales can easily be identified by their images—a glass slipper, a bean stalk and talking harp, golden eggs, a bloody handkerchief, a red riding hood, and so on. Related to these images are the motifs on which most tales rely. In art, a motif is a repeated figure or element in a larger design (decorative fads are easily recognized by their motifs—ducks or geese or hearts and flowers, and so on). Similarly, in literature, a motif is a narrative element that we find recurring in various tales, defined by folklorist Stith Thompson as "the smallest element in a tale having power to persist in tradition." Motifs undoubtedly helped the teller in remembering and the audiences in comprehending the tales. Examples of popularly used motifs include magical transformations (a beast is transformed into a handsome prince, usually after some expression of true love), the use of magical objects, the appearance of deceitful animals (or helpful animals), and the making of foolish bargains.

Magic. Many folktale motifs are examples of magic—helpful animals, transformations from human to beast and beast to human, granted wishes, and so on. One important stylistic feature of the folktale is that the magic, when it appears, is always greeted by the characters with matter-of-factness. Folktale characters acknowledge magic as an almost normal part of life. No one is ever amazed or disbelieving when a wolf speaks politely, or a fairy godmother materializes out of thin air, or an elf make exotic promises. This accepting attitude toward magic on the part of every folktale character further distances the folktale from reality, and it provides an important distinction between folk literature and much of literary fantasy. In many literary fantasies (heroic fantasy being one of the exceptions), magical occurrences are not necessarily taken for granted, but may be regarded with surprise, awe, and disbelief. (Both Alice and Dorothy, those most famous of child travelers in literary fantasies, are in constant wonder at the characters and circumstances they encounter.)

ISSUES IN FOLK LITERATURE

Since they were first collected and committed to paper in the late seventeenth and eighteenth centuries, folktales have been at the center of various controversies generally centering on their suitability for children. At the heart of most early controversies was the concern over violence and lack of moral instruction in folktales. Today objections are raised over social attitudes the stories portray. Evidently, the folktales remain as vital as ever.

VIOLENCE

Among the issues most often discussed regarding folk literature is the prevalence of violence. Foolish and irresponsible little pigs are devoured, wolves are cooked in boiling water, witches are pushed into hot ovens, characters are mutilated in any number of ways—folktales have their fair share of violent acts. Certainly much of this violence is the product of earlier, less squeamish eras (and the same can be said for the violence in Mother Goose rhymes). But before we express our indignation over these violent elements and seek to exorcise them from stories for the young, perhaps we should consider the excessively graphic and despicably gruesome violence on television or in the cinema. Modern violence—not the least of which is found in children's Saturday morning cartoons—is often gratuitous, without sense or purpose other than to arouse or titillate the audience. This is clearly different from folktale violence, which is always handled without graphic description and seldom included without motivation. Violence perpetrated by the wicked always results in their downfall and, usually, in their deaths; violence perpetrated by the good is always a response to evil. It is interesting that, when given the choice, children most often prefer versions of "Little Red Riding Hood" in which the grandmother is devoured and the wolf is ultimately killed—as opposed to those versions in which the ravenous wolf, after inexplicably tying up grandmother and tossing her in the closet, is miraculously reformed and promises to be good henceforth.

FOLKTALES AS PSYCHOTHERAPY

In a controversial study of folktales, the psychiatrist Bruno Bettelheim suggests that folktales, through their rich symbolism and evocative story patterns, actually fulfill unconscious psychological needs in some children. Bettelheim argues that children are able to vent anxieties and hostilities through the vicarious experience of art and literature, with folktales providing an especially healthy and much-needed emotional outlet. Bettelheim's thesis encourages close Freudian readings of folktales and sees them laden with symbolism, particularly sexual. He notes how many folktales, for instance, end in marriages, suggesting that they are coming-of-age tales, stories of awakening sexual maturity. He further argues that the violence in folktales gives children a vicarious means of coping with their inner frustrations (that is, it is better to direct our hatred toward a wicked stepmother or witch in a story than toward our own mother). Bettelheim also advocates that the tales not be tampered with or expurgated in any way and that they not be illustrated (for illustrations can inhibit a child's imagination). Critics of Bettelheim find him too extreme in his Freudian interpretations, but his theories do add an interesting dimension to the study of folktales and should not be summarily dismissed. (For a sampling of Bettelheim's theory, see the discussion on "Psychoanalytical Approaches" in Chapter 4.)

ANTIFEMINISM

Perhaps more potentially damaging than the violence or the sexuality is the depiction of negative female stereotypes (the frail young girl in need of a good man) or the unfortunate deprecation of stepmothers in general. The popular story of "Cinderella" has come under the most severe attack (although "Sleeping Beauty" and "Snow White" are not markedly different). These stories seem to suggest that a woman's purpose in life is to find a Prince Charming and that all she really has going for her are her looks and a docile, sweet personality (see the discussion in Chapter 4 on "Feminist Criticism"). Modern attitudes demand that we attempt to balance our selection of folktales—it is possible to find folktales with more assertive female role models ("Mollie Whuppie" and "Kate Crackernuts" are just two examples). And we should also consider the possibility of contemporary adaptations of old folktales. Some of the "politically correct" versions are great fun and actually not out of character with the fluid nature of the oral tale (see Garner's *Politically Correct Bedtime Stories*).

COLLECTORS, RETELLERS, AND ADAPTERS

Almost as soon as human beings invented the art of writing, they began to record their oral tales—on stone, on papyrus, and on paper. So far as Western culture is concerned, virtually the entire body of ancient Greek literature consists of renderings and retellings of their myths, legends, and fables. The ancient Romans followed this practice similarly. The ancient Jews recorded their stories with a rich mixture of history and legend. The Christian Middle Ages built up a body of literature on the legendary lives of the saints as well as on the glorified deeds of heroes. But by and large, the vast majority of folktales remained only in oral form, except for a few recorded by such medieval writers as Chaucer in *The Canterbury Tales* and Boccaccio in *The Decameron*. Consequently, these stories survived chiefly by word of mouth until the seventeenth and eighteenth centuries when writers began to collect them and put them down on paper.

Among the first and most famous of these writers was Charles Perrault whose *Tales of Mother Goose* made such stories as "Cinderella," "Sleeping Beauty," and "Little Red Riding Hood," standard fare in children's literature. In the early nineteenth century, the famous Grimm brothers gathered together German folktales, which included, not surprisingly, versions of "Cinderella" ("Aschenputtel") and "Little Red Riding Hood" ("Little Red Cap"), as well as such familiar favorites as "Snow White and the Seven Dwarfs."

These early collections were not for children, and many people found folktales too harsh and sought to protect children from these stories. But children, of course, devoured the tales anyway. Ever since Joseph Jacobs and Andrew Lang began collecting tales in the late nineteenth century, folktales have been largely the property of children. The twentieth century has seen an explosion in the interest in folklore, and countless collections of tales from all over the world have appeared. The most famous modern adaptations have been the animated films of Walt Disney. The Disney films have been immensely popular, but they are not without their detractors. Some critics argue that the Disney versions are awash with sentimentality, that they condescend to children and lack the power of the original tales. Still others claim that the folktales were intended to be popularized, that their very form invites new adaptations, and that Disney has captured anew some of the magic of the folktales.

Although not a controversial issue, a recent trend has been for authors to write parodies of folktales. The most famous are Jon Scieszka's works, including *The True Story of the Three Little Pigs* (as told by A. Wolf), which turns the story upside down, telling it from the wolf's point of view. As with all parodies, the effect works best if we first know the original tale. These works, like the "politically correct" tales, can be tremendously delightful and help introduce children to varying points of view as well as literary parody. Nor are they necessarily out of step with the nature of the folktale. We should remember that folktales have been continually adapted over the centuries to meet the changing needs of society. They are remarkably resilient and, having survived for centuries, will be likely to endure for generations to come—a testament to their ageless wonder.

WORK CITED

Erdoes, Richard, and Alfonso Ortiz, eds. *American Indian Myths and Legends*. New York: Pantheon, 1984.

RECOMMENDED READINGS

Bettelheim, Bruno. *The Uses of Enchantment: The Meaning and Importance of Fairy Tales*. New York: Knopf, 1976.

Bosma, Betty. *Fairy Tales, Fables, Legends, and Myths: Using Folk Literature in Your Classroom*, 2nd ed. New York: Teachers College Press, 1993.

Campbell, Joseph. *The Hero with a Thousand Faces*, 2nd ed. Princeton, NJ: Princeton University Press, 1968.

Chase, Richard. *American Folk Tales and Songs*. New York: Dover, 1971.

Cook, Elizabeth. *The Ordinary and the Fabulous*. Cambridge: Cambridge University Press, 1969.

Krappe, Alexander H. *The Science of Folklore* (1929). New York: Norton, 1964.

Luthi, Max. *Once Upon a Time: On the Nature of Fairy Tales*. Bloomington: Indiana University Press, 1976.

Petrone, Penny. *Native Literature in Canada: From the Oral Tradition to the Present*. Oxford: Oxford University Press, 1990.

Storr, Catherine. "Folk and Fairy Tales." *Children's Literature in Education* 17 (Spring 1986): 63–70.

Tatar, Maria. *Off With Their Heads*. Princeton: Princeton University Press, 1992.

Thompson, Stith. *The Folktale*. New York: Holt, Rinehart and Winston, 1951.

Walker, Virginia, and Mary E. Lunz. "Symbols, Fairy Tales and School-Age Children." *The Elementary School Journal* November 1976: 94–100.

Yolen, Jane. *Touch Magic*. New York: Philomel, 1981.

Zipes, Jack. *Breaking the Magic Spell: Radical Theories of Folk and Fairy Tales*. Austin, TX: University of Texas Press, 1979.

———. *Fairy Tales and the Art of Subversion: The Classical Genre for Children and the Process of Civilization*. London: Heinemann, 1983.

COLLECTIONS OF FOLK LITERATURE, MYTHS, AND LEGENDS

Below is a brief selection from the vast number of collected folktales, fables, riddles, myths, and legends that are available. They are classified as either (1) Folktales and Fables, (2) Myths, Epics, and Legends, or (3) Literary Fairy Tales. Check the bibliography following chapter 6 for picture-book versions.

FOLKTALES AND FABLES

Aesop's Fables. Illus. Fritz Kredel. New York: Grosset, 1947.

Asbjornsen, Peter, and Jorgen Moe. *East O' the Sun and West O' the Moon*. New York: Dover, 1970. (Scandinavian folktales)

Bierhorst, John, ed. *Lightning Inside You: And Other Native American Riddles*. New York: Morrow, 1992.

———. *The White Deer and Other Stories Told by the Lenape*. New York: Morrow, 1995.

Bloch, Marie Halun. *Ukranian Folk Tales*. New York: Coward, McCann, 1964.

Briggs, Katharine. *British Folk Tales*. New York: Pantheon, 1977.

Bushnaq, Inea, trans. *Arab Folktales*. New York: Pantheon, 1986.

Calvino, Italo, ed. *Italian Folktales*. New York: Pantheon, 1980.

Chandler, Robert, trans. *Russian Folk Tales*. New York: Shambhala/Random House, 1980.

Chase, Richard. *The Jack Tales*. Boston: Houghton Mifflin, 1971. (American tall tales)

Cole, Joanna, sel. *Best-Loved Folktales of the World*. Garden City, NY: Doubleday, 1982.

Demi, adaptor. *A Chinese Zoo: Fables and Proverbs*. New York: Harcourt, 1987.

de Wit, Dorothy. *The Talking Stone: An Anthology of Native American Tales and Legends*. New York: Greenwillow, 1979.

Fang, Linda, reteller. *The Ch'i-lin Purse: A Collection of Ancient Chinese Stories*. New York: Farrar, Straus & Giroux, 1995.

Finger, Charles. *Tales from Silver Lands*. New York: Doubleday, 1924. (Central American folktales)

Gág, Wanda. *Tales from Grimm*. New York: Coward, McCann & Geoghegan, 1981.

Garner, James Finn. *Politically Correct Bedtime Stories*. New York, Macmillan, 1994.

Glassie, Henry. *Irish Folk Tales*. New York: Pantheon, 1985.

Grimm, Jakob, and Wilhelm Grimm. *Household Stories*. Trans. Lucy Crane. New York: Dover, 1963.

Haley, Gail E, reteller-illustrator. *Mountain Jack Tales*. New York: Penguin, 1992.

Hamilton, Virginia. *In the Beginning: Creation Stories from Around the World*. New York: Harcourt Brace Jovanovich, 1988.

———. *The People Could Fly*. New York: Knopf, 1985. (African-American folktales)

Hausman, Gerald, collector-reteller. *How Chipmunk Got Tiny Feet: Native American Origin Stories*. New York: HarperCollins, 1995.

Haviland, Virginia. *Favorite Tales Told in India*. Boston: Little, Brown, 1973.

Hodges, Margaret, reteller. *Hauntings: Ghosts and Ghouls from Around the World*. Boston: Little, Brown, 1991.

Hoogasian-Villa, Susie. *One Hundred Armenian Tales*. Detroit: Wayne State University Press, 1966.

Jacobs, Joseph. *Celtic Fairy Tales*. New York: Dover, 1968.

———. *English Fairy Tales*. New York: Dover, 1967.

Jaffe, Nina, and Steve Zeitlin. *While Standing on One Foot: Puzzle Stories and Wisdom Tales from the Jewish Tradition*. Illus. John Segal. New York: Holt, 1993.

James, Grace, reteller. *Green Willow and Other Japanese Fairy Tales*. New York: Avenel, 1987.

Joseph, Lynn. *The Mermaid's Twin Sister: More Stories from Trinidad*. New York: Clarion, 1994.

Kherdian, David, reteller. *Feathers and Tails: Animal Fables from around the World*. New York: Putnam, 1992.

Lang, Andrew. *The Blue Fairy Book* (1889). New York: Dover, 1965.

Lester, Julius. *Black Folktales*. New York: Richard W. Baron, 1969.

Lyons, Mary E., sel. *Raw Head, Bloody Bones: African-American Tales of the Supernatural*. New York: Scribner's, 1991.

Manitonquat (Medicine Story), reteller. *The Children of the Morning Light: Wampanoag Tales*. Illus. Mary F. Arquette. New York: Macmillan, 1994.

Neil, Philip, reteller. *Fairy Tales of Eastern Europe*. Boston: Houghton Mifflin, 1991.

Nic Leodhas, Sorche. *Thistle and Thyme: Tales and Legends from Scotland*. New York: Holt, Rinehart and Winston, 1962.

Opie, Iona, and Peter Opie. *The Classic Fairy Tales*. New York: Oxford University Press, 1974.

Phelps, Ethel Johnson. *The Maid of the North: Feminist Folk Tales from Around the World*. New York: Holt, Rinehart and Winston, 1981.

Ross, Gayle. *How Rabbit Tricked Otter and Other Cherokee Trickster Stories*. Illus. Murv Jacob. New York: HarperCollins, 1994.

Schwartz, Alvin, reteller. *Ghosts!: Ghostly Tales from Folklore*. New York: HarperCollins, 1991.

Schwarz, Howard, and Barbara Rush, reteller. *The Diamond Tree: Jewish Tales from Around the World*. New York: HarperCollins, 1991.

Singer, Isaac Bashevis. *Zlateh the Goat and Other Stories*. New York: Harper, 1966. (Yiddish folktales)

Tehranchian, Hassan, adaptor. *Kalilah and Dimnah: Fables from the Middle East*. New York: Harmony, 1985.

Vuong, Lynette Dyer. *The Golden Carp and Other Tales from Vietnam*. Illus. Manabu Saito. New York: Lothrop, 1993.

Wolkstein, Diane. *The Magic Orange and Other Haitian Folktales*. New York: Knopf, 1978.

Yeats, W. B., and Lady Gregory. *A Treasury of Irish Myth, Legend, and Folklore*. New York: Avenel, 1986.

Yep, Laurence, reteller. *Tongues of Jade*. New York: HarperCollins, 1991. (Chinese)

Yolen, Jane, ed. *Favorite Folktales from Around the World*. New York: Pantheon, 1986.

Zipes, Jack, trans. *Beauties, Beasts, and Enchantment: Classic French Fairy Tales*. New York: Penguin, 1991.

MYTHS, EPICS, AND LEGENDS

Colum, Padraic. *The Children of Odin: The Book of Northern Myths* (1920). New York: Macmillan, 1984.

———. *The Children's Homer: The Adventures of Odysseus and the Tale of Troy* (1919). New York: Macmillan, 1982.

———. *The Golden Fleece and the Heroes Who Lived Before Achilles* (1921). New York: Macmillan, 1983.

Coolidge, Olivia. *Greek Myths*. Boston: Houghton Mifflin, 1949.

D'Aulaire, Ingri, and Edgar Parin D'Aulaire. *D'Aulaire's Book of Greek Myths*. New York: Doubleday, 1962.

Erdoes, Richard, and Alfonso Ortiz, eds. *American Indian Myths and Legends*. New York: Pantheon, 1984.

Goldston, Robert, reteller. *The Legend of the Cid*. Indianapolis: Bobbs-Merrill, 1963.

Green, Roger Lancelyn. *Heroes of Greece and Troy: Retold from the Ancient Authors*. Illus. Heather Copley and Christopher Chamberlain. New York: Walck, 1961.

Hieatt, Constance, reteller. *Sir Gawain and the Green Knight*. Illus. Walter Lorraine. New York: Crowell, 1967.

Jaffrey, Madhur. *Seasons of Splendour: Tales, Myths & Legends of India*. Illus. Michael Foreman. Harmondsworth, UK: Puffin, 1987.

Kingsley, Charles. *The Heroes*. New York: Dutton, 1963.

McKinley, Robin. *The Outlaws of Sherwood*. New York: Greenwillow, 1988.

Philip, Neil. *The Tale of Sir Gawain*. Illus. Charles Keeping. New York: Philomel, 1987.

Pyle, Howard. *Some Merry Adventures of Robin Hood*. New York: Scribner's, 1954.

Sherwood, Merriam, trans. *The Song of Roland*. New York: McKay, 1938.

Sutcliff, Rosemary. *Beowulf*. London: Bodley Head, 1961 (Later published in the United States as *Dragon Slayer*).

———. *The Light Beyond the Forest: The Quest for the Holy Grail*. New York: Dutton, 1980.

Thompson, Brian. *The Story of Prince Rama*. New York: Viking, 1985.

Thompson, Vivian L. *Hawaiian Tales of Heroes and Champions*. New York: Holiday House, 1971.

Westwood, Jennifer, reteller. *Gilgamesh and Other Babylonian Tales*. New York: Coward McCann, 1970.

LITERARY FAIRY TALES

Andersen, Hans Christian. *The Complete Fairy Tales and Stories*. Trans. Erik Christian Haugaard. New York: Doubleday, 1974. (Numerous editions of single tales are also available.)

Bomans, Godfried. *The Wily Witch and All the Other Fairy Tales and Fables*. Illus. Wouter Hoogendijk. Owings Mills, MD: Stemmer, 1977.

Fleischman, Sid. *The Whipping Boy*. New York: Morrow, 1986.

Gardner, John. *Dragon, Dragon and Other Tales*. New York: Knopf, 1975.

Kingsley, Charles. *The Water-Babies* (1863). Several modern editions.

Macdonald, George. *At the Back of the North Wind* (1871). Several modern editions.

———. *The Light Princess* (1864). Several modern editions.

———. *The Princess and the Curdie* (1877). Several modern editions.

———. *The Princess and the Goblin* (1872). Several modern editions.

Thurber, James. *Many Moons*. New York: Harbrace, 1943.

Chapter 9

~

POETRY

Perhaps one of the loveliest descriptions of poetry comes from the poet Paul Roche who remarked that poetry is like a stained-glass window: It lets the light shine through but exists for its own beauty. In their anthology of poetry for children, *Knock at a Star*, X. J. and Dorothy Kennedy answer the question, "What do poems do?" with the following:

1. They make us laugh—from the nonsense of Lear to the comedy of Shel Silverstein, good children's poets have recognized this as one of the best ways into the child's world.
2. They tell us stories—they can contain scenes, characters, and action.
3. They give us messages—poets usually have points to make, ideas to get across, and even comic verse often offers food for thought.
4. They share feelings with us—from joy to sorrow to anger to excitement to serenity, poets ask us to come into their world and, for a time, to share their deepest feelings and sensations, and the poet is often well aware of our feelings as well.
5. They start us wondering—the poet forces us to see things in ways we may never have thought of before and encourages us to stretch our minds and exercise our imaginations.

POETRY FOR THE VERY YOUNG

Toddlers and preschoolers respond readily to the beauty of poetry. Infants and preschoolers are captivated by the sounds of "Pat-a-cake, pat-a-cake," or "Hickory dickory dock." And Lewis Carroll's "Jabberwocky" remains a pleasure to listen to and to read, however obscure its meaning. It should not be surprising that children demonstrate an early love of the rhythms of language. As noted in Chapter 6, nursery rhymes offer cognitive, emotional, and social benefits as well as entertainment to children. This early exposure to the wonder of language is crucial. Poetry and music spring from the same impulse, and it may even be that the love of poetry and music is a natural impulse, for both echo the rhythmic patterns of nature. It seems quite likely that music, dancing, and poetry are all parts of our earliest artistic expression.

But poetry is as much an appeal to the mind's eye as it is to the ear. Once children begin to comprehend meaning through language, they begin to demand vivid mental images in their stories and poems. Imagery in literature is simply the quality that allows language to paint pictures with words. The Mother Goose rhymes are filled with memorable mental pictures: Miss Muffet on her tuffet, Jack and Jill tumbling down the hill, another Jack suspended in midair over a candlestick, and the miserable Old Woman attempting to corral her unruly children into an oversized shoe. It is no accident that nursery rhymes are among the most illustrated of children's literature. The vivid pictures conveyed by the words almost beckon the artist's brush and pen.

THE KINDS OF POETRY

When we talk about poetry, it is easy to get bogged down with complex terminology and obscure references, and it is certainly not necessary for children to be able to recognize and label poetic techniques. But if we are to appreciate fully the craft of the poet, it is helpful if we have at least a passing acquaintance with the poet's techniques and a vocabulary with which we may discuss poetry. Many different kinds of poetry exist, but we can identify two broad categories—narrative poetry, which first and foremost tells a story, and lyric poetry, which primarily conveys the poet's intellectual and emotional responses.

NARRATIVE POETRY

A *narrative poem* is a story in verse. (To narrate, of course, means simply to tell a story.) The most accessible narrative poems for children are ballads. Ballads are typically straightforward and easy to understand; like a story, they include a setting, character, and events with a climax. Many readers find ballads less intimidating than the shorter, more compact lyric poems. The typical ballad follows a four-line scheme with the second and fourth lines rhyming, such as in this famous opening stanza to the anonymous ballad, "Barbara Allen's Cruelty":

In Scarlet town, where I was born,
There was a fair maid dwellin',

Made every youth cry Well-a-way!
Her name was Barbara Allen.

As with most good story beginnings, we are given a definite setting and introduced to the main character, the beautiful Barbara Allen. Ballads have been popular since the Middle Ages and have proven quite adaptable. They are frequently tragic and plaintive, such as this example of an anonymous ballad from the American West, called "The Dying Cowboy" or "The Streets of Laredo":

Let sixteen gamblers come handle my coffin,
Let sixteen young cowboys come sing me a song,
Take me to the green valley and lay the sod o'er me,
For I'm a poor cowboy and I know I've done wrong.

Occasionally ballads are set to music, and the perennial favorite "Wreck of the Edmund Fitzgerald" by Gordon Lightfoot is an interesting example of a modern-day shipping disaster supplying the inspiration for a modern-day ballad. And country and western music thrives on the ballad form.

Not all narrative poems are ballads. In fact, among the world's oldest literature are the 3,000-year-old Sumerian epic, *Gilgamesh*, and the great narrative poems of Homer, *The Iliad* and *The Odyssey*. These are lengthy stories in the form of poetry that were actually intended to be recited to audiences (rather than read by them). A hundred years ago, lengthy narrative poems still enjoyed some popularity, and Robert Browning's "The Pied Piper of Hamelin" and Henry Wadsworth Longfellow's "The Song of Hiawatha" are examples of nineteenth-century narrative verse still found in print. The early twentieth-century poet Alfred Noyes wrote narrative poems imbued with drama on subjects that appeal to readers in the upper elementary years— "The Highwayman" and "A Song of Sherwood" are examples. More recently, the comical poems of Shel Silverstein in *Where the Sidewalk Ends* and *A Light in the Attic* combine the qualities of narrative poetry with nonsense verse and are immensely popular.

In a narrative poem, we look for a storylike structure, with a beginning, a middle, and an end. We look for character motivation (if not development), and we look for an underlying theme (the monumental theme of the triumph and tragedy of war or the tender theme of the forsaken lover are examples).

LYRIC POETRY

Lyric poetry is a far more personal expression of the poet's response to a subject. Unlike a narrative poem, a lyric does not so much tell a story as it does describe the feeling of a moment. Lyrics tend to focus on a single experience and are usually briefer than narrative poems. In the absence of an exciting story, the lyric must depend heavily on musical qualities. There seems to be an endless variety of stanza forms in lyric poetry, and new ones are still being created.

Haiku. *Haiku* is of Japanese origin and consists typically of 17 syllables divided into three lines and is usually on the subject of nature and our relationship to nature, such as this by Ruby Lytle*:

> The moon is a week old—
> A dandelion to blow
> Scattering star seed.

In this haiku, the image of the stars as tiny seeds blown from the moon, a whispery soft dandelion puff gone to seed, brings us closer to the starry night sky and reminds us of the interconnectedness of all nature. Haiku in English possesses a subtle rhythm, but typically does not rhyme. Its strength lies in its suggestive quality. Successful haiku uses metaphor to give us a fresh and imaginative look at something we may view as quite ordinary.

Cinquain. The *cinquain* is a five-line stanza apparently of medieval origin. The term once seems to have included any five-line poem (*cinq* is French for "five"), but Adelaide Crapsey, in her volume entitled *Verse*, created more precise rules stipulating that the five lines should contain two, four, six, eight, and two syllables respectively. Her inspiration may have been the Japanese haiku, although little real similarity between the two forms exists. The poet Myra Cohn Livingston sees the cinquain as a sort of mathematical puzzle, in which the writer must find expressions of the correct number of syllables placed in an intelligible order. Notice the pattern of syllables (2, 4, 6, 8, 2) in Adelaide Crapsey's cinquain, entitled "November Night." Notice how the poet plays on the double meaning of the last word:

> Listen . . .
> With faint dry sound,
> Like steps of passing ghosts,
> The leaves, frost-crisp'd, break from the trees
> And fall.

Concrete Poetry. When the words of a poem are so arranged that they form a pictorial representation of the poem's subject, we have what is called a *concrete poem*. These are really not new, for the English metaphysical poets were practicing this sort of poetry in the seventeenth century. George Herbert, for example, wrote "The Altar" so that the lines formed the shape of an altar; also popular were poems in the shapes of crosses and pyramids, and Herbert's "Easter Wings" was designed to suggest angel wings. In the twentieth century, much more liberty has been taken

---

* What Is the Moon?" by Ruby Lytle, © 1965 by Charles E. Tuttle Co., Inc. of Tokyo, Japan. Reprinted by permission.

with this sort of thing, such as in this example by Robert Froman, in which the poet defines what he calls "A Seeing Poem"*:

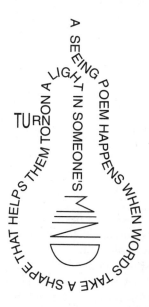

Limerick.   Among the most popular poetic forms with children is the *limerick*, a five-line humorous poem, the first, second, and fifth lines rhyming, and the third and fourth rhyming. Part of the fun of the limerick is its playful rhythm, and part is in its broad humor. The following limerick has been attributed to President Woodrow Wilson:

> I sat next to the Duchess at tea;
> It was just as I thought it would be;
>   Her rumblings abdominal
>   Were simply phenomenal,
> And everyone thought it was me.

The limerick's form is easily imitated, and young children can have a great deal of fun creating their own.

Free Verse.   The twentieth century has popularized *free verse*, which adheres to no predetermined rules, but establishes its own criteria for rhyming and rhythmical patterns. Free verse is much more demanding on the poet than most readers suppose, and it requires the same thoughtful choice of words and sentence patterns

---

* Taken from *Seeing Things: A Book of Poems* by Robert Froman. Copyright © by Robert Froman. Reprinted by permission of the author.

as the more rigid stanza forms. The following example, "The Fog,"* by Carl Sandburg, focuses on a single concrete image:

> The fog comes
> on little cat feet.
> It sits looking
> over harbor and city
> on silent haunches
> and then, moves on.

There are potentially as many stanza forms as there are poets. Perhaps the best we can do for children is to make them aware of the vast array of choices open to them as both readers and writers of poetry, and in this way try to prevent the misconceptions that arise about what a poem is.

THE LANGUAGE OF POETRY

Poetry—like all literature—depends upon the effective union of form and content, but poetry is at once more compact than most literature and more reliant upon certain literary devices for its effect. As we have already emphasized, the most memorable poems are both pleasing to the ear and stimulating to the mind.

IMAGERY

Imagery refers simply to mental pictures created by words. Since words are the poem's medium, their selection is the most crucial aspect of the poem's creation.

Direct Images. Imagery is said to be *direct* when a poet describes something by appealing to one or more of our sensory faculties. For example, images may be *visual*, referring to things we can see, or images may be *tactile*, appealing to our sense of touch. When Walter de la Mare writes "Through the green twilight of a hedge / I peered with cheek on the cool leaves pressed," he is using first visual imagery—*green twilight*—and then tactile—*cool leaves*. We also find *auditory* images, which suggest the sounds of things, as when Eve Merriam writes of a wrecking ball in her poem, "Bam, Bam, Bam"†:

> Crash goes a chimney,
> Pow goes a hall,

---

* "Fog" from CHICAGO POEMS by Carl Sandburg, copyright 1916 by Holt, Rinehart and Winston, Inc. and renewed 1944 by Carl Sandburg, reprinted by permission of Harcourt Brace & Company.

† Excerpted from BAM BAM BAM by Eve Merriam. (A Bill Martin Book for Henry Holt and Company.) Text copyright © 1966 by Eve Merriam. © Renewed 1994 by Dee Michel and Guy Michel. Reprinted by permission of Marian Reiner.

> Zowie goes a doorway,
> Zam goes a wall.

Olfactory images suggest the smells of things, as in these lines from Shakespeare that mingle sound imagery with that of scent: "[The music] came o'er my ear like the sweet sound / That breathes upon a bank of violets, / Stealing and giving odor!" Dante Gabriel Rosetti suggests another olfactory image: "I know the grass beyond the door / The sweet keen smell." *Kinesthetic* images refer to actions or motions, as do these lines from Alan Cunningham's "At Sea":

> A wet sheet and a flowing sea,
>   A wind that follows fast
> And fills the white and rustling sail
>   And bends the gallant mast

And *gustatory* images suggest the tastes of things. These images are less common than others, but it is perhaps taste, texture, and color that Mary O'Neill had in mind when she wrote that "Brown is cinnamon / and morning toast" or that gray is "The bubbling of oatmeal mush."

Indirect Images.   Images may also be *indirect*, describing one object or idea by comparing it to another with which we are more familiar. (It, of course, makes no sense to compare two things neither of which the readers knows or understands.) The three common methods of comparison are through similes, metaphors, and personification.

A *simile* is a stated comparison, employing a connective such as "like" or "as"; take Robert Burns's famous line: "My love is like a red, red rose." The unfamiliar entity, so far as the reader is concerned, is "My love" (presumably the poet's sweetheart), and the familiar is the "red, red rose" (a flower that is familiar to his audience). It is true that we may, as readers/listeners, have somewhat different conceptions and attitudes about the "red, red rose" (someone with an allergy to roses may not share the general population's fondness for them). However, most people think of roses as examples of extraordinary delicacy and beauty, and we would certainly respond in another way had the poet written, "My love is like a mighty oak." The point is that the poet's object was not to confuse us, but, rather, to help us understand his deep and passionate feelings about his lover.

A *metaphor* is an implied comparison—one not directly stated with words such as "like" and "as." Metaphors are often more subtle to grasp. In a brief poem, "City,"* by Langston Hughes, the poet implies a comparison of a city in the morning with a songbird:

> In the morning the city
> Spreads its wings
> Making a song
> In stone that sings.

This simple poem gives us an exhilarating feeling about the city. The short, musical lines, with their repeating *s* and *ing* and short *i* sounds, and their end rhyme, help to convey a sense of the animated and joyous life in the bustling city. The effective metaphor helps us to understand the poet's message and attitude or tone.

Personification is by its nature metaphorical, although not all metaphors are examples of personification. Personification occurs when a poet gives human qualities to an inanimate object, an abstract idea, or a force of nature. James Stephens is using personification when he writes: "The Night was creeping on the ground! / She crept and did not make a sound. . . ." It is also personification when Eleanor Averitt writes of the November wind that she "has plucked the trees / like pheasants, held / between her knees."

SOUND PATTERNS

Rhythm. Most poems are written expressly for oral delivery, and, consequently, how they sound is extremely important. All poetry is musical, and, as in music, rhythm is a fundamental quality in poetry. Babies respond to rhythmical patterns almost from birth, whether it be swaying or rocking or a simple caressing of the back. Who is to say that our first sensory experience is not, in fact, prenatal—that steady, rhythmical pulsation of our mother's body and the gentle undulations of the embryonic fluids sweeping about us? And, of course, rhythm is everpresent in nature, the orbiting of the planets and the rhythmical birth, flourishing, death, and rebirth revealed to us through the changing seasons. Rhythm—be it in nursery rhymes or Shakespeare—is inseparable from poetry.

Simply defined, *rhythm* is the pattern of stressed and unstressed syllables in a poem. (This pattern is also called *meter*.) The smallest unit of rhythmical pattern is called a *foot*. There are many variations of metrical feet, each having from two to three syllables. The most common are the following:

> *Iamb* (two syllables with the emphasis on the second: "When **wál**-king **in** a **tí**-ny **ráin**")
> *Trochee* (two syllables with the emphasis on the first: "**Síng** a **sóng** of **súb**-ways")
> *Anapest* (three syllables with the emphasis on the last: "In the **mórn**-ing the **cí**-ty' ")
> *Dactyl* (three syllables with the emphasis on the first: "**Sky'**-scra-per, **sky'**-scra-per, **Scrápe** me some **sky'**")

Nursery rhymes tend to have very regular rhythms: "**Má**-ry **hád** a **lít**-tle **lámb**" (regular trochees). Following their example, much of the verse for the very young repeats similar singsong patterns. But if children are ever to appreciate poetry more fully, they must be brought beyond the notion that perfect, unvaried meter is the only rhythmical option available to poetry. Much poetry combines more than one rhythmical pattern to achieve a particular effect. When we read poetry to children, it is important that we ourselves are aware of any subtleties of rhythm the poem may contain, so that we may gain the best effect from our reading.

Rhyme.   *Rhyme*, the second important element of sound patterns, is achieved through the similarity of sound that exists between two or more words. When it comes to poetry for children, we customarily place too much emphasis on end rhymes—that is, rhyming "June" with "moon" and "spoon" and "soon." In fact, rhyme can occur anywhere sounds are repeated.

Alliteration, for example, is the repetition of initial sounds in two or more words, such as the *b* and *l* sounds in these lines by A. E. Housman:

> **B**y **b**rooks too **b**road for **l**eaping,
> The **l**ightfoot **b**oys are **l**aid.

Assonance is the repetition of identical vowel sounds, such as the long *a*, long *u*, and long *i* sounds in these lines by Carl Sandburg: "Let me be the **great nail** holding a skyscraper thr**ough blue nights** into white stars."

Consonance is the repetition of consonant sounds within words, often with a variation in adjoining vowels, such as the *f* and *d* sounds in these lines by William Jay Smith:

> Butter**f**lies . . .
> Gli**d**ing over **f**ield and stream—
> Like **f**ans unfol**d**ing in a **d**ream.

Obviously, too much of any repetitive sound pattern becomes noticeable and begins to detract from the content. The good poet knows just how much to include to make music, and just when to stop before the result is tongue-tying racket.

SHARING POETRY WITH CHILDREN

Studies of children's poetry preferences suggest, among other things, that children prefer poetry they can understand, that they prefer humorous poetry, that they prefer new poems to older ones, and that they do not like serious and contemplative poems (see Terry). However, such studies can be dangerous if we use them to determine what poetry we will share with children. This would result in a further narrowing of taste among children and deprive many children of fresh and imaginative poetry that they just might enjoy. Nor is it desirable that we provide children only with what they like or think they like. After all, an important part of education is broadening experiences. But it is useful to know what prejudices and preconceptions children may have about poetry, so that we have some idea of where we must go. Too often in the schools, we labor under the misconception that poetry is obscure (a puzzle to be unravelled by English teachers), "pretty"(without any particular meaning), and frivolous. These are the very misconceptions that are passed on to children—the very children who could not get enough of Mother Goose rhymes or the delightful verses of Jack Prelutsky, Shel Silverstein, and others. And many of these children may have dabbled in writing poetry themselves in early elementary school. It is important that the approach to poetry in the classroom build on the early love of rhythm, rhyme, and figurative language and that enjoyment be the goal.

Reading poetry is ideally a regular part of a child's reading program (rather than an intensive two-week unit to be forgotten as quickly as it was begun). Most poetry is best read aloud, and—in the classroom, at least—it is best read frequently and not saved up for a marathon weeklong poetry drill once a year. There are wonderful poems suitable for special occasions (or even ordinary occasions—poems for a partly cloudy day, for instance). Poetry offers endless possibilities—a well-presented poem can fill a relatively small time slot in a day and provide some welcome, joyous relief. If we begin to think of poetry in this fashion, we may begin to dispel some of the notions of drudgery and perplexity that often surround poetry.

It is important to eliminate those tedious academic exercises (memorizing irrelevant poems, counting meters, scanning lines, and so on) that typically form the academic study of poetry. There is nothing wrong with discussing these matters with children and showing them how they might make use of them in their own poems, but it can be disastrous to make meaningless exercises of them.

The writing of original poetry may be encouraged and even required (but only after the children have caught the "poetry bug"), and some children will find it fun and rewarding. Encouraging children to form collections of their own favorite poems is also an enriching experience (and every adult presenting poetry to children should do the same). Requiring students to memorize poems can result in happy experiences for some children, but it quickly devolves into drudgery for others. We need to be aware of children's individual differences and personal preferences.

Helping children to read their favorite poems effectively is always a worthwhile exercise. Inexperienced readers tend to want to dramatize the rhythm or the rhyme of a poem, to make a deliberate pause at the end of a line whether the poet has punctuated it or not, and to overemphasize the singsong quality. Children learn best by example. We can demonstrate the effective reading of poetry, paying close attention to the poet's punctuation, avoiding a lapse into inappropriate nursery-rhyme rhythm, carefully enunciating the words, and emphasizing the meaning of those words by using natural and not artificial inflections. Practice in reading poetry is the key to accomplishment. Ideally, the reading of poetry will become a much anticipated part of the daily schedule—both a delight and a refreshment.

SELECTING POEMS
AND ANTHOLOGIES

Too often children are asked to read poems that were clearly intended for adults. And then we wonder why the children are confused or bored. The truth is that much of the poetry of our most revered poets speaks about adult emotions and adult perceptions of the world. How can we expect children to identify with these subjects? We certainly need not expect them to do so; there are plenty of very good poems for young readers. We do not need to raid adult literature for suitable examples.

Every classroom and home should include a generous supply of poetry books, both anthologies and books by individual poets. With the wealth of good poetry available, every child—no matter how resistant to poetry—is bound to find some favorites. The key is, of course, to supply a wide and varied sampling—poems on all subjects, poems representing myriad stanza forms and rhyme schemes and rhythms.

A great number of poetry anthologies can be found on the market today. We can rely on a few guidelines to help us select an anthology of quality. Following are some of the important characteristics found in the best anthologies (and these guidelines vary with the purpose of the anthology):

1. The selection includes both familiar and new poets.
2. The selection includes a significant number of new poems and not simply old poems that can already be found in many anthologies.
3. The selection includes a balance of light and serious poems.
4. The poems *show* the reader (through effective imagery, metaphor, personification) rather than *tell* the reader the poet's thoughts.
5. The poems reflect a variety of verse forms.
6. The illustrations (if the book is illustrated) complement the poems without overpowering them.

As with all children's literature, if we wish to instill a love of reading poetry in children, we must begin with ourselves. The poet is a visionary, one who sees the world in fresh and unusual ways, and one who is capable of sharing that vision with the rest of us. We have been notoriously unsuccessful in conveying this notion of poetry to young people. It is important that we overcome our own fears and apprehensions about poetry so that we may share in its bounty. But, as with everything else in creation, the more we understand about poetry, and the better we come to know it, the richer our experience with it will be. And few literary forms offer so much in pleasure and knowledge than poetry. Lovers of poetry are not born, but made through patient and careful nurturing.

WORKS CITED

Hughes, Langston. *Collected Poems*. New York: Knopf, 1994.
Kennedy, X. J., and Dorothy Kennedy, eds. *Knock at a Star: A Child's Introduction to Poetry*. Illus. Karen Ann Weinhaus. Boston: Little, Brown, 1982.

Lytle, Ruby. *"What Is the Moon?"* Tokyo: Charles E. Tuttle Co., Inc.
Sandburg, Carl. "Fog." In *Chicago Poems*. New York: Holt, Rinehart and Winston, 1916.
Smith, William Jay, and Louise Bogan. *The Golden Journey*. Chicago: Contemporary Books, 1990.

RECOMMENDED READINGS

Baskin, Barbara Holland, Karen H. Harris, and Coleen C. Salley. "Making the Poetry Connection." *The Reading Teacher* 30 (Dec. 1976): 259–265.

Ciardi, John, and Miller Williams. *How Does a Poem Mean?* 2nd ed. Boston: Houghton Mifflin, 1975.

Fisher, Carol J., and Margaret A. Natarella. "Of Cabbages and Kings: Or What Kinds of Poetry Children Like." *Language Arts* 56: 4 (April 1979): 380–385.

Higginson, William J., with Penny Harter. *The Haiku Handbook: How to Write, Share and Teach Haiku*. New York: McGraw-Hill, 1985.

Hopkins, Lee Bennet. *Pass the Poetry Please*. New York: Citation Press, 1972.

Hurst, Carol. "What to Do with a Poem." *Early Years* 11(February 1980): 28–29, 68.

Kennedy, X. J. " 'Go and Get Your Candle Lit!' An Approach to Poetry." *Horn Book Magazine* 57: 3 (June 1981): 273–279.

Krogness, Mary Mercer. "Imagery and Image Making." *Elementary English* 51: 4 (April 1974): 488–490.

Larrick, Nancy, ed. *Somebody Turned on a Tap in These Kids*. New York: Delacorte, 1971.

Lewis, Marjorie. "Why Is a Poem a Four-Letter Word?" *School Library Journal* 23: 9 (May 1977): 38–39.

Livingston, Myra. *Climb into the Bell Tower: Essays on Poetry*. New York: HarperCollins, 1990.

————. *Poem-Making: Ways to Begin Writing Poetry*. New York: HarperCollins, 1991.

Shapiro, Jon E. *Using Literature and Poetry Affectively*. Newark, DE: International Reading Association, 1979.

Steiner, Barbara. "Writing Poetry for Children." *Writer's Digest* Feb. 1986: 34–35.

Terry, Ann. *Children's Poetry Preferences: A National Survey of the Upper Elementary Grades*. Urbana, IL: National Council of Teachers of English, 1984.

SELECTED BIBLIOGRAPHY OF POETRY BOOKS FOR CHILDREN

POETRY ANTHOLOGIES

Abdul, Raoul, ed. *The Magic of Black Poetry*. Illus. Dane Burr. New York: Dodd, 1972.

Adoff, Arnold, ed. *Celebrations: A New Anthology of Black American Poetry*. Chicago: Follett, 1977.

————. *The Poetry of Black America: An Anthology of the 20th Century*. New York: Harper, 1973.

Arbuthnot, May Hill, and Shelton L. Root, eds. *Time for Poetry*. Illus. Arthur Paul. Glenview, IL: Scott, Foresman, 1968.

Blishen, Edward, comp. *Oxford Book of Poetry for Children*. Illus. Brian Wildsmith. New York: Watts, 1963.

Bober, Natalie S., comp. *Let's Pretend: Poems of Flight and Fancy*. Illus. Bill Bell. New York: Viking, 1986.

Bryan, Ashley, sel. and illus. *All Night, All Day: A Child's First Book of African-American Spirituals*. New York: Atheneum, 1991.

Carlson, Lori M., ed. *Cool Salsa: Bilingual Poems on Growing Up Latino in the United States*. New York: Holt, 1994.

Carter, Anne, sel. *Birds, Beasts, and Fishes: A Selection of Animal Poems*. New York: Macmillan, 1991.

Cole, William, comp. *Poems of Magic and Spells*. Illus. Peggy Bacon. Cleveland: World, 1960.

———. *A Zooful of Animals*. Illus. Lynn Munsinger. Boston: Houghton Mifflin, 1992.

de Gasztold, Carmen Bernos, sel. *Prayers from the Ark*. Trans. Rumer Godden. Illus. Barry Moser. New York: Viking, 1992.

de la Mare, Walter, ed. *Come Hither*, 3rd ed. Illus. Warren Chappell. New York: Knopf, 1957.

———. *Tom Tiddler's Ground*. Illus. Margery Gill. New York: Knopf, 1962.

Demi, sel. and illus. *In the Eyes of the Cat: Japanese Poetry for All Seasons*. Trans. Tze-si Huang. New York: Holt, 1992.

Dunning, Stephen, Edward Lueders, and Hugh Smith, comps. *Reflections on a Gift of Watermelon Pickle*. Glenview, IL: Scott, Foresman, 1967.

———. *Some Haystacks Don't Even Have Any Needle*. Glenview, IL: Scott, Foresman, 1969.

Elledge, Scott, ed. *Wider than the Sky: Poems to Grow Up With*. New York: Harper, 1990.

Feelings, Tom, comp.-illus. *Soul Looks Back in Wonder*. New York: Dial, 1993.

Gordon, Ruth, sel. *Pierced by a Ray of Sun: Poems about the Times We Feel Alone*. New York: HarperCollins, 1995.

Houston, James, ed. *Songs of the Dream People*. New York: Atheneum, 1972. (Eskimo and other Native America poems)

Janesczko, Paul B., sel. *Looking for your Name: A Collection of Contemporary Poems*. New York: Jackson/Orchard/Watts, 1993.

———. *The Place My Words Are Looking For: What Poets Say about and through Their Work*. New York: Bradbury, 1990.

———. *Preposterous: Poems of Youth*. New York: Watts, 1991.

Jones, Hettie, sel. *The Trees Stand Shining: Poetry of the North American Indians*. Illus. Robert Andrew Parker. New York: Dial, 1971.

Larrick, Nancy, ed. *Piping Down the Valleys Wild*. Illus. Ellen Raskin (1968). New York: Dell, 1982.

Livingston, Myra Cohn, comp. *Dilly Dilly Piccalilli: Poems for the Very Young*. New York: McElderry, 1989. (Nonsense verse)

Moore, Lilian, ed. *Go with the Poem*. New York: McGraw-Hill, 1979.

———. *Sunflakes: Poems for Children*. Illus. Jan Ormerod. New York: Clarion, 1992.

Moore, Lilian, and Judith Thurman, comps. *To See the World Afresh*. New York: Atheneum, 1974.

Nye, Naomi Shihab, sel. *This Same Sky: A Collection of Poems from around the World*. New York: Macmillan, 1992.

Opie, Iona, and Peter Opie, eds. *The Oxford Book of Children's Verse*. New York: Oxford, 1973.

Orozco, José-Luis, sel.-arr. *De Colores and Other Latin-American Folk Songs for Children*. New York: Dutton, 1994.

Sullivan, Charles, ed. *Imaginary Gardens: American Poetry and Art for Young People*. New York: Abrams, 1989.

Townsend, John Rowe, comp. *Modern Poetry*. Philadelphia: Lippincott, 1974.

Whipple, Laura, comp. *Animals Animals*. Illus. Eric Carle. New York: Philomel, 1989.

BOOKS BY INDIVIDUAL POETS

Adoff, Arnold. *All the Colors of the Race*. Illus. John Steptoe. New York: Lothrop, 1982.

———. *Street Music: City Poems*. Illus. Karen Barbour. New York: HarperCollins, 1995.

Armour, Richard. *A Dozen Dinosaurs*. Illus. Paul Galdone. New York: McGraw-Hill, 1970.

Blake, William. *Songs of Innocence and Experience*. Illus. Harold Jones. New York: Barnes, 1961.

Bodeker, N. M. *Water Pennies: And Other Poems*. Illus. Erik Blegvad. New York: McElderry, 1991.

Cawthorne, William Alexander. *Who Killed Cockatoo?* Illus. Rodney McRea. New York: Farrar, Straus & Giroux, 1989. (Australian adaptation of "Who Killed Cock Robin?")

Chandra, Deborah. *Balloons and Other Poems*. Illus. Leslie Bowman. New York: Farrar, Straus & Giroux, 1990.

Ciardi, John. *The Man Who Sang the Sillies*. Illus. Edward Gorey. Philadelphia: Lippincott, 1961.

———. *The Reason for the Pelican*. Illus. Madeleine Gekiere. Philadelphia: Lippincott, 1959.

Coatsworth, Elizabeth. *Under the Green Willow*. Illus. Janina Domanska. New York: Macmillan, 1971.

cummings, e. e. *Hist Whist*. Illus. Deborah Kogan Ray. New York: Crown, 1989.

de la Mare, Walter. *Peacock Pie*. Illus. Barbara Cooney. New York: Knopf, 1961.

Dickinson, Emily. *Letter to the World*. Ed. Rumer Godden. Illus. Prudence Seward. New York: Macmillan, 1969.

Eliot, T. S. *Old Possum's Book of Practical Cats*. Illus. Edward Gorey. New York: Harcourt, Brace, Jovanovich, 1982.

Farjeon, Eleanor. *Then There Were Three*. Illus. Isobel and John Morton-Sale. Philadelphia: Lippincott, 1965.

Field, Rachel. *Poems*. New York: Macmillan, 1957.

Fisher, Aileen. *Cricket in a Thicket*. Illus. Feodor Rojankovsky. New York: Scribner's, 1963.

———. *Feathered Ones and Furry*. Illus. Eric Carle. New York: Crowell, 1971.

Fleischman, Paul. *I Am Phoenix: Poems for Two Voices*. Illus. Ken Nutt. New York: Harper, 1985.

———. *A Joyful Noise: Poems for Two Voices*. New York: Harper, 1988.

Fletcher, Ralph. *I Am Wings: Poems about Love*. New York: Macmillan, 1994.

Froman, Robert. *Seeing Things: A Book of Poems*. New York: Crowell, 1974.

Frost, Robert. *Birches*. Illus. Ed Young. New York: Holt, 1988.

Giovanni, Nikki. *Spin a Soft Black Song*. Illus. George Martins. New York: Hill and Wang, 1985.

Greenfield, Eloise. *Night on Neighborhood Street*. Illus. Jan Spivey Gilchrist. New York: Dial, 1991.

Hughes, Langston. *The Dream Keeper and Other Poems*. New York: Knopf, 1994.

Hughes, Ted. *Moon-Whales and Other Moon Poems*. Illus. Leonard Baskin. New York: Viking, 1976.

Issa. *A Few Flies and I: Haiku by Issa*. Trans. R. H. Blyth and Nobuyaki Yuasa. Ed. Jean Merrill and Ronni Solbert. New York: Pantheon, 1969.

Kennedy, X. J. *Chastlies, Goops & Pincushions: Nonsense Verse*. Illus. Ron Barrett. New York: McElderry, 1989.

Kuskin, Karla. *Near the Window Tree*. New York: Harper, 1975.

Lear, Edward. *The Complete Nonsense Book*. Ed. Lady Strachey. New York: Dodd, 1942.

———. *The Quangle-Wangle's Hat*. Illus. Helen Oxenbury. New York: Watts, 1969.

Lewis, J. Patrick. *A Hippopotamusn't: And Other Animal Verses*. Illus. Victoria Chess. New York: Dial, 1990.

Livingston, Myra Cohn. *The Way Things Are and Other Poems*. Illus. Jenni Oliver. New York: Atheneum, 1974.

———. *Whispers and Other Poems*. Illus. Jacueline Chwast. New York: Harcourt, 1958.

McCord, David. *One at a Time: His Collected Poems for the Young*. Illus. Henry Kane. Boston: Little, Brown, 1977.

Mahy, Margaret. *Nonstop Nonsense*. Illus. Quentin Blake. New York: McElderry, 1989.

Merriam, Eve. *The Singing Green: New and Selected Poems for All Seasons*. New York: Morrow, 1992.

———. *There Is No Rhyme for Silver*. Illus. Joseph Schindelman. New York: Atheneum, 1962.

Milne, A. A. *The World of Christopher Robin*. Illus. Ernest Shephard. New York: Dutton, 1924.

Moore, Lilian. *Adam Mouse's Book of Poems*. Illus. Kathleen Garry McCord. New York: Atheneum, 1992.

Nash, Ogden. *The Adventures of Isabel*. Illus. James Marshall. Boston: Little, Brown, 1991.

———. *Custard and Company: Poems by Ogden Nash*. Comp. and illus. Quentin Blake. Boston: Little, Brown, 1980.

O'Neill, Mary. *Hailstones and Halibut Bones*. Illus. John Wallner. New York: Doubleday, 1989.

Prelutsky, Jack. *The Dragons Are Singing Tonight*. New York: Greenwillow, 1993.

———. *Ride a Purple Pelican*. New York: Greenwillow, 1986.

———. *The Sheriff of Rottenshot*. Illus. Victoria Chess. New York: Greenwillow, 1982.

———. *Something Big Has Been Here*. Illus. James Stevenson. New York: Greenwillow, 1990.

Richards, Laura. *Tirra Lirra: Rhymes Old and New*. Illus. Marguerite Davis. Boston: Little, Brown, 1955.

Roethke, Theodore. *Dirty Dinky and Other Creatures*. Sel. Beatrice Roethke and Stephen Lushington. New York: Doubleday, 1973.

Schwartz, Alvin, sel. *And the Green Grass Grew All Around: Folk Poetry from Everyone*. Illus. Sue Truesdell. New York: Harper, 1992.

Seabrooke, Brenda. *Judy Scuppernong*. Illus. Ted Lewin. New York: Dutton, 1990.

Service, Robert W. *The Shooting of Dan McGrew*. Illus. Ted Harrison. Boston: Godine, 1988.

Silverstein, Shel. *A Light in the Attic*. New York: Harper, 1981.

———. *Where the Sidewalk Ends*. New York: Harper, 1974.

Soto, Gary. *A Fire in My Hands: A Book of Poems*. Illus. James M. Cardillo. New York: Scholastic, 1991. (Poems about Hispanic culture)

Starbird, Kaye. *The Covered Bridge House*. Illus. Jim Arnosky. New York: Four Winds, 1979.

Stevenson, James. *Sweet Corn: Poems*. New York: Greenwillow, 1995.

Stevenson, Robert Louis. *A Child's Garden of Verses*. (1905). Illus. Jessie Willcox Smith. New York: Scribner's, 1969.

Swenson, May. *The Complete Poems to Solve*. New York: Macmillan, 1993.

Viorst, Judith. *If I Were in Charge of the World and Other Worries*. Illus. Lyn Cherry. New York: Atheneum, 1969.

Whitman, Walt. *Voyages: Poems by Walt Whitman*. Sel. Lee Bennett Hopkins. Illus. Charles Mikolaycak. New York: Harcourt, 1988.

Wilbur, Richard. *Opposites*. New York: Harcourt, 1973.

Willard, Nancy. *Household Tales of Moon and Water*. New York: Harcourt, 1982.

———. *A Visit to William Blake's Inn*. Illus. Alice and Martin Provensen. New York: Harcourt, 1981.

Worth, Valerie. *All the Small Poems and Fourteen More*. Illus. Natalie Babbitt. New York: Farrar, Straus & Giroux, 1994.

Chapter 10

FANTASY

Who does not recall fondly the enduring figures of the great fantasies—Alice, Dorothy and her motley companions, the irrepressible Mr. Toad of Toad Hall, Peter Pan, Wilbur the pig and Charlotte the spider? These characters are fixed indelibly on the cultural consciousness of our society and have helped to shape our imaginations. It is difficult to exaggerate the influence that fantasy reading has on a young mind.

Fantasy may be simply defined as any story of the impossible, a tale including events that contradict the laws of the natural world; but we must distinguish it from folk literature, which is certainly the root of all fantasy. In contrast with the folktale, which is part of the oral tradition, has no discoverable author, and is subject to myriad variations, fantasy is a literary work, written by an individual or individuals. Although we can frequently find "retellings" or "adaptations" of fantasy stories—Walt Disney has adapted Grahame's *Wind in the Willows*, A. A. Milne's *Winnie-the-Pooh*, and Carroll's *Alice in Wonderland*, for example—it is possible to point to the original text and see what the author actually wrote. Another extremely important distinction is that fantasy lacks the traditional aspects of folk literature. Whereas the teller of a folktale relies on the audience's familiarity with such traditional elements as magical objects, enchanted places, stereotypical characters, and so on, the fantasy writer creates anew in each work the setting, the "rules" of the fantasy, the nature of the characters, and so on. Consequently, fantasy is more complex in structure than the folktale, with generally deeper character development, more detailed settings, and more intricate plots. And, as a written work, fantasy typically has a more polished style than the folktale.

The first important fantasies specifically for children appeared in the nineteenth century. Hans Christian Andersen, in addition to retelling traditional tales, wrote original fairy stories heavily influenced by the folk tradition. But it is Lewis Carroll's *Alice in Wonderland* (1865) that is remembered as one of the pioneers in book-length fantasy for children. (It is also considered one of the first children's books written primarily for the pleasure of children without heavy underlying didacticism.) Since that time, modern fantasy has prospered, producing some of the most memorable works of children's literature. Other early classics in modern fantasy for children include Carlo Collodi's *The Adventures of Pinocchio* (1881), Jules Verne's popular works of science fiction (*Twenty Thousand Leagues Under the Sea* (1870) and others), L. Frank Baum's *The Wonderful Wizard of Oz* (1900), Kenneth Grahame's *The Wind in the Willows* (1908), and A. A. Milne's *Winnie-the-Pooh* (1926).

TYPES OF FANTASY

We have many ways of distinguishing types of fantasy, and each method has its drawbacks. But, since all fantasies contain some form of enchantment, some unreality, it makes a great deal of sense to classify fantasies according to the predominant type of enchantment. We will briefly consider some of the more common of these.

ANIMAL FANTASY

In *animal fantasies* the magic is, of course, that the animals talk and display some human traits. Young children are particularly fascinated by animals and, in fact, see them as possessing human characteristics—having familial relationships similar to humans, enjoying pleasures similar to humans, and even going to some animal heaven when they die. So it is only natural that among the favorite fantasies of children are those using animals as the main characters.

There are essentially two ways that an author may present animal characters in a fantasy. Kenneth Grahame, in his classic, *The Wind in the Willows*, creates animals who talk and behave almost entirely as humans. The animals live in houses (Mr. Toad inhabits a sprawling English manor house), use furniture and human modes of transportation, wear clothes, and even eat human food. So realistically does Grahame portray his characters that readers usually do not question the incongruity of a water rat and a mole eating cold chicken for a picnic lunch. The world is almost entirely inhabited by such fantastic characters, and the few humans who enter it are portrayed satirically.

On the other hand, E. B. White, in his classic, *Charlotte's Web*, depicts animals living in a predominately human world. Hence, Wilbur the pig lives like a pig in a barnyard, eats like a pig, and generally has all the habits of a pig. The only differences between Wilbur and any other pig we might expect to find on a farm are that Wilbur (along with the other barnyard animals) talks and he experiences human emotions—love, fear, loneliness, and so on. Wilbur and his animal friends may speak to and be understood by the child, Fern, but the animals never speak to adult humans. Charlotte, likewise, lives the life of a spider; we see her entrap a fly and suck its blood, for example, an activity that at first horrifies even Wilbur the pig. As is customary in animal fantasy, Wilbur and his friends exhibit human personality traits—Charlotte is kind and wise, Templeton is greedy and selfish, Wilbur is lovable—but not human customs (we would be disturbed if Wilbur should suddenly take to wearing a spiffy jacket and top hat).

In all cases of animal fantasy, the premise is that the animals have human feelings. We can emphathize with them, and from their behavior we can learn something about ourselves and humanity in general. Consequently, it is possible for us to draw significant conclusions about human behavior from reading either *The Wind in the Willows* or *Charlotte's Web*. By the same token, we learn very little reliable information about animal behavior. In other words, animal fantasy constitutes a form of literary symbolism, the animal characters symbolizing human counterparts, and these fantasies are often vehicles for exploring human emotions, values, and relationships.

TOY FANTASY

Similar to the animal fantasy is the *toy fantasy*, in which talking toys—usually dolls or stuffed animals—are the major characters. But there are the distinct differences. A frequent theme in toy fantasy is the desire of the toys to become human. Collodi's *Pinocchio* is the classic of this type, in which the wooden puppet comes to life and wants nothing more than to become a real, live boy—a fact accomplished after a series of harrowing experiences that presumably make him worthy of the gift of life. Margery Nicholson's *The Velveteen Rabbit* is another perennial favorite with a similar theme, as is Leo Lionni's picture-book fantasy *Alexander and the Wind-up Mouse*. The implication is, of course, that it is much better to be a living, breathing human being than an inanimate object—although, curiously enough, the toys generally exhibit human traits before their magical transformations.

Other toy fantasies depict toys who are apparently contented with their lot, happy to interact with each other or with a loving child caretaker. A. A. Milne's *Winnie-the-Pooh* is the most famous example of this type of fantasy. Each of the toys, all of which are stuffed animals, has his or her own peculiar personality, and the prospect of becoming human is not a possibility (nor does it seem desirable). In another example of this type, Rachel Field's *Hitty, Her First Hundred Years*, the first-person memoirs of a doll over an entire century, we see some of the peculiar advantages of a toy protagonist, who can enjoy virtual immortality (barring wear and tear or natural disintegration, of course) and thereby witness the parade of history.

ECCENTRIC AND EXTRAORDINARY CHARACTERS

Many fantasies contain humor, but some fantasies feature slapstick, exaggeration, and eccentricity. Typically, the focus of this type of fantasy is an eccentric or magical character or characters. Modern-day fantasies featuring the extraordinary or eccentric character are frequently humorous. Jean Merrill's *The Pushcart War* about a mythical conflict between truckers and carters in New York comes to mind. Others have as their focus a character who may possess some extraordinary power, such as P. L. Travers's *Mary Poppins*, about a nanny with an enchanted umbrella among other powers, or Astrid Lindgren's *Pippi Longstocking*, about an irrepressible young girl with extraordinary powers, or Hugh Loftis's *Dr. Dolittle*, who can communicate with the animals. These fantasies all emphasize the charm of eccentricity and the advantages of being different. Since many are written for children in the middle grades, when peer pressure to conform is at a peak, these stories may help to encourage a sense of individuality and to focus on the need to achieve one's own identity.

One of the masters of the fantasy of eccentricity is Roald Dahl, author of such childhood favorites as *Charlie and the Chocolate Factory*, *James and the Giant Peach*, and *Matilda*. His books are filled with characters both comical and grotesque (which has made him the source of much controversy among adults, but very popular with children). *Charlie and the Chocolate Factory* and *James and the Giant Peach* combine the fantasy of extraordinary character with that of the enchanted journey. These books include journeys—one through a remarkable chocolate factory and the other across the Atlantic in a giant, magical peach—that are reminiscent of the journeys of folk heroes. The downtrodden and outcast hero follows a path to both greater maturity and worldly riches. Dahl's work evokes a surrealistic quality that is at once fascinating and disturbing. The inventive fantasy writer will inevitably create his or her own special kind of fantasy.

ENCHANTED JOURNEYS AND IMAGINARY LANDS

The journey motif is one of the oldest in literature, going back to Homer's *Odyssey* and beyond. The great advantage to sending fictional characters on a journey is that the possibilities for plot variations are virtually endless. Everyone is familiar with those fantasies that take a character—almost always a child—from the real world into an other world, a sort of never-never land where all manner of wondrous things can occur. These fantasies are especially popular with younger readers, and some of these tales include the most famous books of childhood—Lewis Carroll's *Alice in Wonderland*, L. Frank Baum's *The Wizard of Oz*, and Sir James Barrie's *Peter Pan*. Enchanted journeys typically begin in the real world (called the *primary world*), and then, by some device—such as a cyclone or a rabbit hole—the principal character is allowed to enter the enchanted realm (called the *secondary world*).

The journey may have some purpose (Dorothy wants to find the Emerald City and ultimately a way back home; Alice wants to find the Queen's Garden), but that purpose is usually overshadowed by the thrill and delight offered by the extraordinary events that can happen in the secondary world. The credibility of these stories is typically aided by the fact that the fanciful events can only happen in the secondary world and not in the primary world—the Wicked Witch has no authority in Kansas. The plots of these tales are frequently quite loose—sometimes episodic, simply stringing together a series of adventures—and we rely on the central character (the human child) to be our touchstone with reality. Alice and Dorothy judge everything they see in Wonderland and Oz, respectively, by the standards they knew at home.

Joan Aiken has written several fantasies that are quasi-historical, in that they are set in an eighteenth-century England that never was. *The Wolves of Willoughby Chase* and *Black Hearts in Battersea* are both melodramatic novels that include eccentric characters and inventive schemes that could only succeed in a fantasy. The Moomintroll fantasies by the Finnish writer Tove Janssen (who writes in Swedish) describe an entire fantasy world with marvelous creatures who live in a gentle, distant valley with friends as peculiar as they are. The Moomintroll family is introduced in *Tales from Moominvalley* and their adventures are followed through nine books that are now available in English.

Another type of secondary world is the land of miniaturized characters. Jonathan Swift is usually singled out as creating the prototype for this form, with his description of the journey to Lilliput in the first book of *Gulliver's Travels*; however, the adventures of the diminutive folktale hero, Tom Swift, predate Swift. Modern examples include L. Frank Baum's depiction of the Munchkins in *The Wonderful Wizard of Oz* and Mary Norton's *The Borrowers*, the tale of a family of miniature people living in the walls of a house (they are the ones responsible for all the items that inexplicably disappear). Carol Kendall's *The Gammage Cup*, about the struggles of the Minnipin society against their ancient enemies, the Mushroom People, contains many of the features of heroic fantasy, just on a smaller scale. Young readers are attracted to these miniature worlds because they can identify with the diminutive characters and because these stories often depict the clever triumph of the small and weak characters over the larger, but duller, bullies of the world.

HEROIC OR QUEST FANTASY

Alice and Dorothy, although they perform several acts that might be interpreted as heroic, remain clearly grounded in the primary world, the touchstone against which the wonders of the fantasy world are measured. However, in the *heroic fantasy* (sometimes referred to as *quest fantasy* or *high fantasy*), we share the heroic exploits of a hero or heroine engaged in a monumental struggle against a seemingly all-powerful evil, and the fate of an entire civilization often depends on the outcome of the struggle. Whereas the enchanted journey may be quite episodic, the heroic fantasy is usually more tightly woven, with all the action directed toward a single purpose—the triumph of good over evil.

Primary and secondary worlds are variously treated in heroic fantasies. Sometimes, as in Susan Cooper's "The Dark Is Rising" series, the fantasy is set in the real or primary world, which is threatened by dark forces. In Cooper's series, most of the fantasy, although it takes place technically in the primary world, occurs on a psychological level understood only by certain "chosen" humans in the stories. In other heroic fantasies, the story begins in the primary world and contains a passage to the secondary world. C. S. Lewis's *The Lion, the Witch and the Wardrobe* is one of the best-known examples, the children getting to the secondary world of Narnia through the back of an old wardrobe in an English country house. (Passages to secondary worlds are not restricted to heroic fantasies, however. Alice's rabbit hole and looking-glass and Dorothy's cyclone are among the most famous passageways in literature.) And finally, many heroic fantasies, such as Ursula Le Guin's *Earthsea* cycle or Tolkien's *Lord of the Rings* trilogy, take place entirely in imaginary worlds inhabited by imaginary creatures (sometimes humanlike, sometimes not) in no way connected to the world as we know it. These works contain no passage between our world and the fantasy world, but focus on self-contained fictional worlds.

Heroic fantasies are most often structured around the hero's or heroine's *quest*—this frequently turns out to be a quest for identity, although the hero or heroine usually does not realize that at first. The fate of a nation or a people is often dependent upon the success or failure of the quest, and the hero or heroine becomes a figure of adulation and may even be rewarded with a crown by the story's end. The central character acts decisively, is altruistic, and eventually becomes the savior of a people. The plot typically consists of a series of remarkable *adventures*—usually impediments that the central character must overcome in order to achieve the quest. Because of the seriousness of the themes—the necessity for good to overcome evil, the defense of an entire society, the search for the rightful ruler, and so on—humor is either absent or a decidedly secondary element in heroic fantasy. (Lloyd Alexander's *Prydain* cycle, based on Welsh legend, is a good example of heroic fantasy employing humorous elements, usually in the form of comic characters. However, the hero, if sympathetic, is always quite serious.) Most heroic fantasies do not shy away from tragedy, and the message is frequently that good is not accomplished without some significant sacrifice. Heroic fantasy owes a great deal to the traditional märchen or wonder tales of folk literature, from which are derived themes and plot structures, even characters and settings. If we understand the folktales, we are more likely to understand heroic fantasy.

SUPERNATURAL AND TIME FANTASY

Supernatural and time fantasy are among the most popular fantasy types, including ghost and witch stories, stories of mysterious and unexplained occurrences, and stories of time travel—explained or otherwise. All are set in the natural world, and the fantasy element is often seen as a disturbing situation that must be corrected before the story ends. Ghost stories are perennial favorites with many young people. Robert Bright's *Georgie and the Robbers* is a picture book about a shy ghost, and the cartoon figure of Casper the Friendly Ghost (now a popular film) has a long history. But older children often prefer more threatening ghosts; indeed, the more horrifying and gruesome the story is, the better some seem to like it. Many people have deep within them something of the ambulance chaser. Nevertheless, the most thrilling tales of the supernatural are not those that dramatize and glamorize the blood and horror, but those that leave something for our imaginations. Penelope Lively's *The Ghost of Thomas Kempe* is a popular and well-told example of a modern ghost story. Devoid of any grisly horror, Lively's novel explores the potential problems that a ghost from an earlier time might have in the modern world.

Related to the supernatural tales are those stories that involve playing tricks with time—a ghost, after all, is simply a human presence operating in a time other than that in which it lived. Philippa Pearce's *Tom's Midnight Garden* explores movement in and out of time, and deals sensitively and seriously with human relationships. In a similar vein are Lucy Boston's *Green Knowe* books and Alan Garner's *The Owl Service*, the latter of which is a somewhat sophisticated tale of the occult, drawing on mysterious ancient powers.

SCIENCE FICTION AND SPACE FANTASY

Mary Shelley's *Frankenstein* (1818) is usually credited with being the first true work of *science fiction*, followed by the works of Jules Verne (*Twenty Thousand Leagues Under the Sea* and *From Earth to the Moon Direct*), which achieved great popularity in the mid-nineteenth century. Today science fiction has a following among young readers who make up in enthusiasm what they may lack in actual numbers. Science fiction is speculative writing, usually focusing on life in the future, either on earth or on some other planet. The principal types of science fiction include stories about aliens from outer space, many of which include stories set in the present or near future (John Christopher's *When the Tripods Came*), stories about the future, often on other planets (Sylvia Engdahl's *Enchantress from the Stars*), and stories about space travel or time travel (Madeleine L'Engle's *A Wrinkle in Time*). Many variations on these patterns exist.

Much of science fiction is devoted to dramatizing the wonders of technology (although science fiction is not especially scientific). Science fiction, in fact, closely resembles heroic fantasy, with magic being replaced by technology, and the plots often unfold mighty struggles between the forces of good and evil, with the fate of civilization hanging in the balance. As one critic notes, "How different, after all, is a wizard with a magic wand from a scientist with a microminiaturized matter-transformer? The reader does not know how either gadget works" (Roberts 90).

There is typically little humor in science fiction because the science fiction writer often wants to create the illusion that the world depicted is one that might exist. We are therefore asked to take it seriously, and there is little room for flippancy or lightheartedness. (The exception may be science fiction written for the younger reader; these works are largely space travel adventures—Ruthven Todd's *Space Cat*—or perhaps robot stories—Lester Del Rey's *The Runaway Robot*.)

Some works that we categorize as science fiction may be better termed *space fantasy*. This is the term preferred by Sylvia Engdahl, whose *Enchantress from the Stars* and *The Far Side of Evil*, among other works, are set in the future on distant planets, but otherwise are little concerned with scientific or technological achievements. Engdahl's works, despite their futuristic worlds, are usually preferred by readers who are not science fiction buffs. Engdahl treats her futuristic setting as simply the framework through which she conveys her sense of the development of human civilization, socially and psychologically rather than scientifically and technologically.

There is, in fact, a strong didactic strain in science fiction, and many works deal with ethical problems we face as scientific and technological progress outpace our development as human beings. Consequently, the question as to whether technological discoveries will be used for humanity's benefit or its destruction frequently becomes a theme of science fiction. Madeleine L'Engle, best known for *A Wrinkle in Time*, addresses such issues in her science fiction.

SPECIAL CHARACTERISTICS OF FANTASY

Zilpha Snyder suggests that, regardless of the type, there are two things children demand from fantasy—that it contain no nonsense and that it contain no treachery (230). These, at first, may appear to be curious requirements, but they are quite important. Even though fantasy presents situations that we know to be impossible, we do expect them to be presented as if they *were* possible. Consequently, children insist that writers of fantasy establish certain rules that operate within the fantasy world itself and that the writers abide by those rules. Also, children insist that the fantasy not be unfairly taken away at the book's end (such as pretending that it never happened, that it was all a dream, and so on). Such a betrayal on the writer's part usually generates a groan from readers. After all, part of the readers' delight in fantasy is that of being completely absorbed into the fantasy, and, once having made that commitment, readers do not like to find out that it has all been a trick or an elaborate deception. For example, the end of the movie version of *The Wizard of Oz* implies that the entire adventure was just a dream, but Baum played no such trick on his readers. According to the original book, Dorothy *really* went to Oz and returned to Kansas. Baum wants us to believe in that magical land, and so do we want to believe.

ORIGINALITY

In addition to the general characteristics that we expect of all fiction, we expect good fantasy to meet some special requirements. Perhaps above all, we expect fantasy to be *original*. From a stylistic point of view, neither *The Wizard of Oz* nor *Peter Pan* is particularly well written, but the ideas in these works are so imaginative and so original that the stories remain with us throughout our lives. The characters of good fantasy—Alice, Mr. Toad of Toad Hall, Winnie-the-Pooh, the Scarecrow and the Tin Woodsman—remain indelibly marked in our minds, and we inevitably measure every new character against these mainstays.

BELIEVABILITY

Secondly, we expect good fantasy to be *believable*. This may sound contradictory, but, in fact, fantasy may have to seem more believable than a realistic work. Readers want to believe in the fantasy, and we often resent it when an incompetent writer includes something that we immediately recognize as silly. ("Silly" is, of course, a relative term. We tolerate certain behavior in a toy fantasy such as *Winnie-the-Pooh* that we would not tolerate in C. S. Lewis's heroic fantasy *The Lion, the Witch and the Wardrobe*. It is the writer who, in the creation of the fantasy, sets the limits, and those limits must not be overstepped.) A good writer achieves believability in fantasy by several means:

1. *The massing of detail* provides us with vivid descriptions of things seen and heard, and when we can visualize the scenes we are more apt to believe that the fantasy world does indeed exist. Whereas folktales are virtually devoid of physical description, fantasies are often lush with details and the writers make the fantasies believable by fleshing them out and giving them substance.

2. *Maintaining consistency* is essential in good fantasy. Rules are established for every secondary world—there is only one way to get into the fantasy world, drinking from a certain fountain bestows immortality, the villain can be killed only by a special sword, and so on. The writer must abide by whatever rules are established.

3. *Restraining the fantastic* establishes limits on a fantasy and sets boundaries that prevent it from slipping into sheer absurdity. A fantasy in which "anything goes" is really no fun. The wizards in Le Guin's *Earthsea* cycle possess magical powers, but those powers are made more believable because they have their limitations, and Le Guin, once creating those limitations, makes sure her characters do not exceed these bounds.

4. Finally, good fantasy is rooted in *reality* and in *human nature*. Even if the characters are not human or not of this world, the good fantasy writer realizes that readers are human and that if the readers are to identify with the characters and the situations, they must be, disguised or otherwise, human characters and situations. Mr. Toad of Toad Hall may look like a toad, but he acts like a human and has human weaknesses. Winnie-the-Pooh, toy though he is, is capable of human adventures and exhibits human responses to those adventures (despite his protest that he is only a bear of little brain). Most fantasy, despite its wondrous dress, is imbued with a strong sense of reality and a deep seriousness. The imaginary world captures us; the underlying reality of it all moves us.

THE REWARDS OF FANTASY

Fantasy holds many treasures for us, not the least of which is the stimulation of our imaginations. Fantasy writer Joan Aiken has summarized what she sees to be the practical value of a developed imagination. In addition to amusing us, Aiken points out, our imagination keeps us hopeful, enabling us to see the myriad possibilities that life offers. It helps us to solve problems by allowing us to see things from different and fresh perspectives. It helps us see the points of view of others, thus serving as a check to fanaticism. Aiken goes further to suggest that the imagination is a bit like a muscle—if we do not exercise it, it becomes weak and ineffectual. Reading is the best way of exercising our imaginations. Although Aiken does not suggest that reading fantasy is a better exercise of the imagination than reading realism or nonfiction, we can safely say that fantasy does require a bit *more* exercise. Fantasy demands more of the reader than does realistic fiction, for fantasy creates not only its own characters and plots, but also its own special laws with which we as readers must become acquainted.

Through the medium of fantasy, writers are able to explore complex ideas on a symbolic level that would be difficult to convey to young readers otherwise. Natalie Babbitt's *Tuck Everlasting* can cause us to think of the implications of immortality on earth, its advantages and disadvantages, in a way that would be impossible for a realistic story and tedious in nonfictional treatise. Fantasy is perfectly suited to the thoughtful exploration of philosophical issues at a level that can be understood and appreciated by the child reader. It raises questions and demands the exploration of uncharted realms of thought. And for those who are ready to accept the challenges of fantasy, the rewards can be manifold.

WORKS CITED

Aiken, Joan. "On Imagination." *The Horn Book* Nov./Dec. 1984: 735–741.

Roberts, Thomas J. "Science Fiction and the Adolescent." *Children's Literature: The Great Excluded* 2 (1973): 87–91.

Snyder, Zilpha Keatley. "Afterword." *Tom's Midnight Garden* by Philippa Pearce. New York: Dell, 1986.

RECOMMENDED READINGS

Alexander, Lloyd. "High Fantasy and Heroic Romance." *Horn Book Magazine* 47:6 (Dec. 1971): 577–584.

Attebery, Brian. *The Fantasy Tradition in American Literature: From Irving to Le Guin.* Bloomington: Indiana University Press, 1980.

Babbitt, Natalie. "Fantasy and the Classic Hero." *School Library Journal.* October 1987: 25–29.

Cameron, Eleanor. *The Green and Burning Tree.* Boston: Little, Brown, 1969.

Dickinson, Peter. "Fantasy: The Need for Realism." *Children's Literature in Education* 17:1 (1986): 39–51.

Egoff, Sheila. *Worlds Within: Children's Fantasy from the Middle Ages to Today.* Chicago: American Library Association, 1988.

Engdahl, Sylvia. "The Changing Role of Science Fiction in Children's Literature." *Horn Book Magazine* 47:5 (Oct. 1971): 449–455.

Hume, Kathryn. *Fantasy and Mimesis.* New York and London: Methuen, 1984.

Kuznets, Lois. *When Toys Come Alive: Narratives of Animations, Metamorphosis and Development.* New Haven, CT: Yale University Press, 1994.

Le Guin, Ursula. *The Language of the Night.* Ed. Susan Wood. New York: G. P. Putnam's Sons, 1979.

Lewis, C. S. "Three Ways of Writing for Children." *Horn Book Magazine* 39:5 (Oct. 1963): 459–469.

Marcus, Leonard S. "Picture Books Animals: How Natural a History?" *The Lion and the Unicorn* 7/8 (1983/84): 127–139.

Raynor, Mary. "Some Thoughts on Animals in Children's Books" *Signal* 29 (May 1979): 81–87.

Sale, Roger. *Fairy Tales and After: From Snow White to E. B. White*. Cambridge, MA: Harvard University Press, 1978.

Singer, Jerome. "Fantasy: The Foundation of Serenity." *Psychology Today* July 1976: 33–37.

Tolkien, J. R. R. *Tree and Leaf*. Boston: Houghton Mifflin, 1965.

Waggoner, Diana. *The Hills of Faraway: A Guide to Fantasy*. New York: Atheneum, 1978.

Wood, Michael. "Coffee Break for Sisyphus: The Point of Science Fiction." *New York Review of Books* 2 October 1975: 3–4, 6–7.

SELECTED BIBLIOGRAPHY
OF FANTASY FICTION

ANIMAL FANTASIES FOR YOUNGER READERS (GRADES 2–5)

Banks, Lynn Reid. *The Magic Hare*. New York: Morrow, 1993.

Bond, Michael. *A Bear Called Paddington*. Boston: Houghton Mifflin, 1960.

———. *Paddington at Large*. Boston: Houghton Mifflin, 1963.

———. *The Tales of Olga da Polga*. New York: Penguin, 1971.

Cleary, Beverly. *Runaway Ralph*. New York: Morrow, 1970.

Ets, Marie Hall. *Mister Penny*. New York: Viking, 1935.

King-Smith, Dick. *Ace: The Very Important Pig*. New York: Crown, 1990.

———. *Babe, the Gallant Pig*. New York: Random House, 1983.

Lawson, Robert. *Ben and Me*. Boston: Little, Brown, 1939.

———. *Rabbit Hill*. New York: Viking, 1944.

———. *The Tough Winter*. New York: Viking, 1970.

Marshall, James. *Rats on the Roof and Other Stories*. New York: Dial, 1991.

Rey, Hans A. *Curious George*. Boston: Houghton Mifflin, 1941.

Selden, George. *The Cricket in Times Square*. Illus. Garth Williams. New York: Farrar, Straus & Giroux, 1960.

Sharp, Margery. *Miss Bianca*. Boston: Little, Brown, 1962.

———. *The Rescuers*. Boston: Little, Brown, 1959.

Steig, William. *Abel's Island*. New York: Farrar, Straus & Giroux, 1976.

———. *Dominic*. New York: Farrar, Straus & Giroux, 1972.

Titus, Eve. *Basil in Mexico*. Illus. Paul Galdone. New York: McGraw-Hill, 1976.

White, E. B. *Charlotte's Web*. New York: Harper, 1952.

———. *Stuart Little*. New York: Harper, 1945.

———. *The Trumpet of the Swan*. New York: Harper, 1970.

ANIMAL FANTASIES FOR OLDER
READERS (GRADES 6 AND UP)

Adams, Richard. *Watership Down*. New York: Macmillan, 1974.

Grahame, Kenneth. *The Wind in the Willows* (1908). Several modern editions.

Jacques, Brian. *Mareil of Redwall*. New York: Philomel, 1992.

———. *Mattimeo*. New York: Philomel, 1990.

———. *Mossflower*. New York: Philomel, 1988.

———. *Redwall*. New York: Philomel, 1987.

Jarrell, Randall. *The Animal Family*. Illus. Maurice Sendak. New York: Pantheon, 1965.
———. *The Bat-Poet*. New York: Macmillan, 1964.
Lisle, Janet Taylor. *Forest*. New York: Jackson, 1993.
O'Brien, Robert. *Mrs. Frisby and the Rats of NIMH*. New York: Atheneum, 1971.

TOY FANTASIES FOR YOUNGER READERS (GRADES 2–5)

Bailey, Caroline Sherwin. *Miss Hickory*. New York: Viking, 1968.
Collodi, Carlo [pseud. for Carlo Lorenzini]. *The Adventures of Pinocchio* (1883). Several modern editions.
Field, Rachel. *Hitty, Her First Hundred Years*. New York: Macmillan, 1929.
Godden, Rumer. *The Dolls' House*. New York: Viking, 1962.
———. *Impunity Jane*. New York: Viking, 1964.
Lionni, Leo. *Alexander and the Wind-Up Mouse*. New York: Pantheon, 1969.
Milne, A. A. *The House at Pooh Corner* (1928). Illus. Ernest Shepard. New York: Dutton, 1961.
———. *Winnie-the-Pooh* (1926). Illus. Ernest Shepard. New York: Dutton, 1961.
Nicholson, Margery. *The Velveteen Rabbit*. Illus. Michael Hague. New York: Holt, Rinehart & Winston, 1983.

TOY FANTASIES FOR OLDER READERS (GRADES 6 AND UP)

Banks, Lynn Reid. *The Indian in the Cupboard*. New York: Doubleday, 1981.
———. *The Return of the Indian*. New York: Doubleday, 1986.
———. *The Secret of the Indian*. New York: Doubleday, 1989.
Clarke, Pauline. *The Return of the Twelves*. New York: Coward-McCann, 1964. (British title: *The Twelve and the Genii*)
Griffith, Helen V. *Caitlin's Holiday*. New York: Greenwillow, 1990.
Hoban, Russell. *The Mouse and His Child*. New York: Harper, 1967.
Kennedy, Richard. *Amy's Eyes*. New York: Harper, 1985.
Winthrop, Elizabeth. *The Castle in the Attic*. New York: Holiday, 1985.

FANTASY OF THE EXTRAORDINARY: CHARACTERS AND SITUATIONS—BOOKS FOR YOUNGER READERS (GRADES 2–5)

Allard, Harry. *The Stupids Die*. Illus. James Marshall. Boston: Houghton Mifflin, 1981.
———. *The Stupids Step Out*. Illus. James Marshall. Boston: Houghton Mifflin, 1974.
Atwater, Richard, and Florence Atwater. *Mr. Popper's Penguins*. Illus. Robert Lawson. Boston: Little, Brown, 1938.
Dahl, Roald. *Charlie and the Chocolate Factory*. New York: Knopf, 1964.
———. *James and the Giant Peach*. New York: Knopf, 1961.
———. *Matilda*. New York: Viking, 1988.
DuBois, William Pene. *Twenty-One Balloons*. New York: Viking, 1947.
Kastner, Erich. *The Little Man*. Trans. James Kirkup. Illus. Rick Schreiter. New York: Knopf, 1966.
Lindgren, Astrid. *Pippi Longstocking*. New York: Viking, 1950.
Loftis, Hugh. *The Adventures of Dr. Dolittle*. Philadelphia: Lippincott, 1920.
Travers, P. L. *Mary Poppins*. New York: Harcourt, 1934.

FANTASY OF THE EXTRAORDINARY: CHARACTERS AND SITUATIONS—BOOKS FOR OLDER READERS (GRADES 6 AND UP)

Farmer, Penelope. *The Summer Birds*. New York: Harcourt, 1962.
Kipling, Rudyard. *Puck of Pook's Hill* (1906). Various modern editions.
Merrill, Jean. *The Pushcart War*. Reading, MA: Scott/Addison, 1964.
Rodgers, Mary. *Freaky Friday*. New York: Harper, 1972.
———. *Summer Switch*. New York: Harper, 1982.

ENCHANTED JOURNEYS AND IMAGINARY WORLDS—BOOKS FOR YOUNGER READERS (GRADES 2–5)

Babbitt, Natalie. *Kneeknock Rise*. New York: Farrar, Straus & Giroux, 1970.
———. *The Search for Delicious*. New York: Farrar, Straus & Giroux, 1969.
Barrie, Sir James. *Peter Pan*. New York: Scribner's, 1950.
Baum, L. Frank. *The Wonderful Wizard of Oz* (1900). Several modern editions.
Carroll, Lewis. *Alice's Adventures in Wonderland*. Illus. John Tenniel. London: Macmillan, 1984.
Fleischman, Sid. *The Midnight Horse*. New York: Morrow, 1990.
Norton, Mary. *The Borrowers*. New York: Harcourt, 1953.
———. *The Borrowers Afield*. New York: Harcourt, 1955.

ENCHANTED JOURNEYS AND IMAGINARY WORLDS—BOOKS FOR OLDER READERS (GRADES 6 AND UP)

Aiken, Joan. *Black Hearts in Battersea*. New York: Doubleday, 1964.
———. *The Wolves of Willoughby Chase*. New York: Doubleday, 1963.
Janssen, Tove. *Comet in Moominland* (1961). Trans. Elizabeth Portch. New York: Farrar, Straus & Giroux, 1990.
———. *Finn Family Moomintroll* (1948). Trans. Elizabeth Portch. New York: Farrar, Straus & Giroux, 1989.
———. *Moominsummer Madness* (1964). Trans. Thomas Warburton. New York: Farrar, Straus & Giroux, 1991.
Juster, Norton. *The Phantom Tollbooth*. New York: Random House, 1961.
Kendall, Carol. *The Gammage Cup*. New York: Harcourt, 1959.
Lagerlof, Selma. *The Wonderful Adventures of Nils* (1906). Various modern editions.
McKinley, Robin. *A Knot in the Grain and Other Stories*. New York: Greenwillow, 1994.
Pedley, Ethel C. *Dot and the Kangaroo*. London: Burleigh, 1899.
Snyder, Zilpha Keatley. *Song of the Gargoyle*. New York: Delacorte, 1991.
Steele, Mary Q. *Journey Outside*. New York: Viking, 1969.
Townsend, John Rowe. *The Fortunate Isles*. New York: Lippincott, 1989.
Wein, Elizabeth E. *The Winter Prince*. New York: Atheneum, 1993.

HEROIC FANTASIES FOR OLDER
READERS (GRADES 6 AND UP)

Alexander, Lloyd. "The Prydain Chronicles": *The Book of Three* (1964); *The Black Cauldron* (1965); *The Castle of Llyr* (1965); *Taran Wanderer* (1967); *The High King* (1968); New York: Holt.

Cooper, Susan. "The Dark Is Rising" series: *Over Sea, Under Stone* (1966); *The Dark Is Rising* (1973); *Greenwitch* (1974); *The Grey King* (1975); New York: Atheneum.

Doyle, Debra, and James D. Macdonald. *Knight's Wyrd*. New York: Harcourt, 1992.

Le Guin, Ursula. "The Earthsea Cycle" series: *A Wizard of Earthsea* (1968); *The Tombs of Atuan* (1971); *The Farthest Shore* (1972); *Tehanu: The Last Book of Earthsea* (1990); New York: Atheneum.

Lewis, C. S. "The Narnia Chronicles": *The Lion, the Witch and the Wardrobe* (1950); *Prince Caspian, The Return to Narnia* (1951); *The Voyage of the "Dawn Treader"* (1952); *The Silver Chair* (1953); *The Horse and His Boy* (1954); *The Magician's Nephew* (1954); *The Last Battle* (1956); New York: Macmillan.

McCaffrey, Anne. *Dragondrums*. New York: Atheneum, 1979.

———. *Dragonsinger*. New York: Atheneum, 1977.

———. *Dragonsong*. New York: Atheneum, 1976.

McKinley, Robin. *The Hero and the Crown*. New York: Greenwillow, 1985.

Mayne, William. *Antar and the Eagles*. New York: Delacorte, 1990.

Tolkien, J. R. R. *The Hobbit*. Boston: Houghton Mifflin, 1938. (Followed by the *Lord of the Rings* trilogy.)

Yolen, Jane. *Dragon's Blood*. New York: Delacorte, 1982.

SUPERNATURAL AND TIME FANTASIES
FOR YOUNGER READERS (GRADES 2–5)

Aiken, Joan. *A Foot in the Grave*. New York: Viking, 1992.

Babbitt, Natalie. *Tuck Everlasting*. New York: Farrar, Straus & Giroux, 1975.

Norton, Mary. *Bed-Knob and Broomstick*. Illus. Erik Blegvad. New York: Harcourt, 1957.

Yolen, Jane, and Martin H. Greenberg, eds. *Things That Go Bump in the Night: A Collection of Original Stories*. New York: Harper, 1989.

SUPERNATURAL AND TIME FANTASIES
FOR OLDER READERS (GRADES 6 AND UP)

Boston, Lucy. *The Children of Greene Knowe*. New York: Harcourt, 1964.

Cameron, Eleanor. *The Court of the Stone Children*. New York: Dutton, 1973.

Cobalt, Martin [pseud. for William Mayne]. *Pool of Swallows*. New York: Nelson, 1974.

Dunlop, Eileen. *Elizabeth, Elizabeth*. New York: Holt, 1977.

———. *The Valley of Deer*. New York: Holiday, 1989.

Farmer, Penelope. *A Castle of Bone*. New York: Philomel, 1982.

———. *Charlotte Sometimes*. New York: Harcourt, 1969.

Garfield, Leon. *Mister Corbett's Ghost*. New York: Pantheon, 1968.

———. *The Restless Ghost: Three Stories*. New York: Pantheon, 1969.

Garner, Alan. *The Owl Service*. New York: Walck, 1968.

Hamilton, Virginia. *Sweet Whispers, Brother Rush*. New York: Philomel, 1982.

Hunter, Mollie. *The Haunted Mountain*. New York: Harper, 1972.

Lindbergh, Anne. *Nick of Time*. Boston: Little, Brown, 1994.

Lively, Penelope. *The Ghost of Thomas Kempe*. Illus. Antony Maitland. New York: Dutton, 1973.

Lunn, Janet. *The Root Cellar*. New York: Scribner's, 1983.

Mayne, William. *Earthfasts*. New York: Dutton, 1967.

———. *A Game of Dark*. New York: Dutton, 1971.

Morgan, Helen. *The Witch Doll*. New York: Viking, 1992.

Nesbit, E. *The Enchanted Castle*. Harmondsworth, UK: Penguin, 1979.

Pearce, Philippa. *Tom's Midnight Garden*. New York: Dell, 1986.

Pearson, Kit. *A Handful of Time*. New York: Viking, 1988.

Price, Susan. *Ghost Song*. New York: Farrar, Straus & Giroux, 1992.

Schmidt, Annie M. G. *Minnie*. New York: Milkweed, 1994.

Walsh, Jill Paton. *A Chance Child*. New York: Farrar, Straus & Giroux, 1978.

Westall, Robert. *The Devil on the Road*. New York: Greenwillow, 1979.

Woodruff, Elvira. *The Magnificent Mummy Maker*. New York: Scholastic, 1994.

SCIENCE FICTION AND SPACE FANTASY FOR YOUNGER READERS (GRADES 2–5)

Cameron, Eleanor. *Wonderful Flight to the Mushroom Planet*. Illus. Robert Henneberger. Boston: Little, Brown, 1954.

Del Rey, Lester. *The Runaway Robot*. Philadelphia: Westminster, 1965.

Todd, Ruthven. *Space Cat*. Illus. Paul Galdone. New York: Scribner's, 1952.

SCIENCE FICTION AND SPACE FANTASY FOR OLDER READERS (GRADES 6 AND UP)

Clarke, Arthur C. *Dolphin Island*. New York: Holt, 1963.

Christopher, John. *Beyond the Burning Lands*. New York: Macmillan, 1971.

———. *When the Tripods Came*. New York: Dutton, 1988.

———. *The White Mountains*. New York: Macmillan, 1967.

Cresswell, Helen. *The Watchers: A Mystery of Alton Towers*. New York: Macmillan, 1994.

Dickinson, Peter. *Eva*. New York: Delacorte, 1989.

Engdahl, Sylvia. *Enchantress from the Stars*. New York: Macmillan, 1970.

———. *The Far Side of Evil*. New York: Macmillan, 1971.

Hamilton, Virginia. *Justice and Her Brothers*. New York: Greenwillow, 1978.

Heinlein, Robert. *Have Space Suit—Will Travel*. New York: Scribner's, 1958.

Lawrence, Louise. *Moonwind*. New York: Harper, 1986.

L'Engle, Madeleine. *A Wrinkle in Time*. New York: Farrar, Straus & Giroux, 1962.

Norton, Andre. *Moon of Three Rings*. New York: Viking, 1966.

Oppel, Kenneth. *Dead Water Zone*. New York: Joy Street, 1993.

Rubenstein, Gillian. *Beyond the Labyrinth*. New York: Watts, 1990.

Sleator, William. *Strange Attractors*. New York: Dutton, 1989.

Verne, Jules. *Twenty Thousand Leagues Under the Sea* (1870). New York: Penguin, 1987.

Wells, H. G. *The Time Machine*. New York: Bantam, 1982.

———. *War of the Worlds*. New York: Putnam, 1978.

Chapter 11

CONTEMPORARY AND HISTORICAL REALISM

CONTEMPORARY REALISM

Realistic fiction is set in the world as we know it, governed by the laws of the natural world as we understand them, and intended to provide a believable verisimilitude to life as we experience it. This is in contrast to fantasy, which ignores the natural laws and establishes its own set of rules. In this chapter, we will discuss both contemporary and historical realism—contemporary being those works set in the present (by this we usually mean the writer's present, naturally realizing that in time every writer's present will become the reader's past), and historical realism being those works deliberately set in a past that must be recreated for the reader. Although by definition realistic fiction is a story that is *possible*, it need not always be especially *probable*. Realistic fiction may contain very ordinary or quite exaggerated characters and mundane or preposterous plots, but it does not violate the essential rules of nature. Reality is its touchstone.

TYPES OF CONTEMPORARY REALISM

Equally as diverse as fantasy, realism, whether it be in the form of a novel or a short story, can address every imaginable subject and take an infinite number of approaches. In an effort to suggest the range of contemporary realism, we will classify realistic stories into broad thematic groups—adventure and survival stories, domestic fiction, social realism, psychological realism, and animal stories. The lines are not easily drawn, however, and we often find a work that, because of the writer's inventiveness and ingenuity, refuses to fit neatly into a single category. And there are an increasing number of books that no longer fit the old definition of fantasy and realism (Virginia Hamilton's *Sweet Whispers, Brother Rush* comes to mind). The following divisions constitute the mere convenience of a classification. Most of the works discussed in this chapter are novels, but in recent years the contemporary realistic short story has appeared more prominently—Marion Dane Bauer and Martha Brooks have both produced fine short story collections for young people. Short stories rely on a compressed style, a sharply focused theme, skilfully drawn characters, and usually evocative imagery. The following classification can apply to short stories as well as novels.

Adventure Stories.   Perhaps the most popular types of realistic fiction among young readers today are adventure stories of one sort or another. The very earliest novels were adventure stories, going back to Miguel de Cervantes' *Don Quixote* (1605), Daniel Defoe's *Robinson Crusoe* (1719), and Jonathan Swift's *Gulliver's Travels* (1726) (adult works, all of which have proven popular in one form or another among children). The adventure story is characterized by exciting, fast-moving plots; unusual, often bizarre, characters; and frequently exotic settings. The characters are often sharply defined, with strong and daring heroes and dastardly villains. In many ways, the adventure story occupies a place in that misty territory between the boundaries of fantasy and realism, for it is often the tale of the improbable (whereas fantasy is the tale of the impossible and pure realism the tale of the possible).

The nineteenth century was rife with hack writers who cranked out formulaic adventure books primarily for boys. But some very fine stories were written as well, with thoughtful themes and well-drawn characters, including the already-mentioned *Treasure Island* by Robert Louis Stevenson and *Huckleberry Finn* and *Tom Sawyer* by Mark Twain, which are classic adventure stories. We can identify some specific variations on adventure stories as well.

Survival Stories.   Among the best of the modern adventure stories are the *survival stories*, adventures that focus on an individual or individuals pitted against the forces of nature, which the protagonist must either outwit or (more likely) unite with in order to survive. *Robinson Crusoe* is often regarded as the granddaddy of the survival story, and the Swiss writer Johann David Wyss modeled *The Swiss Family Robinson* (1812) on Defoe's work. But whereas Defoe and Wyss have their heroes taming the wild tropical paradise where they are stranded and carving out lives of considerable comfort, modern versions of the survival story depict their heroes or heroines humbled before the forces of nature. Rather than taming the wild and forcing the environment to conform to human whims, modern-day protagonists in survival stories adapt their lifestyles to their surroundings. These heroes and heroines learn to live in harmony with the natural world and often come to respect it above the civilizing forces of humanity. Some even go so far as to adopt the ways of the wild animals inhabiting their environment—such as Karana in Scott O'Dell's *Island of the Blue Dolphins* (set on an island off the California coast) and Julie in Jean Craighead George's *Julie of the Wolves* (set in the arctic wilds). Theodore Taylor's *The Cay* and Harry Mazer's *Snowbound* and *The Island Keeper* are other examples of this popular form of fiction, with Mazer's works representing a combination of the adventure story with the problem novel. Felice Holman's *Slake's Limbo* provides a new twist to the survival story, with the hero surviving in the grim world of the New York City subway system.

Mystery or Detective Stories.   As with the adventure and survival stories, the mystery and detective stories are forms of romance, escapist fiction creating a world somehow more exciting, more dangerous, and more beautiful than we imagine our own to be. The *mystery*, first popularized in the early nineteenth century by Edgar Allan Poe and later by Arthur Conan Doyle, the creator of Sherlock Holmes, has long been a favorite of young readers. Series with detectives such as Nancy Drew, the Hardy Boys, the Bobbsey Twins, and Donald Sobol's Encyclopedia Brown are enormously popular. The mystery always involves the solving of a puzzle—typically, but in children's stories not necessarily, a crime—and, consequently, depends heavily upon plot intricacy and clever twists. The success of a mystery depends upon an ingenious crime, the clever planting of clues, and an appealing detective. The puzzle must not be too easily solved or the reader will lose interest. And the solution to the puzzle must seem logical once all the pieces are put together or the reader will feel deceived. The mystery writer must keep a delicate balance, knowing just how much to reveal and when.

Among the fine mysteries for young readers is E. L. Konigsburg's *From the Mixed-Up Files of Mrs. Basil E. Frankweiler*, which recounts the exploits of a young brother and sister detective as they follow clues to the unraveling of a mystery, largely set in the Metropolitan Museum of Art. Ellen Raskin's *The Westing Game* likewise depicts a young detective searching out the word clues of a cleverly devised mystery, containing numerous surprising twists. Virginia Hamilton's *The House of Dies Drear* may be regarded as a mystery of sorts, weaving suspense into a tale of a boy examining his African-American heritage. Hamilton has the uncanny ability to take seemingly ordinary people and places and weave an almost magical story. Her characters are so richly developed that we come to believe in even the most bizarre of them.

We should note that although they are often lumped together, mysteries, spy thrillers, and crime or police procedural stories are not all the same, and each attracts its own audience. The spy thriller reached its peak of popularity with Ian Fleming's 007 series; however, since the decline of the West's great nemesis, the Soviet Union, the spy novel has lost some of its appeal. The crime novel is one in which the culprit or culprits are known from the beginning—they are usually very unsavory characters—and our interest is in how the authorities trap them. Both the spy thriller and the crime novel depend a great deal on such techniques as high speed chase scenes and shootouts and other action-packed devices—and most are aimed at adult or young adult audiences.

Humorous Adventures.   Our ability to laugh may be largely responsible for our successful survival in today's complex society. Children love to laugh, and most elementary school children will choose a humorous book over any other type. With a few notable exceptions, most children's books include humor, but some are built entirely on humorous situations, such as Robert McCloskey's *Homer Price* or Beverly Cleary's *Ramona* series or Peggy Parish's *Amelia Bedelia* series or the elaborate tall tales of Sid Fleischman. We find several different types of humor in children's realism:

1. *The humor of character* revolves around an eccentric personality, such as the irrepressible "Grand Rascal," Uncle Will, in Sid Fleischman's *Chancy and the Grand Rascal;*
2. *The humor of situation* deals with surprising, awkward, or ridiculous situations, such as when the doughnut machine goes wild in *Homer Price*;
3. *The humor of language* depends upon misunderstandings, plays on words, or verbal irony, such as that found in the *Amelia Bedelia* books when Amelia, a maid, takes literally everything her employers ask her to do (imagine what happens when she is asked to "dress the turkey" or "draw the curtains").

In one way or another, most of the adventure stories we have been describing are examples of escapist literature, books to take the readers away from the ordinary, the everyday, to places where exciting things happen. These books provide a respite from which most readers return refreshed, even exhilarated, in which case a temporary escape is a good thing.

Domestic Realism.   While nineteenth-century boys were reading adventure stories, girls enjoyed family stories or domestic realism. These stories share features of the eighteenth-century domestic romance, which focused on the everyday manners, customs, and mores of society. It is not surprising that young readers should be interested in reading stories about home and family, since those are the principal focus of their childhood experiences. Unlike the mystery or adventure story with its dramatic plot sequence, domestic fiction more commonly uses an episodic plot. This narrative structure is especially well suited to the family story since it is often built around the daily details and activities, the squabblings, the schemings, the reconciliations, in which families are normally engaged.

The British author Charlotte Yonge is usually credited with writing the first domestic novel for young people: *The Daisy Chain* (1862). But the American writers were the ones who ultimately became most comfortable with this type, beginning with Louisa May Alcott's *Little Women* (1867). Alcott, drawing on her own girlhood experiences, presents us with a realistic portrayal of mid-nineteenth-century American family life with all its ups and downs. For Alcott, the family is a constant source of strength and stability, the parents are idealized role models, and the troubles of the outside world are kept at bay by the family's industry and good humor.

Alcott's successors (and there were many) include Margaret Sidney, author of the once enormously popular *The Five Little Peppers and How They Grew*. Unlike Alcott, Sidney was not able to restrain the sentimental, and her story of the destitute, but virtuous, Pepper family is too saccharine for most modern readers. The children are all self-sacrificing and dutiful, always doing more than their fair share for the family's well-being. The mother seems to draw strength from her poverty, and no one ever complains. Their patience and goodness are rewarded in the end with the almost miraculous bestowal of good fortune. In response to the public demand of that time, Sidney wrote numerous sequels.

Frances Hodgson Burnett's *The Secret Garden* is a refreshing change from the overly sweet domestic romance, for her heroine, Mary Lennox, is initially a rather unpleasant orphan placed in an even more unpleasant home—that of her wealthy, but very mysterious, uncle. It is the story of Mary's growth into a loving, caring human being, symbolized by the rejuvenation, at Mary's hands, of a neglected garden. *The Secret Garden* contains mystery and suspense, as well as engaging characters, making it one of the most enduring of childhood stories, and it is also difficult to pigeonhole, for although it celebrates the virtues of family life, it certainly is not a domestic tale in any traditional sense.

The Canadian writer Lucy Maud Montgomery created an equally appealing character in *Anne of Green Gables* and its sequels, set on Prince Edward Island in the first decade of the twentieth century. Anne is an orphaned child who is placed in a foster home with an elderly man and his sister who originally wanted a boy. The book combines sensitively drawn characters and gentle humor, while avoiding sentimentality. In recent years, Montgomery's stories have found new life in the form of a popular televison series produced by Disney, *Avonlea*, based loosely on characters created by Montgomery and using Montgomery's romantic Prince Edward Island setting.

Two notable writers, Eleanor Estes (of the *Moffat* series) and Elizabeth Enright (of the *Melendy* series), produced successful domestic fiction in the 1930s and 1940s. Both take a romantic view of the family and present us with households that, even on the brink of poverty, are filled with warmth and caring. Estes' works are set in the era of World War I, whereas Enright's stories take place a generation later in the 1940s.

In the 1950s and 1960s, writers such as Beverly Cleary (*Ramona the Pest* and *Ramona the Brave*, among others) and Madeleine L'Engle (*Meet the Austins* and its sequels) continued the tradition of Estes and Enright, depicting stable family units knit together with love. But with the dramatic change in the family structure in the latter half of the twentieth century, the romantic family scenes described by Estes, Enright, Cleary, and L'Engle are becoming rare in literature—particularly in books for older readers. Today we more commonly find, in place of the happy family unit once exemplified by such television programs as *Father Knows Best*, *The Donna Reed Show*, and *Leave It to Beaver*, stories of emotionally charged situations, broken homes, and nontraditional domestic arrangements. Cleary herself recognized and adapted to this transformation with her Newbery Award–winning book, *Dear Mr. Henshaw*, about a young boy coping with his parents' divorce. Bill and Vera Cleaver's *Where the Lilies Bloom* describes the trials of an Appalachian family of poor orphaned children who survive and are held together chiefly through the valiant efforts of the thirteen-year-old middle sister. Virginia Hamilton's *M. C. Higgins, the Great*, also about a mountain family—this one African-American—likewise addresses the issues of family survival and family pride in the face of an increasingly insensitive technological world.

Alternative families—single parents, gay parents, foster parents, and so on—are becoming more and more common in our society. (Over half of all marriages end in divorce, for example.) Consequently, it is important that children understand that families need not conform to historical norms to be happy or successful. Norma Klein's *Mom, the Wolfman and Me*, about an unwed mother and her daughter, was in the vanguard of stories about such alternative lifestyles. As can be seen, the trend of the domestic novel in the twentieth century has been toward greater realism and less sentimentality. This change has been inevitably necessitated by the changing nature of the family—a perfect example of the response of art to life.

Social Realism.   *Social realism* focuses on societal problems—poverty, crime, education, working conditions, corruption—and how those problems affect the characters in the novel. It could be argued that Horatio Alger, Jr., the nineteenth-century writer of boy's success stories, was a pioneer in writing social realism for young people, with his stories of children growing up in the poverty of America's big cities. His heroes generally succeed in gaining respectability (which is what they always wanted) largely because they are morally upright individuals—and not because they necessarily work harder than anybody else.

However, social realism for young people has really come into its own in the latter half of the twentieth century, which has produced many decidedly unromantic works openly examining the important social issues facing the world. Common subjects found in stories of social realism include racial struggles, the effects of poverty, urban crime, problems of the aged and the disabled, and the effects of war. Bill and Vera Cleaver's *Where the Lilies Bloom* deals with the plight of the rural poor and combines features of the family story and social realism. Some novels dealing with social issues take on the appearance of survival fiction—Holman's *Slake's Limbo* is an excellent example. In an age when technology threatens the individual's sense of identity and, at times, even the nature of society and civilization as we know it, we may well feel that growing up in a city slum or an Appalachian hovel is as much a challenge as being abandoned on a desert island or in the frozen Arctic reaches.

Typically, the novels of social realism offer hope amid the struggle, although the message is usually that, if hardship is to be overcome, it will be through perseverance and determination and not through some happy accident. S. E. Hinton's *The Outsiders*, published in 1967, is about the plight of inner-city youth plagued by poverty and lack of guidance. It was one of the books heralding what has come to be called the *new realism*. The new realism is characterized by frankness, absence of sentimentality, and, in some cases, a diminishing of hope. Robert Cormier's novels (including *I Am the Cheese, The Chocolate War, Beyond the Chocolate War, Bumblebees Fly Anyway*, and others) take a much bleaker look at society than most books for young people. In his works, adults and children alike are often depicted in the worst possible light—self-serving, vicious, unscrupulous, even downright evil. Society as Cormier paints it takes on an Orwellian flavor—Big Brother is watching every move, spies lurk around every corner and even infiltrate the sanctity of the home. Adults criticize Cormier's unhappy—even grimly depressing—endings but he has remained consistently popular with adolescents, proving once again that adults have underestimated the capacity of the young to deal with serious issues.

Our growing social awareness has brought to the forefront the issues of people with special needs. We now see stories about children with emotional, physical, and intellectual disabilities. In many of these books, the theme is the need for society's increased awareness of and deeper sensitivity for the individuals with special needs. Books are available on a variety of special needs, from learning disabilities such as dyslexia (Rose Blue's *Me and Einstein*) to physical disabilities such as immobility (Carolyn Meyer's *Killing the Kudu*) to emotional problems (James Bennett's *I Can Hear the Mourning Dove*). Another issue to which children should be made sensitive is that of aging. Many see it in their grandparents and older relatives and friends, but our society has a habit of removing the elderly from sight, putting them away in nursing homes, perhaps because they remind us all of our own mortality. Society would be far better off if our children had a greater understanding of the aging process and a deeper sense of commitment to our aging population.

Psychological Realism. *Psychological realism* focuses on the individual's emotional reaction and adjustment to life's experiences. Common subjects found in the stories of psychological realism include adjusting to friendships, coming to terms with sexuality, accepting death, and facing personal crises that inevitably accompany growing up. In many respects, virtually all children's books are about growing up and maturing, from picture books such as Bernard Waber's *Ira Sleeps Over* to the most sophisticated of young adult novels. But in some stories, the chief focus is on the personal development of the central character—it may be emotional development, social adjustment, sexual maturity, and so on. Growing up is not easy, and most of us take directions poorly; we must learn through our own experiences.

As has been mentioned before, few subjects are any longer taboo in books for young readers—and that is as it should be. It is far better for children and young adults to learn about a delicate or difficult subject at the hands of an intelligent and sensitive writer rather than on the back streets from ill-informed friends. Judy Blume became a sensation with her problem novels on various issues of concern to emerging adolescents. Her *Are You There, God? It's Me, Margaret* focuses in part on a girl's coming to terms with menstruation and the psychological confusion surrounding it. *Tiger Eyes*, also by Blume, is a fine story about a young girl adjusting to the tragic murder of her father, which took place just as she herself was coming into sexual maturity.

The problem novel, an invention of the 1960s and persisting today, has been extremely popular with many adolescents, who readily identify with the characters, their feelings and predicaments. Problem novels have been used as part of *bibliotherapy*, a process by which young people are assisted in coping with personal problems through directed reading, and some professionals maintain that bibliotherapy can be an effective means of coping. On the other hand, other writers and critics have held that problem novels themselves often encourage a self-indulgence that only makes matters worse (see, especially, Nodelman 1981). Teenagers, according to this theory, read only about other teenagers just like themselves who suffer the same traumas as they do, and this results in an inflated view of their problems. In other words, rather than giving them a fresh outlook on the problems, the books allow them to wallow in self-pity that eventually narrows instead of widens their world. Of course, it should be pointed out that teenagers often have an inflated view of their own tribulations—the books they read do not create that dilemma. However, truly effective bibliotherapy is that which expands the reader's experiences, broadens the reader's mind, and thus multiplies the reader's possible responses to problems. At its worst, the problem novel becomes formulaic, predictable, and sometimes sensationalized, often implying that problems have simple solutions. At its best, the problem novel explores significant psychological issues with sensitivity, and it gives us vivid characters with depth of emotion.

But not all stories of psychological adjustment are formula problem novels. Many are finely crafted works with keen psychological insights, multifaceted characters, and compelling plots. Writers such as Irene Hunt (in *Up a Road Slowly*), Katherine Paterson (in *The Great Gilly Hopkins* and *Bridge to Terabithia*), and Zibby Oneal (in *The Language of Goldfish* and *In Summer's Light*) sensitively explore the personal difficulties facing young people in the process of maturing, but more importantly, there is the implicit faith in the resilience and ultimate good sense of young people.

Realistic Animal Stories.   Realistic animal stories first appeared in the late nineteenth and early twentieth centuries (most earlier animal stories were fantasies), and they emerged from North America. The Canadians Ernest Thompson Seton (*Wild Animals I Have Known*) and Charles G. D. Roberts (*Red Fox*) wrote stories depicting animals realistically, but giving them personalities. Jack London's popular *White Fang* and *Call of the Wild* soon followed. The animals in these stories live as animals, behave as animals, and are not empowered with human speech (although some may argue they are given human emotions).

Of course, young readers have always had soft spots for animals of all kinds, and animal stories have proved to be among the most enduring of modern children's literature. They are frequently inspiration for movies. Often these books focus on the relationship between an animal and a youthful human companion, such as in Marjorie Kinnan Rawlings's *The Yearling*, or Mary O'Hara's *My Friend Flicka* and Eric Knight's *Lassie Come Home*. One of the most loved of all is Wilson Rawls's *Where the Red Fern Grows*, about two hunting dogs and their boy-master. Farley Mowat's comical true-life adventure, *Owls in the Family*, is found in the nonfiction section of the library, since it is autobiographical, and it is an excellent example of the sometimes fine line that exists between fiction and reality.

Some animal stories focus on the animal and not on the animal-human relationship. An early Newbery Award–winner, Dhan Gopal Mukerji's *Gay-Neck, the Story of a Pigeon*, keeps its focus on the central animal character. Marguerite Henry's books about horses, *Misty of Chincoteague*, *King of the Wind*, and others, remain among the best animal stories of this sort. Also popular is Sheila Burnford's *The Incredible Journey*, in which a cat and two dogs undertake a hazardous trip across the Canadian wilderness. Some readers feel that Burnford oversteps the limits of credibility, with the animals assuming too much of human nature to be totally believable as animals. This criticism suggests one of the difficulties of writing realistic animal fiction. But for many readers, making the animal characters too human is a minor technical flaw that does not essentially detract from the appeal of the story.

HISTORICAL REALISM

Historical realism consists of stories set in the past, usually realistic, although in the past 30 years there has been a trend toward combining historical realism with other types of realism, so we can find historical fantasy (as in Joan Aiken's *The Black Hearts in Battersea*), historical tall tales (as in Sid Fleischman's *By the Great Horn Spoon!*), and historical mystery stories (Leon Garfield's *Footsteps*). The distinguishing feature of historical realism is that it seeks to recreate the aura of a time past, reconstructing characters, events, movements, ways of life, and the spirit of a bygone day. It is important to note that not all works set in the past can be strictly considered historical novels. Stevenson's *Treasure Island* (1883), for example, is set in the 1740s according to the text, but indeed very little in the book distinguishes the time period—the story would scarcely change if it were moved a hundred years backwards or forwards. In true historical realism, the time period is at the core of the story, and the writer assumes an obligation to faithfully convey a distinctive historical period. Purists insist that true historical fiction must include an actual historical personage.

Historical realism often fits into one of the other classes of realism we have identified. It may be, for instance, a domestic novel, such as Patricia MacLachlan's beautiful tale, *Sarah, Plain and Tall*, a unified work—albeit a very brief one—which sensitively explores the perceptions and feelings of a pioneer girl as she adjusts to a new stepmother (an experience all too common in the old West). Or it may be psychological realism, such as Gillian Avery's *Maria Escapes* (about a young Victorian woman's struggle for identity). Or it may be an adventure story, such as Leon Garfield's *Smith* and *The Drummer Boy* or Rosemary Sutcliff's *Mark of the Horse Lord*. Or it may be social realism, such as Irene Hunt's *Across Five Aprils* (about the hardships caused by the Civil War), or Yoshiko Uchida's *Journey to Topaz* (the story of the Japanese-American internment during World War II), or Paula Fox's *The Slave Dancer* (about American slave trade in the 1840s), or James and Christopher Collier's *My Brother Sam Is Dead*, and Esther Forbes's *Johnny Tremain* (both about the Revolutionary War). Historical realism is a rich field and includes some of the finest writing for young people.

THE DEVELOPMENT OF HISTORICAL REALISM

Historical realism, like fantasy, sprang from the romantic movement of the early nineteenth century, and both appeal to the romantic desire to escape from the present. The late nineteenth century saw a flowering of historical realism for children, beginning with Charlotte Yonge's *The Dove in the Eagle's Nest* (1866) and including such popular writers as G. A. Henty and R. L. Stevenson (in such novels as *Kidnapped* [1886], which, unlike *Treasure Island*, is appropriately labeled *historical realism*). Rudyard Kipling's *Puck of Pook's Hill* (1906) is rightly considered a historical time-travel fantasy. In the United States, most nineteenth-century writers of historical realism looked to American history for their inspiration, but the most famous of them all, Howard Pyle, drew on medieval settings in *The Merry Adventures of Robin Hood* (1883) and *Otto of the Silver Hand* (1888).

With World War I, historical realism fell into decline, perhaps partly as a result of the disillusionment resulting from that conflict. A revival occurred in the 1930s, and for the next 30 or more years historical realism flourished. It became more eclectic, drawing on the histories of various cultures from ancient Ethiopia (Elizabeth Coatsworth's *The Princess and the Lion*) to Roman Britain (Rosemary Sutcliff's *The Lantern Bearers*) to the Spanish explorations of sixteenth-century America (Scott O'Dell's *The King's Fifth*). Many historical novels won major book awards and enjoyed great popularity. Then the 1970s saw the youth rebellion and the subsequent rejection of the past and an insistence on "relevance." All this cast shadows on history in general and on the historical novel in particular. The genre has not yet recovered its former popularity, although some very fine historical realism is being written for children today.

The most successful historical novels today are those that attempt to reassess and understand the past, rather than to extol it. For example, in contrast to celebrating the patriotic glory of the Revolutionary War, Christopher and James Lincoln Collier paint a far more realistic (some would say cynical) picture in *My Brother Sam Is Dead*. Mildred Taylor reveals the ugliness of racial injustice in the South of the 1930s in *Roll of Thunder, Hear My Cry*. And many powerful stories of the inhumanity and sacrilege of World War II have been published, including fictional accounts (Lois Lowry's *Number the Stars*) and others based on firsthand experience (Hans Richter's *Friedrich*).

QUALITIES OF HISTORICAL REALISM

Unobtrusive History.   Historical realism depends heavily on a believable and reasonably accurate setting and often includes actual historical personages, but it is *not* history. The events are creations of the author's imagination. Unlike realism set in contemporary times, historical realism must provide considerably more background for the reader. The more remote and unfamiliar the historical period, the more background the author must supply, including political and social history, customs, and even psychological attitudes. It would be unrealistic, for example, for an Egyptian slave or medieval peasant to embrace a democratic way of life. Additionally, the writer must be aware of the state of science and technology during the period covered in a historical novel. For instance, an author of contemporary realism need not explain modern methods of preserving food for us, because most of us already know that we just throw it in the freezer. But when writing about the American frontier of the mid-nineteenth century, a writer might have to briefly describe an ice house or the methods of preserving meat, such as salting or smoking.

On the other hand, readers are not reading the book primarily to learn about such things; the writer's task is instead to include such information as unobtrusively as possible. Joan Blos, herself a writer of some fine historical realism (*A Gathering of Days* and *Brothers of the Heart*), has noted some of the pitfalls writers of historical realism should avoid:

1. overloading the text with historical background information so that it sounds more like a history text than a novel;
2. having characters reveal this information in an artificial and inappropriate fashion, so that they seem to be instructing us;
3. using language unsuited to the historical time—a child of the rural nineteenth century should not be talking like a modern city dweller. (38–39)

The apparatus of writing, in other words, should never get in the way of the story.

Authenticity.   If historical realism is not going to give us the flavor of the historical period, then it might as well be set in contemporary times. We expect the atmosphere to be authentic, to evoke the period, to be filled with the sights, sounds, smells, and textures of the historical period. So Marguerite de Angeli opens her novel of Medieval England, *The Door in the Wall*, with "Robin drew the coverlet close about his head and turned his face to the wall. He covered his ears and shut his eyes, for the sound of the bells was deafening. All the bells of London were ringing the hour of Nones" (7).

Part of the flavor of a period is the language the people speak. We know that nineteenth-century Americans did not speak the same way that twentieth-century Americans do. The following brief passage from Irene Hunt's Civil War story, *Across Five Aprils*, clearly shows how certain language is acceptable and even appropriate in historical realism that would be out of place in a contemporary story:

> The young man got to his feet grinning. "Sure, Red, glad to oblige. Hear you been blowin' off at the mouth at some of the cracker-barrel heroes agin."
>
> Milton shrugged. "Word gets around fast."
>
> "Ben Harris was in fer a minute." The young man shook his head. "You jest ain't goin' to be happy till you git dressed up in tar and feathers, are you, Red?"
>
> (78)

The passage refers, of course, to an actual nineteenth-century practice of covering victims with tar and feathers—a not-too-subtle means of public chastisement.

This brings us to another aspect of authenticity, and that is faithfulness to the facts. Historical realism is not bound by the same rules as historical writing, but to be effective and not dismissed as purely fanciful, historical realism ought to give us a fair depiction of the society. Only satire or nonsense would tolerate a story about

George Washington plotting out Revolutionary War strategy on a computer. But the conscientious writer of historical realism is meticulous in the use of details faithful to the period, and a great deal of research goes into this kind of writing. Historical novelists read not only other historical works about the period, but also material written during the period—letters, newspapers, documents, books. Only in this way can they acquire a sense of what it may have been like to live in the era.

Sensitivity.   Finally, an issue of growing importance is the need for writers to view history with a new sensitivity. White supremacy and nineteenth-century imperialism are no longer the accepted norms. The day is past when we can excuse insensitive American Westerns depicting idealized cowboys pitted against savage, dehumanized Indians, for example. The capable writer of historical realism recognizes the nature of the historical period and, rather than romanticizing it, provides a balanced and intelligent viewpoint. Ignorance and prejudice have no place in any writing for children, but they can be especially unfortunate in historical realism. It is also regrettable that we find few works of historical realism about the lands outside of Europe and North America. Historical novels set in Asia, Africa, South America, or India are exceedingly rare. Perhaps in the future, budding writers will see the unexplored possibilities in this field.

THE REWARDS OF HISTORICAL REALISM

Historical realism can give us a greater sense of and appreciation for the past. We are compelled to believe that humanity can learn from the mistakes of its past. This is why it is important that our children know about the merciless slaughter of six million innocent Jews and others by Hitler during the 1930s and 1940s. This is why it is important that our children learn of the reprehensible treatment by the European Americans of the Native Americans and the African Americans. Are these historical episodes we want to see repeated? Historical realism can introduce young readers to humanity's past to help them look at the present with a new, enlightened perspective.

We may summarize by saying that a good piece of historical realism

1. tells a good story;
2. conveys the flavor of the historical period;
3. authentically captures the people of the period, their values, and their habits;
4. uses dialogue to make the characters sound authentic but not artificial;
5. faithfully uses historical knowledge to avoid distorting history;
6. fairly and sensitively portrays different sides of the compelling issues of the period; and
7. gives us insight into contemporary problems as well as helps us understand the problems of the past.

Historical realism forms one of the great treasure houses of literature for children.

WORKS CITED

Blos, Joan. "The Overstuffed Sentence and Other Means for Assessing Historical Fiction for Children." *School Library Journal* 31 (November 1985): 38–39.

de Angeli, Marguerite. *The Door in the Wall*. New York: Doubleday, 1949.

Hunt, Irene. *Across Five Aprils*. New York: Follett, 1964. (Civil War)

RECOMMENDED READINGS

Abrahamson, Jane. "Still Playing It Safe: Restricted Realism in Teen Novels." *School Library Journal* 22 (May 1976): 38-39.

Dickinson, Peter. "In Defense of Rubbish." *Children's Literature in Education* 3 (November 1970): 7-10.

Ellis, Anne W. *The Family Story in the 1960's*. New York: Archon, 1970.

Frye, Northrop. *The Educated Imagination*. Bloomington: Indiana University Press, 1964.

Hinton, S. E. "Teenagers Are for Real." *New York Times Book Review* 27 August 1967: 26-29.

Hipple, T., and B. Bartholomew. "The Novels College Freshmen Have Read." *ALAN Review* Winter 1982: 8-10.

Kingston, Carolyn. *The Tragic Mode in Children's Literature*. New York: Teachers College Press, 1974.

McDowell, Miles. "Fiction for Children and Adults: Some Essential Differences." *Children's Literature in Education* 10 (March 1973): 50-63.

Mertz, Maia Pank, and David A. England. "The Legitimacy of American Adolescent Fiction." *School Library Journal* 29 (October 1983): 119-123.

Moorman, Charles. *Kings & Captains: Variations on a Heroic Theme*. Louisville: University of Kentucky Press, 1971.

Moran, Barbara B., and Susan Stienfirst. "Why Johnny (and Jane) Read Whodunits in Series." *School Library Journal* March 1985: 113-117.

Nixon, Joan Lowry. "Clues to the Juvenile Mystery." *The Writer* 90 (February 1977): 23-26.

Nodelman, Perry. "How Typical Children Read Typical Books." *Children's Literature in Education* 12 (Winter 1981): 177-185.

Paterson, Katherine. *Gates of Excellence: On Reading and Writing Books for Children*. New York: Elsevier/Nelson, 1981.

Peck, Richard. "Some Thoughts on Adolescent Literature." *News from ALAN* Sept/Oct. 1975: 4-7.

Rees, David. *The Marble in the Water*. Boston: The Horn Book, 1980.

———. *Painted Desert, Green Shade: Essays on Contemporary Writers for Children and Young Adults*. Boston: The Horn Book, 1984.

Soderbergh, Peter A. "The Stratemeyer Strain: Educators and the Juvenile Series Book, 1900-1980." In *Only Connect*, 2nd ed, ed. Sheila Egoff, G. T. Stubbs, and L. F. Ashely. New York: Oxford, 1980.

Wilkin, Binnie Tate. *Survival Themes in Fiction for Children and Young People*. New York: Scarecrow, 1978.

SELECTED BIBLIOGRAPHY OF CONTEMPORARY REALISM

The following list is a representative sampling of realistic fiction classified according to the categories outlined in the chapter and by approximate reader age. Remember that many books quite easily fit into more than one category and that readers develop at different paces. Chapter 3 includes a bibliography of realistic fiction focusing on the various cultural groups found in the United States.

ADVENTURE STORIES (INCLUDING SURVIVAL STORIES, MYSTERIES, AND HUMOROUS STORIES) FOR YOUNGER READERS (GRADES 2–5)

Blume, Judy. *Tales of a Fourth Grade Nothing*. New York: Dutton, 1972. (Humor)
Cleary, Beverly. *Ellen Tebbits*. New York: Morrow, 1951. (Humor)
———. *Henry Huggins*. New York: Morrow, 1950. (Humor)
———. *Ramona the Brave*. New York: Morrow, 1975. (Humor)
———. *Ramona the Pest*. New York: Morrow, 1968. (Humor)
Fine, Anne. *Alias, Madame Doubtfire*. Boston: Little, Brown, 1988. (Humor)
Fitzhugh, Louise. *Harriet the Spy*. New York: Harper, 1964. (Humor)
Fleishman, Sid. *Chancy and the Grand Rascal*. Boston: Little, Brown, 1966. (Humor)
———. *The Ghost in the Noonday Sun*. New York: Dell, 1965. (Humor)
———. *Humbug Mountain*. Boston: Little, Brown, 1978. (Humor)
Konigsburg, E. L. *From the Mixed-Up Files of Mrs. Basil E. Frankweiler*. New York: Atheneum, 1967. (Mystery)
McCloskey, Robert. *Centerburg Tales*. New York: Viking, 1951. (Humor)
———. *Homer Price*. New York: Viking, 1943. (Humor)
Parish, Peggy. *Amelia Bedelia*. New York: Harper, 1963. (Humor)
Shecter, Ben. *Inspector Rose*. New York: Harper, 1969. (Mystery)
Sobol, Donald. *Encyclopedia Brown Saves the Day*. Nashville, TN: Nelson, 1970. (Mystery)

ADVENTURE STORIES (INCLUDING SURVIVAL STORIES, MYSTERIES, AND HUMOROUS STORIES) FOR OLDER READERS (GRADES 6 AND UP)

Corcoran, Barbara. *A Star to the North*. Philadelphia: Lippincott, 1970. (Survival)
George, Jean Craighead. *Julie of the Wolves*. New York: Harper, 1972. (Survival)
———. *My Side of the Mountain*. New York: Dutton, 1959. (Survival)
Holman, Felice. *Slake's Limbo*. New York: Scribner's, 1974. (Survival)
Houston, James. *Frozen Fire*. New York: Atheneum, 1977. (Survival)
———. *Long Claw: An Arctic Adventure*. New York: Atheneum, 1981. (Survival)
Mazer, Harry. *The Island Keeper*. New York: Delacorte, 1981. (Survival)
———. *Snowbound*. New York: Dell, 1973. (Survival)
O'Dell, Scott. *Island of the Blue Dolphins*. Boston: Houghton Mifflin, 1960. (Survival)
Raskin, Ellen. *The Westing Game*. New York: Dutton, 1978. (Mystery)
Speare, Elizabeth George. *The Sign of the Beaver*. Boston: Houghton Mifflin, 1983. (Survival)

Stevenson, Robert Louis. *Treasure Island* (1883). Various modern editions. (Adventure)

Streiber, Whitley. *Wolf of Shadows*. New York: Knopf, 1985. (Survival)

Taylor, Theodore. *The Cay*. New York: Doubleday, 1969. (Survival)

Twain, Mark. *The Adventures of Huckleberry Finn* (1884). Various modern editions. (Adventure)

————. *The Adventures of Tom Sawyer* (1876). Various modern editions. (Adventure)

Watson, Harvey. *Bob War and Poke*. Boston: Houghton Mifflin, 1991.

Westall, Robert. *The Kingdom by the Sea*. New York: Farrar, Straus & Giroux, 1991. (Mystery)

————. *A Place to Hide*. New York: Scholastic, 1994. (Mystery)

DOMESTIC REALISM—BOOKS FOR YOUNGER READERS (GRADES 2–5)

Cleary, Beverly. *Dear Mr. Henshaw*. New York: Morrow, 1983.

Enright, Elizabeth. *Thimble Summer*. New York: Holt, 1938.

Estes, Eleanor. *The Moffats*. New York: Harcourt, 1941.

Gates, Doris. *Blue Willow*. New York: Viking, 1940.

Lowry, Lois. *Attaboy, Sam!* Boston: Houghton Mifflin, 1992.

MacLachlan, Patricia. *Sarah, Plain and Tall*. New York: Harper, 1985.

Sawyer, Ruth. *Roller Skates*. New York: Viking, 1936.

Sidney, Margaret. *The Five Little Peppers and How They Grew* (1880). Various modern editions.

Sorenson, Virginia. *Miracles on Maple Hill*. New York: Harcourt, 1956.

Wiggin, Kate Douglas. *Rebecca of Sunnybrook Farm* (1903). Various modern editions.

DOMESTIC REALISM—BOOKS FOR OLDER READERS (GRADES 6 AND UP)

Alcott, Louisa May. *Little Women* (1868–1869). Various modern editions.

Burnett, Francis Hodgson. *The Secret Garden* (1909). Various modern editions.

Cleaver, Bill, and Vera Cleaver. *Where the Lilies Bloom*. Philadelphia: Lippincott, 1969.

Ellis, Sarah. *Out of the Blue*. New York: McElderry, 1995.

Hermes, Patricia. *Mama, Let's Dance*. Boston: Little, Brown, 1991.

Hickman, Janet. *Jericho*. New York: Greenwillow, 1994.

Klein, Norma. *Mom, the Wolfman and Me*. New York: Pantheon, 1972.

L'Engle, Madeleine. *Meet the Austins*. New York: Vanguard, 1960.

MacLachlan, Patricia. *Cassie Binegar*. New York: HarperCollins, 1982.

————. *Journey*. New York: Delacorte, 1991.

Montgomery, L. M. *Anne of Green Gables* (1908). Various modern editions.

Namioka, Lensey. *Yang the Youngest and His Terrible Ear*. Boston: Little, Brown, 1992.

Paterson, Katherine. *The Great Gilly Hopkins*. New York: Crowell, 1978.

————. *Jacob Have I Loved*. New York: Crowell, 1980.

Peck, Robert. *A Day No Pigs Would Die*. New York: Knopf, 1972.

Porter, Eleanor. *Pollyanna* (1913). Various modern editions.

Spyri, Johanna. *Heidi* (1884). Various modern editions.

Voight, Cynthia. *Dicey's Song*. New York: Atheneum, 1982.

————. *Homecoming*. New York: Atheneum, 1981.

————. *A Solitary Blue*. New York: Atheneum, 1983. (Father-son relationship)

SOCIAL REALISM—BOOKS FOR YOUNGER READERS (GRADES 2–5)

Blue, Rose. *Me and Einstein*. New York: Human Sciences, 1979. (Dyslexia)

Clymer, Eleanor. *The Get-Away Car*. New York: Dutton, 1978. (Aging)

Fox, Paula. *How Many Miles to Babylon?* Port Washington, NY: White, 1967. (Race)

Hanson, Joyce. *Yellow Bird and Me*. New York: Houghton Mifflin, 1986. (Learning disability)

Marek, Margot. *Different, Not Dumb*. New York: Watts, 1985. (Learning disability)

Mathis, Sharon Bell. *The Hundred Penny Box*. New York: Viking, 1975. (Aging)

Myers, Walter Dean. *Me, Mop, and the Moondance Kid*. New York: Dell, 1985. (Adoption)

SOCIAL REALISM—BOOKS FOR OLDER READERS (GRADES 6 AND UP)

Bennett, James. *I Can Hear the Mourning Dove*. Boston: Houghton Mifflin, 1990. (Emotional illness)

Bonham, Frank. *Durango Street*. New York: Dutton, 1965. (Race)

———. *The Nitty Gritty*. New York: Dutton, 1968. (Race)

Brooks, Jerome. *Uncle Mike's Boy*. New York: Harper, 1973. (Mental retardation)

Bunting, Eve. *Summer Wheels*. San Diego: Harcourt Brace Jovanovich, 1992. (Aging)

Byars, Betsy. *Summer of the Swans*. New York: Viking, 1970. (Mental retardation)

Childress, Alice. *A Hero Ain't Nothin' but a Sandwich*. New York: Coward, 1973. (Drugs)

Cormier, Robert. *Beyond the Chocolate War*. New York: Knopf, 1985. (Struggle with evil)

———. *The Chocolate War*. New York: Pantheon, 1974. (Struggle with evil)

———. *I Am the Cheese*. (Struggle with evil)

Cunningham, Julia. *Dorp Dead*. New York: Pantheon, 1965. (Allegorical struggle with evil)

Fleischman, Paul. *The Half-a-Moon Inn*. New York: Harper, 1980. (Muteness)

Graham, Lorenz. *North Town*. New York: Crowell, 1965. (Race)

Greene, Bette. *Summer of My German Soldier*. New York: Dial, 1973. (Prejudice)

Hamilton, Virginia. *The Planet of Junior Brown*. New York: Macmillan, 1971. (Emotional problems)

Hicyilmaz, Gaye. *Against the Storm*. Boston: Little, Brown, 1992. (Set in modern Turkey)

Hinton, S. E. *The Outsiders*. New York: Viking, 1967. (Teenage gangs)

Hunter, Kristen. *Soul Brothers and Sister Lou*. New York: Scribner's, 1958. (Race)

Levoy, Myron C. *A Shadow Like a Leopard*. New York: Harper, 1981. (Aging)

Lipsyte, Robert. *The Brave*. New York: HarperCollins, 1991.

Marsden, John. *Letters from the Inside*. Boston: Houghton Mifflin, 1994.

Meyer, Carolyn. *Killing the Kudu*. New York: Macmillan, 1990. (Mobility)

Myers, Walter Dean. *It Ain't All for Nothin'*. New York: Viking, 1978. (Crime)

———. *Scorpions*. New York: Harper, 1988. (Gangs)

Nelson, Theresa. *Earthshine*. New York: Jackson, 1994. (AIDS)

Peck, Richard. *Those Summer Girls I Never Met*. New York: Delacorte, 1988. (Aging)

Skinner, David. *The Wrecker*. New York: Simon, 1995. (Social misfit)

Spinelli, Jerry. *Maniac Magee*. Boston: Little, Brown, 1990. (Race)

Voight, Cynthia. *When She Hollers*. New York: Scholastic, 1994.

Wright, Betty Ren. *Getting Rid of Marjorie*. New York: Holiday House, 1981. (Aging)

PSYCHOLOGICAL REALISM—BOOKS FOR YOUNGER READERS (GRADES 2–5)

Byars, Betsy. *The Cybil War*. New York: Viking, 1981. (Friendship)

Fine, Anne. *Flour Babies*. Boston: Little, Brown, 1994. (Personal responsibility)

Greene, Bette. *Philip Hall Likes Me. I Reckon Maybe*. New York: Dial, 1974. (Boy-girl relationships)

Greene, Constance. *The Ears of Louis*. New York: Viking, 1974. (Self-acceptance)

Konigsburg, E. L. *Jennifer, Hecate, Macbeth, William McKinley, and Me, Elizabeth*. New York: Atheneum, 1967. (Friendship)

MacLachlan, Patricia. *Baby*. New York: Delacorte, 1993. (Death)

Naylor, Phyllis Reynolds. *Alice in Rapture, Sort of*. New York: Atheneum, 1989. (Boy-Girl friendship)

Paterson, Katherine. *Bridge to Terabithia*. New York: Crowell, 1977. (Death of a friend)

———. *Come Sing, Jimmy Jo*. New York: Dutton, 1985. (Self-acceptance)

Smith, Doris Buchanan. *A Taste of Blackberries*. New York: Crowell, 1973. (Death of a friend)

PSYCHOLOGICAL REALISM—BOOKS FOR OLDER READERS (GRADES 6 AND UP)

Avi. *Nothing but the Truth: A Documentary Novel*. New York: Watts, 1991.

Block, Francesca Lia. *Weetzie Bat*. New York: HarperCollins, 1989. (Alternative lifestyles in a work of surrealism)

Blue, Marion Dane. *Am I Blue?: Coming Out of the Silence*. New York: HarperCollins, 1994. (Homosexuality)

Blume, Judy. *Are You There, God? It's Me, Margaret*. New York: Bradbury, 1970.

———. *Tiger Eyes*. Scarsdale, NY: Bradbury, 1981. (Death of a parent)

Brooks, Martha. *Paradise Café and Other Stories*. Boston: Little, Brown, 1988. (Relationships and various themes)

———. *Traveling On into the Light and Other Stories*. New York: Kroupa, 1994.

Cole, Brock. *Celine*. New York: Farrar, Straus & Giroux, 1989. (Relationships)

———. *The Goats*. New York: Farrar, Straus & Giroux, 1987. (Relationships)

Cormier, Robert. *The Bumblebee Flies Anyway*. New York: Pantheon, 1983. (Terminal illness)

Crutcher, Chris. *Staying Fat for Sarah Byrnes*. New York: Morrow, 1993. (Child abuse)

Daly, Maureen. *Seventeenth Summer*. New York: Dodd, 1942. (First love)

Danziger, Paula. *The Cat Ate My Gymsuit*. New York: Delacorte, 1974. (Personal adjustment)

Fox, Paula. *The Eagle Kite*. New York: Jackson/Orchard, 1995. (Homosexuality)

Garden, Nancy. *Annie on My Mind*. New York: Farrar, Straus & Giroux, 1982. (Lesbianism)

Honeycutt, Natalie. *Ask Me Something Easy*. New York: Watts, 1991.

Hunt, Irene. *Up a Road Slowly*. New York: Follett, 1967. (Coming of age)

Hunter, Mollie. *A Sound of Chariots*. New York: Harper, 1972. (Death of a parent)

Kerr, M. E. *Deliver Us from Evie*. New York: HarperCollins, 1994. (Homosexuality)

Knowles, John. *A Separate Peace*. New York: Macmillan, 1960. (Death of a friend)

Lipsyte, Robert. *One Fat Summer*. New York: Harper, 1977. (Obesity)

Lowry, Lois. *A Summer to Die*. Boston: Houghton Mifflin, 1977. (Terminal illness)

Murrow, Liza Ketchum. *Twelve Days in August*. New York: Holiday House, 1993. (Sexuality)

Naylor, Phyllis Reynolds. *Reluctantly Alice*. New York: Atheneum, 1991. (Sexuality)

Oneal, Zibby. *In Summer Light*. New York: Viking, 1985. (Death of a parent)

———. *The Language of Goldfish*. New York: Random House, 1980. (Mental illness)

Peck, Richard. *Remembering the Good Times*. New York: Delacorte, 1985. (Friend's suicide)

———. *Secrets of the Shopping Mall*. New York: Delacorte, 1979. (Running away)

Raskin, Ellen. *Figgs & Phantoms*. New York: Dutton, 1974. (Death)

Rylant, Cynthia. *A Couple of Kooks and Other Stories about Love*. New York: Orchard, 1990. (Love and sexuality)

Scoppettone, Sandra. *Trying Hard to Hear You*. New York: Harper, 1981. (Homosexuality)

Shannon, George. *Unlived Affections*. New York: Harper, 1989. (Gay parent)

Wilson, Budge. *The Leaving*. New York: Philomel, 1992.

Woodson, Jacqueline. *I Hadn't Meant to Tell You This*. New York: Delacorte, 1994. (Sexual abuse)

Wynne-Jones, Tim. *Some of the Kinder Planets*. New York: Kroupa, 1995. (Short stories about relationships and various themes)

Zindel, Paul. *The Pigman*. New York: Harper, 1968. (Old Age)

REALISTIC ANIMAL STORIES FOR ALL AGES

Burnford, Sheila. *The Incredible Journey*. Boston: Little, Brown, 1961.

Byars, Betsy. *The Midnight Fox*. New York: Viking, 1968.

Cleary, Beverly. *Socks*. New York: Morrow, 1973.

DeJong, Meindert. *Hurry Home, Candy*. New York: Harper, 1953.

Gates, Doris. *Little Vic*. New York: Viking, 1951.

George, Jean. *The Cry of the Crow*. New York: Harper, 1980.

Gipson, Fred. *Old Yeller*. New York: Harper, 1956.

Griffiths, Helen. *The Greyhound*. New York: Doubleday, 1964.

———. *The Wild Heart*. New York: Doubleday, 1963.

Henry, Marguerite. *King of the Wind*. New York: Rand, 1948.

———. *Misty of Chincoteague*. New York: Rand, 1947.

Kjelgaard, Jim. *Big Red*. New York: Holiday, 1956.

James, Will. *Smoky, the Cow Horse*. New York: Scribner's, 1926.

London, Jack. *The Call of the Wild* (1903). Various modern editions.

Mowat, Farley. *Owls in the Family*. Boston: Little, Brown, 1962.

Mukerji, Dhan Gopal. *Gay-Neck, the Story of a Pigeon*. New York: Dutton, 1927.

Naylor, Phyllis Reynolds. *Shiloh*. New York: Atheneum, 1991.

Rawlings, Marjorie Kinnan. *The Yearling*. New York: Scribner's, 1938.

Rawls, Wilson. *Where the Red Fern Grows*. New York: Doubleday, 1961.

Reaver, Chap. *Bill*. New York: Delacorte, 1994.

SELECTED BIBLIOGRAPHY OF HISTORICAL REALISM

The following bibliography lists a few of the many books of historical realism available for young readers. These have been classified according to broad regional and chronological categories, and most of these titles are for readers at about the fourth- and fifth-grade reading level and above. Also check out the bibliography following Chapter 13 for some other titles relating to historical subjects.

ANCIENT, MEDIEVAL, AND RENAISSANCE EUROPEAN HISTORY

Behn, Harry. *The Faraway Lurs*. New York: Putnam, 1963. (Ancient World)

Brennan, J. H. *Shiva: An Adventure of the Ice Age*. New York: Lippincott, 1989.

Chute, Marchette. *The Innocent Wayfaring*. New York: Dutton, 1955.

Cushman, Karen. *Catherine, Called Birdy*. New York: Clarion, 1994. (Medieval)

———. *The Midwife's Apprentice*. New York: Clarion, 1995. (Medieval)

Gray, Elizabeth Janet. *Adam of the Road*. New York: Viking, 1942. (Medieval England)

Haugaard, Erik Christian. *Hakon of Rogen's Saga*. Boston: Houghton Mifflin, 1963. (Medieval Norse)

———. *Leif the Unlucky*. Boston: Houghton Mifflin, 1982. (Medieval Norse)

———. *Orphans of the Wind*. New York: Dell, 1966. (Medieval Norse)

Hunter, Mollie. *The Spanish Letters*. New York: Funk, 1967.

———. *The Stronghold*. New York: Harper, 1974. (Ancient Scotland)

Ish-Kishor, Sulamith. *A Boy of Old Prague*. New York: Pantheon, 1963.

Kelly, Eric P. *The Trumpeter of Krakow*. New York: Macmillan, 1928. (Medieval Poland)

Konigsburg, E. L. *A Proud Taste for Scarlet and Miniver*. New York: Atheneum, 1973. (Medieval)

———. *The Second Mrs. Giaconda*. New York: Atheneum, 1975. (Renaissance Italy)

McGraw, Eloise Jarvis. *Mara, Daughter of the Nile*. New York: Coward, 1961.

Pilar, Molina Llorente. *The Apprentice*. New York: Farrar, Straus & Giroux, 1993. (Renaissance Florence)

Pyle, Howard. *Men of Iron*. 1890. Various modern editions. (Medieval)

———. *Otto of the Silver Hand*. 1888. Various modern editions. (Medieval)

Speare, Elizabeth George. *The Bronze Bow*. Boston: Houghton Mifflin, 1961. (Ancient Rome)

Stolz, Mary. *Zekmet the Stone Carver: A Tale of Ancient Egypt*. Illus. Deborah Nourse Lattimore. New York: Harcourt, 1988.

Sutcliff, Rosemary. *The Lantern Bearers*. New York: Walck, 1959.

———. *The Mark of the Horse Lord*. New York: Walck, 1965. (Early Britain)

Tarr, Judith. *His Majesty's Elephant*. New York: Harcourt, 1993. (Early Medieval France)

Treace, Geoffrey. *The Red Towers of Granada*. New York: Vanguard, 1967.

Treece, Henry. *The Centurion*. Illus. Mary Russon. New York: Meredith, 1967. (Ancient Rome)

Turner, Ann. *Time of the Bison*. Illus. Beth Peck. New York: Macmillan, 1987. (Pre-history)

MODERN EUROPEAN HISTORY SINCE THE RENAISSANCE

Anderson, Rachel. *Black Water*. New York: Holt, 1995.

Avery, Gillian. *Maria Escapes*. New York: Simon & Schuster, 1992. (Originally published in 1957 in England as *The Warden's Niece*.)

Garfield, John. *December Rose*. New York: Viking, 1986. (Eighteenth-Century England)

———. *Smith*. New York: Pantheon, 1967. (Eighteenth-Century England)

———. *The Sound of Coaches*. New York: Viking, 1974. (Eighteenth-Century England)

Hesse, Karen. *Letters from Rifka*. New York: Holt, 1992.

Holman, Felice. *The Wild Children*. New York: Scribner's, 1983.

Hunter, Mollie. *The Ghosts of Glencoe*. New York: Funk, 1969.

Lowry, Lois. *Number the Stars*. Boston: Houghton Mifflin, 1989. (World War II)

Monjo, F. N. *The Sea Beggar's Son*. New York: Coward, 1975.

Orlev, Uri. *The Island on Bird Street*. Trans. Hillel Halkin. Boston: Houghton Mifflin, 1984.

Pelgrom, Els. *The Winter When Time Was Frozen*. Trans. Maryka and Rafael Rudnik. New York: Morrow, 1980.

Peyton, K. M. *The Edge of the Cloud*. Cleveland: World, 1970.

————. *Flambards*. Cleveland: World, 1968.

Richter, Hans Peter. *Friedrich*. New York: Holt, 1970. (World War II)

Serraillier, Ian. *The Silver Sword*. New York: Criterion, 1959.

Siegal, Aranka. *Grace in the Wilderness: After the Liberation, 1945–1948*. New York: Farrar, Straus & Giroux, 1985.

————. *Upon the Head of the Goat: A Childhood in Hungary, 1939–1944*. New York: Farrar, Straus & Giroux, 1981.

NORTH AMERICAN AND NATIVE AMERICA HISTORY

Armer, Laura Adams. *Waterless Mountain*. New York: McKay, 1931.

Avi. *The Barn*. New York: Jackson, 1994.

————. *Encounter at Easton*. New York: Pantheon, 1980.

Bawdin, Nina. *Carrie's War*. New York: Lippincott, 1973.

Beatty, Patricia. *Jayhawker*. New York: Morrow, 1991.

Blos, Joan. *A Gathering of Days*. New York: Scribner's, 1979. (Nineteenth Century)

Brenner, Barbara. *Wagon Wheels*. Illus. Don Bolognese. New York: Harper, 1978. (Nineteenth Century)

Brink, Carol Ryrie. *Caddie Woodlawn* (1936). Various modern editions. (Nineteenth Century)

Bulla, Clyde. *A Lion to Guard Us*. New York: Crowell, 1978.

Collier, James Lincoln, and Christopher Collier. *My Brother Sam Is Dead*. New York: Four Winds Press, 1974. (Revolutionary War)

Dorris, Michael. *Guests*. New York: Hyperion, 1994. (Pre-Columbian America)

————. *Morning Girl*. New York: Hyperion, 1992. (Pre-Columbian America)

Dyer, T. A. *A Way of His Own*. Boston: Houghton Mifflin, 1981. (Pre-Columbian North America)

Fleischman, Paul. *The Borning Room*. New York: Harper, 1991. (Nineteenth Century)

————. *Coming-and-Going Man*. New York: Harper, 1985.

Forbes, Esther. *Johnny Tremain*. Boston: Houghton Mifflin, 1946. (American Revolution)

Fox, Paula. *The Slave Dancer*. New York: Bradbury, 1973. (Early Nineteenth Century)

Fritz, Jean. *The Cabin Faced West*. New York: Coward, 1958. (Late Eighteenth Century)

Garrigue, Sheila. *The Eternal Spring of Mr. Ito*. New York: Bradbury, 1985.

Hudson, Jan. *Sweetgrass*. New York: Philomel, 1989.

Lasky, Kathryn. *Beyond the Burning Time*. New York: Scholastic, 1994. (Colonial America)

Lyons, Mary E. *Letters from a Slave Girl: The Story of Harriet Jacobs*. New York: Scribner's, 1992.

Myers, Walter Dean. *The Glory Field*. New York: Scholastic, 1994.

O'Dell, Scott. *The King's Fifth*. Boston: Houghton Mifflin, 1966. (Sixteenth Century)

————. *Sing Down the Moon*. Boston: Houghton Mifflin, 1970. (Nineteenth Century)

Paterson, Katherine. *Lyddie*. New York: Dutton, 1991.

Pellowski, Anne. *Winding Valley Farm: Annie's Story*. New York: Philomel, 1982.

Petry, Ann. *Tituba of Salem Village*. New York: Crowell, 1964.

Reeder, Carolyn. *Shades of Gray*. New York: Macmillan, 1989.

Richter, Conrad. *The Light in the Forest*. New York: Knopf, 1953. (Nineteenth Century)

Rostokowski, Margaret I. *After the Dancing Days*. New York: Harper, 1986.

Sebestyen, Ouida. *Words by Heart*. Boston: Little, Brown, 1979. (Early Twentieth Century)
Speare, Elizabeth George. *The Sign of the Beaver*. Boston: Houghton Mifflin, 1983.
————. *The Witch of Blackbird Pond*. Boston: Houghton Mifflin, 1958. (Colonial America)
Taylor, Mildred. *Let the Circle Be Unbroken*. New York: Dial, 1981. (1930s)
————. *Roll of Thunder, Hear My Cry*. New York: Dial, 1976. (1930s)
Wilder, Laura Ingalls. *By the Shores of Silver Lake* (1939). New York: Harper, 1953.
————. *Farmer Boy* (1933). New York: Harper, 1953.
————. *Little House in the Big Woods* (1932). New York: Harper, 1953.
————. *Little House on the Prairie* (1935). New York: Harper, 1953.
————. *Little Town on the Prairie* (1941). New York: Harper, 1953.
————. *The Long Winter* (1940). New York: Harper, 1953.
————. *On the Banks of Plum Creek* (1937). New York: Harper, 1953.
————. *Those Happy Golden Years* (1943). New York: Harper, 1953.

OTHER TIMES AND PLACES

Bosse, Malcolm. *The Examination*. New York: Farrar, Straus & Giroux, 1994. (Medieval China)
De Jenkins, Lyll Becerra. *The Honorable Prison*. New York: Lodestar, 1988. (South America)
DeJong, Meindert. *The House of Sixty Fathers*. New York: Harper, 1956. (China)
Dickinson, Peter. *The Dancing Bear*. Boston: Little, Brown, 1972. (Byzantium)
Disher, Gary. *The Bamboo Flute*. Boston: Houghton, 1993. (1930s Australia)
Fyson, J. G. *The Three Brothers of Ur*. Illus. Victor G. Ambrus. New York: Coward, 1966.
Ho Minfong. *The Clay Marble*. New York: Farrar, Straus & Giroux, 1991. (Cambodia)
Holman, Felice. *Wild Children*. New York: Scribner's, 1983. (Russia)
Lewis, Elizabeth Foreman. *Young Fu of the Upper Yangtze*. New York: Holt, 1932. (China)
Namioka, Lensey. *Island of Ogres*. New York: Harper, 1989. (Japan)
Paterson, Katherine. *The Master Puppeteer*. New York: T. Crowell, 1976. (Japan)
————. *Of Nightingales That Weep*. New York: T. Crowell, 1974. (Japan)
————. *Rebels of the Heavenly Kingdom*. New York: T. Crowell, 1983. (China)
————. *The Sign of the Chrysanthemum*. New York: T. Crowell, 1973. (Japan)
Ritchie, Rita. *The Golden Hawks of Genghis Kahn*. New York: Dutton, 1958.
————. *Secret Beyond the Mountains*. New York: Dutton, 1960. (China)
————. *The Year of the Horse*. New York: Dutton, 1957. (China)
Walsh, Jill Paton. *The Emperor's Winding Sheet*. New York: Farrar, Straus & Giroux, 1978. (Constantinople)
Yep, Laurence. *The Serpent's Children*. New York: Harper, 1984. (China)

Chapter 12

∾

BIOGRAPHY

A *biography* is a literary work describing the life—or part of the life—of an individual. When a person writes the story of his or her own life, we call the work an *autobiography*. We separate our discussion of biographies from other nonfiction primarily because biographies (and autobiographies) have traditionally been regarded as a sort of subgenre of literature, unlike other informational books. The biographer Paul Murray Kendall notes that biography lies between history and literature—and has never been fully embraced by either (3). Nevertheless, biography is a very old genre—the Gospels, in fact, are among the earliest biographies, describing, as they do, the life of Christ. And today, biography has a devoted following (perhaps smaller than we should wish). Through biographies we are reminded of the common thread of humanity that runs through us all. Biography can inspire us with portraits of the indomitable human spirit, or it can arouse us from complacency with portraits of human malice and insensitivity. The good biography probably does a little of both.

This century has seen many fine writers—both for children and adults—earn their literary reputations as biographers (Esther Forbes, Jean Fritz, James Daugherty, Ingri and Edgar Parin d'Aulaire, and Russell Freedman, to name just a few). The field of biography has yielded a rich and varied harvest.

APPROACHES TO BIOGRAPHY

There are three approaches to biography for children: (1) the authentic biography, which values faithful adherence to facts; (2) the fictionalized biography, which values dramatic narrative; and (3) biographical fiction, which values a good story over hard facts. Each has its peculiar strengths and appeal.

AUTHENTIC BIOGRAPHY

If a biography attempts to convey the factual information of a person's life and times faithfully, we call it an *authentic biography*. An authentic biography will not use any facts that cannot be supported by solid and reliable research. Consequently, if dialogue is used (which is not common in authentic biography) it must be dialogue that can be substantiated by historical documents (such as letters or diaries) or reliable personal recollections. Although authentic biography attempts to be accurate in its presentation of the facts, we must remember that even the most thorough and honest biographer cannot be free from bias or completely objective. By ignoring some facts and highlighting others, it is possible to slant even the most solid evidence, and readers need to be aware of such slanting.

James Daugherty was a pioneer of fine authentic biography for young people; his *Poor Richard* (a life of Benjamin Franklin), *Daniel Boone*, and *Abraham Lincoln* are justly celebrated. More recently, the works of Jean Fritz and Russell Freedman have established still more exacting standards for young people's biography. In fact, Freedman's *Lincoln: A Photobiography* won the coveted Newbery Medal. This work is marked by careful research, rare and fascinating photographs from the period, and an honest, unsentimental portrayal of one of the great figures of American history. The book should be a model for all future biographers.

FICTIONALIZED BIOGRAPHY

In writing for young people, some biographers have found it inviting to dramatize certain events—to give characters dialogue or perhaps even to invent believable scenes—presumably to make the story more interesting. These *fictionalized biographies* are readily recognizable by their dialogue. That is, if we are reading a biography of Benjamin Franklin and find extended conversations between young Franklin and his brother or his parents, we can be fairly certain that the author has invented these discussions, for it is unlikely that such details are recorded in any surviving record. A sound fictionalized biography will not tamper with the basic facts of history, but it will dramatize scenes and create conversations. Naturally, since its boundaries between truth and fiction are not precisely defined, fictionalized biography cannot be regarded with the same reliability as authentic biography, and it should be acknowledged as leisure reading. Jean Lee Latham's *Carry On, Mr. Bowditch* is a good example of fictionalized biography. Most of this book consists of dramatized scenes depicting events that occurred in the late eighteenth century—scenes with dialogue to which no modern biographer could have been privy.

BIOGRAPHICAL FICTION

Biographical fiction should properly be considered as fiction and is thus classified in most libraries. Robert Lawson's wonderfully entertaining *Ben and Me*, for example, ostensibly describes the life of Benjamin Franklin as told by Amos, an irascible mouse that inhabits the great man's fur hat. Amos is an incurable egotist and takes most of the credit for Franklin's great works, describing how the Declaration of Independence was actually the work of mice fighting for their own liberty and how Amos was responsible for the "first" French Revolution—that of the French mice. It is all a great deal of fun, but it is not, by any stretch of the imagination, a biography of Franklin nor is it history. It is more appropriately evaluated by the standards of fantasy. A more serious work of biographical fiction is E. L. Konigsburg's *A Proud Taste for Scarlet and Miniver*, a life of the great medieval English queen, Eleanor of Aquitaine. Eleanor's story is related by some of the principal figures in her life, a churchman, a nobleman, and her mother-in-law, all from their points of view in heaven. The story is both entertaining and historically quite accurate—an example of the blurring of the division between the genres of fiction and nonfiction.

THE FORMS OF BIOGRAPHY

In addition to these differences in approach, biographies also differ in their content: A biography that covers a subject's entire life is called a *complete biography*. A *partial biography* is one that covers only part of a subject's life. A *collective biography* includes stories of a group of individuals who share some common ground. Of course, each of these types can be either authentic or fictionalized biographies.

COMPLETE BIOGRAPHIES

We can find a multitude of complete biographies, which, as the name suggests, examine the whole of the subject's life from the cradle to the grave. A complete biography may be simple—such as Aliki's charming picture-book biographies (*The Story of Johnny Appleseed*, for example) or complex—such as Russell Freedman's works (*Lincoln: A Photobiography, Eleanor Roosevelt*, and others). Jean Fritz has produced a number of very brief biographies, which are nonetheless complete in that they survey the entire life of the subject. Fritz has successfully distilled the essence of the lives of her subjects (all figures of the American Revolution) into works of under 50 pages, and she writes with a warm sense of humor that helps to bring her subjects closer to her readers. Since complete biographies necessitate bringing together a considerable amount of information that may be only loosely related, these are often the most difficult to unify. However, most biographers tie their works together by focusing on specific themes in an individual's life.

PARTIAL BIOGRAPHIES

Occasionally, biographies will appear that focus on only one period or one aspect of a subject's life. These partial biographies allow the author to focus more clearly on a specific theme. For example, Johanna Johnston's fictionalized biography of Harriet Beecher Stowe—*Harriet and the Runaway Book*—focuses chiefly on Mrs. Stowe's writing of *Uncle Tom's Cabin*. Esther Hautzig's autobiographical *The Endless Steppe: Growing Up in Siberia* recounts five years in the author's youth spent in forced labor. And, of course, one of the most famous of all partial autobiographical works is Anne Frank's *The Diary of a Young Girl*. Of necessity, biographies of living persons are technically partial biographies, since the life is not yet completed.

Occasionally series of books have appeared focusing on the childhoods of famous Americans. Unfortunately, some have not been well written, and at times we find them using fabricated dialogue, for example, between young Thomas Jefferson and his friends, making them sound as if they were midwestern schoolchildren of the mid-twentieth century. However, these books remind us that in biographies young readers are not very much interested in the events of childhood and adolescence. The activities of an accomplished adult—the usual subject of a biography—may not always be suitable or readily accessible material for young readers. Max Bolliger's *David*, which follows the life of King David up until he became king of Israel, is a good example of a partial biography for young readers that focuses on the subject's formative years. On the other hand, F. N. Monjo's *Poor Richard in France* concentrates on Benjamin Franklin's mature years as the American emissary to the French capital during the American Revolution.

COLLECTIVE BIOGRAPHIES

Many biographical works briefly examine the lives of several people who are linked by a common thread—scientists, first ladies, sports figures, and musicians, for example. Collective biographies may take two general forms. Most commonly, a brief biographical sketch is provided for each individual included, forming a collection of short biographies. Henrietta Buckmaster's *Women Who Shaped History* deals with such influential women as Dorothea Dix, Harriet Tubman, and Mary Baker Eddy. One of the most famous of all collective biographies is John F. Kennedy's best-selling *Profiles in Courage*, which has been edited for younger audiences. A second type weaves into a single narrative the lives of two or more people who worked in collaboration. Jane Goodsell's biography of the founders of the famed clinic that bears their name, *The Mayo Brothers*, is an example.

The collective biography emphasizes above all the theme of an individual's life and work, and it further allows us to place that theme in a larger perspective. An additional benefit of the collective biography is that it can serve as a catalyst for further reading, prompting young readers to explore the life of one or more of the subjects involved, or perhaps to seek out biographies of others whose lives played on the same themes.

THE ELEMENTS OF BIOGRAPHICAL WRITING

Five basic elements of biographical writing should be considered when we read and evaluate biographies: subject, accuracy, balance, style, and theme.

SUBJECT

A subject's fame and glory are no guarantee that the biography will be interesting. Throughout the Middle Ages and the Renaissance, biographical writing generally focused on either saints or royalty, and in both cases the purpose was to glorify the subject. Only in the twentieth century has biography become truly democratized—now it is possible to locate biographies of artists, teachers, mathematicians, and scoundrels. There are really no limits when it comes to the choice of a biographical subject. The biographer's role is to present the life in an interesting manner (by choosing the right facts and expressing them in the right way, not by inventing facts). We expect a biography to convey a sense of the historical period and the geographic place in which the subject lived. Obviously, the more remote the historical period or the more distant and unfamiliar the place, the more background is needed. And finally, the good biography not only reveals to us the life of the subject, but it contributes to our broader and deeper understanding of humankind. In other words, when we are finished reading the biography we should not only feel that we know more about the subject's life, but we should feel that we know more about people in general. If not, the biography becomes little more than a vehicle for idle gossip.

ACCURACY

The material of a good biography is both accurate and authentic. Even in fictionalized biography, we expect the author to faithfully convey the *essence* of the character, if not always the specific details of the life. The good biography bears evidence of careful research—Jean Fritz has shown us through her use of endnotes that this can be done even in biographies for younger readers. We expect that there are no glaring omissions that would distort the reader's view or understanding of the subject. However, as one critic remarks: "Children's biography does not always present the whole truth about a subject. If a life contains tragic or unsavory aspects, these are generally omitted" (Gottlieb 174). There is disagreement over this issue, with some feeling that children may not have the emotional and intellectual capacity to handle certain themes, and others believing that the implied dishonesty in omitting these elements is a worse offense. Most biographers of Benjamin Franklin, for example, do not make a point of mentioning that his son was illegitimate, but Jean Fritz, in her biography *What's the Big Idea, Ben Franklin?*, explains simply in an endnote that we do not know who the son's mother was, a bold admission in a book for elementary children. Fritz's solution seems reasonable, combining honesty with discretion.

The illustrations in a good biography pay careful attention to authenticity and are appropriately juxtaposed with the text. We can again turn to biographies of Benjamin Franklin for an example. Several biographies for young people include illustrations of the famous kite-flying episode and depict a young boy, representing Franklin's son, accompanying Franklin in the storm. In fact, Franklin's son was a grown man of over 20 when the incident occurred. Careless illustration may cast doubt—rightly or wrongly—on the validity of the text.

It has only been in the last few years that biographers have begun to include supplementary material—notes, bibliographies, indexes—in their books for young people. Naturally, very young children will benefit little from such materials, but children in the middle and upper elementary grades are not too young to learn about footnotes, endnotes, references, maps, and indexes. The works of Milton Meltzer (not primarily a biographer but a social historian) and Russell Freedman are not only given added authority by their inclusion of supplementary materials, they also suggest that these writers hold their readers in high regard, seeing them as discerning and inquisitive individuals. In general, the writer of a good biography avoids oversimplification, sentimentality, and overt didacticism.

BALANCE

Early biographical writing tended to focus on the glorious exploits of "captains and kings," and the subjects were often idealized and treated as virtual superhumans. When a biographer presents an idealized portrait of an apparently superhuman hero, there is the danger that young readers may come to believe that success is unattainable by ordinary people. Today we prefer biographies that reveal the human side of people, their errors in judgment, their personality flaws, their peculiar and eccentric habits, and so on. These inclusions should not cause us to think less of the individual, but should give us a greater capacity for sympathetic or empathetic understanding.

This does not mean that we want our heroes debunked—a fault that is found often in popular biographies for adults (which focus on the perversions, sexual escapades, and criminal activities of public officials, sports heroes, movie stars, and so on). Young people want heroes or heroines to believe in. But we should not forget that even heroes and heroines have their weaknesses, and that what sets them apart from others is that they are able to triumph in spite of these weaknesses. It is probably better for our egos if we learn as Jean Fritz points out in *Where Was Patrick Henry on the 29th of May?* that Patrick Henry achieved fame and respectability despite a streak of laziness. Or we may gain a new perspective when we learn, as Russell Freedman points out in *Lincoln: A Photobiography*, that Abraham Lincoln was self-conscious about his appearance. Freedman tells us that "When a rival called him 'two-faced' during a political debate, Lincoln replied: 'I leave it to my audience. If I had another face, do you think I'd wear this one?'" (1). Typically, readers want to believe in the characters, to see them as flesh and blood individuals, and to feel comfortable with their heroes.

STYLE

Sometimes a writer achieves what might have been thought the impossible—producing an incredibly dull book about an incredibly fascinating subject. A dull biography may result from an unwise selection of material, but more likely it is the result of a dry literary style. The good biographer writes with a style that is interesting, accessible, and appropriate to the subject. Necessary background material is carefully woven into the narrative—young people generally prefer action and dialogue to lengthy description. Dialogue, when it is used, is believable and authentic to the period. Eighteenth-century farm boys are not to sound like twentieth-century urban dwellers.

Naturally, the vocabulary and sentence structure of a good biography are suited to the intended audience, but need not be without reasonable challenge—remember, boredom results either from the absence of any challenge or from an overwhelming challenge. Another means of attracting and keeping the reader's interest is through humor. Jean Fritz effectively employs humor in her biographies without diminishing the stature of her subjects, and in the example quoted above from Freedman, we see that humor can help endear the subject to the readers. Because humor is so important to the healthy human existence, it is difficult to understand why it appears so seldom in biography.

THEME

Finally, the theme of a good biography is both significant and sound. The theme clarifies the writer's attitude toward the character. The good biographer will try to shed new light on the subject, or clear up old misunderstandings. This is not to suggest that biography should be didactic, but without a theme to hold it together a biography is simply a loose collection of facts (something like a *Guinness Book of Records*— interesting to read in bits and pieces, but hardly a gripping story). Sometimes the theme is evident from the title. Jean Fritz's *The Double Life of Pocahontas* suggests the theme of a tragic woman caught between the conflicting values of two very different ways of life—that of her native Indian culture and that of her adoptive English culture. (However, Fritz's work has been criticized for trivializing the story of Pocahontas and ignoring the plight of the Native Americans at the hands of the European settlers; in other words, it is thought to lack balance.) Milton Meltzer's *Benjamin Franklin: The New American* advances a rather standard view of Franklin as a man of rich and varied character with boundless physical energy and intellectual curiosity. And Freedman's portrait of Lincoln shows the sixteenth president as an extraordinarily complex and often troubled man, not without his significant shortcomings, but whose greatest strength was his sincere and warm humanity.

It is undoubtedly futile to hope that we have seen the last of the didactic biographies, those well-intentioned books that presume to teach us virtue through the examples of our heroes. But this is not to suggest that good biographies should contain no message at all for its readers. On the contrary, the best biographies are built upon very profound themes—themes that speak to the strength and resilience of the human spirit, themes that remind us that the life well lived is its own reward.

Not all young readers will become enthralled with biography, but those who do become passionate about it. Publishers have attempted to satisfy the appetites of these aficionados by producing the biography series. Dell has published its "Famous Americans Series," consisting of very brief biographies, widely varying in quality, and lacking such apparatus as indexes or bibliographies. Puffin's "Women of Our Time Series" includes some very fine authors, including Milton Meltzer on Betty Friedan and Patricia Reilly Giff on Mother Theresa. These are authentic biographies, but they still adopt the format of a fictional work, lacking indexes, source lists, notes, and so on. We may hope that some of the recent excellent contributions to the field will pave the way for more biographies of high standards—biographies with uncompromising integrity and a healthy respect for the intellectual and emotional capacities of young readers.

SPECIAL CHARACTERISTICS
OF AUTOBIOGRAPHY

Autobiography has some of its own special characteristics that set it apart from biography. Obviously, autobiographies are not complete lives—since they are written in the midst of one's life. Often, an autobiographer will write only about one part of his or her life—childhood and adolescence, for example, or early adult years, or specific career experiences. Autobiography is usually more informal than biography, sometimes appearing in the form of memoirs or reminiscences. Individuals may feel they have no need to research their own lives, and therefore rely on their memories and recollections to supply them with information. For example, specific dates are frequently missing from autobiographies, perhaps because the writers feel no need to prove authenticity. After all, they probably think, who should know their lives better than they themselves? Likewise, autobiographies typically lack references, often even tables of contents and indexes.

By the same token, we must be wary of what a writer says in an autobiography, for it is difficult to find a more potentially biased source about an individual's life than the individual him- or herself. This does not mean that the autobiographer always puts him- or herself in the best light. Henry Adams's famous autobiography for adult readers, *The Education of Henry Adams*, is remarkably self-effacing and modest. Readers would hardly guess that the writer was a highly respected teacher, scholar, and public servant. Autobiographies are not necessarily reliable sources of facts about people.

On the other hand, the autobiography can be an indispensable source for discovering an individual's character traits, likes and dislikes, innermost feelings—these things are not easily hidden. The unique personal perspective of the autobiography can tell us things we will find no place else. It also has the advantage of immediacy—if it is well written—of making us feel as if we are right there next to the subject, sharing his or her life experiences.

Regrettably, few autobiographies are written especially for children. This is perhaps not surprising, for individuals who feel their lives are worth recording usually prefer to write for adult readers. However, recent years have seen more and more autobiographical writing for young readers. The series of autobiographical picture books about famous children's illustrators, including *Self-Portrait: Margot Zemach* and *Self-Portrait: Erik Blegvad*, provides an interesting variation on the autobiography whereby artists not only tell their own life stories, they illustrate them as well. These are some of the finer examples of autobiographies for children. A market surely exists for good, brief autobiographies for children by some of their favorite authors. Betsy Byars's *The Moon and I*, Phyllis Reynolds Naylor's *How I Came to Be a Writer*, and Roald Dahl's *Boy: Tales of Childhood* are three examples. Aside from providing positive role models and uplifting examples, autobiographies are excellent sources for encouraging children to think about their own life experiences and to record those experiences in a diary or journal. Both biography and autobiography can inspire us all to examine our own lives and bring us to a deeper understanding of ourselves.

WORKS CITED

Gottlieb, Robin. "On Nonfiction Books for Children: Tradition & Dissent." *Wilson Library Journal* October 1974: 174-177.

Kendall, Paul Murray. *The Art of Biography*. New York: Norton, 1985.

RECOMMENDED READINGS

Aiken, Joan. "Interpreting the Past." *Children's Literature in Education* 16 (Summer 1985): 67-83.

Berry, Thomas Elliott, ed. *The Biographer's Craft*. New York: Odyssey, 1967.

Blos, Joan. "The Overstuffed Sentence and Other Means for Assessing Historical Fiction for Children." *School Library Journal* 31 (November 1985): 38-39.

Bowen, Catherine Drinker. *Biography: The Craft and the Calling*. Boston: Little, Brown, 1968.

Burton, Hester. "The Writing of Historical Novels." In *Children and Literature: Views and Reviews*, ed. Virginia Haviland. Glenview, IL: Scott, Foresman, 1973.

Carr, Jo. "What Do We Do About Bad Biographies?" In *Beyond Fact*, ed. Jo Carr. Chicago: American Library Association, 1982.

Coolidge, Olivia. "My Struggle with Facts." *Wilson Library Bulletin* October 1974: 146-151.

Fisher, Margery. "Life Course or Screaming Force." *Children's Literature in Education* Autumn 1976: 107-127.

Forman, Jack. "Biography for Children: More Facts, Less Fiction." *Library Journal* 97 (September 15, 1972): 2968-2969.

Fritz, Jean. "George Washington, My Father, and Walt Disney." *Horn Book Magazine* 52 (April 1976): 191-198.

Garfield, Leon. "Historical Fiction for Our Global Times." *The Horn Book* November/December 1988: 736-742.

Groff, Patrick. "Biography: The Bad or the Bountiful." *Top of the News* April 1973: 210-217.

Higgins, Judith. "Biographies They Can Read." *School Library Journal* 18 (April 1971): 33-34.

Jurich, Marilyn. "What's Left Out of Biography for Children?" *Children's Literature* 1 (1972): 143-151.

Lochhead, Marion. "Clio Junior: Historical Novels for Children." In *Only Connect*, 2d ed., eds. Sheila Egoff, G. T. Stubbs, and L. F. Ashely. New York: Oxford University Press, 1980.

Marcus, Leonard. "Life Drawing: Some Notes on Children's Picture Book Biographies." *The Lion and the Unicorn* 4 (Summer 1980): 15-31.

Moore, Ann W. "A Question of Accuracy: Errors in Children's Biographies." *School Library Journal* 31 (Feb. 1985): 34-35.

Morman, Charles. *Kings & Captains: Variations on a Heroic Theme*. Louisville: University of Kentucky Press, 1971.

Rahn, Suzanne. "An Evolving Past: The Story of Historical Fiction and Nonfiction for Children." *The Lion and the Unicorn* 15 (June 1991): 1-26.

Segel, Elizabeth. "In Biographies for Young Readers, Nothing Is Impossible." *The Lion and the Unicorn* 4 (Summer 1980): 4-14.

Wilms, Denise M. "An Evaluation of Biography." In *Jump Over the Moon*, eds. Pamela Barron and Jennifer Burley. New York: Holt, Rinehart and Winson, 1984.

SELECTED BIBLIOGRAPHY OF BIOGRAPHIES AND AUTOBIOGRAPHIES

Since many writers specialize in biographical writing, look for other biographies by the writers represented on this list. If the subject of the biography is not obvious from the title, it has been supplied in brackets next to the entry. The recommended reading levels are approximations only, since every young reader develops at a different pace.

BIOGRAPHIES FOR YOUNGER READERS (GRADES 2–5)

Adler, David A. *Christopher Columbus, Great Explorer*. New York: Holiday House, 1991.

Aliki (pseud. of Aliki Brandenburg). *The Story of Johnny Appleseed*. Englewood Cliffs, NJ: Prentice-Hall, 1963.

————. *A Weed Is a Flower: The Life of George Washington Carver*. Englewood Cliffs, NJ: Prentice-Hall, 1965.

Bolliger, Max. *David*. Illus. Edith Schindler. New York: Delacorte, 1967.

Bulla, Clyde. *Songs of St. Francis*. Illus. Valenti Angelo. New York: Crowell, 1952. (St. Francis of Assisi)

————. *Squanto, Friend of the Pilgrims*. Illus. Peter Burchard. New York: Crowell, 1954.

————. *Washington's Birthday*. Illus. Don Bolognese. New York: Crowell, 1957.

Daugherty, James. *Abraham Lincoln*. New York: Viking, 1943.

————. *Daniel Boone*. New York: Viking, 1939.

d'Aulaire, Ingri, and Edgar Parin d'Aulaire. *Abraham Lincoln*. New York: Doubleday, 1939.

————. *Columbus*. New York: Doubleday, 1959.

Faber, Doris. *Eleanor Roosevelt: First Lady of the World*. New York: Viking, 1985.

Fritz, Jean. *Bully for You, Teddy Roosevelt!* New York: Putnam, 1991.

————. *Can't You Make Them Behave, King George?* Illus. Tomie de Paola. New York: Coward-McCann, 1977. (King George III)

————. *The Double Life of Pocahontas*. New York: Putnam, 1983.

————. *Homesick: My Own Story*. New York: Putnam, 1982. (Autobiography)

————. *Make Way for Sam Houston*. New York: Putnam, 1986.

————. *Where Was Patrick Henry on the 29th of May?* Illus. Margot Tomes. New York: Coward-McCann, 1975.

Gish, Lillian, and Selma Lanes. *An Actor's Life for Me*. New York: Viking, 1987.

Goodsell, Jane. *Eleanor Roosevelt*. New York: Crowell, 1970.

———. *The Mayo Brothers*. New York: Crowell, 1972.

Greenfield, Eloise. *Mary McLeod Bethune*. New York: Crowell, 1977.

———. *Rosa Parks*. New York: Crowell, 1973.

Hyman, Trina Schart. *Self-Portrait: Trina Schart Hyman* (1981). New York: HarperCollins, 1989.

Johnston, Johanna. *Harriet and the Runaway Book: The Story of Harriet Beecher Stowe and Uncle Tom's Cabin*. New York: Harper, 1977.

Judson, Clara Ingram. *Abraham Lincoln, Friend of the People*. Chicago: Wilcox and Follett, 1950.

———. *Admiral Christopher Columbus*. Chicago: Follett, 1965.

Lawrence, Jacob. *Harriet and the Promised Land*. New York: Windmill, 1968. (One-time slave and heroine of the underground railroad Harriet Tubman)

Monjo, F. N. *The One Bad Thing About Father*. New York: Harper, 1970. (Theodore Roosevelt)

———. *Poor Richard in France*. New York: Holt, 1973. (Benjamin Franklin)

Peet, Bill. *Bill Peet: An Autobiography*. Boston: Houghton Mifflin, 1989.

Provensen, Alice, and Martin Provensen. *The Glorious Flight: Across the Channel with Louis Bleriot*. New York: Viking, 1983.

Raboff, Ernest. *Marc Chagall*. New York: Doubleday, 1968.

———. *Pablo Picasso*. New York: Doubleday, 1968.

Shippen, Katherine. *Leif Eriksson: First Voyager to America*. New York: Harper, 1951.

Stanley, Diane. *Peter the Great*. New York: Four Winds, 1986.

BIOGRAPHIES FOR OLDER READERS (GRADES 6 AND UP)

Adoff, Arnold. *Malcolm X*. Illus. John Wilson. New York: Crowell, 1970.

Asimov, Isaac. *Breakthroughs in Science*. Boston: Houghton Mifflin, 1960.

Blegvad, Erik. *Self-Portrait: Erik Blegvad*. Reading, MA: Addison-Wesley, 1979.

Brooks, Polly Schoyer. *Queen Eleanor: Independent Spirit of the Medieval World*. Philadelphia: Lippincott, 1983.

Bruchac, Joseph. *A Boy Called Slow: The True Story of Sitting Bull*. New York: Philomel, 1995.

Buckmaster, Henrietta. *Women Who Shaped History*. New York: Macmillan, 1966.

Burleigh, Robert. *Flight: The Journey of Charles Lindbergh*. New York: Philomel, 1991.

Carter, Dorothy S. *Queen Hatshepsut*. Illus. Cecil Leslie. New York: Faber, 1978.

Clayton, Ed. *Martin Luther King: The Peaceful Warrior*. Englewood Cliffs, NJ: Prentice-Hall, 1968.

Cleary, Beverly. *A Girl from Yamhill: A Memoir*. New York: Morrow, 1988.

Collier, James Lincoln. *Louis Armstrong: An American Success Story*. New York: Macmillan, 1985.

Coolidge, Olivia. *Tom Paine: Revolutionary*. New York: Scribner's, 1969.

———. *Winston Churchill and the Story of Two World Wars*. Boston: Houghton Mifflin, 1960.

Dahl, Roald. *Boy: Tales of Childhood*. New York: Farrar, Straus & Giroux, 1984.

Davidson, Margaret. *The Story of Eleanor Roosevelt*. New York: Four Winds, 1969.

De Trevino, Elizabeth Borton. *I, Juan de Pareja*. New York: Farrar, Straus & Giroux, 1965.

Duncan, Lois. *Chapters: My Growth as a Writer*. Boston: Little, Brown, 1982.

Eaton, Jeanette. *America's Own Mark Twain*. Illus. Leonard Everett Fisher. New York: Morrow, 1958.

Ferris, Jeri. *Native American Doctor: The Story of Susan LaFlesche Picotte*. Minneapolis: Carolrhoda, 1991.

Fisher, Leonard Everett. *Galileo*. New York: Macmillan, 1992.

Freedman, Russell. *Eleanor Roosevelt: A Life of Discovery*. New York: Clarion, 1993.

————. *Franklin Delano Roosevelt*. New York: Clarion, 1990.

————. *Indian Chiefs*. New York: Holiday House, 1987.

————. *Lincoln: A Photobiography*. New York: Clarion, 1987.

————. *The Wright Brothers: How They Invented the Airplane*. New York: Holiday, 1991.

Hamilton, Virginia. *W. E. B. DuBois: A Biography*. New York: Crowell, 1972.

Hanff, Helene. *Queen of England: The Story of Elizabeth I*. New York: Doubleday, 1969.

Haskins, James. *The Story of Stevie Wonder*. New York: Lothrop, 1976.

Henry, Marguerite, and Wesley Dennis. *Benjamin West and His Cat Grimalkin*. Illus. Wesley Dennis. Indianapolis: Bobbs-Merrill, 1947. (Early American artist Benjamin West)

Hoyt-Goldsmith, Diane. *Hoang Anh: A Vietnamese-American Boy*. New York: Holiday, 1992.

Kennedy, John F. *Profiles in Courage*. New York: Harper, 1964. (Abridged for young readers; stories of courageous Americans)

Kherdian, David. *The Road from Home: The Story of an Armenian Girl*. New York: Greenwillow, 1979.

Komroff, Manuel. *Mozart*. Illus. Warren Chappell. New York: Knopf, 1956.

Konigsburg, E. L. *A Proud Taste for Scarlet and Miniver*. New York: Dell, 1973. (Fictionalized account of the life of Eleanor of Aquitaine)

Lacy, Leslie Alexander. *Cheer the Lonesome Traveler: The Life of W. E. B. DuBois*. New York: Dial, 1970.

Latham, Jean Lee. *Carry On, Mr. Bowditch*. Boston: Houghton Mifflin, 1955.

Lipsyte, Robert. *Jim Thorpe: 20th-Century Jock*, New York: Harper, 1993.

Littlefield, Bill. *Champions: Stories of Ten Remarkable Athletes*. Boston: Little, Brown, 1993.

McKissack, Patricia C. *Jesse Jackson: A Biography*. New York: Scholastic, 1989.

McNeer, May. *America's Mark Twain*. Illus. Lynd Ward. Boston: Houghton Mifflin, 1962.

Mathis, Sharon Bell. *Ray Charles*. New York: Crowell, 1973.

Meigs, Cornelia. *Invincible Louisa*. Boston: Little, Brown, 1968.

Meltzer, Milton. *Benjamin Franklin: The New American*. New York: Watts, 1984.

————. *Dorothea Lange: Life Through the Camera*. New York: Viking, 1985.

————. *Langston Hughes: A Biography*. New York: Crowell, 1968.

Mitchison, Naomi. *African Heroes*. New York: Farrar, Straus & Giroux, 1969.

Naylor, Phyllis Reynolds. *How I Came to Be a Writer* (1978). New York: Aladdin, 1987.

Oneal, Zibby. *Grandma Moses: Painter of Rural America*. New York: Viking, 1986.

Reef, Catherine. *Walt Whitman*. New York: Clarion, 1995.

Rylant, Cynthia. *Best Wishes*. Photographs by Carlo Ontal. Katonah, NY: Richard C. Owen, 1992. (Autobiography)

Sandburg, Carl. *Abe Lincoln Grows Up*. Illus. James Daugherty. New York: Harcourt, 1928.

Shiels, Barbara. *Winners: Women and the Nobel Prize*. Minneapolis: Dillon, 1985.

Sills, Leslie. *Inspirations: Stories about Women Artists*. Morton Grove, IL: Whitman, 1989.

Singer, Isaac Bashevis. *A Day of Pleasures: Stories of a Boy Growing Up in Warsaw*. New York: Farrar, Straus & Giroux, 1969.

Sis, Peter. *Follow the Dream*. New York: Knopf, 1991. (Christopher Columbus)

Stanley, Fay. *The Last Princess: The Story of Princess Ka'iulani of Hawai'i*. New York: Four Winds, 1991.

Stanley, Jerry. *I Am an American: A True Story of Japanese Internment*. New York: Crown, 1994.

Stoddard, Hope. *Famous American Women*. New York: Crowell, 1970.

Swift, Hildegarde. *From the Eagle's Wing: A Biography of John Muir*. Illus. Lynd Ward. New York: Morrow, 1962.

Tobias, Tobi. *Marian Anderson*. New York: Crowell, 1972.

Turner, Robyn Montana. *Georgia O'Keeffe*. Boston: Little, Brown, 1991.

———. *Rosa Bonheur*. Boston: Little, 1991.

van der Rol, Ruud, and Rian Verhoeven. *Anne Frank: Beyond the Diary*. New York: Viking, 1993.

Wadsworth, Ginger. *Rachel Carson: Voice for the Earth*. Minneapolis: Lerner, 1992.

Weidhorn, Manfred. *Jackie Robinson*. New York: Atheneum, 1993.

Yates, Elizabeth. *Amos Fortune, Free Man*. New York: Dutton, 1950.

Yolen, Jane. *A Letter from Phoenix Farm*. Photographs by Jason Stemple. Katonah, NY: Richard C. Owen, 1992. (Autobiography)

Zemach, Margot. *Self-Portrait: Margot Zemach*. Reading, MA: Addison-Wesley, 1978.

Chapter 13

INFORMATIONAL BOOKS

Adults are not accustomed to thinking of books on history, travel, science, or human behavior as "literature." Instead, these informational or nonfiction works are usually seen as functional, their purpose being to convey information rather than to entertain or inspire us. But in children's literature the distinction has always been fuzzy. One of the reasons may be that children themselves do not clearly distinguish between fiction and nonfiction. Indeed, sometimes the lines seem to disappear altogether. Joanna Cole's very popular "Magic School Bus" series are picture books about an unconventional science teacher who believes in hands-on experience and has at her disposal a school bus capable of taking the class to the center of the earth, for example, to study rocks (in *The Magic School Bus: Inside the Earth*). In this case, through fantasy fiction, young readers are introduced to the field of geology.

Adults sometimes seem to expect their nonfiction to be flat and utilitarian, but children demand works that are alive with imagination. Consequently, in informational books for children we find that creativity and fine writing are as important as accuracy. We might add here that there is absolutely no reason adults should not make the same demands of their informational books as do children—but in our society adults seem to value information over aesthetics and content over form.

TYPES OF INFORMATIONAL BOOKS

For the purposes of this chapter, we shall take "informational books" to mean any works that deal exclusively with factual material and are clearly intended above all to instruct young readers. In Chapter 6, we briefly discussed the first informational books children are likely to encounter—the concept books. Now we will consider the wider realm of informational books. Informational books for young people are available on virtually any imaginable topic. We shall attempt to simplify our discussion by grouping these works into four broad (and occasionally overlapping) subject categories.

LANDS AND PEOPLES

This is admittedly a very broad category, encompassing history, geography, anthropology, sociology, and religion, to name a few subjects. Most of the children's books dealing with lands and peoples fit into one of the following categories:

1. books about the past,
2. books about places,
3. books about societies and cultures (our own and others), and
4. book about religions.

Consider how many of our world's problems have resulted from our failure to understand and empathize with the other people who share this planet. We only dimly understand our own culture, let alone those of distant foreign peoples. By being introduced to other cultures, other civilizations, we not only learn about them, but we learn more about ourselves. Additionally, tolerance is often a happy byproduct of this knowledge. Bigotry and fear are usually the result of ignorance. Any book that makes young readers aware of the world and the people around them will contribute to our efforts toward global understanding.

It is possible to learn a great deal about people and places through well-written realistic fiction and even through the traditional folktales. However, in addition to these fictional works, it is important that children also read factual accounts to receive a fuller understanding and appreciation of a culture. Recent years have seen the appearance of some very fine informational books written for the very young. Aliki (pseudonym for Aliki Brandenburg) has been among the most consistently successful in bringing stories of lands and peoples to children in the lower grades (for example, *Mummies Made in Egypt*). Books about history, geography, and cultures figure even more prominently in reading for children in the middle elementary years. Leonard Everett Fisher has created two outstanding series of first-rate informational books—one on colonial American crafts and one on nineteenth-century American commerce and industry. (His *Pumpers, Boilers, Hooks and Ladders* is suitable for a younger audience, and such works as *The Factories, The Railroads*, and *The Schoolmasters* are suited to fourth, fifth, and sixth graders.) Fisher gives us a clear text and powerful illustrations, two of the most important features in any informational book for young readers.

Milton Meltzer has produced superb works on some rather complex facets of American history. His books include *In Their Own Words: A History of the American Negro; Brother Can You Spare a Dime? The Great Depression: 1929–1933*; and *Bread and Roses: The Struggle of American Labor, 1865–1915*. Meltzer's works are distinguished by their thorough scholarship. He treats his young readers with great respect, never condescending to them; he includes bibliographies and indexes (two features not always found in informational books for young people); and he prefers to use period photographs to illustrate his works (a feature that gives them a great deal of authenticity).

In addition to his biographies mentioned in Chapter 12, Russell Freedman has written such historical works as *Cowboys of the Wild West*, presenting a fascinating history that corrects some of our misconceptions about cowboys. Through his use of photographs and an exciting writing style, Freedman suggests that the reality was even more compelling than the myth. Modern social concerns are documented in Brent Ashabranner's *Children of the Maya*, a photo-essay about Central American natives attempting to rebuild their lives in Florida after escaping from persecution in their homeland. Books such as Walter Dean Myers's *Now Is Your Time!: The African-American Struggle for Freedom* seek to address an inadequacy that has plagued us so long in books about African Americans and their contribution to American society.

In the field of religion, not only do children need to learn about their own religious heritage, they need to become acquainted with other religions and to learn respect for other beliefs. There are some particularly useful books about Jewish traditions, such as Howard Greenfield's *Passover* and *Rosh Hashanah and Yom Kippur* or Karla Kuskin's *Jerusalem, Shining Still*. Alice Bach and J. Cheryl Exum have retold some of the stories of the Old Testament to provide a feminine point of view in *Miriam's Well: Stories about Women in the Bible*. Anton Powell's *The Rise of Islam* describes the earlier history of that important world religion. And Elizabeth Seeger's *Eastern Religions* explores the religious faith of the Orient. In an age when religion is still capable of firing passions to violence, the more knowledge we have of other faiths the more likely we are to learn tolerance for them.

SCIENCE AND NATURE

Millicent Selsam, herself a fine science writer for children, tells us that "a good science book is not just a collection of facts" (62). The fault of many school textbooks is that they provide voluminous, static facts and overlook the more important total picture. (This is true of texts on all subjects, not science alone.) Or, to cite an old, but not inappropriate, cliché, these books prevent us from seeing the forest because of the trees. A good science book, Selsam contends, demonstrates the workings of the scientific method as well as conveys "something of the beauty and excitement of science" (65).

The major types of books found in this category of science and nature include

1. books about the life sciences, including studies of animals and plants;
2. books about managing the environment, which combine the life sciences and the earth sciences;
3. books about the earth or physical sciences, including natural laws and outer space; and
4. books about the abstract world of mathematics.

As might be expected, informational books about animals are among the most popular of the science books—particularly with younger readers. We are told that the most frequently consulted entry in a young people's encyclopedia is that on dogs. Children in the very early years find almost any book about animals appealing. In recent years, a number of very good books have appeared on unusual or threatened animal species, including the puffin, the panda, the bald eagle, and some largely unheard of species, such as the hoiho in Adele Vernon's *The Hoiho: New Zealand's Yellow-Eyed Penguin*, and some surprising ones such as several breeds of American farm animals close to extinction, as described in Catherine Paladino's *Our Vanishing Farm Animals*.

The plant world can be equally fascinating to younger children, as demonstrated in such books as Gail Gibbons's *From Seed to Plant* and Ruth Heller's *The Reason for a Flower*. Both books illustrate one of nature's most elemental tales, the growth of a plant from a tiny seed. Since this process can easily be witnessed at home or in a schoolroom over a relatively short period of time, hands-on experience can follow the reading of these books. We also know that it is not only the animal world that is threatened with extinction, and we are beginning to see books alerting young children to the potential disappearance of our plant life as well. Barbara Taylor's series, including *Coral Life, Desert Life, Pond Life*, and *Rain Forests*, introduces the very young to the concept of the ecosystem—plants and animals working together to maintain the balance of nature and ensure the survival of the planet.

Laurence Pringle's *Living in a Risky World* encourages young readers to think about modern civilization and the implications of its lifestyle, particularly the effects of its pollutants (acid rain, carcinogens, and other environmental hazards). A book such as this demonstrates that the scientific world is not divorced from our everyday world or from the complicated ethical issues that face humanity. This work pointedly examines the ethics of science and technology in the modern world—the title suggests both the substance and the theme. As we face the ethical dilemma of humanity's responsibility to the earth, and as polution, overpopulation, and reckless development take their toll, it becomes more imperative that we begin educating our young children about the delicate ecosystem in which we all must live out our lives.

Books about the earth sciences include such works as Joanna Cole's *The Magic School Bus: Inside the Earth*, mentioned previously, and Seymour Simon's *Earthquakes*, which not only provides elementary scientific information on the description and cause of earthquakes but also practical information such as what to do when one occurs. Franklyn Branley's *Light and Darkness* and Claire Llewellyn's *My First Book of Time* both focus on physics, albeit quite fundamental. Probably the most popular of these types of books are those not about the earth at all, but those about the physical nature of outer space. Astronaut Sally Ride in *To Space and Back* (coauthored with Susan Okie) describes her experiences on the space shuttle flight, and this book serves a dual purpose of presenting up-to-date information of general interest and of dispelling feminine stereotyping in career choices. These works, as might be expected, date rather more rapidly than most publications, and there is the constant need for up-to-date works, as scientific discoveries reveal new facts, engender new theories, and provide for new technologies. Franklyn Branley's *Uranus: The Seventh Planet* was written in 1976 and included the most up-to-date information on our giant distant neighbor. But the visit of Voyager 2 to the planet in 1986 prompted Seymour Simon to write *Uranus*, much of the earlier information on the planet having become obsolete.

David Macauley's near monumental *The Way Things Work* explores all the realms of the earth sciences—mechanics, physics (even nuclear physics), electronics, and chemistry. With amazing clarity and simplicity and with the help of hundreds of clever drawings, Macauley explains a phenomenal number of complex ideas and processes. This is a book with enormous appeal for adults as well as young people. Among the books on mathematical subjects are Mitsumasa Anno's imaginatively illustrated *Anno's Math Games* in two volumes and Jane Jonas Srivastava's *Statistics*, an introduction for middle elementary school children. Given the highly publicized deficiency that most American children apparently exhibit in mathematical skills, this would seem to be a ripe field for imaginative writers who are capable of bringing this abstract science to life.

Sometimes a science book skirts the border between science and art. Jim Arnosky's *Secrets of a Wildlife Watcher* is a firsthand account of ways to locate and observe animals in the wild. This work is also an example of how science writing can be brought to a practical level. In at least two later books, Arnosky takes his scientific knowledge and puts it to recreational use: *Fish in a Flash!: A Personal Guide to Spin-Fishing* and *Sketching Outdoors in Spring*. So we find a segue into a new class of informational books, the fine and applied arts, and we are reminded that where there is art, science is never far afield, and vice versa.

FINE AND APPLIED ARTS

The creative impulses of humanity have produced everything from architectural monuments (as illustrated by David Macauley's carefully detailed *Cathedral* and *Castle*) to oil paintings (as presented in Ernest Raboff's series, "Art for Children," on the major artists of the Western world) to such practical arts as the invention of writing (as graphically described in Leonard Everett Fisher's *Alphabet Art*). Children can read about dance (Arnold Haskell's *The Wonderful World of Dance*), music (Langston Hughes's *The First Book of Jazz*), gardening (Marc Brown's *Your First Garden Book*), and the theater (Walter Hodge's *Shakespeare's Theater*)—in titles that only begin to scratch the surface.

Picture books make good introductions to art and artists, for reproductions of their works can be included. Some good books to begin with are Alice Elizabeth Chase's *Looking at Art*, which describes the various ways that artists have viewed the world, or Robert Hofsinde's *Indian Arts*, which reminds us that that art, culture, and history are all wrapped up together. In recent years, many books for children about individual artists have appeared.

In this category, we also include books on sports, which can certainly be viewed as artistic expression (indeed, a skill such as ice skating, as described in Jonah and Laura Kalb's *The Easy Ice Skating Book*, has developed into a highly refined performing art). And too, we should not forget the various craft and hobby books, such as Ferne Geller Cone's *Crazy Crocheting*, which describes a time-honored folk art form. Combining sports and the art of writing is William Jaspersohn's *Magazine: Behind the Scenes at* Sports Illustrated. This photo-essay may have an immediate appeal to sports buffs, but its focus is actually on the writing, editing, illustrating, and printing of a magazine. This is a book focusing quite clearly on an applied art—art put to a practical, everyday purpose.

HUMAN DEVELOPMENT AND BEHAVIOR

Books about human development and behavior include all those dealing with the cycle of life—especially birth, growth, sexuality, and death—and interpersonal relationships. These issues are treated frequently in picture storybooks (Martha Alexander's *Nobody Asked Me If I Wanted a Baby Sister* and Judith Viorst's book about the death of a pet, *The Tenth Good Thing About Barney*, are two good examples). Such works are not, of course, *informational* books, the primary purpose of which is to impart facts; however, fiction is probably the most effective way of conveying complex psychological concepts to young readers. But for older readers, stories of human behavior have a great impact if they are factual. The success of the so-called docu-drama, a movie based on an actual event, suggests that adults also find true stories equally as engrossing as fiction.

Eda LeShan's *What Makes Me Feel This Way?* is written for upper elementary-aged children and deals with personal emotions. A growing number of informational books address personal responses to human predicaments. Jill Krementz specializes in writing frankly about difficult human problems. In *How It Feels When Parents Divorce*, Krementz uses firsthand accounts from children of divorced parents. Appropriately, the book is illustrated with photographs, intensifying the reality of the subject.

Physical disabilities are too frequently ignored in books for children, and Ron Roy's *Move Over, Wheelchairs Coming Through!* is a welcome addition to informational books. Subtitled *Several Young People in Wheelchairs Talk About Their Lives*, this is a fascinating and moving account that provides an admirable combination of frankness and sensitivity for its topic. As we have seen, there is virtually no limit to the sort of psychological or sociological problems that children's literature might discuss. Our society's penchant for therapy has at last spilled over into the realm of children's books.

EVALUATING INFORMATIONAL BOOKS

As with biographies, informational books must necessarily be evaluated by quite different standards from fiction, but an evaluation, nevertheless, is quite crucial. Readers, adults and children alike, have a tendency to accept unquestioningly whatever they see in print, particularly if the work purports to be "informational." The following criteria may help in evaluating these books.

PURPOSE AND AUDIENCE

An informational book is more successful if its *purpose and audience* are clear from the very beginning. An illustrated book for very young readers about life in the seventeenth-century court of King Louis XIV of France (Aliki's *The King's Day*) is not meant to give us an assessment of the Sun King or a perspective of the French people in his day. Its purpose is narrowly defined and appropriate to its audience. Aliki illustrates the fantastic ritual surrounding the monarch and give us the flavor of royal France of 300 years ago. At the other end of the spectrum are Milton Meltzer's carefully researched and documented social histories and David Macauley's works on physics and architecture. It is helpful to determine what the writer's purpose is, for whom the book is written, and how successfully the goals have been met.

The secret of a good informational book is to present material that is new and challenging, without being intimidating. But we should not take this to mean that facts for younger readers should be sugarcoated. Life is difficult enough without our complicating it with delusions and misconceptions.

ACCURACY AND OBJECTIVITY

A fiction writer must be a keen observer of human nature, but not necessarily an "expert" in any particular field of study. The author of an informational book, however, may need specialized training in the subject about which he or she is writing. This is less true for writers of picture concept books for preschoolers than it is for juvenile authors. (One need not be a linguist to create a good alphabet book or a mathematician to create a good counting book.) But it should go without saying that an informational book with glaring errors is not a good thing.

Authors of informational books for older children tend to specialize—Franklyn Branley in physics and astronomy, Leonard Everett Fisher in historical crafts and trades, Millicent Selsam in natural history, Vicki Cobb in chemistry, and so on. Interested readers begin to recognize familiar names and seek out books by certain writers in a field. Also, the upper elementary years are not too early for children to begin thinking about the authors behind the books and their qualifications. Sometimes biographical notes in the books themselves provide this information, but additional information can be garnered from library card catalogues, books about writers (such as *Something About the Author* or *The Dictionary of Literary Biography*), and in books about children's literature. Naturally, much of the burden for determining the accuracy of a work will lie with adults, but we should take every opportunity to show children the importance of *accuracy* and encourage them to question accuracy in their reading.

Objectivity in informational books is an important asset. A good book presents a balanced point of view, weighs all the available evidence, and draws conclusions based on that evidence. Jim Murphy's recent account of the Chicago fire, *The Great Fire*, is a good example of a book that provides a variety of viewpoints, including firsthand reports. Additionally, Murphy carefully examines the various problems the city faced in fighting the fire—human error, inefficient organization of the firefighters, and so on—problems that prevented a successful response. Murphy's book shows us that a historical account can be balanced and faithful to the facts as well as exciting to read. The old saying has it that truth is stranger than fiction, and if that is true the writer of nonfiction should have no need to embellish the facts.

In addition to presenting a balanced view of the information, the good writer of nonfiction should give us up-to-date information. Informational books, as we have noted, become rather quickly dated—science books become outdated when new discoveries and theories supercede the old; books on history, art, and human behavior become outdated as new material is uncovered and as society's attitudes change. For example, a survey of books on Christopher Columbus will reveal such a change. Early books (such as Ingri and Edgar Parin d'Aulaire's *Columbus*, 1955) depict Columbus as a noble hero, whereas more recent studies (notably David Adler's *Christopher Columbus, Great Explorer*, 1991, and Milton Meltzer's *Christopher Columbus and the World Around Him*, 1990) reveal Columbus's mercenary side, as well as his heinous treatment of the Native American population. In the area of human behavior, we can find an example of changing attitudes in books on sexuality, including a rising number of works for children on the issue of homosexuality (for example, Roger Sutton's *Hearing Us Out: Voices from the Gay and Lesbian Community*, 1994). Just because an informational book is new does not mean that is better than anything that came before it, and many older books remain solid sources of information. Nevertheless, the publication date of an informational book can be quite significant.

FORMAT AND ORGANIZATION

A book that is well laid out can go a long way in making the information less intimidating for young readers. Readers young and old prefer books that are easy to follow—and a book does not have to be simplistic to be easy to follow. We look for clear and logical organization: from simple to complex ideas in the case of science and art, or chronologically in the case of history. Organizational aids (such as headings and subheadings) and supplementary aids (such as a table of contents, a glossary, an index, and a bibliography) are especially desirable in more complex books for older children.

Illustrations must be carefully placed in the text (preferably next to the material they are illustrating). Captions should be included if they are appropriate. We should expect illustrations both to increase our knowledge and to provide aesthetic pleasure. Photographs are frequently used to illustrate informational books, for they can provide a sense of reality and authenticity (particularly in history books, nature books, and books about people). Books on science and nature can benefit from photographs as well. Photography, of course, is an art—and not just any photograph will do. A well done photograph can be beautiful and moving and will do more than simply identify an object.

This is not to suggest that photographs are the only effective means of illustrating informational books. However, when graphic or painterly techniques are used to illustrate these works they ought not trivialize the subject (can you imagine a cartoon book about divorce or the death of parent?) or unnecessarily sentimentalize it. Leonard Everett Fisher opted for black and white scratchboard illustrations for his history works, and they are appropriately simple without suggesting that colonial life was a bed of roses. Regardless of the medium and style of the illustrative material, the important thing is that the illustrations contribute to the essentially instructional value of the book.

STYLE

As was suggested above, school textbooks are notoriously dull reading—in part, because they are obliged to convey a great deal of information in a short space. But informational books can be entertaining. Certainly, the first virtue of any informational book is clarity—without this, the book is a failure. An informational book, not only through its choice of facts, but through its choice of words (diction) and sentence structure (syntax) can be stimulating reading. A good writer will suit both diction and syntax to the intended audience's age level. (We have already noted that boredom results from the material or the style being either too simple or too difficult for the reader.)

Where it is appropriate, humor can add enjoyment to informational books—so long as it neither mocks nor obscures an issue. And humor can help to make the material less intimidating. Appropriate similes and metaphors not only make interesting reading, they can also clarify complicated or unfamiliar ideas. David Macauley's *The Way Things Work* treats some extremely complicated concepts, but he ties the entire work together by using cartoon figures of woolly mammoths to demonstrate the various properties and scientific principles involved. For example, the mammoths are used to represent "force" or "effort." (The cartoon figures, incidentally, do not trivialize the subject matter in this case; instead they help to make accessible some extraordinarily complex ideas—such as jet propulsion and the operation of computers.) In this way, Macauley uses metaphor to illustrate an otherwise abstract concept, and humor to make his explanations understandable and enjoyable. The comical cartoons in Joanna Cole's "The Magic School Bus" books depict wisecracking students at the mercy of their eccentric teacher, Ms. Frizzle. Humor is a tool that helps many people to learn material more quickly and remember it longer.

INFORMATIONAL BOOKS AS LITERATURE

Informational books for young people should be books that excite young readers to do further reading, books that young readers want to return to again and again—not only for information, but for enjoyment. It is quite right to expect that a nonfictional work be well written, beautifully illustrated, imaginatively laid out, as well as up-to-date, accurate, and thought-provoking. Fortunately, it is possible today to find books for children by writers who know their subjects well and who are able to convey their love and enthusiasm to others—it is the ideal formula for the informational book.

WORK CITED

Selsam, Millicent E. "Writing About Science for Children." In *Beyond Fact: Nonfiction for Children and Young People*, ed. Jo Carr. Chicago: American Library Association, 1982.

RECOMMENDED READINGS

Bacon, Betty. "The Art of Nonfiction." *Children's Literature in Education* 14 (Spring 1981): 3-14

Carr, Jo, ed. *Beyond Fact: Nonfiction for Children and Young People*. Chicago: American Library Association, 1982.

Carter, Betty, and Richard F. Abrahamson. *Nonfiction for Young Adults: From Delight to Wisdom*. Phoenix, AZ: Oryx Press, 1991.

Chamberlain, Larry. "Enchantment Isn't Everything: A New Way of Looking at Lands and Peoples." *School Library Journal* (1978): 25-26.

Fisher, Margery. *Matters of Fact: Aspects of Non-Fiction for Children*. New York: Crowell, 1972.

Kobrin, Beverly. *Eyeopeners! How to Choose and Use Children's Books About Real People, Places, and Things*. New York: Viking, 1988.

Mallet, Margaret. *Making Facts Matter: Reading Non-fiction 5-11*. London: Paul Chapman, 1992.

Meltzer, Milton. "Where Do All the Prizes Go? The Case for Nonfiction." *Horn Book Magazine* 52 (February 1976): 17-23.

Norris, Lynn. "Extending Curiosity: Children's Informational Books." *Idaho Librarian* October 1975: 126-128.

Sutherland, Zena. "Information Pleases—Sometimes." *Wilson Library Journal* 49 (October 1974): 17-23.

———. "Science as Literature." *Literary Trends* 22:4 (April 1974): 485-489.

SELECTED BIBLIOGRAPHY
OF INFORMATIONAL BOOKS

The books in this list simply represent a cross-section of the wealth of nonfictional reading available for young readers. These books are categorized according to the four broad classifications outlined in this chapter; however, these are only general guidelines, and frequently books cross boundaries. For example, Franklyn Branley's *The Mystery of Stonehenge* may fit comfortably into both "Lands and People" as an historical work and into "Science and Nature" for its scientific explanation of that Stone Age phenomenon.

LANDS AND PEOPLES—BOOKS FOR YOUNGER READERS (GRADES 2–5)

Aliki (pseud. for Aliki Brandenburg). *Corn Is Maise—The Gift of the Indians*. New York: Crowell, 1976.

———. *The King's Day: Louis XIV of France*. New York: Crowell, 1989.

———. *A Medieval Feast*. New York: Crowell, 1983.

———. *Mummies Made in Egypt*. New York: Crowell, 1979.

Baylor, Byrd. *When Clay Sings*. Illus. Tom Bakhi. New York: Scribner's, 1972.

Branley, Franklyn. *The Mystery of Stonehenge*. New York: Crowell, 1969.

Commager, Henry Steele. *The First Book of American History*. Illus. Leonard Everett Fisher. New York: Watts, 1957.

Coolidge, Olivia. *Tales of the Crusades*. Boston: Houghton Mifflin, 1970.

Fisher, Leonard Everett. *The Factories*. New York: Holiday, 1979.

———. *The Hospitals*. New York: Watts, 1980.

———. *The Peddlers*. New York: Watts, 1968.

———. *The Railroads*. New York: Holiday, 1979.

———. *The Schoolmasters*. New York: Watts, 1967.

Foster, Genevieve. *The World of William Penn*. New York: Scribner's, 1973.

———. *The Year of the Pilgrims—1620*. New York: Scribner's, 1969.

Keegan, Marcia. *Pueblo Boy: Growing Up in Two Worlds*. New York: Dutton, 1991.

Kuskin, Karla. *Jerusalem, Shining Still*. New York: Harper, 1987.

LANDS AND PEOPLES—BOOKS FOR OLDER READERS (GRADES 6 AND UP)

Ashabranner, Brent. *Children of the Maya*. New York: Dodd, Mead & Co., 1986.

———. *Land of Yesterday, Land of Tomorrow: Discovering Chinese Central Asia*. New York: Cobblehill, 1992.

Bach, Alice, and J. Cheryl Exum. *Miriam's Well: Stories about Women in the Bible*. New York: Delacorte, 1991.

Bealer, Alex W. *Only the Names Remain: The Cherokees and the Trail of Tears*. Boston: Little, Brown, 1972.

Berck, Judith. *No Place to Be: Voices of Homeless Children*. Boston: Houghton Mifflin, 1991.

Bontemps, Arna. *Story of the Negro*, 3rd ed. New York: Knopf, 1958.

Caselli, Giovanni. *The First Civilizations*. New York: Bedrick, 1985.

Chaikin, Miriam, adapter. *Exodus*. Illus. Charles Mikolaycak. New York: Holiday Mifflin, 1987.

———. *Sound the Shofar: The Story and Meaning of Rosh Hashanah and Yom Kippur*. Boston: Houghton Mifflin, 1986.

Chang, Ina. *A Separate Battle: Women and the Civil War*. New York: Dutton, 1991.

Chubb, Thomas Caldecot. *The Byzantines*. Cleveland: World, 1959.

Colman, Penny. *Rosie the Riveter: Women Working on the Home Front in World War II*. New York: Crown, 1995.

Freedman, Russell. *Cowboys of the Wild West*. New York: Tickner & Fields, 1985.

———. *Immigrant Kids*. New York: Dutton, 1980.

———. *An Indian Winter*. New York: Holiday, 1992.

Greenfeld, Howard. *Chanukah*. New York: Holt, 1976.

———. *The Hidden Children*. New York: Clarion, 1993.

———. *Passover*. New York: Holt, 1978.

————. *Rosh Hashanah and Yom Kippur*. New York: Holt, 1979.

Hughes, Langston. *The First Book of Africa*, rev. ed. New York: Watts, 1964.

Jacobs, Francine. *The Tainos: The People Who Welcomed Columbus*. New York: Putnam, 1992.

Kimmel, Eric A. *Bar Mitzvah: A Jewish Boy's Coming of Age*. New York: Viking, 1995.

Meltzer, Milton. *Brother Can You Spare a Dime? The Great Depression: 1929-33*. New York: New American Library, 1977.

————. *Columbus and the World Around Him*. New York: Watts, 1990.

————. *The Hispanic Americans*. New York: Crowell, 1982.

Murphy, Jim. *Across America on an Emigrant Train*. New York: Clarion, 1993.

————. *The Great Fire*. New York: Scholastic, 1995. (The Chicago fire)

Myers, Walter Dean. *Now Is Your Time!: The African-American Struggle for Freedom*. New York: HarperCollins, 1991.

Price, Christine. *Made in Ancient Egypt*. New York: Dutton, 1970.

Rylant, Cynthia. *Appalachia: The Voices of Sleeping Birds*. New York: Harcourt, 1991.

Schwartz, Alvin. *The City and Its People: The Story of One City's Government*. New York: Dutton, 1967.

Seeger, Elizabeth. *Eastern Religions*. New York: T. Crowell, 1973.

Snelling, John. *Buddhism*. New York: Watts, 1986.

Stanley, Jerry. *I Am an American: A True Story of Japanese Internment*. New York: Crown, 1994.

Van Loon, Hendrik Willem. *The Story of Mankind*, rev. ed. New York: Liveright, 1951.

SCIENCE AND NATURE—BOOKS FOR YOUNGER READERS (GRADES 2–5)

Anno, Mitsumasa. *Anno's Math Games*. New York: Philomel, 1987.

————. *Anno's Math Games II*. New York: Philomel, 1987.

Branley, Franklyn. *Air Is All Around You*. New York: Crowell, 1986.

————. *Light and Darkness*. New York: Crowell, 1975.

————. *Uranus: The Seventh Planet*. New York: Crowell, 1988.

Brown, Laurie Krasny, and Marc Brown. *Dinosaurs to the Rescue!: A Guide to Protecting Our Planet*. Boston: Little, Brown, 1992.

Cobb, Vicki. *The Scoop of Ice Cream*. Boston: Little, Brown, 1985.

————. *Sneakers Meet Your Feet*. Boston: Little, Brown, 1985.

Cole, Joanna. *The Magic School Bus: Inside the Earth*. Illus. Bruce Degen. New York: Scholastic, 1987.

Heller, Ruth. *The Reason for a Flower*. New York: Scholastic, 1983.

Lauber, Patricia. *The Friendly Dolphins*. New York: Random House, 1963.

————. *Summer of Fire: Yellowstone 1988*. New York: Watts, 1991.

————. *Tales Mummies Tell*. New York: Crowell, 1985.

Llewellyn, Claire. *My First Book of Time*. Boston: Houghton Mifflin, 1992.

Machotka, Hana. *Breathtaking Noses*. New York: Morrow, 1992.

————. *What Neat Feet!* New York: Morrow, 1991.

Mendoza, George. *The Digger Wasp*. New York: Dial, 1969.

Paladino, Catherine. *Our Vanishing Farm Animals: Saving America's Rare Breeds*. Boston: Little, Brown, 1991.

Patent, Dorothy Hinshaw. *Where the Bald Eagles Gather*. Photographs by William Munoz. Boston: Houghton Mifflin, 1984.

Peters, Lisa Westberg. *Water's Way*. New York: Arcade, 1991.

Ride, Sally, and Susan Okie. *To Space and Back*. New York: Lothrop, 1986.

Simon, Seymour. *Earthquakes*. New York: Morrow, 1991.

————. *Mars*. New York: Morrow, 1987.

————. *Uranus*. New York: Morrow, 1987.

Srivastava, Jane Jonas. *Statistics*. New York: Crowell, 1973.

Taylor, Barbara. *Coral Reef*. Boston: Houghton Mifflin, 1992.

————. *Desert Life*. Boston: Houghton Mifflin, 1992.

————. *Pond Life*. Boston: Houghton Mifflin, 1992.

————. *Rain Forest*. Boston: Houghton Mifflin, 1992.

Vernon, Adele. *The Hoiho: New Zealand's Yellow-Eyed Penguin*. New York: Putnam, 1991.

SCIENCE AND NATURE—BOOKS FOR OLDER READERS (GRADES 6 AND UP)

Anderson, Joan. *Earth Keepers*. New York: Harcourt, 1993.

Arnosky, Jim. *Secrets of a Wildlife Watcher*. New York: Lothrop, 1983.

Brandenburg, Jim. *An American Safari: Adventures on the North American Prairie*. New York: Walker, 1995.

George, Jean Craighead. *Spring Comes to the Ocean*. New York: Crowell, 1965.

Gibbons, Gail. *From Seed to Plant*. New York: Holiday, 1991.

————. *The Puffins Are Back!* New York: HarperCollins, 1991.

————. *Recycle!: A Handbook for Kids*. Boston: Little, Brown, 1992.

Gross, Ruth Belov. *A Book about Pandas*. New York: Scholastic, 1974.

————. *Snakes*. New York: Four Winds, 1975.

Macauley, David. *The Way Things Work*. Boston: Houghton Mifflin, 1988.

Pringle, Laurence. *City and Suburbs: Exploring Ecosystems*. New York: Macmillan, 1975.

————. *The Hidden World: Life Under a Rock*. New York: Macmillan, 1977.

————. *Living in a Risky World*. New York: Morrow, 1989.

FINE AND APPLIED ARTS—BOOKS FOR YOUNGER READERS (GRADES 2–5)

Ancona, George. *Cutters, Carvers and the Cathedral*. New York: Lothrop, 1995. (St. John the Divine, New York City)

Bellville, Cheryl Walsh. *Theater Magic: Behind the Scenes at a Children's Theater*. Minneapolis: Carolrhoda, 1986.

Brown, Marc. *Your First Garden Book*. Boston: Little, Brown, 1981.

Florian, Douglas. *A Carpenter*. New York: Greenwillow, 1991.

————. *A Potter*. New York: Greenwillow, 1991.

Kalb, Jonah, and Laura Kalb. *The Easy Ice Skating Book*. Illus. Sandy Kossin. Boston: Houghton Mifflin, 1981.

Krementz, Jill. *A Very Young Rider*. New York: Knopf, 1977.

Lasky, Kathryn. *Puppeteer*. New York: Macmillan, 1985.

Macauley, David. *Castle*. Boston: Houghton Mifflin, 1977.

————. *Cathedral: The Story of Its Construction*. Boston: Houghton Mifflin, 1973.

————. *Pyramid*. Boston: Houghton Mifflin, 1975.

Marks, Mickey K. *OP-Tricks: Creating Kinetic Art*. Philadelphia: Lippincott, 1972.

Raboff, Ernest. *Michelangelo Buonarroti*. New York: Harper, 1988.

————. *Pablo Picasso*. New York: Harper, 1987.

————. *Van Gogh*. New York: Harper, 1988.

Rodari, Florian. *A Weekend with Picasso*. New York: Rizzoli, 1991.

Skira-Venturi, Rosabianca. *A Weekend with Renoir*. New York: Rizzoli, 1991.

Skira-Venturi, Rosabianca. *A Weekend with Van Gogh*. New York: Rizzoli, 1994.

Streatfield, Noel. *A Young Person's Guide to Ballet*. London: Warne, 1985.

FINE AND APPLIED ARTS—BOOKS FOR OLDER READERS (GRADES 6 AND UP)

Arnosky, Jim. *Fish in a Flash!: A Personal Guide to Spin-Fishing*. New York: Bradbury, 1991.

————. *Sketching Outdoors in Spring*. New York: Lothrop, 1987.

Batterberry, Ariane, and Michael Batterberry. *The Pantheon Story of American Art for Young People*. New York: Pantheon, 1976.

Beardsley, John. *Pablo Picasso*. New York: Abrams, 1991.

Bierhorst, John. *A Cry from the Earth: Music of the North American Indians*. New York: Four Winds, 1979.

Chase, Alice Elizabeth. *Famous Artists of the Past*. Bronx, NY: Platt & Munk, 1964.

————. *Looking at Art*. New York: T. Crowell, 1966.

Cone, Ferne Geller. *Crazy Crocheting*. Illus. Rachel Osterlof. Photographs by J. Morton Cone. New York: Atheneum, 1981.

Cooper, Miriam. *Snap! Photography*. New York: Messner, 1981.

Duncan, Lois. *The Circus Comes Home: When the Greatest Show on Earth Rode the Rails*. New York: Doubleday, 1993.

Fisher, Leonard Everett. *Alphabet Art*. New York: Four Winds, 1978.

————. *Calendar Art*. New York: Four Winds, 1987.

Greenberg, Jan, and Sandra Jordan. *The Painter's Eye: Learning to Look at Contemporary American Art*. New York: Delacorte, 1991.

Haskell, Arnold. *The Wonderful World of Dance*. New York: Doubleday, 1969.

Hodges, C. Walter. *Shakespeare's Theatre*. New York: Coward-McCann, 1964.

Hofsinde, Robert (Gray-Wolf). *Indian Arts*. New York: Morrow, 1971.

Hughes, Langston. *The First Book of Jazz*. New York: Watts, 1955.

Jaspersohn, William. *Magazine: Behind the Scenes at* Sports Illustrated. Boston: Little, Brown, 1983.

Kohl, Herbert. *A Book of Puzzlements: Play and Invention with Language*. New York: Schocken, 1981.

Naylor, Penelope. *Black Images: The Art of West Africa*. New York: Doubleday, 1973.

St. George, Judith. *The Brooklyn Bridge: They Said It Couldn't Be Built*. New York: Putnam, 1982.

————. *The Panama Canal: Gateway to the World*. New York: Putnam, 1989.

Tinkelman, Murray. *Rodeo: The Great American Sport*. New York: Greenwillow, 1982.

Weiss, Harvey. *How to Make Your Own Books*. New York: Crowell, 1974.

Wolf, Diane. *Chinese Writing*. New York: Holt, Rinehart & Winston, 1975.

HUMAN DEVELOPMENT AND BEHAVIOR—BOOKS FOR YOUNGER READERS (GRADES 2–5)

Banish, Roslyn. *A Forever Family*. New York: HarperCollins, 1992.

Bernstein, Joanne, and Stephen Gullo. *When People Die*. New York: Dutton, 1977.

Cole, Joanna. *The New Baby at Your House*. New York: Morrow, 1985.

Engel, Joel. *Handwriting Analysis Self-Taught*. New York: Elsevier/Nelson, 1980.

Giblin, James Cross. *From Hand to Mouth: Or How We Invented Knives, Forks, Spoons, and Chopsticks & the Table Manners to Go with Them*. New York: Crowell, 1987.

Kamien, Janet. *What If You Couldn't . . . ?* New York: Scribner's, 1979.

LeShan, Eda. *What's Going to Happen to Me? When Parents Separate or Divorce*. New York: Four Winds, 1978.

————. *When a Parent Is Very Sick*. New York: Atlantic, 1986.

Perl, Lila. *The Great Ancestor Hunt: The Fun of Finding Out Who You Are*. Boston: Houghton Mifflin, 1989.

Rofes, Eric E. *The Kids Book About Death and Dying*. Boston: Little, Brown, 1985.

HUMAN DEVELOPMENT AND BEHAVIOR—BOOKS FOR OLDER READERS (GRADES 6 AND UP)

Bode, Janet. *Death Is Hard to Live With: Teenagers and How They Cope with Loss*. New York: Delacorte, 1993.

Brooks, Bruce. *Boys Will Be*. New York: Holt, 1993.

Harris, Robie H. *It's Perfectly Normal: A Book about Changing Bodies, Growing Up, Sex, and Sexual Health*. Cambridge, MA: Candlewick, 1994.

Jennes, Aylette. *Families: A Celebration of Diversity, Commitment, and Love*. Boston: Houghton Mifflin, 1990.

Krementz, Jill. *How It Feels When Parents Divorce*. New York: Knopf, 1984.

Meltzer, Milton. *The Landscape of Memory*. New York: Viking, 1987.

Roy, Ron. *Move Over, Wheelchairs Coming Through!* Illus. R. Hausherr. New York: Clarion, 1985.

Schwartz, Alvin. *Telling Fortunes: Love Magic, Dream Signs, and Other Ways to Learn the Future*. Philadelphia: Lippincott, 1987.

Sutton, Roger. *Hearing Us Out: Voices from the Gay and Lesbian Community*. Boston: Little, Brown, 1994.

Terkel, Susan N., and Janice Rench. *Feeling Safe, Feeling Strong: How To Avoid Sexual Abuse and What to Do If It Happens to You*. Minneapolis, MN: Lerner, 1984.

Appendix

~

CHILDREN'S BOOK
AWARDS

Every year numerous book awards are presented to works of children's literature, both for writing and for illustration. These awards are sponsored by various organizations, each with its own set of criteria. In addition, several awards are presented to individuals recognizing lifetime achievement in children's literature. Included here are some, but not all, of the more prestigious awards. The award-selection process is not infallible, and often some very excellent works have been overlooked whereas some award-winning works have not altogether successfully stood the test of time. In general, these lists can suggest—in addition to specific titles—authors and illustrators who produce works of high quality. But we should by no means be slaves to book award lists.

Included in the following lists are awards presented not only to writers in English, but some international awards. It is good that we make a concerted effort to acquaint ourselves not only with American and English children's authors, but with writers the world over. Perhaps in time, more of these foreign language books for children will be available in translation as we realize how important intercultural communication is to global understanding.

AMERICAN BOOK AWARDS

THE NEWBERY MEDAL

The Newbery Medal was named for John Newbery, the British entrepreneur who pioneered children's book publishing in the eighteenth century. The award is, however, an American award, presented annually by the American Library Association to the most distinguished contribution to children's literature published in the United States. Runners-up are termed Honor Books. As with any such award, there has not always been general agreement with the decisions. However, the list does include some of the finest writing for young people over the last seventy years.

1922   *The Story of Mankind* by Hendrik Willem van Loon, Liveright
Honor Books: *The Great Quest* by Charles Hawes, Little, Brown;
Cedric the Forester by Bernard Marshall, Appleton; *The Old Tobacco Shop: A True Account of What Befell a Little Boy in Search of Adventure* by William Bowen, Macmillan; *The Golden Fleece and the Heroes Who Lived before Achilles* by Padraic Colum, Macmillan; *Windy Hill* by Cornelia Meigs, Macmillan

1923   *The Voyages of Doctor Dolittle* by Hugh Lofting, Lippincott
Honor Books: No record

1924   *The Dark Frigate* by Charles Hawes, Little, Brown
Honor Books: No record

1925   *Tales from Silver Lands* by Charles Finger, Doubleday
Honor Books: *Nicholas: A Manhattan Christmas Story* by Anne Carroll Moore, Putnam; *Dream Coach* by Anne Parrish, Macmillan

1926   *Shen of the Sea* by Arthur Bowie Chrisman, Dutton
Honor Book: *Voyagers: Being Legends and Romances of Atlantic Discovery* by Padraic Colum, Macmillan

1927   *Smoky, The Cowhorse* by Will James, Scribner's
Honor Books: No record

1928   *Gayneck, The Story of a Pigeon* by Dhan Gopal Mukerji, Dutton
Honor Books: *The Wonder Smith and His Son: A Tale from the Golden Childhood of the World* by Ella Young, Longmans; *Downright Dencey* by Caroline Snedeker, Doubleday

1929   *The Trumpeter of Krakow* by Eric P. Kelly, Macmillan
Honor Books: *Pigtail of Ah Lee Ben Loo* by John Bennett, Longmans, Green (McKay); *Millions of Cats* by Wanda Gág, Coward, McCann & Geoghegan; *The Boy Who Was* by Grace Hallock, Dutton; *Clearing Weather* by Cornelia Meigs, Little, Brown; *Runaway Papoose* by Grace Moon, Doubleday; *Tod of the Fens* by Elinor Whitney, Macmillan

1930   *Hitty, Her First Hundred Years* by Rachel Field, Macmillan
Honor Books: *Daughter of the Seine: The Life of Madame Roland* by Jeanette Eaton, Harper; *Pran of Albania* by Elizabeth Miller, Doubleday; *Jumping-off Place* by Marian Hurd McNeely, Longmans, Green (McKay); *Tangle-coated Horse and Other Tales: Episodes from the Fionn Saga* by Ella Young, Longmans, Green (McKay); *Vaino: A Boy of New England* by Julia Davis Adams, Dutton; *Little Blacknose* by Hildegarde Swift, Harcourt Brace Jovanovich

1931   *The Cat Who Went to Heaven* by Elizabeth Coatsworth, Macmillan
Honor Books: *Floating Island* by Anne Parrish, Harper; *The Dark Star of Itza: The Story of a Pagan Princess* by Alida Malkus, Harcourt Brace Jovanovich; *Queer Person* by Ralph Hubbard, Doubleday; *Mountains Are Free* by Julia Davis Adams, Dutton; *Spice and the Devil's Cave* by Agnes Hewes, Knopf; *Meggy Macintosh* by Elizabeth Janet Gray, Doubleday; *Garram the Hunter: A Boy of the Hill Tribes* by Herbert Best, Doubleday; *Ood-Le-Uk the Wanderer* by Alice Lide and Margaret Johansen, Little, Brown

1932 *Waterless Mountain* by Laura Adams Armer, Longmans, Green (McKay)
   Honor Books: *The Fairy Circus* by Dorothy P. Lathrop, Macmillan; *Calico Bush* by Rachel Field, Macmillan; *Boy of the South Seas* by Eunice Tietjens, Coward, McCann & Geoghegan; *Out of the Flame* by Eloise Lownsbery, Longmans, Green (McKay); *Jane's Island* by Marjorie Allee, Houghton Mifflin; *Truce of the Wolf and Other Tales of Old Italy* by Mary Gould Davis, Harcourt Brace Jovanovich

1933 *Young Fu of the Upper Yangtze* by Elizabeth Foreman Lewis, Winston
   Honor Books: *Swift Rivers* by Cornelia Meigs, Little, Brown; *The Railroad to Freedom: A Story of the Civil War* by Hildegarde Swift, Harcourt Brace Jovanovich; *Children of the Soil: A Story of Scandinavia* by Nora Burglon, Doubleday

1934 *Invincible Louisa: The Story of the Author of "Little Women"* by Cornelia Meigs, Little, Brown
   Honor Books: *The Forgotten Daughter* by Caroline Snedeker, Doubleday; *Swords of Steel* by Elsie Singmaster, Houghton Mifflin; *ABC Bunny* by Wanda Gág, Coward, McCann & Geoghegan; *Winged Girl of Knossos* by Erik Berry, Appleton; *New Land* by Sarah Schmidt, McBride; *Big Tree of Bunlahy: Stories of My Own Countryside* by Padraic Colum, Macmillan; *Glory of the Seas* by Agnes Hewes, Knopf; *Apprentice of Florence* by Ann Kyle, Houghton Mifflin

1935 *Dobry* by Monica Shannon, Viking
   Honor Books: *Pageant of Chinese History* by Elizabeth Seeger, Longmans, Green (McKay); *Davy Crockett* by Constance Rourke, Harcourt Brace Jovanovich; *Day on Skates: The Story of a Dutch Picnic* by Hilda Van Stockum, Harper

1936 *Caddie Woodlawn* by Carol Ryrie Brink, Macmillan
   Honor Books: *Honk, the Moose* by Phil Strong, Dodd, Mead; *The Good Master* by Kate Seredy, Viking; *Young Walter Scott* by Elizabeth Janet Gray, Viking; *All Sail Set: A Romance of the Flying Cloud* by Armstrong Sperry, Winston

1937 *Roller Skates* by Ruth Sawyer, Viking
   Honor Books: *Phoebe Fairchild: Her Book* by Lois Lenski, Stokes; *Whistler's Van* by Idwal Jones, Viking; *Golden Basket* by Ludwig Bemelmans, Viking; *Winterbound* by Margery Bianco, Viking; *Audubon* by Constance Rourke, Harcourt Brace Jovanovich; *The Codfish Musket* by Agnes Hewes, Doubleday

1938 *The White Stag* by Kate Seredy, Viking
   Honor Books: *Pecos Bill* by James Cloyd Bowman, Little Brown; *Bright Island* by Mabel Robinson, Random House; *On the Banks of Plum Creek* by Laura Ingalls Wilder, Harper

1939 *Thimble Summer* by Elizabeth Enright, Holt, Rinehart and Winston
   Honor Books: *Nino* by Valenti Angelo, Viking; *Mr. Popper's Penguins* by Richard and Florence Atwater, Little, Brown; *"Hello the Boat!"* by Phillis Crawford, Holt, Rinehart and Winston; *Leader by Destiny: George Washington, Man and Patriot* by Jeanette Eaton, Harcourt Brace Jovanovich; *Penn* by Elizabeth Janet Gray, Viking

1940 *Daniel Boone* by James Daugherty, Viking
   Honor Books: *The Singing Tree* by Kate Seredy, Viking; *Runner of the Mountain Tops: The Life of Louis Agassiz* by Mabel Robinson, Random House; *By the Shores of Silver Lake* by Laura Ingalls Wilder, Harper; *Boy with a Pack* by Stephen W. Meader, Harcourt Brace Jovanovich

1941 *Call It Courage* by Armstrong Sperry, Macmillan
   Honor Books: *Blue Willow* by Doris Gates, Viking; *Young Mac of Fort Vancouver* by Mary Jane Carr, Crowell; *The Long Winter* by Laura Ingalls Wilder, Harper; *Nansen* by Anna Gertrude Hall, Viking

1942 *The Matchlock Gun* by Walter D. Edmonds, Dodd, Mead
   Honor Books: *Little Town on the Prairie* by Laura Ingalls Wilder, Harper; *George Washington's World* by Genevieve Foster, Scribner; *Indian Captive: The Story of Mary Jemison* by Lois Lenski, Lippincott; *Down Ryton Water* by Eva Roe Gaggin, Viking

1943 *Adams of the Road* by Elizabeth Janet Gray, Viking
   Honor Books: *The Middle Moffat* by Eleanor Estes, Harcourt Brace Jovanovich; *Have You Seen Tom Thumb?* by Mabel Leigh Hunt, Lippincott

1944 *Johnny Tremain* by Esther Forbes, Houghton Mifflin
   Honor Books: *These Happy Golden Years* by Laura Ingalls Wilder, Harper; *Fog Magic* by Julia Sauer, Viking; *Rufus M.* by Eleanor Estes, Harcourt Brace Jovanovich; *Mountain Born* by Elizabeth Yates, Coward, McCann & Geoghegan

1945 *Rabbit Hill* by Robert Lawson, Viking
   Honor Books: *The Hundred Dresses* by Eleanor Estes, Harcourt Brace Jovanovich; *The Silver Pencil* by Alice Dalgliesh, Scribner; *Abraham Lincoln's World* by Genevieve Foster, Scribner; *Lone Journey: The Life of Roger Williams* by Jeanette Eaton, Harcourt Brace Jovanovich

1946 *Strawberry Girl* by Lois Lenski, Lippincott
   Honor Books: *Justin Morgan Had a Horse* by Marguerite Henry, Rand McNally; *The Moved-Outers* by Florence Crannell Means, Houghton Mifflin; *Bhimsa, the Dancing Bear* by Christine Weston, Scribner; *New Found World* by Katherine Shippen, Viking

1947 *Miss Hickory* by Carolyn Sherwin Bailey, Viking
   Honor Books: *Wonderful Year* by Nancy Barnes, Messner; *Big Tree* by Mary and Conrad Buff, Viking; *The Heavenly Tenants* by William Maxwell, Harper; *The Avion My Uncle Flew* by Cyrus Fisher, Appleton; *The Hidden Treasure of Glaston* by Eleanore Jewett, Viking

1948 *The Twenty-One Balloons* by William Pene du Bois, Viking
   Honor Books: *Pancakes-Paris* by Claire Huchet Bishop, Viking; *Le Lun, Lad of Courage* by Carolyn Treffinger, Abingdon; *The Quaint and Curious Quest of Johnny Longfoot, The Shoe-Kings Son* by Catherine Besterman, Bobbs-Merrill; *The Cow-tail Switch, and Other West African Stories* by Harold Courlander, Holt, Rinehart and Winston; *Misty of Chincoteague* by Marguerite Henry, Rand McNally

1949 *King of the Wind* by Marguerite Henry, Rand McNally
   Honor Books: *Seabird* by Holling C. Holling, Houghton Mifflin; *Daughter of the Mountains* by Louise Rankin, Viking; *My Father's Dragon* by Ruth S. Gannett, Random House; *Story of the Negro* by Arna Bontemps, Knopf

1950 *The Door in the Wall* by Marguerite de Angeli, Doubleday

Honor Books: *Tree of Freedom* by Rebecca Caudill, Viking; *The Blue Cat of Castle Town* by Catherine Coblentz, Longmans, Green (McKay); *Kildee House* by Rutherford Montgomery, Doubleday; *George Washington* by Genevieve Foster, Scribner; *Song of the Pines: A Story of Norwegian Lumbering in Wisconsin* by Walter and Marion Havighurst, Winston

1951 *Amos Fortune, Free Man* by Elizabeth Yates, Aladdin
Honor Books: *Better Known as Johnny Appleseed* by Mabel Leigh Hunt, Lippincott; *Gandhi, Fighter without a Sword* by Jeanette Eaton, Morrow; *Abraham Lincoln, Friend of the People* by Clara Ingram Judson, Follett; *The Story of Appleby Capple* by Anne Parrish, Harper

1952 *Ginger Pye* by Eleanor Estes, Harcourt Brace Jovanovich
Honor Books: *Americans before Columbus* by Elizabeth Baity, Viking; *Minn of the Mississippi* by Holling C. Holling, Houghton Mifflin; *The Defender* by Nicholas Kalashnikoff, Scribner; *The Light at Tern Rock* by Julia Sauer, Viking; *The Apple and the Arrow* by Mary and Conrad Buff, Houghton Mifflin

1953 *Secret of the Andes* by Ann Nolan Clark, Viking
Honor Books: *Charlotte's Web* by E. B. White, Harper; *Moccasin Trail* by Eloise McGraw, Coward, McCann & Geoghegan; *Red Sails to Capri* by Ann Weil, Viking; *The Bears on Hemlock Mountain* by Alice Dalgliesh, Scribner; *Birthdays of Freedom*, Vol. 1, by Genevieve Foster, Scribner

1954 *. . . and Now Miguel* by Joseph Krumgold, Crowell
Honor Books: *All Alone* by Claire Huchet Bishop, Viking; *Shadrach* by Meindert DeJong, Harper; *Hurry Home Candy* by Meindert DeJong, Harper; *Theodore Roosevelt, Fighting Patriot* by Clara Ingram Judson, Follett; *Magic Maize* by Mary and Conrad Buff, Houghton Mifflin

1955 *The Wheel on the School* by Meindert DeJong, Harper
Honor Books: *The Courage of Sarah Noble* by Alice Dalgliesh, Scriber; *Banner in the Sky* by James Ullman, Lippincott

1956 *Carry On, Mr. Bowditch* by Jean Lee Latham, Houghton Mifflin
Honor Books: *The Secret River* by Marjorie Kinnan Rawlings, Scribner; *The Golden Name Day* by Jennie Linquist, Harper; *Men, Microscopes, and Living Things* by Katherine Shippen, Viking

1957 *Miracles on Maple Hill* by Virginia Sorensen, Harcourt Brace Jovanovich
Honor Books: *Old Yeller* by Fred Gipson, Harper; *The House of Sixty Fathers* by Meindert DeJong, Harper; *Mr. Justice Holmes* by Clara Ingram Judson, Follett; *The Corn Grows Ripe* by Dorothy Rhoads, Viking; *Black Fox of Lorne* by Marguerite de Angeli, Doubleday

1958 *Rifles for Watie* by Harold Keith, Crowell
Honor Books: *The Horsecatcher* by Mari Sandoz, Westminster; *Gone-Away Lake* by Elizabeth Enright, Harcourt Brace Jovanovich; *The Great Wheel* by Robert Lawson, Viking; *Tom Paine, Freedom's Apostle* by Leo Gurko, Crowell

1959 *The Witch of Blackbird Pond* by Elizabeth George Speare, Houghton Mifflin
Honor Books: *The Family under the Bridge* by Natalie Savage Carlson, Harper; *Along Came a Dog* by Meindert DeJong, Harper; *Chucaro: Wild Pony of the Pampas* by Francis Kalnay, Harcourt Brace Jovanovich; *The Perilous Road* by William O. Steele, Harcourt Brace Jovanovich

1960 *Onion John* by Joseph Krumgold, Crowell

Honor Books: *My Side of the Mountain* by Jean George, Dutton; *America Is Born* by Gerald W. Johnson, Morrow; *The Gammage Cup* by Carol Kendall, Harcourt Brace Jovanovich

1961 *Island of the Blue Dolphins* by Scott O'Dell, Houghton Mifflin
Honor Books: *America Moves Forward* by Gerald W. Johnson, Morrow; *Old Ramon* by Jack Schaefer, Houghton Mifflin; *The Cricket in Times Square* by George Selden, Farrar, Straus & Giroux

1962 *The Bronze Bow* by Elizabeth George Speare, Houghton Mifflin
Honor Books: *Frontier Living* by Edwin Tunis, World; *The Golden Goblet* by Eloise McCraw, Coward, McCann & Geoghegan; *Belling the Tiger* by Mary Stolz, Harper

1963 *A Wrinkle in Time* by Madeline L'Engle, Farrar, Straus & Giroux
Honor Books: *Thistle and Thyme: Tales and Legends from Scotland* by Sorche Nic Leodhas, Holt, Rinehart and Winston; *Men of Athens* by Olivia Coolidge, Houghton Mifflin

1964 *It's Like This, Cat* by Emily Cheney Neville, Harper
Honor Books: *Rascal* by Sterling North, Dutton; *The Loner* by Ester Wier, McKay

1965 *Shadow of a Bull* by Maia Wojciechowska, Atheneum
Honor Book: *Across Five Aprils* by Irene Hunt, Follett

1966 *I, Juan de Pareja* by Elizabeth Borten de Trevino, Farrar, Straus & Giroux
Honor Books: *The Black Cauldron* by Lloyd Alexander, Holt, Rinehart and Winston; *The Animal Family* by Randall Jarrell, Pantheon; *The Noonday Friends* by Mary Stolz, Harper

1967 *Up a Road Slowly* by Irene Hunt, Follett
Honor Books: *The King's Fifth* by Scott O'Dell, Houghton Mifflin; *Zlateh the Goat and Other Stories* by Isaac Bashevis Singer, Harper; *The Jazz Man* by Mark H. Weik, Atheneum

1968 *From the Mixed-Up Files of Mrs. Basil E. Frankweiler* by E. L. Konigsburg, Atheneum
Honor Books: *Jennifer, Hecate, Macbeth, William McKinley, and Me, Elizabeth* by E. L. Konigsburg, Atheneum; *The Black Pearl* by Scott O'Dell, Houghton Mifflin; *The Fearsome Inn* by Isaac Bashevis Singer, Scribner; *The Egypt Game* by Zilpha Keatley Snyder, Atheneum

1969 *The High King* by Lloyd Alexander, Holt, Rinehart and Winston
Honor Books: *To Be a Slave* by Julius Lester, Dial Press; *When Shlemiel Went to Warsaw and Other Stories* by Isaac Bashevis Singer, Farrar, Straus & Giroux

1970 *Sounder* by William H. Armstrong, Harper
Honor Books: *Our Eddie* by Sulamith Ish-Kishor, Pantheon; *The Many Ways of Seeing: An Introduction to the Pleasures of Art* by Janet Gaylord Moore, World; *Journey Outside* by Mary Q. Steele, Viking

1971 *Summer of the Swans* by Betsy Byars, Viking
Honor Books: *Kneeknock Rise* by Natalie Babbitt, Farrar, Straus & Giroux; *Enchantress from the Stars* by Sylvia Louise Engdahl, Atheneum; *Sing Down the Moon* by Scott O'Dell, Houghton Mifflin

1972 *Mrs. Frisby and the Rats of NIMH* by Robert C. O'Brien, Atheneum
Honor Books: *Incident at Hawk's Hill* by Allan W. Eckert, Little, Brown;

The Planet of Junior Brown by Virginia Hamilton, Macmillan; *The Tombs of Atuan* by Ursula K. Le Guin, Atheneum; *Annie and the Old One* by Miska Miles, Little, Brown; *The Headless Cupid* by Zilpha Keatley Snyder, Atheneum

1973 *Julie of the Wolves* by Jean Craighead George, Harper
Honor Books: *Frog and Toad Together* by Arnold Lobel, Harper; *The Upstairs Room* by Johanna Reiss, Crowell; *The Witches of Worm* by Zilpha Keatley Snyder, Atheneum

1974 *The Slave Dancer* by Paula Fox, Bradbury
Honor Book: *The Dark Is Rising* by Susan Cooper, Atheneum

1975 *M. C. Higgins, the Great* by Virginia Hamilton, Macmillan
Honor Books: *Figgs & Phantoms* by Ellen Raskin, Dutton; *My Brother Sam Is Dead* by James Lincoln Collier and Christopher Collier, Four Winds; *The Perilous Gard* by Elizabeth Marie Pope, Houghton Mifflin; *Philip Hall Likes Me. I Reckon Maybe* by Bette Greene, Dial Press

1976 *The Grey King* by Susan Cooper, Atheneum
Honor Books: *The Hundred Penny Box* by Sharon Bell Mathis, Viking; *Dragonwings* by Laurence Yep, Harper

1977 *Roll of Thunder, Hear My Cry* by Mildred D. Taylor, Dial Press
Honor Books: *Abel's Island* by William Steig, Farrar, Straus & Giroux; *A String in the Harp* by Nancy Bond, Atheneum

1978 *Bridge to Terabithia* by Katherine Paterson, Crowell
Honor Books: *Ramona and Her Father* by Beverly Cleary, Morrow; *Anpao: An American Indian Odyssey* by Jamake Highwater, Lippincott

1979 *The Westing Game* by Ellen Raskin, Dutton
Honor Book: *The Great Gilly Hopkins* by Katherine Paterson, Crowell

1980 *A Gathering of Days: A New England Girl's Journal 1830-32* by Joan Blos, Scribner
Honor Book: *The Road from Home: The Story of an American Girl* by David Kherdian, Greenwillow (Morrow)

1981 *Jacob Have I Loved* by Katherine Paterson, Cromwell
Honor Books: *The Fledgling* by Jane Langton, Harper; *A Ring of Endless Light* by Madeleine L'Engle, Farrar, Straus & Giroux

1982 *A Visit to William Blake's Inn: Poems for Innocent and Experienced Travelers* by Nancy Willard, Harcourt Brace Jovanovich
Honor Books: *Ramona Quimby, Age 8* by Beverly Cleary, Morrow; *Upon the Head of the Goat: A Childhood in Hungary, 1939-1944* by Aranka Siegal, Farrar, Straus & Giroux

1983 *Dicey's Song* by Cynthia Voigt, Atheneum
Honor Books: *Blue Sword* by Robin McKinley, Morrow; *Dr. DeSoto* by William Steig, Farrar, Straus & Giroux; *Graven Images* by Paul Fleischman, Harper; *Homesick: My Own Story* by Jean Fritz, Putnam; *Sweet Whisper, Brother Rush* by Virginia Hamilton, Philomel (Putnam)

1984 *Dear Mr. Henshaw* by Beverly Cleary, Morrow
Honor Books: *The Wish Giver* by Bill Brittain, Harper; *Sugaring Time* by Kathryn Lasky, Macmillan; *The Sign of the Beaver* by Elizabeth George Speare, Houghton Mifflin; *A Solitary Blue* by Cynthia Voigt, Atheneum

1985 *The Hero and the Crown* by Robin McKinley, Greenwillow (Morrow)
Honor Books: *The Moves Make the Man* by Bruce Brooks, Harper; *One-Eyed Cat* by Paula Fox, Bradbury; *Like Jake and Me* by Mavis Jukes, Knopf

1986 *Sarah, Plain and Tall* by Patricia MacLachlan, Harper
Honor Books: *Commodore Perry in the Land of the Shogun* by Rhoda Blumberg, Lothrop; *Dogsong* by Gary Paulsen, Bradbury

1987 *The Whipping Boy* by Sid Fleischman, Greenwillow (Morrow)
Honor Books: *On My Honor* by D. Bauer, Clarion; *Volcano: The Eruption and Healing of Mount St. Helens* by Patricia Lauber, Bradbury; *A Fine White Dust* by Cynthia Rylant, Bradbury

1988 *Lincoln: A Photobiography* by Russell Freedman, Clarion/Houghton Mifflin
Honor Books: *After the Rain* by Norma Fox Mazer, Morrow; *Hatchet* by Gary Paulsen, Bradbury

1989 *Joyful Noise: Poems for Two Voices* by Paul Fleischman, Harper
Honor Books: *In the Beginning* by Virginia Hamilton, Harcourt Brace Jovanovich; *Scorpions* by Walter Dean Myers, Harper

1990 *Number the Stars* by Lois Lowry, Houghton Mifflin
Honor Books: *Afternoon of the Elves* by Janet Taylor Lisle, Orchard Books/Watts; *The Winter Room* by Gary Paulsen, Orchard Books/Watts; *Shabanu: Daughter of the Wind* by Suzanne Fisher Staples, Knopf

1991 *Maniac Magee* by Jerry Spinelli, Little, Brown
Honor Book: *The True Confessions of Charlotte Doyle* by Avi, Orchard

1992 *Shiloh* by Phillis Reynolds Naylor, Atheneum
Honor Books: *Nothing But the Truth* by Avi, Orchard; *The Wright Brothers: How They Invented the Airplane* by Russell Freedman, Holiday

1993 *Missing May* by Cynthia Ryland, Orchard
Honor Books: *The Dark-Thirty: Southern Tales of the Supernatural* by Patricia McKissack, Knopf; *Somewhere in the Darkness* by Walter Dean Myers, Scholastic; *What Hearts* by Bruce Brooks, HarperCollins

1994 *The Giver* by Lois Lowry, Houghton, Mifflin
Honor Books: *Eleanor Roosevelt: A Life of Discovery* by Russell Freedman, Clarion/Houghton, Mifflin; *Dragon's Gate* by Laurence Yep, HarperCollins; *Crazy Lady* by Jane Leslie Conly, HarperCollins

1995 *Walk Two Moons* by Sharon Creech, HarperCollins
Honor Books: *Catherine, Called Birdy* by Karen Cushman, Clarion; *The Ear, the Eye, and the Arm* by Nancy Farmer, Orchard

1996 *The Midwife's Apprentice* by Karen Cushman, Houghton, Mifflin
Honor Books: *What Jamie Saw* by Carolyn Coman, Front Street; *The Watsons Go to Birmingham—1963* by Christopher Paul Curtis, Delacorte; *Yolanda's Genius* by Carol Fenner, Simon; *The Great Fire* by Jim Murphy, Scholastic

THE CALDECOTT MEDAL

Named for the British illustrator Randolph Caldecott, the Caldecott Medal has been awarded annually since 1938 by the American Library Association to the most distinguished picture book published in America. Runners up are given Honor Awards. Although the passage of time has not always validated the awards and many fine books have been overlooked, the awards list does provide a roll call of some of the best in children's books. The Caldecott Award is given to the illustrator and honors the pictorial art rather than the text.

1938 *Animals of the Bible* by Helen Dean Fish, illustrated by Dorothy P. Lathrop, Stokes
  Honor Books: *Seven Simeon: A Russian Tale* by Boris Artzybasheff, Viking; *Four and Twenty Blackbirds: Nursey Rhymes of Yesterday Recalled for Children of To-Day* by Helen Dean Fish, illustrated by Robert Lawson, Stokes

1939 *Mei Li* by Thomas Handforth, Doubleday
  Honor Books: *The Forest Pool* by Laura Adams Arner, Longmans, Green (McKay); *Wee Gillis* by Munro Leaf, illustrated by Robert Lawson, Viking; *Snow White and the Seven Dwarfs* by Wanda Gág, Coward, McCann & Geoghegan; *Barkis* by Clare Newberry, Harper; *Andy and the Lion: A Tale of Kindness Remembered or the Power of Gratitude* by James Daugherty, Viking

1940 *Abraham Lincoln* by Ingri and Edgar Parin d'Aulaire, Doubleday
  Honor Books: *Cock-a-Doodle Doo: The Story of a Little Red Rooster* by Berta and Elmer Hader, Macmillan; *Madeleine* by Ludwig Bemelmans, Simon & Schuster; *The Ageless Story* by Lauren Ford, Dodd, Mead

1941 *They Were Strong and Good* by Robert Lawson, Viking
  Honor Book: *April's Kittens* by Clare Newberry, Harper

1942 *Make Way for Ducklings* by Robert McCloskey, Viking
  Honor Books: *An American ABC* by Maud and Miska Petersham, Macmillan; *In My Mother's House* by Ann Nolan Clark, illustrated by Velino Herrera, Viking; *Paddle-to-the-Sea* by Holling C. Holling, Houghton Mifflin; *Nothing at All* by Wanda Gág, Coward, McCann & Geoghegan

1943 *The Little House* by Virginia Lee Burton, Houghton Mifflin
  Honor Books: *Dash and Dart* by Mary and Conrad Buff, Viking; *Marshmallow* by Clare Newberry, Harper

1944 *Many Moons* by James Thurber, illustrated by Louis Slobodkin, Harcourt Brace Jovanovich
  Honor Books: *Small Rain: Verses from the Bible* selected by Jessie Orton Jones, illustrated by Elizabeth Orton Jones, Viking; *Pierre Pigeon* by Lee Kingman, illustrated by Arnold E. Bare, Houghton Mifflin; *The Mighty Hunter* by Berta and Elmer Hader, Macmillan; *A Child's Good Night Book* by Margaret Wise Brown, illustrated by Jean Charlot, W. R. Scott; *Good Luck Horse* by Chih-Yi Chan, illustrated by Plato Chan, Whittlesey

1945 *Prayer for a Child* by Rachel Field, illustrated by Elizabeth Orton Jones, Macmillan
  Honor Books: *Mother Goose: Seventy-Seven Verses with Pictures*, illustrated by Tasha Tudor, Walck; *In the Forest* by Marie Hall Ets, Viking; *Yonie Wondernose* by Marguerite de Angeli, Doubleday; *The Christmas Anna Angel* by Ruth Sawyer, illustrated by Kate Seredy, Viking

1946 *The Rooster Crows . . .*, illustrated by Maud and Miska Petersham, Macmillan
  Honor Books: *Little Lost Lamb* by Golden MacDonald, illustrated by Leonard Weisgard, Doubleday; *Sing Mother Goose* by Opal Wheeler, illustrated by Marjorie Torrey, Dutton; *My Mother Is the Most Beautiful Woman in the World* by Becky Reyher, illustrated by Ruth Gannett, Lothrop; *You Can Write Chinese* by Kurt Wiese, Viking

1947 *The Little Island* by Golden MacDonald, illustrated by Leonard Weisgard, Doubleday.

Honor Books: *Rain Drop Splash* by Alvin Tresselt, illustrated by Leonard Weisgard, Lothrop; *Boats on the River* by Marjorie Flack, illustrated by Jay Hyde Barnum, Viking; *Timothy Turtle* by Al Graham, illustrated by Tony Palazzo, Viking; *Pedro, The Angel of Olvera Street* by Leo Politi, Scribner; *Sing in Praise: A Collection of the Best Loved Hymns* by Opal Wheeler, illustrated by Marjorie Torrey, Dutton

1948 *White Snow, Bright Snow* by Alvin Tresselt, illustrated by Roger Duvoisin, Lothrop

Honor Books: *Stone Soup: An Old Tale* by Marcia Brown, Scribner; *McElligot's Pool* by Dr. Seuss, Random House; *Bambino the Clown* by George Schreiber, Viking; *Roger and the Fox* by Lavinia Davis, illustrated by Hildegard Woodward, Doubleday; *Song of Robin Hood* edited by Anne Malcolmson, illustrated by Virginia Lee Burton, Houghton Mifflin

1949 *The Big Snow* by Berta and Elmer Hader, Macmillan

Honor Books: *Blueberries for Sal* by Robert McCloskey, Viking; *All Around the Town* by Phillis McGinley, illustrated by Helen Stone, Lippincott; *Juanita* by Leo Politi, Scribner; *Fish in the Air* by Kurt Wiese, Viking

1950 *Song of the Swallows* by Leo Politi, Scribner

Honor Books: *America's Ethan Allen* by Stewart Holbrook, illustrated by Lynd Ward, Houghton Mifflin; *The Wild Birthday Cake* by Lavinia Davis, illustrated by Hildegard Woodward, Doubleday; *The Happy Day* by Ruth Krauss, illustrated by Marc Simont, Harper; *Bartholomew and the Oobleck* by Dr. Seuss, Random House; *Henry Fisherman* by Marcia Brown, Scribner

1951 *The Egg Tree* by Katherine Milhouse, Scribner

Honor Books: *Dick Whittington and His Cat* by Marcia Brown, Scribner; *The Two Reds* by William Lipkind, illustrated by Nicholas Mordvinoff, Harcourt Brace Jovanovich; *If I Ran the Zoo* by Dr. Seuss, Random House; *The Most Wonderful Doll in the World* by Phyllis McGinley, illustrated by Helen Stone, Lippincott; *T-Bone, the Baby Sitter* by Clare Newberry, Harper

1952 *Finders Keepers* by William Lipkind, illustrated by Nicholas Mordvinoff, Harcourt Brace Jovanovich

Honor Books: *Mr. T. W. Anthony Woo: The Story of a Cat and a Dog and a Mouse* by Marie Hall Ets, Viking; *Skipper John's Cook* by Marcia Brown, Scribner; *All Falling Down* by Gene Zion, illustrated by Margaret Bloy Graham, Harper; *Bear Party* by William Pene du Bois, Viking; *Feather Mountain* by Elizabeth Olds, Houghton Mifflin

1953 *The Biggest Bear* by Lynd Ward, Houghton Mifflin

Honor Books: *Puss in Boots* by Charles Perrault, illustrated and translated by Marcia Brown, Scribner; *One Morning in Maine* by Robert McCloskey, Viking; *Ape in a Cape: An Alphabet of Odd Animals* by Fritz Eichenberg, Harcourt Brace Jovanovich; *The Storm Book* by Charlotte Zolotow, illustrated by Margaret Bloy Graham, Harper; *Five Little Monkeys* by Juliet Kepes, Houghton Mifflin

1954 *Madeline's Rescue* by Ludwig Bemelmans, Viking

Honor Books: *Journey Cake, Ho!* by Ruth Sawyer, illustrated by Robert

McCloskey, Viking; *When Will the World Be Mine?* by Miriam Schlein, illustrated by Jean Charlot, W. R. Scott; *The Steadfast Tin Soldier* by Hans Christian Andersen, illustrated by Marcia Brown, Scribner; *A Very Special House* by Ruth Krauss, illustrated by Maurice Sendak, Harper; *Green Eyes* by A. Birnbaum, Capitol

1955 *Cinderella, or the Little Glass Slipper* by Charles Perrault, translated and illustrated by Marcia Brown, Scribner
Honor Books: *Book of Nursey and Mother Goose Rhymes,* illustrated by Marguerite de Angeli, Doubleday; *Wheel on the Chimney* by Margaret Wise Brown, illustrated by Tibor Gergely, Lippincott; *The Thanksgiving Story* by Alice Dalgliesh, illustrated by Helen Sewell, Scribner

1956 *Frog Went A-Courtin* edited by John Langstaff, illustrated by Feodor Rojankovsky, Harcourt Brace Jovanovich
Honor Books: *Play with Me* by Marie Hall Ets, Viking; *Crow Boy* by Taro Yashima, Viking

1957 *A Tree Is Nice* by Janice May Udry, illustrated by Marc Simont, Harper
Honor Books: *Mr. Penny's Race Horse* by Marie Hall Ets, Viking; *1 is One* by Tasha Tudor, Walck; *Anatole* by Eve Titus, illustrated by Paul Galdone, McGraw-Hill; *Gillespie and the Guards* by Benjamin Elkin, illustrated by James Daugherty, Viking; *Lion* by William Pene du Bois, Viking

1958 *Time of Wonder* by Robert McCloskey, Viking
Honor Books: *Fly High, Fly Low* by Don Freeman, Viking; *Anatole and the Cat* by Eve Titus, illustrated by Paul Galdone, McGraw-Hill

1959 *Chanticleer and the Fox* adapted from Chaucer and illustrated by Barbara Cooney, Crowell
Honor Books: *The House That Jack Built: A Picture Book in Two Languages* by Antonio Frasconi, Harcourt Brace Jovanovich; *What Do You Say, Dear?* by Sesyle Joslin, illustrated by Maurice Sendak, Scott; *Umbrella* by Taro Yashima, Viking

1960 *Nine Days to Christmas* by Marie Hall Ets and Aurora Labastida, illustrated by Marie Hall Ets, Viking
Honor Books: *Houses from the Sea* by Alice E. Goudey, illustrated by Adrienne Adams, Scribner; *The Moon Jumpers* by Janice May Udry, illustrated by Maurice Sendak, Harper

1961 *Baboushka and the Three Kings* by Ruth Robbins, illustrated by Nicolas Sidjakov, Parnassus
Honor Book: *Inch by Inch* by Leo Lionni, Obolensky

1962 *Once a Mouse . . .* by Marcia Brown, Scribner
Honor Books: *The Fox Went Out on a Chilly Night: An Old Song* by Peter Spier, Doubleday; *Little Bear's Visit* by Else Holmelund Minarik, illustrated by Maurice Sendak, Harper; *The Day We Saw the Sun Come Up* by Alice E. Goudey, illustrated by Adrienne Adams, Scribner

1963 *The Snowy Day* by Ezra Jack Keats, Viking
Honor Books: *The Sun Is a Golden Earring* by Natalia M. Belting, illustrated by Bernarda Bryson, Holt, Rinehart and Winston; *Mr. Rabbit and the Lovely Present* by Charlotte Zolotow, illustrated by Maurice Sendak, Harper

1964 *Where the Wild Things Are* by Maurice Sendak, Harper
Honor Books: *Swimmy* by Leo Lionni, Pantheon Books; *All in the Morning Early* by Sorche Nic Leodhas, illustrated by Evaline Ness, Holt, Rinehart and Winston; *Mother Goose and Nursey Rhymes* illustrated by Philip Reed, Atheneum

1965 *May I Bring a Friend?* by Beatrice Schenk de Regniers, illustrated by Beni Montresor, Atheneum
Honor Books: *Rain Makes Applesauce* by Julian Scheer, illustrated by Marvin Bileck, Holiday; *The Wave* by Margaret Hodges, illustrated by Blair Lent, Houghton Mifflin; *A Pocketful of Cricket* by Rebecca Caudill, illustrated by Evaline Ness, Holt, Rinehart and Winston

1966 *Always Room for One More* by Sorche Nic Leodhas, illustrated by Nonny Hogrogian, Holt, Rinehart and Winston
Honor Books: *Hide and Seek Fog* by Alvin Tresselt, illustrated by Roger Duvoisin, Lothrop; *Just Me* by Marie Hall Ets, Viking; *Tom Tit Tot* by Evaline Ness, Scribner

1967 *Sam, Bangs & Moonshine* by Evaline Ness, Holt, Rinehart and Winston
Honor Book: *One Wide River to Cross* by Barbara Emberley, illustrated by Ed Emberley, Prentice-Hall

1968 *Drummer Hoff* by Barbara Emberley, illustrated by Ed Emberley, Prentice-Hall
Honor Books: *Frederick* by Leo Lionni, Pantheon; *Seashore Story* by Taro Yashima, Viking; *The Emperor and the Kite* by Jane Yolen, illustrated by Ed Young, World

1969 *The Fool of the World and the Flying Ship* by Arthur Ransome, illustrated by Uri Shulevitz, Farrar, Straus & Giroux
Honor Book: *Why the Sun and the Moon Live in the Sky: An African Folktale* by Elphinstone Dayrell, illustrated by Blair Lent, Houghton Mifflin

1970 *Sylvester and the Magic Pebble* by William Stieg, Windmill (Simon & Schuster)
Honor Books: *Goggles!* by Ezra Jack Keats, Macmillan; *Alexander and the Wind-Up Mouse* by Leo Lionni, Pantheon; *Pop Corn and Ma Goodness* by Edna Mitchell Preston, illustrated by Robert Andrew Parker, Viking; *Thy Friend, Obadiah* by Brinton Turkle, Viking; *The Judge: An Untrue Tale* by Harve Zemach, illustrated by Margot Zemach, Farrar, Straus & Giroux

1971 *A Story—A Story: An African Tale* by Gail E. Haley, Atheneum
Honor Books: *The Angry Moon* by William Sleator, illustrated by Blair Lent, Little, Brown; *Frog and Toad Are Friends* by Arnold Lobel, Harper; *In the Night Kitchen* by Maurice Sendak, Harper

1972 *One Fine Day* by Nonny Hogrogian, Macmillan
Honor Books: *If All the Seas Were One Sea* by Janina Domanska, Macmillan; *Moja Means One: Swahili Counting Book* by Muriel Feelings, illustrated by Tom Feelings, Dial Press; *Hildilid's Night* by Cheli Duran Ryan, illustrated by Arnold Lobel, Macmillan

1973 *The Funny Little Woman* retold by Arlene Mosel, illustrated by Blair Lent, Dutton
Honor Books: *Anansi the Spider: A Tale from the Ashanti* adapted and illustrated by Gerald McDermott, Holt, Rinehart and Winston; *Hosie's Alphabet* by Hosea Tobias and Lisa Baskin, illustrated by Leonard Baskin, Viking; *Snow White and the Seven Dwarfs* translated by Randall Jarrell, illustrated by Nancy

Elkholm Burkert, Farrar, Straus & Giroux; *When Clay Sings* by Byrd Baylor, illustrated by Tom Bahti, Scribner

1974 *Duffy and the Devil* by Harve Zemach, illustrated by Margot Zemach, Farrar, Straus & Giroux

Honor Book: *Three Jovial Huntsmen* by Susan Jeffers, Bradbury; *Cathedral: The Story of Its Construction* by David Macauley, Houghton Mifflin

1975 *Arrow to the Sun* adapted and illustrated by Gerald McDermott, Viking

Honor Books: *Jambo Means Hello: A Swahili Alphabet Book* by Muriel Feelings, illustrated by Tom Feelings, Dial Press

1976 *Why Mosquitoes Buzz in People's Ears* retold by Verna Aardema, illustrated by Leo and Diane Dillon, Dial Press

Honor Books: *The Desert Is Theirs* by Byrd Baylor, illustrated by Peter Parnall, Scribner; *Strega Nona* retold and illustrated by Tomie de Paola, Prentice-Hall

1977 *Ashanti to Zulu: African Traditions* by Margaret Musgrove, illustrated by Leo and Diane Dillon, Dial Press

Honor Books: *The Amazing Bone* by William Steig, Farrar, Straus & Giroux; *The Contest* retold and illustrated by Nonny Hogrogian, Greenwillow (Morrow); *Fish for Supper* by M. B. Goffstein, Dial Press; *The Golem: A Jewish Legend* by Beverly Brodsky McDermott, Lippincott; *Hawk, I'm Your Brother* by Byrd Baylor, illustrated by Peter Parnall, Scribner

1978 *Noah's Ark* by Peter Spier, Doubleday

Honor Books: *Castle* by David Macaulay, Houghton Mifflin; *It Could Always Be Worse* retold and illustrated by Margot Zemach, Farrar, Straus & Giroux

1979 *The Girl Who Loved Wild Horses* by Paul Goble, Bradbury

Honor Books: *Freight Train* by Donald Crews, Greenwillow (Morrow); *The Way to Start a Day* by Byrd Baylor, illustrated by Peter Parnall, Scribner

1980 *Ox-Cart Man* by Donald Hall, illustrated by Barbara Cooney, Viking

Honor Books: *Ben's Trumpet* by Rachel Isadora, Greenwillow (Morrow); *The Treasure* by Uri Shulevitz, Farrar, Straus & Giroux; *The Garden of Abdul Gasazi* by Chris Van Allsburg, Houghton Mifflin

1981 *Fables* by Arnold Lobel, Harper

Honor Books: *The Bremen-Town Musicians* by Ilse Plume, Doubleday; *The Grey Lady and the Strawberry Snatcher* by Molly Bang, Four Winds; *Mice Twice* by Joseph Low, Atheneum; *Truck* by Donald Crews, Greenwillow (Morrow)

1982 *Jumanji* by Chris Van Allsburg, Houghton Mifflin

Honor Books: *A Visit to William Blake's Inn: Poems for Innocent and Experienced Travelers* by Nancy Willard, illustrated by Alice and Martin Provensen, Harcourt Brace Jovanovich; *Where the Buffaloes Begin* by Olaf Baker, illustrated by Stephen Gammell, Warne; *On Market Street* by Arnold Lobel, illustrated by Anita Lobel, Greenwillow (Morrow); *Outside Over There* by Maurice Sendak, Harper

1983 *Shadow* by Blaise Cendrars, illustrated by Marcia Brown, Scribner

Honor Books: *When I Was Young in the Mountains* by Cynthia Rylant, illustrated by Diane Goode, Dutton; *Chair for My Mother* by Vera B. Williams, Morrow

1984 *The Glorious Flight: Across the Channel with Louis Blériot July 25, 1909* by Alice and Martin Provenson, Viking
Honor Books: *Ten, Nine, Eight* by Molly Bang, Greenwillow (Morrow); *Little Red Riding Hood* by Trina Schart Hyman, Holiday House

1985 *Saint George and the Dragon* by Margaret Hodges, illustrated by Trina Schart Hyman, Little, Brown
Honor Books: *Hansel and Gretel* by Rika Lesser, illustrated by Paul O. Zelinsky, Dodd, Mead; *The Story of the Jumping Mouse* by John Steptoe, Lothrop; *Have You Seen My Duckling?* by Nancy Tafuri, Greenwillow (Morrow)

1986 *The Polar Express* by Chris van Allsburg, Houghton Mifflin
Honor Books: *The Relatives Came* by Cynthia Rylant, illustrated by Stephen Gammell, Bradbury; *King Bidgood's in the Bathtub* by Audrey Wook, illustrated by Don Wood, Harcourt Brace Jovanovich

1987 *Hey, Al* by Arthur Yorinks, illustrated by Richard Egielski, Farrar, Straus & Giroux
Honor Books: *The Village of Round and Square Houses* by Ann Grifalconi, Little, Brown; *Alphabatics* by Suse MacDonald, Bradbury; *Rumpelstiltskin* by Paul O. Zelinsky, Dutton

1988 *Owl Moon* by Jane Yolen, illustrated by John Schoenherr, Philomel (Putnam)
Honor Books: *Mufaro's Beautiful Daughter* by John Steptoe, Lothrop

1989 *Song and Dance Man* by Karen Ackerman, illustrated by Stephen Gammell, Knopf
Honor Books: *Goldilocks* by James Marshall, Dial Press; *The Boy of the Three-Year Nap* by Dianne Snyder, illustrated by Allen Say; *Mirandy and Brother Wind* by Patricia McKissack, illustrated by Jerry Pinkney, Knopf; *Free Fall* by David Wiesner, Lothrop

1990 *Lon Po Po: A Red-Riding Hood Story from China* by Ed Young, Philomel (Putnam)
Honor Books: *Hershel and the Hanukkah Goblins* by Eric Kimmel, illustrated by Trina Schart Hyman, Holiday; *Color Zoo* by Lois Ehlert, Lippincott; *Bill Peet: An Autobiography* by Bill Peet, Houghton Mifflin; *The Talking Eggs* retold by Robert D. San Souci, illustrated by Jerry Pinkney, Dial

1991 *Black and White* by David Macaulay, Houghton, Mifflin
Honor Books: *Puss'n Boots* by Charles Perrault, illustrated by Fred Marcellino, Farrar; *"More, More, More," Said the Baby: 3 Love Stories* by Vera Williams, Greenwillow

1992 *Tuesday* by David Wiesner, Clarion
Honor Book: *Tar Beach* by Faith Ringgold, Crown

1993 *Mirette on the High Wire* by Emily Arnold McCully, Putnam
Honor Books: *Seven Blind Mice* by Ed Young, Philomel; *The Stinky Cheese Man and Other Fairly Stupid Tales* by Jon Scieszka, illustrated by Lane Smith, Viking; *Working Cotton* by Sherley Anne Williams, illustrated by Carole Byard, Harcourt

1994 *Grandfather's Journey* by Allen Say, Houghton
Honor Books: *Peppe the Lamplighter* by Elisa Bartone, illustrated by Ted Lewin, Lothrop; *In the Small, Small Pond* by Denise Fleming, Holt; *Owen* by Keven Henkes, Greenwillow; *Raven: A Trickster Tale from the Pacific Northwest* by Gerald McDermott, Harcourt; *Yo! Yes?* by Chris Raschka, Orchard

1995 *Smoky Night* by Eve Bunting, illustrated by David Diaz, Harcourt
   Honor Books: *Swamp Angel* by Anne Isaacs, illustrated by Paul O. Zelin-
      sky, Dutton; *John Henry* retold by Julius Lester, illustrated by Jerry Pinkney,
      Dial; *Time Flies* by Eric Rohmann, Crown

1996 *Officer Buckle and Gloria* by Peggy Rathmann, Putnam
   Honor Books: *Alphabet City* by Stephen T. Johnson, Viking Penguin;
      Zin! Zin! Zin! A Violin! by Lloyd Moss, illustrated Marjorie Priceman, Simon;
      The Faithful Friend by Robert D. San Souci, illustrated by Brian Pinkney, Si-
      mon; *Tops & Bottoms* by Janet Stevens, Harcourt

BOSTON GLOBE–HORN BOOK AWARDS

Awarded annually since 1967 and sponsored jointly by *The Boston Globe* and *The Horn Book Magazine*, two prizes originally were given—one to recognize the outstanding text and one the outstanding illustration. Beginning in 1976, the categories were redefined: Outstanding Fiction or Poetry, Outstanding Nonfiction, and Outstanding Illustration.

1967 Text: *The Little Fishes* by Erik Haugaard, Houghton Mifflin
   Illustration: *London Bridge Is Falling Down* by Peter Spier, Doubleday
1968 Text: *The Spring Rider* by John Lawson, Crowell
   Illustration: *Tikki Tikki Tembo* by Arlene Mosel, illus. Blair Lent, Holt
1969 Text: *A Wizard of Earthsea* by Ursula K. Le Guin, Houghton Mifflin
   Illustration: *The Adventures of Paddy Pork* by John S. Goodall, Harcourt
1970 Text: *The Intruder* by John Rowe Townsend, Lippincott
   Illustration: *Hi, Cat!* by Ezra Jack Keats, Macmillan
1971 Text: *A Room Made of Windows* by Eleanor Cameron, Little, Brown
   Illustration: *If I Built a Village* by Kazue Mizumura, Crowell
1972 Text: *Tristan and Iseult* by Rosemary Sutcliff, Dutton
   Illustration: *Mr. Gumpy's Outing* by John Burningham, Holt, Rinehart and Winston
1973 Text: *The Dark Is Rising* by Susan Cooper, McElderry/Atheneum
   Illustration: *King Stork* by Trina Schart Hyman, Little, Brown
1974 Text: *M. C. Higgins, The Great* by Virginia Hamilton, Macmillan
   Illustration: *Jambo Means Hello* by Muriel Feelings, illus. Tom Feelings, Dial
1975 Text: *Transport 7-41-R* by T. Degens, Viking
   Illustration: *Anno's Alphabet* by Mitsumasa Anno, Crowell
1976 Fiction: *Unleaving* by Jill Paton Walsh, Farrar, Straus & Giroux
   Nonfiction: *Voyaging to Cathay: Americans in the China Trade* by Al-
      fred Tamarin and Shirley Glubok, Viking
   Illustration: *Thirteen* by Remy Charlip and Jerry Joyner, Parents
1977 Fiction: *Child of the Owl.* by Laurence Yep, Harper
   Nonfiction: *Chance, Luck and Destiny* by Peter Dickinson, Little, Brown
   Illustration: *Granfa' Grig Had a Pig and Other Rhymes* by Wallace
      Tripp, Little, Brown
1978 Fiction: *The Westing Game* by Ellen Raskin, Dutton
   Nonfiction: *Mischling, Second Degree: My Childhood in Nazi Germany*
      by Ilse Koehn, Greenwillow
   Illustration: *Anno's Journey* by Mitsumasa Anno, Philomel

1979 Fiction: *Humbug Mountain* by Sid Fleischman, Little, Brown
Nonfiction: *The Road From Home: The Story of an Armenian Girl* by
David Kherdian, Greenwillow
Illustration: *The Snowman* by Raymond Briggs, Random House

1980 Fiction: *Conrad's War* by Andrew Davies, Crown
Nonfiction: *Building: The Fight Against Gravity* by Mario Salvadori,
McElderry/Atheneum
Illustration: *The Garden of Abdul Gasazi* by Chris Van Allsburg,
Houghton, Mifflin

1981 Fiction: *The Leaving* by Lynn Hall, Scribner
Nonfiction: *The Weaver's Gift* by Kathryn Lasky, Warne
Illustration: *Outside Over There* by Maurice Sendak, Harper

1982 Fiction: *Playing Beatie Bow* by Ruth Park, Atheneum
Nonfiction: *Upon the Head of the Goat: A Childhood in Hungary,
1939-1944* by Aranka Siegal, Farrar, Straus & Giroux
Illustration: *A Visit to William Blake's Inn: Poems for Innocent and Experienced Travelers* by Nancy Willard, illus. by Alice and Martin Provensen

1983 Fiction: *Sweet Whispers, Brother Rush* by Virginia Hamilton, Philomel
Nonfiction: *Behind Barbed Wire: The Imprisonment of Japanese Amer-
icans During World War II* by Daniel S. David, Dutton
Illustration: *A Chair for My Mother* by Vera B. Williams, Greenwillow

1984 Fiction: *A Little Fear* by Patricia Wrightson, McElderry/Atheneum
Nonfiction: *The Double Life of Pocahontas* by Jean Fritz, Putnam
Illustration: *Jonah and the Great Fish* retold and illus. by Warwick Hut-
ton, McElderry/Atheneum

1985 Fiction: *The Moves Make the Man* by Bruce Brooks, Harper
Nonfiction: *Commodore Perry in the Land of the Shogun* by Rhoda
Blumberg, Lothrop
Illustration: *Mama Don't Allow* by Thatcher Hurd, Harper

1986 Fiction: *In Summer Light* by Zibby Oneal, Viking/Kestrel
Nonfiction: *Auks, Rocks and the Odd Dinosaur* by Peggy Thompson,
Crowell
Illustration: *The Paper Crane* by Molly Bang, Greenwillow

1987 Fiction: *Rabble Starkey* by Lois Lowry, Houghton, Mifflin
Nonfiction: *Pilgrims of Plimouth* by Marcia Sewall, Atheneum
Illustration: *Mufaro's Beautiful Daughters* by John Steptoe, Lothrop

1988 Fiction: *The Friendship* by Mildred Taylor, Dial
Nonfiction: *Anthony Burns: The Defeat and Triumph of a Fugitive
Slave* by Virginia Hamilton, Knopf
Illustration: *The Boy of the Three-Year Nap* by Diane Snyder, Houghton, Mifflin

1989 Fiction: *The Village by the Sea* by Paula Fox, Franklin Watts
Nonfiction: *The Way Things Work* by David Macaulay, Houghton Mifflin
Illustration: *Shy Charles* by Rosemary Wells, Dial

1990 Fiction: *Maniac Magee* by Jerry Spinelli, Little, Brown
Nonfiction: *The Great Little Madison* by Jean Fritz, Putnam
Illustration: *Lon Po Po: A Red-Riding Hood Story from China* retold and illus-
trated by Ed Young, Philomel

1991 Fiction: *The True Confessions of Charlotte Doyle* by Avi, Orchard
Nonfiction: *Appalachia: The Voices of Sleeping Birds* by Cynthia Rylant, illustrated by Barry Moser, Harcourt
Illustration: *The Tale of the Mandarin Ducks* retold by Katherine Paterson, illustrated by Leo and Diane Dillon, Lodestar

1992 Fiction: *Missing May* by Cynthia Rylant, Orchard
Nonfiction: *Talking with Artists* by Pat Cummings, Bradbury
Illustration: *Seven Blind Mice* by Ed Young, Philomel

1993 Fiction: *Ajeemah and His Son* by James Berry, Harper
Nonfiction: *Sojourner Truth: Ain't I a Woman?* by Patricia C. and Fredrick McKissack, Scholastic
Illustration: *The Fortune-Tellers* by Lloyd Alexander, illustrated by Trina Schart Hyman, Dutton

1994 Fiction: *Scooter* by Vera B. Williams, Greenwillow
Nonfiction: *Eleanor Roosevelt: A Life of Discovery* by Russell Freedman, Clarion
Illustration: *Grandfather's Journey* by Allen Say, Houghton

1995 Fiction: *Some of the Kinder Planets* by Tim Wynne-Jones, Kroupa/Orchard
Nonfiction: *Abigail Adams: Witness to a Revolution* by Natalie S. Bober, Atheneum
Illustration: *John Henry* retold by Julius Lester, illustrated by Jerry Pinkney, Dial

THE MILDRED L. BATCHELDER AWARD

Presented annually by the American Library Association, this award recognizes the most outstanding children's book originally translated from a language other than English. (Unless otherwise indicated, the author is also the translator.)

1968 *The Little Man* by Erich Kastner, translated by James Kirkup, illustrated by Rich Schreiter, Knopf, 1966

1969 *Don't Take Teddy* by Babbis Friis-Baastad, translated by Lise Somme McKinnon, Scribner, 1967

1970 *Wildcat under Glass* by Alki Zei, translated by Edward Fenton, Holt, Rinehart and Winston, 1968

1971 *In the Land of Ur: The Discovery of Ancient Mesopotamia* by Hans Baumann, Stella Humphries, illustrated by Hans Peter Renner, Pantheon Books, 1969

1972 *Friedrich* by Hans Peter Richter, translated by Edite Kroll, Holt, Rinehart and Winston, 1970

1973 *Pulga* by Siny Rose Van Iterson, translated by Alexander and Alison Gode, Morrow, 1971

1974 *Petros' War* by Alki Zei, translated by Edward Fenton, Dutton, 1972

1975 *An Old Tale Carved Out of Stone* by Aleksandr M. Linevski, translated by Maria Polushkin, Crown, 1973

1976 *The Cat and Mouse Who Shared a House* by Ruth Hurlimann, translated by Anthea Bell, Walck, 1974

1977 *The Leopard* by Cecil Bodker, illustrated by Gunnar Poulsen, Antheneum, 1975

1978 No award

1979 *Konrad* by Christine Nostlinger, translated by Anthea Bell, illustrated by Carol Nicklaus, Watts, 1977
      Rabbit Island by Jorg Steiner, translated by Ann Conrad Lammers, illustrated by Jorg Muller, Harcourt Brace Jovanovich, 1978

1980 *The Sound of Dragon's Feet* by Alki Zei, translated by Edward Fenton, Dutton, 1979

1981 *The Winter When Time Was Frozen* by Els Pelgrom, translated by Raphael and Maryka Rudnik, Morrow, 1980

1982 *The Battle Horse* by Harry Kullman, translated by George Blecher and Lone Thygesen-Blecher, Bradbury, 1981

1983 *Hiroshima no Pika* by Toshi Maruki, Lothrop, 1982

1984 *Ronia, the Robber's Daughter* by Astrid Lindgren, translated by Patricia Crampton, Viking, 1983

1985 *The Island on Bird Street* by Uri Orlev, translated by Hillel Halkin, Houghton Mifflin, 1984

1986 *Rose Blanche* by Christophe Gallaz and Roberto Innocenti, translated by Martha Coventry and Richard Graglia, illustrated by Roberto Innocenti, Creative Education, 1985

1987 *No Hero for the Kaiser* by Rudolf Frank, translated by Patricia Crampton, illustrated by Klaus Steffans, Lothrop, 1986

1988 *If You Didn't Have Me* by Ulf Nilsson, illustrated by Eva Ericksson, translated by Lone Thygesen-Blecher and George Blecher, McElderry

1989 *Crutches* by Peter Hartling, Lothrop

1990 *Buster's World* by Branner og Korch, Dutton

1991 *A Handful of Stars* by Rafik Schami, translated by Rika Lesser, Dutton
      Honor Book: *Two Short and One Long* by Nina Ring Aamundsen, Houghton, Mifflin

1992 *The Man from the Other Side* by Uri Orlev, translated by Hillel Halkin, Houghton, Mifflin

1993 No Award

1994 *The Apprentice* by Pilar Molina Llorente, translated by Robin Longshaw, illustrated by Juan Ramón Alonso, Farrar

1995 *Sister Shako and Kolo the Goat* by Vedat Dalokay, Lothrop

THE LAURA INGALLS WILDER AWARD

Named in honor of the beloved author of the Little House books (who was also its first recipient), this award is presented by the Association of Library Service to Children of the American Library Association to the individual, either author or illustrator, whose work has over the years proven to be a significant contribution to children's literature. Originally awarded every five years, it has since 1980 been given every three years.

1954 Laura Ingalls Wilder

1960 Clara Ingram Judson

1965 Ruth Sawyer

1970 E. B. White

1975 Beverly Cleary

1980 Theodore Geisel (Dr. Seuss)

1983 Maurice Sendak

1986 Jean Fritz

1989 Elizabeth George Speare

1992 Marcia Brown

1995 Virginia Hamilton

THE CORETTA SCOTT KING AWARD

Presented annually by the Social Responsibilities Round Table of the American Library Association, this award recognizes an African-American author and illustrator (since 1974) who has made an outstanding contribution to literature for children in the preceding year. The award is named for the widow of civil rights leader and Nobel Peace Prize winner Dr. Martin Luther King, Jr., and it acknowledges the humanitarian work of both Dr. and Mrs. King.

1970 *Martin Luther King, Jr., Man of Peace* by Lillie Patterson, Garrard

1971 *Black Troubadour: Langston Hughes* by Charlemae Rollins, Rand

1972 *17 Black Artists* by Elton C. Fax, Dodd

1973 *I Never Had It Made* by Jackie Robinson (as told to Alfred Duckett), Putnam

1974 Author: *Ray Charles* by Sharon Bell Mathis, Crowell
Illustrator: *Ray Charles* by Sharon Bell Mathis, illustrated by George Ford, Crowell

1975   Author: *The Legend of Africana* by Dorothy Robinson, Johnson
Illustrator: *The Legend of Africana* by Dorothy Robinson, illustrated by Herbert Temple, Johnson

1976 Author: *Duey's Tale* by Pearl Bailey, Harcourt.
Illustrator: No Award

1977 Author: *The Story of Stevie Wonder* by James Haskins, Lothrop
Illustrator: No Award

1978 Author: *Africa Dream* by Eloise Greenfield, Day/Crowell
Illustrator: *Africa Dream* by Eloise Greenfield, illustrated by Carole Bayard, Day/Crowell

1979 Author: *Escape to Freedom* by Ossie Davis, Viking
Illustrator: *Something on My Mind* by Nikki Grimes, illustrated by Tom Feelings, Dial

1980 Author: *The Young Landlords* by Walter Dean Myers, Viking
Illustrator: *Cornrows* by Camille Yarbrough, illustrated by Carole Bayard, Coward

1981 Author: *This Life* by Sidney Poitier, Knopf
Illustrator: *Beat the Story-Drum, Pum-Pum* by Ashley Bryan, Atheneum

1982 Author: *Let the Circle Be Unbroken* by Mildred Taylor, Dial
Illustrator: *Mother Crocodile: An Uncle Amadou Tale* from Senegal adapted by Rosa Guy, illustrated by John Steptoe, Delacorte

1983 Author: *Sweet Whispers, Brother Rush* by Virginia Hamilton, Philomel
Illustrator: *Black Child* by Peter Mugabane, Knopf

1984 Author: *Everett Anderson's Good-Bye* by Lucile Clifton, Holt
Illustrator: *My Mama Needs Me* by Mildred Pitts Walter, illustrated by Pat Cummings, Lothrop

1985 Author: *Motown and Didi* by Walter Dean Myers, Viking
   Illustrator: No Award

1986 Author: *The People Could Fly: American Black Folktales* by Virginia Hamilton,
   Knopf
   Illustrator: *Patchwork Quilt* by Valerie Flournoy, illustrated by Jerry
   Pinckney, Dial

1987 Author: *Justin and the Best Biscuits in the World* by Mildred Pitts Walter,
   Lothrop
   Illustrator: *Half Moon and One Whole Star* by Crescent Dragonwagon,
   illustrated by Jerry Pinkney, Macmillan

1988 Author: *The Friendship* by Mildred D. Taylor, Dial
   Illustrator: *Mufaro's Beautiful Daughters: An African Tale* retold and illustrated by John Steptoe, Lothrop

1989 Author: *Fallen Angels* by Walter Dean Myers, Scholastic
   Illustrator: *Mirandy and Brother Wind* by Patricia McKissack, illustrated
   by Jerry Pinkney, Knopf

1990 Author: *A Long Hard Journey* by Patricia and Frederick McKissack, Walker
   Illustrator: *Nathaniel Talking* by Eloise Greenfield, illustrated by Jan
   Spivey Gilchrist, Black Butterfly Press

1991 Author: *Road to Memphis* by Mildred D. Taylor, Dial
   Illustrator: *Aida* retold by Leontyne Price, illustrated by Leo and Diane
   Dillon, Harcourt

1992 Author: *Now Is Your Time! The African-American Struggle for Freedom* by Walter Dean Myers, HarperCollins
   Illustrator: *Tar Beach* by Faith Ringgold, Crown

1993 Author: *The Dark-Thirty: Southern Tales of the Supernatural* by Patricia McKis-
   sack, Knopf
   Illustrator: *Origins of Life on Earth: An African Creation Myth* by David
   A. Anderson, illustrated by Kathleen Atkins Smith, Sight Productions

1994 Author: *Toning the Sweep* by Angela Johnson, Orchard
   Illustrator: *Soul Looks Back in Wonder* compiled and illustrated by Tom
   Feelings, Dial

1995 Author: *Christmas in the Big House, Christmas in the Quarters* by Patricia
   McKissack and Fredrick L. McKissack, illustrated by John Thompson, Scholastic
   Illustrator: *The Creation* by James Weldon Johnson, illustrated by James
   E. Ransom, Holiday

1996 Author: *Her Stories* by Virginia Hamilton, illustrated by Leo and Diane Dillon,
   Scholastic
   Illustrator: *The Middle Passage: White Ships, Black Cargo* by Tom Feel-
   ings, Dial

THE SCOTT O'DELL AWARD FOR HISTORICAL FICTION

Established by the noted children's novelist, Scott O'Dell, and administered by the Advisory
Committee of the Bulletin of the Center for Children's Books, this award is presented to the
most distinguished work of historical fiction set in the New World and written by a citizen
of the United States.

1984 *The Sign of the Beaver* by Elizabeth George Speare, Houghton, Mifflin

1985 *The Fighting Ground* by Avi, Harper

1986 *Sarah, Plain and Tall* by Patricia MacLachlan, Harper

1987 *Streams to the River, River to the Sea: A Novel of Sacagawea* by Scott O'Dell, Houghton, Mifflin

1988 *Charlie Skedaddle* by Patricia Beatty, Morrow

1989 *The Honorable Prison* by Lyll Becerra de Jenkins, Lodestar

1990 *Shades of Gray* by Carolyn Reeder, Macmillan

1991 *A Time of Troubles* by Pieter van Raven, Scribner's

1992 *Stepping on the Cracks* by Mary Downing Hahn, Clarion

1993 *Morning Girl* by Michael Dorris, Hyperion

1994 *Bull Run* by Paul Fleischman, Harper

1995 *Under the Blood-Red Sun* by Graham Salisbury, Delacorte

NATIONAL COUNCIL OF TEACHERS OF ENGLISH AWARD FOR EXCELLENCE IN POETRY FOR CHILDREN

This award is presented every three years (from 1977 through 1982 it was awarded annually) by the National Council of Teachers of English and was established to recognize a living poet's lifetime contribution to poetry for children.

1977 David McCord

1978 Aileen Fisher

1979 Karla Kuskin

1980 Myra Cohn Livingston

1981 Eve Merriam

1982 John Ciardi

1985 Lilian Moore

1988 Arnold Adoff

1991 Valerie Worth

1994 Barbara Juster Esbensen

THE PHOENIX AWARD

The Phoenix Award is given annually by the International Children's Literature Association for a book published exactly twenty years earlier that did not, at the time, win a major award, but which has stood the test of time and merited recognition for its contribution to children's literature. The award was first presented in 1985.

1985 *The Mark of the Horse Lord* by Rosemary Sutcliff, Oxford, 1965

1986 *Queenie Peavy* by Robert Burch, Viking, 1966

1987 *Smith* by Leon Garfield, Constable, 1967

1988 *The Rider and His Horse* by Erik Christian Haugaard, Houghton Mifflin, 1968

1989 *The Night Watchmen* by Helen Cresswell, Faber, 1969

1990 *Enchantress from the Stars* by Sylvia Louise Engdahl, Atheneum, 1970

1991 *A Long Way from Home* by Jane Gardam, Hamish Hamilton, 1971

1992 *A Sound of Chariots* by Mollie Hunter, Hamish Hamilton, 1972

1993 *Carrie's War* by Nina Bawden, Gollancz, 1973

1994 *Of Nightingales That Weep* by Katherine Paterson, Harper, 1974

1995 *Dragonwings* by Laurence Yep, Harper, 1975

1996 *The Stone Book* by Alan Garner, Collins, 1976

INTERNATIONAL AWARDS

THE HANS CHRISTIAN ANDERSEN AWARD

This medal, named for the great Danish storyteller, is presented every two years by the International Board on Books for Young People to a living author and (since 1966) living illustrator whose works have made a significant, international contribution to children's literature.

1956 Eleanor Farjeon (Great Britain)

1958 Astrid Lindgren (Sweden)

1960 Erich Kastner (Germany)

1962 Meindert DeJong (United States)

1964 Rene Guillot (France)

1966 Author: Tove Jansson (Finland)
Illustrator: Alois Carigiet (Switzerland)

1968 Authors: James Kruss (Germany) and Jose Maria Sanchez-Silva (Spain)
Illustrator: Jiri Trnka (Czechoslovakia)

1970 Author: Gianni Rodari (Italy)
Illustrator: Maurice Sendak (United States)

1972 Author: Scott O'Dell (United States)
Illustrator: Ib Spang Olsen (Denmark)

1974 Author: Maria Gripe (Sweden)
Illustrator: Farsid Mesghali (Iran)

1976 Author: Cecil Bodker (Denmark)
Illustrator: Tatjana Mawrine (U. S. S. R.)

1978 Author: Paula Fox (United States)
Illustrator: Otto S. Svend (Denmark)

1980 Author: Bohumil Riha (Czechoslovakia)
Illustrator: Suekichi Akaba (Japan)

1982 Author: Lygia Gojunga Nunes (Brazil)
Illustrator: Zbigniew Rychlicki (Poland)

1984 Author: Christine Nostlinger (Austria)
Illustrator: Mitsumasa Anno (Japan)

1986 Author: Patricia Wrightson (Australia)
Illustrator: Robert Ingpen (Australia)

1988 Author: Annie M. G. Schmidt (Netherlands)
Illustrator: Dusan Kallay (Yugoslavia)

1990 Author: Tormod Haugen (Norway)
Illustrator: Lisbeth Zwerger (Austria)

1992 Author: Virginia Hamilton (U.S.A.)
Illustrator: Keveta Pacovská (Czechoslovakia)

1994 Author: Michio Mado (Japan)
Illustrator: Jörg Müller (Switzerland)

THE KATE GREENAWAY MEDAL

Name for the celebrated nineteenth-century children's illustrator, this medal is awarded annually by the British Library Association to the most distinguished illustrated work for children first published in the United Kingdom during the preceding year. (Unless otherwise noted, the author is also the illustrator. The date given is the year of publication.)

1956 *Tim All Alone* by Edward Ardizzone, Oxford

1957 *Mrs. Easter and the Storks* by V. H. Drummond, Faber

1958 No Award

1959 *Kashtanka and a Bundle of Ballads* by William Stobbs, Oxford

1960 *Old Winkle and the Seagulls* by Elizabeth Rose, illustrated by Gerald Rose, Faber

1961 *Mrs. Cockle's Cat* by Philippa Pearce, illustrated by Anthony Maitland, Kestrel

1962 *Brian Wildsmith's ABC* by Brian Wildsmith, Oxford

1963 *Borka* by John Burningham, Jonathan Cape

1964 *Shakespeare's Theatre* by C. W. Hodges, Oxford

1965 *Three Poor Tailors* by Victor Ambrus, Hamilton

1966 *Mother Goose Treasury* by Raymond Briggs, Hamilton

1967 *Charlie, Charlotte & the Golden Canary* by Charles Keeping, Oxford

1968 *Dictionary of Chivalry* by Grant Uden, illustrated by Pauline Baynes, Kestrel

1969 *The Quangle-Wangle's Hat* by Edward Lear, illustrated by Helen Oxenbury, Heinemann
    Dragon of an Ordinary Family by Margaret May, illustrated by Helen Oxenbury, Heinemann

1970 *Mr. Gumpy's Outing* by John Burningham, Jonathan Cape

1971 *The Kingdom under the Sea* by Jan Pienkowski, Jonathan Cape

1972 *The Woodcutter's Duck* by Krystyna Turska, Hamilton

1973 *Father Christmas* by Raymond Briggs, Hamilton

1974 *The Wind Blew* by Pat Hutchins, Bodley Head

1975 *Horses in Battle* by Victor Ambrus, Oxford
    Mishka by Victor Ambrus, Oxford

1976 *The Post Office Cat* by Gail E. Haley, Bodley Head

1977 *Dogger* by Shirley Hughes, Bodley Head

1978 *Each Peach Pear Plum* by Janet and Allan Ahlberg, Kestrel

1979 *Haunted House* by Jan Pienkowski, Dutton

1980 *Mr. Magnolia* by Quentin Blake, Jonathan Cape

1981 *The Highwayman* by Alfred Noyes, illustrated by Charles Keeping, Oxford

1982 *Long Neck and Thunder Foot* by Michael Foreman, Kestrel
    Sleeping Beauty and Other Favorite Fairy Tales by Michael Foreman, Gollancz

1983 *Gorilla* by Anthony Browne, Julia McRae Books

1984 *Hiawatha's Childhood* by Errol LeCain, Faber

1985 *Sir Gawain and the Loathly Lady* by Selina Hastings, illustrated by Juan Wijngaard, Walker

1986 *Snow White in New York* by Fiona French, Oxford

1987 *Crafty Chameleon* by Adrienne Kennaway, Hodder & Stoughton

1988 *Can't You Sleep, Little Bear?* by Martin Waddell, illustrated by Adrienne Kennaway, Hodder & Stoughton

1989 *War Boy: A Country Childhood* by Michael Foreman, Arcade

1990 *The Whale's Song* by Dyan Sheldon, illustrated by Gary Blythe, Dial

1991 *The Jolly Christmas Postman* by Janet and Allan Ahlberg, Heinemann

1992 *Zoo* by Anthony Browne, Julie MacRae Books

1993 *Black Ships Before Troy* retold by Rosemary Sutcliff, illustrated by Alan Lee, Frances Lincoln

1994 *Way Home* by Libby Hawthorne, Anderson

THE CARNEGIE MEDAL

Awarded by the British Library Association to an outstanding book first published in the United Kingdom, this medal has been awarded annually since it was established in 1937 (the first award being presented to a book published in the preceding year). The date given is the date of publication.

1936 *Pigeon Post* by Arthur Ransome, Cape

1937 *The Family from One End Street* by Eve Garnett, Muller

1938 *The Circus Is Coming* by Noel Streatfield, Dent

1939 *Radium Woman* by Eleanor Doorly, Heinemann

1940 *Visitors from London* by Kitty Barne, Dent

1941 *We Couldn't Leave Dinah* by Mary Treadgold, Penguin

1942 *The Little Grey Men* by B. B., Eyre & Spottiswoode

1943 No Award

1944 *The Wind on the Moon* by Eric Linklater, Macmillan

1945 No Award

1946 *The Little White Horse* by Elizabeth Goudge, Brockhampton Press

1947 *Collected Stories for Children* by Walter de la Mare, Faber

1948 *Sea Change* by Richard Armstrong, Dent

1949 *The Story of Your Home* by Agnes Allen, Transatlantic

1950 *The Lark on the Wind* by Elfrida Vipont Foulds, Oxford

1951 *The Wool-Pack* by Cynthia Harnett, Methuen

1952 *The Borrowers* by Mary Norton, Dent

1953 *A Valley Grows Up* by Edward Osmond, Oxford

1954 *Knight Crusader* by Ronald Welch, Oxford

1955 *The Little Bookroom* by Eleanor Farjeon, Oxford

1956 *The Last Battle* by C. S. Lewis, Bodley Head

1957 *A Grass Rope* by William Mayne, Oxford

1958 *Tom's Midnight Garden* by Philippa Pearce, Oxford

1959 *The Lantern Bearers* by Rosemary Sutcliff, Oxford

1960 *The Making of Man* by I. W. Cornwall, Phoenix

1961 *A Stranger at Green Knowe* by Lucy Boston, Faber

1962 *The Twelve and the Genii* by Pauline Clarke, Faber

1963 *Time of Trial* by Hester Burton, Oxford

1964 *Nordy Banks* by Sheena Porter, Oxford

1965 *The Grange at High Force* by Philip Turner, Oxford

1966 No Award

1967 *The Owl Service* by Alan Garner, Collins

1968 *The Moon in the Cloud* by Rosemary Harris, Faber

1969 *The Edge of the Cloud* by K. M. Peyton, Oxford

1970 *The God Beneath the Sea* by Leon Garfield and Edward Blishen, Kestrel

1971 *Josh* by Ivan Southall, Angus & Robertson

1972 *Watership Down* by Richard Adams, Rex Collings

1973 *The Ghost of Thomas Kempe* by Penelope Lively, Heinemann

1974 *The Stronghold* by Mollie Hunter, Hamilton

1975 *The Machine-Gunners* by Robert Westall, Macmillan

1976 *Thunder and Lightnings* by Jan Mark, Kestrel

1977 *The Turbulent Term of Tyke Tiler* by Gene Kemp, Faber

1978 *The Exeter Blitz* by David Rees, Hamish Hamilton

1979 *Tulku* by Peter Dickinson, Dutton

1980 *City of Gold* by Peter Dickinson, Gollancz

1981 *The Scarecrows* by Robert Westall, Chatto & Windus

1982 *The Haunting* by Margaret Mahy, Dent

1983 *Handles* by Jan Mark, Kestrel

1984 *The Changeover* by Margaret Mahy, Dent

1985 *Storm* by Kevin Crossley-Holland, Heinemann

1986 *Granny Was a Buffer Girl* by Berlie Doherty, Methuen

1987 *The Ghost Drum* by Susan Price, Faber

1988 *Pack of Lies* by Geraldine McCaughrean, Oxford

1989 *My War with Goggle-Eyes* by Anne Fine, Joy Street

1990 *Wolf* by Gillian Cross, Oxford

1991 *Dear Nobody* by Berlie Doherty, Hamish Hamilton

1992 *Flour Babies* by Anne Fine, Hamish Hamilton

1993 *Stone Cold* by Robert Swindells, Hamish Hamilton

1994 *Whispers in the Graveyard* by Theresa Breslin, Methuen

THE CANADIAN LIBRARY AWARD

Presented by the Canadian Library Association since 1947, this award recognizes the most distinguished children's book by a Canadian citizen. Beginning in 1954, an additional award has been presented to a distinguished work published in French. The Association has also presented, since 1971, the Amelia Frances Howard-Gibbon Medal for outstanding illustration by a Canadian illustrator in a children's book published in Canada. In some years no award may be given.

1947 *Starbuck Valley Winter* by Roderick Haig-Brown, Collins

1948 *Kristi's Trees* by Mabel Dunham, Hale

1949 No Award

1950 *Franklin of the Arctic* by Richard S. Lambert, McClelland & Stewart

1951 No Award

1952 *The Sun Horse* by Catherine Anthony Clark, Macmillan of Canada

1953 No Award

1954 *Mgr. de Laval* by Emile S. J. Gervais, Comite des Fondateurs de l'Eglise Canadienne

1955 No Awards

1956 *Train for Tiger Lily* by Louise Riley, Macmillan of Canada

1957 *Glooskap's Country* by Cyrus Macmillan, Oxford

1958 *Lost in the Barrens* by Farley Mowatt, Little
     The Chevalier du Roi by Beatrice Clement, Les Editions de l'Atelier

1959 *The Dangerous Cove* by John F. Hayes, Copp Clark
     Un Drole de Petit Cheval by Helene Flamme, Editions, Lemeac

1960 *The Golden Phoenix* by Marius Barbeau and Michael Hornyansky, Walck
     L'Ete Enchante by Paule Daveluy, Les Editions de l'Atelier

1961 *The St. Lawrence* by William Toye, Oxford
     Plante Vagabondes by Marcelle Gauvreau, Centre de Psychologie et de Pedagogie

1962 *Les Ile du Roi Maha Maha II* by Claude Aubry, Les Editions du Pelican

1963 *The Incredible Journey* by Sheila Burnford, Little, Brown
     Drole d'Automne by Paule Daveluy, Les Editions du Pelican

1964 *The Whale People* by Roderick Haig-Brown, William Collins of Canada
     Feerie by Cecile Chabot, Librairie Beauchemin Ltee

1965 *Tales of Nanabozho* by Dorothy Reid, Oxford
     Le Loup de Noël by Claude Aubry, Centre de Psychologie de Montreal

1966 *Tikta'Liktak* by James Houston, Kestrel
     Le Chene des Tempetes by Andre Mallet-Hobden, Fides
     The Double Knights by James McNeal, Walck
     Le Wapiti by Monique Corriveau, Jeunesse

1967 *Raven's Cry* by Christie Harris, McClelland & Stewart

1968 *The White Archer* by James Houston, Kestrel
     Legendes Indiennes du Canada by Claude Melancon, Editions du Jour

1969 *And Tomorrow the Stars* by Kay Hill, Dodd

1970 *Sally Go Round the Sun* by Edith Fowke, McClelland & Stewart
     La Merveilleuse Histoire de la Naissance by Lionel Gendron, Les Editions de l'Homme

1971 *Cartier Discovers the St. Lawrence* by William Toye, Oxford
     La Surprise de Dame Chenille by Henriette Major, Centre de Psychologie de Montreal

1972 *Mary of Mile 18* by Ann Blades, Tundra

1973 *The Marrow of the World* by Ruth Nichols, Macmillan of Canada
   Le Petit Sapin Qui A Pousse sur une Etoile by Simone Bussieres,
      Presses Laurentiennes

1974 *The Miraculous Hind* by Elizabeth Cleaver, Holt of Canada

1975 *Alligator Pie* by Dennis Lee, Macmillan of Canada

1976 *Jacob Two-Two Meets the Hooded Fang* by Mordecai Richler, Knopf

1977 *Mouse Woman and the Vanished Princess* by Christie Harris, McClelland &
      Stewart

1978 *Garbage Delight* by Dennis Lee, Macmillan

1979 *Hold Fast* by Kevin Major, Clarke, Irwin

1980 *River Runners: A Tale of Hardship and Bravery* by James Houston, McClelland
      & Stewart

1981 *The Violin Maker's Gift* by Donn Kushner, Macmillan of Canada

1982 *The Root Cellar* by Janet Lunn, Lester & Orpen Dennys

1983 *Up to Low* by Brian Doyle, Groundwood

1984 *Sweetgrass* by Jan Hudson, Tree Frog Press

1985 *Mama's Going to Buy a Mockingbird* by Jean Little, Penguin

1986 *Julie* by Cora Taylor, Western

1987 *Shadow in Hawthorne Bay* by Janet Lunn, Scribner

1988 *A Handful of Time* by Kit Pearson, Viking

1989 *Easy Avenue* by Brian Doyle, Groundwood

1990 *The Sky Is Falling* by Kit Pearson, Penguin

1991 *Redwork* by Michael Bedard, Dennys

1992 *Eating Between the Lines* by Keven Major, Doubleday

1993 *Ticket to Curlew* by Celia Barker Lottridge, Groundwood

1994 *Some of the Kinder Planets* by Tim Wynne-Jones, Groundwood

1995 *Summer of the Mad Monk* by Taylor Cora, Greystone

THE AMELIA FRANCES HOWARD-GIBBON MEDAL

Awarded since 1971 by the Canadian Library Association, this medal honors excellence in children's illustration in a book published in Canada. The award must go to a citizen or resident of Canada. Unless otherwise indicated, the author is also the illustrator.

1971 *The Wind Has Wings* ed. by Mary Alice Downie and Barbara Robertson, illus-
      trated by Elizabeth Cleaver, Oxford

1972 *A Child in Prison Camp* by Shizuye Takashima, Tundra

1973 *Au Dela du Soleil/Beyond the Sun* by Jacques de Roussan, Tundra

1974 *A Prairie Boy's Winter* by William Kurelek, Tundra

1975 *The Sleighs of My Childhood/Les Traineaux de Mon Enfance* by Carlos Ital-
      iano, Tundra

1976 *A Prairie Boy's Summer* by William Kurelek, Tundra

1977 *Down by Jim Long's Stage: Rhymes for Children and Young Fish* by Al
      Pittman, illustrated by Pam Hall, Breakwater

1978 *The Loon's Necklace* by William Toye, illustrated by Elizabeth Cleaver, Oxford

1979 *A Salmon for Simon* by Betty Waterton, illustrated by Ann Blades, Douglas & McIntyre

1980 *The Twelve Dancing Princesses* by Laszlo Gal, Methuen

1981 *The Trouble with Princesses* by Douglas Tait, McClelland & Stewart

1982 *Ytek and the Arctic Orchid: An Innuit Legend* by Heather Woodall, Douglas & McIntyre

1983 *Chester's Barn* by Lindee Climo, Tundra

1984 *Zoom at Sea* by Tim Wynne-Jones, illustrated by Ken Nutt, Douglas & McIntyre

1985 *Chin Chiang and the Dragon's Dance* by Ian Wallace, Groundwood

1986 *Zoom Away* by Tim Wynne-Jones, illustrated by Ken Nutt, Douglas & McIntyre

1987 *Moonbeam on a Cat's Ear* by Marie-Louise Gay, Stoddard

1988 *Rainy Day Magic* by Marie-Louise Gay, Hodder & Stoughton

1989 *Amos's Sweater* by Janet Lunn, illustrated by Kim LaFave, Douglas & McIntyre

1990 *Til All the Stars Have Fallen: Canadian Poems for Children* selected by David Booth, illustrated by Kady MacDonald Denton, Kids Can Press

1991 *The Orphan Boy* by Tololwa M. Mollel, illustrated by Paul Morin, Oxford

1992 *Waiting for the Whales* by Ron Lightburn, illustrated by Sheryl McFarlane, Orca Books

1993 *The Dragon's Pearl* by Julie Lawson, illustrated by Paul Morin, Oxford

1994 *Last Leaf First Snowflake to Fall* by Leo Yerxa, Groundwood

1995 *Gifts* by Jo Ellen Bogart, illustrated by Barbara Reid, Scholastic

INDEX